ITALIAN RENAISSANCE TALES

ITALIAN RENAISSANCE TALES contains thirty-nine stories from nineteen authors, spanning the period roughly from 1350 to 1630 when the short narrative that the Italians call *novella* became the dominant form of prose fiction. Originating in Florence in the fourteenth century, it spread throughout Italy and by the sixteenth century collections of *novelle* were hugely popular and influential in Spain, France, and England. In the 250 years during which this eclectic genre flourished, its subject matter expanded to embrace the courtly love story, the fable, the parable, the comic anecdote, and the exotic tale. The most famous example and acknowledged model of the genre is Giovanni Boccaccio's *Decameron* which featured 100 tales told by ten narrators. The Italian Renaissance *novella* provided important source texts for Chaucer (*The Clerk's Tale of Patient Griselda*), Shakespeare (*Romeo and Juliet*, *Othello*, *The Merchant of Venice*), and Webster (*The Duchess of Malfi*), as well as early and unexpectedly violent versions of folk tales such as *Cinderella* and *The Sleeping Beauty*.

ANTHONY MORTIMER is Emeritus Professor at the University of Fribourg, Switzerland, and also taught for many years at the University of Geneva. In addition to his scholarly work on English renaissance poetry, he has produced a series of verse translations: Dante (the *Vita Nuova*), Cavalcanti, Petrarch, Michelangelo, Angelus Silesius, Villon, Baudelaire, and *The Song of Roland*. His version of Luigi Pirandello's *Three Plays* was published in the Oxford World's Classics in 2014.

OXFORD WORLD'S CLASSICS

*For over 100 years Oxford World's Classics have brought
readers closer to the world's great literature. Now with over 700
titles—from the 4,000-year-old myths of Mesopotamia to the
twentieth century's greatest novels—the series makes available
lesser-known as well as celebrated writing.*

*The pocket-sized hardbacks of the early years contained
introductions by Virginia Woolf, T. S. Eliot, Graham Greene,
and other literary figures which enriched the experience of reading.
Today the series is recognized for its fine scholarship and
reliability in texts that span world literature, drama and poetry,
religion, philosophy and politics. Each edition includes perceptive
commentary and essential background information to meet the
changing needs of readers.*

OXFORD WORLD'S CLASSICS

═══

Italian Renaissance Tales

═══

Translated with an Introduction and Notes by
ANTHONY MORTIMER

OXFORD
UNIVERSITY PRESS

OXFORD
UNIVERSITY PRESS

Great Clarendon Street, Oxford, OX2 6DP,
United Kingdom

Oxford University Press is a department of the University of Oxford.
It furthers the University's objective of excellence in research, scholarship,
and education by publishing worldwide. Oxford is a registered trade mark of
Oxford University Press in the UK and in certain other countries

First published as an Oxford World's Classics paperback 2019

Impression: 1

Published in the United States of America by Oxford University Press
198 Madison Avenue, New York, NY 10016, United States of America

British Library Cataloguing in Publication Data

Data available

Library of Congress Control Number: 2019945040

ISBN 978-0-19-879496-7

Printed and bound in Great Britain by
Clays Ltd, Elcograf S.p.A.

ACKNOWLEDGEMENTS

I am grateful to all those who have made my task easier with their example, advice, and practical assistance, and especially to Gloria Allaire, Simona Cain, Emma Depledge, Edoardo Fumagalli, Indira Ghose, Peter Hainsworth, Gordon Nichols, Brian Richardson, and Diego Zancani. I must also thank the librarians of the Bibliothèque universitaire de Genève for their unfailing patience and professionalism.

Finally, it is a pleasure to acknowledge the scrupulous attention given to this volume by Luciana O'Flaherty, Kizzy Taylor-Richelieu, Rowena Anketell, Cheryl Brant, and Peter Gibbs. They have left me with no excuse for any oversights and infelicities that remain.

CONTENTS

INTRODUCTION

THERE are many good reasons why modern readers should find the Italian *novella* worthy of interest. The genre contains the genesis of the realist tradition in fiction and, at the same time, through a variety of framing devices, foregrounds complex and sophisticated relations between author, narrator, and audience. In its vivid and usually concise fashion, it testifies to the values both of urban mercantile society in the great cities of Florence and Venice and of the aristocratic culture of courtesy in the courts of smaller city states. And, of course, it provides the rich source material from which Shakespeare fashioned some of his most popular plays. Finally, however, one suspects that the enduring appeal of these Renaissance tales has remained unchanged over the centuries, being quite simply that of lively stories, with sharply etched characters, recounted without excessive didactic intentions by writers with an acute sense of their audience and a relish for their task.

The short narrative that the Italians call *novella* was the dominant form of vernacular prose fiction in Europe for over two centuries. Originating in Florence in the fourteenth century, it spread first to other regions of Italy and then, in the sixteenth century, to France, England, and Spain. And yet it remains obstinately difficult to formulate anything like a comprehensive and convincing generic definition of the *novella*. Paradoxical as it may sound, what ultimately defines the genre is its lack of generic constraints, its protean capacity to adapt and absorb an extraordinary range of narrative content. Medieval treatises on rhetoric, with their emphasis on Latin texts, could give no account of the essentially new and vernacular kind of narrative that found its fullest and finest expression in the *Decameron*. Boccaccio himself seems to draw attention to this situation when, in his Proem, he tells us that he plans to present 'a hundred tales or fables or parables or histories or whatever we choose to call them' (p. 5; *novelle o favole o parabole o istorie che dir vogliamo*). This may sound at first reading as if he were dismissing the whole question of terminology as irrelevant to his concerns, but the offhand tone is, in fact, deceptive, for the passage gives us first the term *novella* that will henceforth be used by himself and his successors to indicate the genre that he is effectively inventing and then goes on to suggest the narrative precedents that it incorporates and supersedes. The *novella* emerges, indeed, from a wide variety of narrative and didactic sources with roots both classical and medieval in Latin, French, Italian, and Provençal. These include exemplary tales, wise and witty responses and aphorisms, brief biographies, chivalric romance, hagiography, moralizing anecdotes, miraculous occurrences, and love stories. An example of what an author without Boccaccio's genius could make of such rich and disparate material is provided by the collection now known as the *Novellino*, compiled in Florence towards the end of the thirteenth century. This ragtag of a book contains a hundred tales, rarely more than a few pages long and often consisting of no more than a single paragraph. It could be described as a sprawling cultural hybrid where tales that lend themselves to ideal readings as models of behaviour jostle with those that reflect specific aspects of everyday life. Set beside the *Decameron*, the *Novellino* looks woefully unsophisticated; but it does testify to two aspects of contemporary culture that are crucial to the fortune of the *novella*.

The first of these is the awareness of a new reading public who might lack competence in Latin but possessed the kind of literacy in the vernacular that was already essential to the progress and prosperity of Florence's mercantile society. In 1338 the chronicler Villani boasted that the majority of Florentine children were taught to read,[1] and though his statistics have been challenged, all the evidence points to the existence of a newly literate and upwardly mobile class. This is the audience sought by the anonymous author or compiler of the *Novellino* when he states that his primary intention is to provide the lower orders with such 'flowers of speech, courteous phrases, and eloquent answers'[2] as will enable them to imitate their social superiors. Half a century later, the readers of the *Decameron* must have been already a good deal more sophisticated than the target audience of the *Novellino*, but there can be no doubting the fact that the rise of prose vernacular narrative is closely linked to the practical needs of the Florentine Republic. The second aspect of the *Novellino* that to some degree announces the *Decameron* is that any serious or consistent moralizing intention is undermined by the sheer variety of the material. The upshot is that,

---

[1] Giovanni Villani, *Nuova Cronica*, ed. Giuseppe Porta (Parma: Fondazione Pietro Bembo, Ugo Guanda Editore, 1991), iii. 198.

[2] *Il Novellino*, ed. Valeria Mouchet (Milan: Rizzoli, 2008), 42; my trans.

in the long run and despite the stated aim of improving popular literacy, the overall purpose of the book seems to be essentially aesthetic—the pleasure to be had in storytelling for its own sake.

With this in mind, we should look more closely at the term *novella* which has less to do with what we now call 'the novel' than anglophones might think. The term suggests both novelty and also *nuovo* in the medieval Italian sense of what is wondrous, surprising, or remarkable. It follows that the *novella* departs from the didactic emphasis and universalist pretensions of earlier narrative genres in order to privilege exceptional events. It is often locally rooted and responsive to the immediate cultural and social situation. This remains true even when the story itself is derived from ancient sources or when the setting is remote, for the contemporaneity of the *novella* is revealed not only by explicit content, but also by attitude, tone, and language. The *Decameron* reflects the values of mercantile Florence by the sheer economy of its stories—the relative brevity, the unity of action, the sense of closure. There is little time for philosophical digression or psychological analysis, and while the Church is represented as an inescapable fact of social life, there is no real sense of Christianity providing anything like spiritual motivation. Characters are revealed by their deeds and are seen as using their intelligence to act in their world rather than being acted upon. As for language, Boccaccio's style is very flexible and runs the whole gamut between highly formal rhetoric (the speeches of Ghismonda, p. 13) and colloquial backchat (Peronella and her husband, p. 27); but it is certainly true that, as a general rule, the *novella* will have a more vital connection to the everyday vernacular than any other genre of the period.

Boccaccio and the Frame

One of the great problems in writing even a brief history of the Italian *novella* is that it seems to burst onto the literary scene in a fully fledged masterpiece which then becomes the standard by which all other collections of *novelle* can be judged and found wanting. This is an unsatisfactory and misleading way of seeing things: as with the *Canzoniere* of Boccaccio's friend Petrarch, a crucial aspect of the *Decameron*'s greatness lies in its seminal capacity to stimulate works that go beyond imitation and strike out in a variety of new directions.

It is the _Decameron_, however, that establishes the basic characters and themes that will become the stock-in-trade of the _novella_ for more than two centuries—clever deceiving wives, cuckolded husbands, libidinous clergy, sharp-witted artisans, persecuted women, gross practical jokes, melodramatic adulteries, tragic and illicit passions. The fundamental move that prevents all this from becoming a mere jumble like the _Novellino_ is above all the strong authorial presence and sense of control evidenced by the organizing principle of the frame. The idea of a collection of stories organized around a fictional frame is not, of course, an invention of Boccaccio. It originates in the Orient during the golden age of Islam where it gave rise to such texts as _The Thousand and One Nights_ or (a more likely inspiration for the _Decameron_) _The Book of the Seven Sages_ which was already circulating in a Tuscan version, probably translated from French.

How much Boccaccio knew of this oriental tradition is open to question, but there can be no doubt that his use of the frame device was of the utmost importance for the future of the _novella_. The passage establishing the frame at the beginning of the book is too long to be included in this anthology; we shall need, therefore, to give a brief summary. After a brief Proem, Boccaccio embarks on a lengthy and terrifyingly graphic description of the Black Death that struck Florence in 1348 (_Decameron_ 1. 1). He then recounts how seven well-born young ladies met in the church of Santa Maria Novella and decided to leave the city and take refuge in the countryside. Realizing that they might need some protection, they enlist three young men to accompany them. The group (_brigata_ in Italian) then move to the idyllic setting of a villa near Fiesole where they spend their time strolling, dancing, singing, and above all telling stories according to a strictly observed schedule. Every evening all ten members of the group are required to tell a tale relevant to the theme of the day proposed by the member who is taking her or his turn as queen or king of that session. Two days a week are set aside for religious observance and domestic chores so that ten days of storytelling are spread over a fortnight and give us one hundred tales. Two days are left without any obligatory theme, others explore the workings of providence, good or bad fortune, happy or tragic love affairs, and resourceful devices for escaping difficult situations. Vittore Branca has argued that, like Dante's great poem, the _Decameron_ presents an ideal human journey, but this time in the form of a secular human comedy that takes us from the reproof of vice in Day One to the exaltation of virtue in Day Ten,[3] and though this sounds rather too schematic for the mobile irony of Boccaccio, it is possible that the frame of the *Decameron* with its hundred stories owes something to the example of the *Divine Comedy* with its hundred cantos. It is probably more significant that the composition of the *Decameron* coincides roughly with Petrarch's decision to collect his scattered lyric poems into the collection that we now know as *Rerum Vulgarium Fragmenta* or more commonly the *Canzoniere*. In both cases the aim is to raise the literary prestige of shorter vernacular forms by incorporating them into a larger structure where each item can be read at two levels—as an autonomous text and also, through comparison and contrast with other items, as part of a sequence.

One major function of Boccaccio's frame is to draw our attention to the act of storytelling and thus to remind us of the oral origins of his narrative tradition. Every tale has a teller and every teller has an audience; and both teller and audience exist in a precise temporal context. The *Decameron* can, indeed, be seen as thriving on an antithesis between frame and content, between the book's occasion in plague-ridden, death-stricken Florence and the overall life-enhancing quality of the tales it presents. Through the stories that they create, the refugees reaffirm the vitality of their urban values and embody the energies that will restore the city's prosperity.

Boccaccio's Women

The title page of the *Decameron* tells us that the book is also called *Prince Galahalt* (*cognominato Prencipe Galeotto*). In medieval Arthurian stories Sir Galahalt is the go-between who facilitates the adulterous love between Sir Lancelot and Queen Guinevere and it is the reading of one such story that, in the celebrated Paolo and Francesca episode of Dante's *Inferno* (5.70–138), provokes the consummation of a guilty passion: 'A Galahalt was the book and he who wrote it.' With gentle mockery of the poet whom he admired above all others, Boccaccio suggests that his own book, like the story that brought Dante's lovers to damnation, will aid women to satisfy their amorous urges. The implicit promise becomes explicit in the delicately ironic Proem

[3] Vittore Branca, in his edition of Giovanni Boccaccio, *Decameron* (Milan: Mondadori, 1985), introd., pp. xxix–xxxii.

where Boccaccio insists that the consolation his book offers to lovers is particularly intended for women:

And who on earth will deny that this help, for what it is worth, should be offered to fair ladies far more than to men? Through fear and shame they hide the flames of love within their tender breasts and those who have had that experience know how much stronger than an open blaze is that hidden fire. Moreover, constrained as they are by the wishes, the whims, and the orders of fathers, mothers, brothers, and husbands, they spend most of the time sitting almost idle, cramped up in their rooms, wishing one thing and its opposite in the same moment and brooding over thoughts that cannot possibly be always cheerful. (p. 4)

Women in love suffer more than men because of the restrictive conditions under which they live; Boccaccio offers them a new distraction to alleviate their pains. We do not know how many women readers the *Decameron* actually had, but Boccaccio surely had hopes that they would be numerous. The book is not only dedicated to women, it is also dominated by them, and we are shown a wide range of female protagonists who are capable of taking the initiative when extraordinary circumstances allow them to do so. It is they who decide to seek refuge outside the city and it is a woman (Pampinea) who comes up with the idea of a storytelling rota. Many of the comic stories show women strong enough to make the men look weak. Alibech's sexual vigour wears out the young hermit Rustico (p. 9), Madonna Filippa (p. 24) argues well enough to change a cruel and discriminatory law, and the shrewd proletarian Peronella (p. 27) not only manages to extricate herself from a very difficult situation, but also combines pleasure with profit as she simultaneously cuckolds her husband and extracts money from her lover. In a tragic vein the young widow Ghismonda (p. 13) defies the stifling unhealthy affection of her tyrannical father and argues her right to sexual satisfaction with a partner of her choice; the power and dignity of her rhetoric contrasts with the querulous tone of Tancredi who has 'wept like a beaten child'. And yet one can hardly regard the *Decameron* as 'the first major European feminist text'.[4] Boccaccio does not lend himself to this kind of simplification. With a slight shift of perspective, Peronella may be seen as demonstrating typically female dishonesty and Ghismonda as embodying an excessive sexual appetite. In the volume as a whole there are enough

[4] Gloria Allaire (ed.), *The Italian Novella* (London: Routledge, 2013), introd., p. 3.

libidinous and stupid women to obviate any suggestion that Boccaccio has a clear feminist agenda. It is in this context that we need to look at the tale of Patient Griselda (p. 30) which was to enjoy such huge popularity throughout Europe in poetry, the theatre, and the visual arts for close on four centuries and which still provides matter for an ongoing debate. As the concluding story of the final day which has been largely a celebration of virtue, one might expect the heroine to be seen in an unambiguously positive light. Petrarch, whose reaction to the *Decameron* was otherwise rather prissy ('written in prose and for the lower class'; 'the humour is rather too free'), chose to translate the story into what he saw as the more durable medium of Latin precisely because he saw its heroine as an example of 'feminine constancy' and 'conjugal devotion'.[5] But one does not have to be a twenty-first-century feminist to find Griselda's wifely obedience to the sadistic Gualtieri a rather problematic virtue. Indeed, the way in which she accepts without protest what she has every reason to believe is the murder of her children casts a strange light on her femininity. Her apparent docility may appear, in the long run, as a ruthless strategy in a ferocious battle of wills where Griselda's determination to keep her marital vow of obedience outweighs all other considerations and matches her husband's insistence on putting her to the test. It is worth remembering that the narrator of this tale is Dioneo who, throughout the book, has been given the freedom to speak on any topic he chooses and whose pervasive scepticism has often been taken as expressing that of Boccaccio himself. Dioneo's aversion to moral absolutism comes out in his devastatingly obscene conclusion:

Perhaps it would have served him [Gualtieri] right if his choice had fallen on a different kind of woman—one who would have reacted to being driven out in her shift by finding another man to jiggle her muff and maybe give her a new dress as part of the deal. (p. 39)

Petrarch unsurprisingly omits this ending as, indeed, he suppresses the narrator altogether; but one suspects that Dioneo's undermining of the tale's exemplary happy end anticipates the kind of reading that Boccaccio expected from his female audience.

---

[5] Francesco Petrarca, *Res Seniles*, ed. Silvia Rizzo (Florence: Le Lettere, 2017), 17. 3; my trans.

After the Decameron

The century after the *Decameron* saw the *novella* take root throughout Tuscany, but with results that have often been considered disappointing. Great authors, it has been said, exhaust the soil they till and it may well be that Boccaccio had so fully exploited the possibilities for prose fiction available to his generation that his immediate successors were left with nowhere to go. The social and economic context would have to change before the *Decameron* model could be put to new and fruitful use. One may add that in the later years of the fourteenth century, the vernacular as a literary language seemed to be losing ground before the humanist revival of Latin. Boccaccio's own career demonstrates this change of direction in that his work after the *Decameron* is almost exclusively in Latin. It would be a mistake, however, to insist on an oppositional relation between Latin and the vernacular. There was considerable interaction between the two Italian languages and it might be more useful to consider the situation as one of creative bilingualism. Tales from the *Decameron* were translated into Latin by Petrarch ('Patient Griselda') and by the great Florentine chancellor and historian Leonardo Bruni ('Tancredi and Ghismonda'), while Enea Silvio Piccolomini (later Pope Pius II) wrote *Historia de duobus amantibus* (*A Tale of Two Lovers*), an impressive Latin *novella* that owes much to the vernacular example.

That the urban realism introduced by Boccaccio need not entail an elimination of more traditional elements is perfectly demonstrated by a *novella* familiar to students of Shakespeare as a major source of *The Merchant of Venice*. This is 'Giannetto and the Lady of Belmont' (p. 40) which is to be found in a collection known for some obscure reason as *Il Pecorone* (*The Big Sheep*, 1378) and usually attributed to Ser Giovanni Fiorentino. There are fifty tales, many of them more or less plagiarized from the Florentine chronicler Giovanni Villani and represented as having been told alternately by an abbess and her clerical lover over a period of twenty-five days. In the story of Giannetto the timeless folklore motifs are clear enough: from the third son who receives no inheritance, through the three visits to the mysterious lady and the test that he passes only at the third attempt, to the pound of flesh and the concluding episode of the ring. But these are neatly blended with the here and now of fourteenth-century Venice—the role of Jewish moneylenders, the financing of mercantile ventures, the profitable trips to the great trading cities of Syria, the conspicuous consumption, and the complex litigation. When Giannetto leaves his fellow merchants to enter the port where the lady reigns he is moving from one narrative world into another.

Litigation and moneylending are also prominent in the *Trecentonovelle* (1392–7) of Franco Sacchetti. The title obviously invites comparison with the *Decameron*, but Sacchetti makes no attempt to imitate Boccaccio's structural mastery: there is no framing device and what unity the collection possesses is given by the strong authorial presence felt especially in the concluding moral comment on each tale. In his Proem Sacchetti describes himself as 'a rude unlettered man' and admits Boccaccio's stylistic superiority; but what this really suggests is a new aesthetic in which his own more rough-hewn manner will expand the range of the genre through a greater reliance on episodes of which he has personal knowledge or experience, while those who dismiss his stories as mere fiction (*favole*) should know that in many cases he has changed nothing but the names. Taken as a whole, the *Trecentonovelle* give a vivid and entertaining picture of life in late fourteenth-century Florence. The tale of 'Piero Brandani's Son' (p. 55), for example, begins with an animated scene near the courthouse in the centre of the city where the boy is waiting with essential documents for the arrival of his irascible and litigious father. We then move out into the nocturnal world of the Tuscan countryside, peopled by travelling merchants, surly innkeepers, fearsome bandits, and voracious wolves. The death of the wolf and the triumphant return of the young Brandani at the end of the story may be read as a happy if fortuitous victory of urban civilization over rustic barbarism.

Moneylending had been a standard feature of the Florentine economy since well before Sacchetti's time and it was not reserved for prominent banking families like the Bardi (who employed the young Boccaccio), the Pazzi, and the Medici. Small moneylenders also abounded, one of the less successful being the father of Dante more than a century earlier. The Church's blanket condemnation of usury may have done little to check the growth of the practice, but it nevertheless disturbed consciences and stimulated efforts to find some morally acceptable solution to the problem. This is the background to the 'Sermon on Usury' (p. 58) where a Dominican friar gains a larger congregation and, presumably, a fatter purse by promising to prove

that moneylending is not a sin. The size of the congregation that the
friar attracts would suggest that Sacchetti's indignation is not directed
against any particular class, but rather against a generalized materialist
culture that has lost its moral bearings. It has been argued that there
is often something incongruous about the solemn lessons that Sacchetti
draws from his lively narratives, but that can hardly be objected to in
this story which, after a hilarious parody of professional banking jargon,
concludes that 'usury lies in the work itself and not in the name'.

After Sacchetti, the Tuscan *novella* shows signs of tiredeness and
repetition, with only occasional successes. Of the nine stories in
Giovanni Gherardi da Prato's *Paradiso degli Alberti* (*c.*1420–30) the
only memorable tale is that of Catellina (p. 62) where the phantas-
magoric scene at the gallows and the wild nocturnal ride through
Naples anticipate the lurid supernaturalism of Francesco Pona two
centuries later. The forty *novelle* of the Sienese Gentile Sermini
(1424) provide conventional examples of scandalous sexual behaviour
which become interesting when they reveal the fragility of the author's
explicit moral stance as in the story of 'Anselmo Salimbeni and Angelica
Montanini' (p. 68), where a brother persuades his sister to sacrifice
her virginity as a way of paying off a debt of honour towards his friend
who is so moved by the gesture that he decides to marry her. Sermini
suggests that we should 'consider all the acts of courtesy that passed
between them' before deciding 'which of them was the greatest and
most praiseworthy'; but this hardly dissipates the impression that
a rather sordid bargain lurks behind the ostentatiously noble gestures.
A not dissimilar unease emanates from Sabbadino degli Arienti's tale
of 'The Priest and the Friar' (p. 119) in *Le Porrettane* (1483). The
frame for this collection is the presence at the spa of Porretta (hence
the title) of a group of young aristocrats from Bologna. The sense of
a close-knit and socially superior group pervades the tale (told in the
first-person plural) of a band of young bloods from Arezzo whose prank
involves disguising a good-looking young priest as a Florentine girl and
taking him to a rustic feast where he excites the lust of a local friar. In
the stress on male solidarity and the pleasure they all seem to take in the
feminine beauty of the young priest there is more than a hint that the
savage punishment they impose on the friar is some kind of exorcism
for their own unacknowledged desires.

The *beffa*, a more or less elaborate prank or practical joke, is a staple
of the Italian *novella*. It is generally immune from moral judgement

and though the prank in question may have some practical purpose (saving a wayward wife from the wrath of her cuckolded husband as in Boccaccio's tale of Peronella), its essential aim is to celebrate the triumph of intelligence over stupidity. The *beffa* provides ideal material for the *novella* in that it is, of its very nature, short and self-contained. Moreover, as Gioachino Chiarini reminds us,[6] it offers an eminently theatrical kind of plot, since it requires a basic scenario involving some form of fiction or deception which is then worked out in detail by a dramatist or producer within the text, and usually performed by a number of complicit actors who move upon the stage of a clearly defined social and physical space. *The Fat Woodworker* (p. 74), a free-standing text that belongs to no collection, is an extreme example of this kind of *beffa*. The basic scenario is the almost Pirandellian idea of persuading an apparently slow-witted but gifted craftsman that he is, in fact, someone else. This improbable jape seems actually to have taken place in 1409. All the major characters (the woodworker Manetto Ammannatini, the architect Filippo Brunelleschi, the sculptor Donatello, the patrician Tomaso Pecori) have a historical existence, and the story has come down to us in two versions, both derived from oral tradition. One version is that of Ammannatini, the victim of the jape, who seems to have told his story to a Florentine merchant whom he met over thirty years later in the Hungarian city of Buda. The second and more detailed account is that of Brunelleschi who obviously took pride in being the originator and organizer of the *beffa* and recounted the whole tale to anyone who wanted to hear until it came down to his future biographer, Antonio Manetti, who is responsible for the version given in this volume. The prank itself has little in the way of serious motivation. We are told that the company of artist-craftsmen who gather at the house of Pecori feel snubbed by the humble woodworker's unexplained absence, but there is little else to suggest that this *beffa* reflects the group's need to reassert a certain degree of hierarchy. The real motive lies in the restless Brunelleschi's hyperactive urge to demonstrate his intellectual brilliance by pulling off a prank of monumental scale involving the precise deployment of a considerable number of subordinate actors. If the woodworker is chosen as the victim, it is less because of any presumed social inferiority than because

---

[6] Gioachino Chiarini (ed.), *Novelle italiane: Il Quattrocento* (Milan: Garzanti, 1982), introd., p. xxvii.

he is the opposite of Brunelleschi: slow-moving, unsure of himself, something of a dreamer. We have grown accustomed to think of identity as being socially constructed and rarely can that idea have been more fully exploited than it is in the tale of *The Fat Woodworker*. Grasso's status is that of a financially self-sufficient citizen and craftsman, so that such things as the disarray of his tools or his arrest for an unpaid debt amount to direct attacks on his identity. He is also defined by the narrow physical space in which he moves and by the temporal patterns that govern his activity. Throughout the tale we follow his movements around Florence (from his workshop in Piazza San Giovanni to his home near Santa Maria del Fiore, from the Merchants' Court to the house of Matteo's brothers near Santa Felicità on the Costa San Giorgio and back at last to Santa Maria del Fiore) and these precise topographical details do more than underline the story's authenticity; they mirror the formidable mastery of detail that enables Brunelleschi to exploit the weakness of the woodworker and to involve the complex machinery of profession, family, the law, and the Church in his extraordinary enterprise. Few stories have been so well plotted—in every sense of that word.

In the long run, however, it is not Brunelleschi alone who threatens Grasso's identity: it is also Florence itself with its clannish insistence on who belongs where and how, its respect for appearances, its emphasis on the public space, and its belief in man as first and foremost a citizen. Not for nothing does the climactic scene take place in that most representative of public buildings, the cathedral church of Santa Maria del Fiore where, twenty-six years after the discomfiture of the woodworker, Brunelleschi will complete his celebrated dome. In leaving for Hungary Grasso is not only avoiding the ridicule that falls on the victim of an outrageous *beffa*, but also seeking refuge from a society whose agile and competitive spirit has no place for a man of his withdrawn and diffident nature. In a last twist of the story we are told that, when he does return to Florence, Grasso clings to the company of his old tormentor as if the only possible protector of his fragile identity is the man whose genius once came so near to destroying it. The concluding passage, with its list of sources, is an eloquent tribute both to the golden age of Florentine artist-craftsmen and to the power of the oral tradition.

The *Porrettane* of Sabbadino degli Arienti with its courtly Bolognese background may have already suggested that, a century after Boccaccio,

Tuscany was beginning to lose its monopoly over the *novella*; but the truly significant break comes with the *Novellino* of Masuccio Salernitano (Tommaso Guardati). It is the first major Italian work of prose literature to emerge from the Neapolitan cultural area that in the preceding decades had been dominated by humanist Latin or (after 1442) by the Catalan of the city's Aragonese rulers. Composed over roughly a quarter of a century (*c.* 1450–74), the volume superficially recalls the structure of the *Decameron* in that it consists of fifty stories arranged thematically in five sets of ten; but there is no over-arching frame and no attempt to suggest an oral origin for the tales. Instead, each tale is presented as a document written by Masuccio himself and with its own frame, consisting of a dedication to some noble or notable personage in Neapolitan courtly circles, and a concluding moralizing comment. Many of the tales express stereotypical attitudes of anticlericalism and misogyny, but they do so with a moral vehemence and a taste for the monstrous and sensational that we do not find to anything like the same extent in the sunnier dispositions of Boccaccio and Chaucer. The story of 'Saint Griffin's Drawers' (p. 103) offers a case in point and, as so often with the *novella*, the relations between frame and story, teller and tale, deserve particular attention. We begin with the dedication to Giovanni Pontano whose humanist learning and prestige as one of the greatest neo-Latin poets of his time might seem to make him an unlikely recipient for a ribald story in the vernacular—and especially a vernacular so recognizably dialectal as that of Masuccio. But Pontano himself was a lively satirist and one who shared Masuccio's dislike of the clergy. And so, in reproaching Pontano for a vice he does not possess, that of being too eager for the company of friars, Masuccio is, in fact, indulging in a private joke which serves to establish his intimacy with the literary elite. The story begins as a lively if conventional account of an adulterous affair between a lecherous friar and a wayward wife, complete with clever serving-maid and comic cuckold. The atmosphere changes when the Blessed Sacrament is paraded through the streets of Catania wrapped in the friar's stained underwear which is then exposed for veneration as a relic of Saint Griffin. Though one is tempted to admire the friar's sheer effrontery, laughter at this extreme development might well feel somewhat queasy; all the more so because in his authorial comment Masuccio goes on to stress the more repugnant physical details:

the very idea of putting a pair of stinking drawers, swarming with fleas and full of a thousand other kinds of filth, in the chosen vessel and true receptacle of the sacred body of the Son of God. Read the terrible Passion of Christ and you will find that not even the perfidious Jews [...] ever showed him such monstrous contempt as this. (pp. 111–12)

How can this tone of shocked moralizing be reconciled with the initial decision to invent such a story and the sheer gusto with which it is narrated? Perhaps the aim is indeed to teach his readers through temptation, insofar as they are forced to admit that what first appeared to be a laughing matter is something that should have filled them with righteous disgust. Be that as it may, one result of rejecting the overall frame is that Masuccio has no fictional narrators to distance him from responsibility for the stories he tells.

The Novella *and the Genre System*

Masuccio's departures from the *Decameron* model in style and structure may be seen as anticipating the extraordinary extension of the *novella*'s registers, range, and influence in the sixteenth century. The popularity of the *novella* now covered the whole of the Italian peninsula and provided fresh material for more traditional genres such as comedy, tragedy, dialogue, and even, in the case of Ariosto's *Orlando Furioso*, the epic poem. The sheer wealth of content that storytelling (or *novellare*) embraces is vividly celebrated in a famous mid-century letter by Andrea Calmo, a Venetian writer of comedies, who describes a feast where the variety of the food is matched by that of tales that can range from the folklore of Mother Goose and the Mouse Who Went on a Pilgrimage to the tragic loves of Guiscardo and Ghismonda or Pyramus and Thisbe.[7] Castiglione also testifies to the appreciation of the genre in courtly circles by using the pretext of a discussion of types of humour to insert a number of short witty tales into the second book of his hugely influential and much-translated *The Courtier* (1528). It should be stressed, however, that this flowering of the *novella* was not, on the whole, accompanied by any marked improvement in its literary prestige. The only attempt to theorize the *novella* was Francesco Bonciani's *Lezione sopra il comporre delle novelle* (*On the Writing of*

7 Cited by Ruth B. Bottigheimer, *Fairy Tales Framed: Early Forewords, Afterwords and Critical Words* (New York: State University of New York, 2012), 49–52.

Tales, 1574) which, while conceding to the *novella* a certain entertainment value, insisted that its hybridity, its prose medium, and the coarseness of its comic subject matter must deny it any place in the traditional hierarchy of genres. The new moral rigidities of the Counter-Reformation combined with such elitist literary attitudes to create an official climate of suspicion towards the *novella*. Even the *Decameron*, which Bembo's *Prose della volgar lingua* (*On the Vernacular Language*, 1525) had proclaimed as the ideal model for Italian prose, did not escape the general censure, being placed on the Index of Forbidden Books in 1559 and subjected to the indignity of bowdlerization in Florentine editions of 1573 and 1582.

The *novella*'s challenge to the genre system and to the linguistic decorum imposed on Florence by Duke Cosimo de' Medici and the followers of Bembo can be seen clearly in the work of Anton Francesco Grazzini, a versatile and prolific author who courted controversy by rejecting what he saw as the dogmatism and sterility of formal literary conventions derived from a narrowly conceived classicism. The vigour of his arguments in favour of more flexible forms with a grittier realism and deeper popular roots earned him a twenty-year exclusion from the academy that he himself had helped to found. In his unfinished *Le cene* (*The Suppers*), the frame with its six witty young women and four cultivated young men superficially recalls the *Decameron*; but there is nothing like Boccaccio's radical contrast between the plague-ridden city and the pleasant hillside refuge. The occasion here is nothing more serious than a snowstorm (p. 226) and the activity of storytelling is in harmony with the Carnival atmosphere outside. But what matters more than the fiction of the frame is the fact that it contains an explicit appeal to Boccaccio's example. The young people have the *Decameron* with them and they honour Boccaccio's memory not simply by reading him or, more provocatively, by calling him a saint ('I like that *saint*'), but by imitating and perpetuating his pattern of storytelling. Grazzini's point here is, perhaps, that through Boccaccio the *novella* has become rooted in Florentine culture as a genre not to be tampered with by moralists or literary lawgivers. Of the twenty-two stories that survive out of a planned thirty there is one at least, that of the proverbially childish Falananna (*Le cene* 2. 2), that has a comic verve worthy of Boccaccio; but Grazzini's more characteristic achievement lies in *novelle* with tight plotting, economic prose, swift action, vivid dramatic events, and a marked taste for episodes of spectacular cruelty.

'Fazio the Goldsmith' (p. 230), for example, begins with a lurid piece of scene-setting, as the mortally wounded usurer Grimaldi makes his way through a thunderstorm to the cabin of the alchemist whose fires are seen through the open door. It then takes us in some detail through the complex international banking operations employed by Fazio to hide his theft of Grimaldi's gold, before concluding with his execution, the suicide of his wife, and her murder of their two children. The story of 'Lazzero and Gabriello' (p. 241) invites comparison with 'Fazio the Goldsmith'. In both *novelle* the protagonist is caught up in circumstances where he risks being punished for a death that he has witnessed but not caused. He then finds a way out of the problem by secretly appropriating the wealth of the dead man (and in Gabriello's case his identity into the bargain). Though Fazio, as an alchemist, is from the start a somewhat shiftier figure than the poor fisherman, the initial guilt of both characters is lessened by the fact that neither of the dead men have any obvious heirs who are being deprived of their rightful inheritance. And yet Fazio will die an atrocious death and his progeny will die with him, whereas Gabriello founds a distinguished line with the appropriate name of Fortunati. There is no sense here of crime and punishment, no satisfaction of justice either human or divine. Grazzini's world is ruled by chance and offers no occasion for moralizing.

A different kind of challenge both to reigning orthodoxies and to the Boccaccio model is offered by *Le piacevoli notti* (*The Pleasant Nights*, 1550–3) of Grazzini's contemporary Giovan Francesco Straparola. A northern Italian from Caravaggio (like the painter), he breaks with the Tuscan tradition of urban realism by introducing, though not uniformly, elements of folklore such as those we find in the tale of 'Fortunio' (p. 133), with its fabulous setting, its talking animals, its repeated patterns of three, and its beautful princess whose hand is won by the poor disinherited youth. Straparola's work became popular throughout Europe and can probably be credited with inspiring the far livelier and more lasting achievement of Giambattista Basile eighty years later.

Yet another significant development is the emergence of stand-alone stories which do not belong to any collection. One of the most famous of these is Machiavelli's *Fable* (p. 125, sometimes known as *Belphagor*), a brilliant misogynistic squib which inherits a long tradition of folklore about demonic possession and stories of the Devil Who Takes a Wife.

Machiavelli's particular contribution lies in the contrast he develops between the harmonious and rational procedures of Hell and the chaotic and frenzied nature of life on earth—especially in Florence. But undoubtedly the most important of these *novelle spicciolate* (uncollected stories) is Luigi Da Porto's *Story of Two Noble Lovers* (p. 146), the basic elements of which can be traced back through Masuccio's Sienese tale of 'Mariotto and Gannozza' (*Novellino* 23) to the story of Pyramus and Thisbe in Ovid's *Metamorphoses*. It is Da Porto who transfers the setting to Verona, names the lovers as Romeo and Giulietta, and provides the dramatic outline that, through the mediation of Bandello's later version (1554) and Arthur Brooke's poem of *Romeus and Juliet* (1562), will structure Shakespeare's play. The phrase 'dramatic outline' should be given full weight here because it indicates something more than a basic plot. As Ettore Bonora has pointed out,[8] what we remember from Da Porto, as from Shakespeare, is a sequence of vividly realized scenes—the feast at the house of Cappelletti, the balcony scene, the death of Tebaldo, Giulietta's taking of the fatal philtre, the tragic conclusion in the crypt. That all these episodes are accompanied by highly rhetorical set speeches underlines the fact that it is Da Porto who is the true begetter of the Romeo and Juliet story in the dramatic form that we know through Shakespeare.

Cinzio, Bandello, and the Italian Wars

In 1494 King Charles VIII of France brought an army down into Italy in pursuit of his somewhat far-fetched claim to the throne of Naples. The expedition ended in failure when Milan, Venice, and the Papal States formed the League of Venice to oppose French interference; but by showing up the vulnerability and disunity of the peninsula, the episode initiated the Italian Wars where French armies battled with imperial German and Spanish forces while the Italian states sought to save some semblance of autonomy in a confusing series of shifting alliances that ended only with the Treaty of Cateau-Cambrésis in 1559. It is against this chaotic background of military violence and political disintegration that we need to read the work of the two major collections of the sixteenth century, both written by northerners: the

---

[8] Ettore Bonora, 'La novella', in Emilio Cecchi and Natalino Sapegne (eds), *Storia della letteratura italiana*, iv (Milan: Garzanti, 1966), 267–8.

Hecatommithi of Giovambattista Giraldi Cinzio (1565) and the *Novelle* of Matteo Bandello (1554 and 1573).

Cinzio's *Hecatommithi* (from Greek *hekatón*, a hundred) clearly invites comparison with the *Decameron*: we have the same division into ten days with ten stories for each and an apparently similar proem describing a catastrophe from which the storytellers have taken refuge. But the differences are crucial. The catastrophe is not a natural disaster like the plague, but a man-made event, the most horrendous episode of the Italian Wars, the Sack of Rome by the troops of Emperor Charles V in 1527. And the storytellers are not taking refuge in the salubrious hills surrounding the city, but sailing away towards what looks like a definitive exile in Marseilles. For Cinzio the Sack of Rome is a crucial episode in the moral history of the world and his sense of a threat to the divine order in Church and State is underlined by his repeated assertion that many of the German imperial troops are Lutheran heretics. It follows that the *Hecatommithi* have an explicit didactic intention that is alien to the urban bourgeois tradition of the *novella*. In this sense, Marcello Ciccuto is right to see Cinzio's collection as a kind of anti-*Decameron*, a Counter-Reformation corrective to the amoral and detached vision of Boccaccio and his Tuscan imitators.[9] Stylistically, Cinzio brings the *novella* nearer to more elevated genres and this in keeping with a taste for extreme situations and violence.

'Iuriste and Epitia' (p. 285) and 'The Moorish Captain' (p. 270), sources for *Measure for Measure* and *Othello* respectively, demonstrate two rather different aspects of Cinzio's work. 'Iuriste and Epitia' reflects Cinzio's defence of tragicomedy as a dramatic form that gives a happy end to plots that explore serious and potentially tragic themes. Despite the specific reference to Emperor Maximilian and Innsbruck, the tale has the air of an ahistorical moral fable, demonstrating how justice should function under ideal imperial rule. The Emperor insists on the rule of law; a citizen appeals to him against the actions of her local governor; the evil governor is justly sentenced to death, but reprieved in the interests of a greater good. But there is nothing ideal about the world of 'The Moorish Captain'. Here we have the recognizably contemporary setting of Venice's long and ultimately unsuccessful defence of Cyprus against the Turks and the tale itself is one of sordid realism that never rises to tragedy. The distance from

---

[9] Marcello Ciccuto (ed.), *Novelle italiane: Il Cinquecento* (Milan: Garzanti, 1982), 412.

Shakespeare's version is instructive: where Othello stabs Desdemona and then himself, Cinzio's Moor seeks to disguise the murder by beating his wife to death with a sand-filled stocking and then making the roof fall in upon her. There is not much justice to be found in Venetian law: the Moor resists torture and escapes the death sentence, but is sent into exile and murdered by Disdemona's relatives, while the ensign dies after being tortured in a completely different affair. After so much brutality, the conventional conclusion ('Thus God avenged the innocence of Disdemona') comes across as an awkwardly pious afterthought. Too many of Cinzio's serious tales are weakened by this kind of moralizing, though 'Nigella and the Doctor' (p. 280) shows that he could, on occasion, work effectively in a lighter vein.

Matteo Bandello, cleric and courtier, is by far the most prolific and influential author of *novelle* after Boccaccio. He claimed to be indifferent to matters of style, but his rapid, nervous, and sometimes loosely constructed prose has, at its best, a narrative drive that makes up for its lack of elegance. One is reminded of the suggestion, in the Prologue to Marguerite de Navarre's *Heptaméron*, that a too obvious display of rhetorical skill would cast doubt on the veracity of the storyteller. Bandello's desire to be seen as, to some extent, a reliable chronicler may also have led him to abandon the clearly fictional frame of the *Decameron* in favour of a scheme not unlike that of Masuccio. Each story is prefaced by an introductory letter which supposedly recounts the precise circumstances under which he heard the tale narrated and by whom. Thus every story has its own frame and, unlike the *Decameron* or the *Hecatommithi*, the volume has no sequential organization, no thematic sections, and no fixed number of narrators. One result of this scheme is that we get a complex interaction between on the one hand the supposed oral narrator and the audience as presented within the frame and on the other the author (Bandello) who reformulates the story as text for his presumed readers.

The frame typically involves a courtly gathering where some great aristocratic lady connected with the courts of Milan or Mantua (Isabella d'Este, Antonia Bauzia, Costanza Rangoni Fregoso, Cecilia Gallerani, Camilla Scarampa) presides over a series of sophisticated cultural entertainments which Bandello describes in loving and reverential detail. He was himself an assiduous and much-respected courtier and though many of his tales may derive from his wide reading in ancient and modern languages, others such as 'The Countess of

Challant' (p. 169) and 'The Duchess of Amalfi' (p. 207) clearly exploit his inside knowledge of contemporary events. But the evocation of these courtly settings is more than a form of snobbery or a strategy of authentification. It bears witness to the growth of what has been called the Renaissance culture of courtesy which reached the whole of Europe through Baldassare (or Baldesar) Castiglione's *The Courtier* (1528; translated into English by Thomas Hoby, 1561); and indeed the courts that Bandello frequents appear as variants of the court of Urbino where Castiglione sets his famous dialogue. This culture of courtesy is something new in the history of Italian nobility insofar as it attempts to substitute an aesthetic–ethical ideal for the old military ethos which had been irreparably damaged by the failure of the aristocracy to pre-vent the foreign invasions that devastated the country in the first half of the sixteenth century. The *novelle* of Bandello, however, reveal the flaws and strains involved in this attempt to find a new function for the nobility as embodiments of civilized living. For a start there is the contrast between the calm, cultured, and orderly existence that Bandello experiences in the various courts of northern Italy, and the violent, chaotic, and lawless activities that fill so many of his tales of contemporary life. The effect is to suggest that courtly culture is, if not irrelevant, at best a very fragile refuge from a society in crisis, and we recognize its permeability when the same Cardinal of Aragon who hounds the Duchess of Amalfi to her death receives a flattering address from Bandello in the introductory letter to another story (*Novelle* 1. 33). We are also made aware of tensions and contradictions when it comes to the role of birth in the constitution of such an elite. In the introduction to 'The Countess of Challant', for example, Bandello uses the familiar analogy of dogs and horses to emphasize the importance of breeding and reproaches the otherwise prudent Lord Ermes Visconti for not marrying 'a noblewoman, high-born and reared in a noble household' (p. 170). And yet, a few stories later, in 'Giulia of Gazzuolo' (p. 177), we find a peasant girl whose acute sense of honour leads her to a suicide so firmly and stoically performed that 'one can only blame Nature for not giving such a great and valiant spirit a more noble birth' (p. 183). Sir Timbreo (p. 184) is worried about marrying below his rank and needs to be reassured that his bride's family, though decayed in wealth and power, are of thoroughly noble origin.

It would be a mistake, however, to consider Bandello's fiction as consciously designed to express a given ideology or social ideal, even if the culture of courtesy could be considered in these terms. 'I believe that this age of ours, more than all others, is one in which things befall that arouse amazement, compassion, and blame'; that much-quoted passage comes from an introductory letter that starts by condemning the religious and political ravages caused by the Lutheran heresy before going on to a *novella* that gives a sensational if somewhat inaccurate account of the marital mishaps of Henry VIII (*Novelle* 3. 62). As Robin Kirkpatrick points out, serious moral reflection soon gives way to juicy gossip.[10] And the problem of gossip is in itself an essential part of Bandello's subject matter if one thinks of Sir Timbreo's readiness to believe the worst about Fenicia or of the loose talk that destroys the happiness of the Duchess of Amalfi and Antonio Bologna. Bandello's narrative ambition, like the 'dyer's hand' of Shakespeare, is 'subdued to what it works in', and if his work offers no stable viewpoint this is partly because, in the long run, his sheer pleasure in the variety of raw material offered by the unsettled age outweighs all other considerations.

New Directions

At the start of this Introduction, in an attempt to define the nature of Boccaccio's realism, we spoke of a genre that is locally rooted and responsive to the immediate cultural and social situation. Despite the differences between them, that description holds good for almost all the *novellieri* in the two centuries between Sacchetti and Cinzio. It is only after the end of the Italian Wars (1559) and the deaths of Bandello (1561) and Cinzio (1573) that the *novella* loses this kind of relevance and verisimilitude as authors begin to exploit other forms of short fiction. It may be too simple to link this situation with the economic and political stagnation of the Italian states in the late sixteenth and seventeenth centuries, but it is surely significant that the decline of the Boccaccio mode of realism coincides with the gradual fading of the Italian *novella* as a model of vernacular fiction for the rest of Europe.

The most extraordinary transformation of the *novella* in the seventeenth century is Giambattista Basile's collection of stories *Lo cunto de li cunti, overo Lo trattenemiento de' peccerille* (*The Tale of Tales or*

---

[10] Robin Kirkpatrick, *English and Italian Literature from Dante to Shakespeare* (London: Longman, 1995), 235.

Entertainment for Little Ones), published posthumously in 1634–6. The invitation to read the volume in the light of the Boccaccio tradition is more or less implicit in its structure—the frame story, the limited number of narrators, the division of fifty tales into five days that led it to be widely known as the *Pentameron*. But we soon become aware that the *Decameron* model has been invoked only to be subverted. Boccaccio's polished Tuscan has been replaced by Neapolitan dialect; the narrators are not fashionable young men and women, but a bunch of old hags; the stories are all fairy tales that stand in contrast to the Tuscan's urban realism. There are, however, some possible misconceptions that need correcting before Basile's achievement can be properly assessed. The first of these is that with the use of dialect Basile was aiming for a popular or even proletarian public. The fact is that in Italy until quite recently dialect was not a class marker. Most intellectuals were to all intents and purposes bilingual, using the Tuscan-based vernacular as a written language and their own regional dialect for everyday business and communication with family and friends. Nor was Basile alone in using Neapolitan dialect as a literary medium as we can see from his own anthology of Neapolitan poetry, *Le muse napolitane* (1635), and from the work of his contemporary, Giulio Cesare Cortese. Another misconception, encouraged by the subtitle, is that the tales are written for children. Some of them certainly are derived from tales told to children and many of them, as we know, have since been adapted for children. But what are we to make of a Cinderella (Zezolla, p. 296) who murders her first stepmother or of a Sleeping Beauty (Talia, p. 301) who is not woken by a prince's kiss but raped by a king while she lies in a trance? Basile's prose, moreover, is anything but naïve. It is no mere transcription of colloquial speech. Inventive in insult and extravagant in praise, given to hyperbole, delighting in lists and brimming with metaphors, it has a sophisticated exuberance that demands a sophisticated audience and that Italian critics have been more than ready to describe as baroque.

There is, of course, a dark and desperate side to this display of energy. Behind all the linguistic ingenuity, the marvels and monsters, the ogres and the fairy godmothers, what these tales ultimately convey is the sense of how hard it is to live in a world that is radically unpredictable in its rewards and punishments, a world that defies our understanding and resists our presumptuous attempts to shape it for the better. That surely is part of Basile's legacy to the Brothers Grimm and to Hans Christian Andersen, if not to Charles Perrault.

While Basile in Naples was, to all intents and purposes, creating a new genre, far to the north in Venice a group of writers associated with the recently founded Accademia degli Incogniti (Academy of the Unknown) was still producing *novelle* of a more traditional kind. In keeping with the generally freethinking stance of the Academy, these tales exploited conventional themes of eroticism and social satire but rarely demonstrated any marked individual quality. An exception, however, should be made for Francesco Pona. His most famous work is *La lucerna* (*The Lamp*, 1625) which, through the original device of a very communicative soul imprisoned in a student's lamp, exploits the idea of reincarnation as a frame for a wide range of stories, with an emphasis on the horrific and the occult. The tale of Lindori (p. 311), one of five insert stories in his novel *Ormondo* (1635), creates a lingering sense of disquiet with less melodramatic means. The abandoned Lindori reappears to her faithless lover under a succession of varied and fleeting manifestations during his voyage from Crete to Venice, and his reactions give the overall impression of poignant nostalgia for a vision that becomes ever more seductive as it loses its recognizable contours. The *novella* has come a long way from Boccaccio's firm and confident grasp of the here and now.

The Italian Novella *in England*

Dante, Petrarch, and Boccaccio (the 'three crowns' of Italian literature) all have a powerful presence in the work of Chaucer, but the Boccaccio who influences Chaucer is not so much the author of the *Decameron* as the courtly writer of the early Neapolitan period. *Troilus and Criseyde* is a reworking of the *Filostrato* while, in the *Canterbury Tales*, both the Franklin's Tale and the Knight's Tale derive from works of this period, the *Filocolo* and the *Teseida*.

The one story in Chaucer's masterpiece that does have its origin in the *Decameron* is the Clerk's Tale of Patient Griselda which, however, is translated not from Boccaccio's Italian but from Petrarch's Latin version. The differences between the three versions are revealing and have produced a fair amount of commentary. Here it is worth noting that the Chaucerian version is thematically embedded in the marriage debate that runs throughout the *Canterbury Tales*, that the conduct of the marquis is more thoroughly condemned than in Boccaccio or Petrarch, and that Griselda is rendered more human by the insight and sympathy of the narrating clerk. There is no proof that Chaucer ever read the *Decameron*, but he may well have known enough about it to imitate the framing device (plague or pilgrimage) that allows a variety of narrators.

The Italian *novella* really arrived in England during the two decades (1560–80) that precede the great flowering of the Elizabethan theatre to which it contributed in so many ways. The genre was already popular in France thanks to the *Heptaméron* of Marguerite de Navarre and the *Histoires tragiques* adapted from Bandello by Pierre Boiaistuau and François de Belleforest and in fact the material of English collections was often received through the filter of these French versions rather than directly from the original Italian. The English reception of this new Italian genre could not, in any case, be a straightforward affair. One of the results of the Reformation had been to render English attitudes to Italy radically ambivalent. On the one hand Italy provided the standard for courtesy and civility as represented in Castiglione's *The Courtier*; Italy was still the model for excellence in the arts and Italian the only modern vernacular to have created a literature deemed worthy of comparison with that of Greece and Rome; on the other hand Italy was the homeland of the infamous Machiavelli, the home of the papacy and of Catholic idolatry, a byword for violence, treachery, and sexual immorality.

In *The Schoolmaster* (1570) Roger Ascham testifies both to the popularity of the *novella* and to fears of its deleterious influence on the national character:

And yet ten *Morte Arthurs* do not the tenth part so much harm as one of these books made in Italy and translated in England. They open not fond and common ways to vice, but such subtle, cunning, new, and diverse shifts to carry young wills to vanity and young wits to mischief, to teach old bawds new school points, as the single head of an Englishman is not able to invent, nor never was heard of in England before; yea, when Papistry overflowed all. Suffer these books to be read, and they shall soon displace all books of godly learning.[11]

It is in this context that we need to consider the adaptations of Italian originals in the three major English collections of *novelle*: Geoffrey Fenton's *Certain tragical discourses of Bandello* (1567), William Painter's

---

[11] Roger Ascham, *The Schoolmaster*, ed. Lawrence V. Ryan (Ithaca, NY: Cornell University Press, 1967).

The Palace of Pleasure (1566–75), and George Whetstone's *Heptameron of Civil Discourses* (1581). All three seek to avoid reproach by girding the tales with moralizing and didactic comment, a process already begun by Boiaistuau and Belleforest but now reinforced by an aggressively patriotic Protestantism.

It is Fenton, a veteran of Elizabeth's Irish wars, who goes the furthest in this direction with a rhetoric that sometimes reaches an almost hysterical pitch of violence, especially when denouncing his favourite vice of 'whoredom'. Painter's collection started out as a selection of tales with classical origin, but was eventually expanded to include the most varied Elizabethan collection of Italian tales—twenty-four out of one hundred, with eight from Boccaccio, six from Bandello, two from Cinzio, and others from Fiorentino, Straparola, and *Il Pecorone*. For Bandello he relied largely on the French versions, but this indicates a stylistic preference rather than any ignorance of Italian. For Boccaccio, whose literary reputation stood so much higher than that of his other authors, it is clear that he went back to the original text. Painter's moralizing, though persistent, is less intrusive than that of Fenton and does not exclude the sheer recreational value (the 'pleasure' of his title) to be found in reading 'histories':

Pleasant they be, for that they recreate, and refresh wearied minds, defatigated, either with painful travail, or with continual care, occasioning them to shun and avoid heaviness of mind, vain fantasies, and idle cogitations.[12]

George Whetstone is perhaps the most Italianate of the English *novellieri*. He differs significantly from both Fenton and Painter in returning to the device of the frame, imagined here as the Christmas festivities of a group of young people in Ravenna where he claims to have been present himself. The topic of conversation is the nature of marriage and the conditions that make it advisable or not, and among the illustrative tales is that of Promos and Cassandra, an adaptation of Cinzio's 'Iuriste and Epitia' which Whetstone later turned into a play (never performed) and which became a major source of Shakespeare's *Measure for Measure*. Though the discussion is serious enough, the 'civil discourse' of the *brigata* has an urbane elegance and a lightness of touch that reveals Whetstone as an English adept of Castiglione and the culture of courtesy.

---

[12] William Painter, *The Palace of Pleasure*, ed. Joseph Jacobs, 3 vols (New York: Dover, 1966), i. 13, spelling modernized.

An introduction of this kind is no place for a detailed discussion of how the *novella* influences English drama of the period and Shakespeare in particular, but one may perhaps hazard a few general observations. The relative economy of these often sensational stories is for a start more suited to theatrical adaptation than the kind of plot-proliferation that one finds in lengthier prose fiction such as the pastoral romances of Sidney (*Arcadia, c.*1580), Sannazaro (*Arcadia*, 1504), or Montemayor (*Diana*, 1559). Moreover, the *novella*'s use of dialogue and its broad range of registers already anticipates the theatre and is a precious tool in the rapid establishment of character. The Elizabethan translators abound in theatrical metaphors for their work ('a theatre of the world and stage of human misery' as Painter puts it) and indeed many tales, including Da Porto's version of Romeo and Juliet and Bandello's 'Timbreo and Fenicia', are structured around a sequence of clearly defined scenes. And there is more to it than that. The Elizabethan stage restores to the *novelle* the spectacular and open-ended quality that had been diluted by the moral and didactic interventions of English translators. Bandello, as we have seen, insists that his tales recount events that 'arouse amazement' as well as 'compassion and blame', an effect that is inevitably enfeebled by the moralizing of Fenton or Painter which has the effect of reducing the extraordinary to the exemplary. But in *A Merchant's Tale*, *Othello*, *Much Ado About Nothing*, or *The Duchess of Malfi*, Shakespeare and Webster exploit and explore disturbing aporia, ambiguous attitudes, and unresolved tensions in a way that defeats any attempt to apply simple moral criteria. Thus the wheel has come full circle and the Italian tales regain the autonomy that they had lost by being subjected to the dictates of a new national and religious project.

NOTE ON THE TEXTS AND TRANSLATIONS

ENGLISH readers usually come across the Italian *novella* in one of two ways: either by reading the *Decameron* or by discovering the tales that are included in scholarly editions of the relevant Shakespeare plays. The purpose of this anthology is to fill in the gaps and provide an overview of the genre's evolution. We need to see the continuities and discontinuities between Boccaccio and Bandello if we are to gain a fuller appreciation of what the Italian *novella* had to offer our own narrative and dramatic literature.

Selection of the material has not been easy. The major problem was what to do with Boccaccio. There were some persuasive arguments for omitting him altogether. Leaving aside the somewhat otiose question of whether Boccaccio belongs to the early Renaissance or to the late Middle Ages (the simple answer is both), it seemed difficult to give anything like adequate representation to the *Decameron* in a volume designed to cover almost three centuries of Italian storytelling. And was it really necessary to give valuable space to such a popular and readily available classic at the expense of Sacchetti and Masuccio and Cinzio and Bandello, all of whom deserve to be rescued from the margins of literary history? On the other hand, the Italian *novellieri*, right through from Sacchetti to Basile, tend to advertise their relation to Boccaccio and are highly conscious of their place in the genre he created. Omitting Boccaccio would deprive these authors of a large part of the context in which they expected to be read. Readers who know their Boccaccio may well skip the first eight items in this anthology; it is to be hoped that those who do not will feel encouraged to take further steps to repair the deficiency. The frame that introduces narrators and audience is also a problem for the anthologist. It is one of the genre's defining features, and yet there was no way a volume of this length could find space for the elaborate scene-setting of Boccaccio at the beginning of Day One, though I have managed to include the Proem. I have included the Florentine setting of Grazzini and the prefatory letters to the stories of Masuccio and Bandello and, in my Introduction, I have tried to give some account of how framing devices function in the *novella*. Once again, the inadequacy of the gesture does not render it any less necessary.

In selecting the tales I have given a clear preference to the longer and more dramatic *novelle*, choosing especially those stories that have influenced English authors. These are as follows:

Boccaccio:
> 'Tancredi and Ghismonda' (p. 13) for Dryden's poem 'Sigismonda and Guiscardo';
> 'The Pot of Basil' (p. 21) for Keats's poem of the same name;
> 'Patient Griselda' (p. 30) for Chaucer's 'The Clerke's Tale'.

Ser Giovanni Fiorentino:
> 'Giannetto and the Lady of Belmont' (p. 40) for Shakespeare's *Merchant of Venice*.

Luigi da Porto:
> *The Story of Two Noble Lovers* (p. 146) for Shakespeare's *Romeo and Juliet*.

Matteo Bandello:
> 'The Countess of Challant' (p. 169) for *The Insatiable Countess* of Marston and Barkstead;
> 'Timbreo and Fenicia' (p. 184) for Shakespeare's *Much Ado About Nothing*;
> 'The Duchess of Amalfi' (p. 207) for Webster's *The Duchess of Malfi*;
> 'Niccolò d'Este' (p. 218) for Byron's *Parisina*.

Giovambattista Giraldi Cinzio:
> 'The Moorish Captain' (p. 270) for Shakespeare's *Othello*;
> 'Iuriste and Epitia' (p. 285) for Shakespeare's *Measure for Measure*.

I have been prepared to sacrifice some ponderous pranks (*beffe*) and comic adulteries, if only because two or three of the latter ('Peronella and the Jar', p. 27; 'Saint Griffin's Drawers', p. 103; 'Nigella and the Doctor', p. 280) are enough to do duty for a scenario that changes very little over the centuries. I have omitted entirely the brief tales known as *facezie* (from Poggio Bracciolini's Latin *Liber facetiarum*, 1452). The typical *facezia* offers an anecdote leading up to a punch-line as in the *Motti e facezie del piovano Arlotto* (1460–80), a collection of witticisms and aphorisms attributed to a well-known rustic priest. But Renaissance humour often falls flat for the modern reader and this, I believe, is even more the case with the Italian *facezie* than it is with the more famous *Adagiae* of Erasmus.

With the problems of translation we are on more familiar ground. What Auerbach calls the 'intermediate style' of Boccaccio[1] has a remarkable flexibility that encompasses both idyllic and down-to-earth elements, both high-flown rhetoric and lively colloquialism; but any attempt to reproduce its long sentences and sinuous syntax in translation will result in archaic-sounding stodge. Moreover, when, as in this anthology, a single translator is responsible for nineteen authors, there is a risk that all the texts will begin to sound the same. There is, in any case, no way of conveying the regional differences that distinguish a northern *novelliere* like Bandello from a southerner like Masuccio or a Tuscan like Grazzini. As for the Neapolitan dialect of Basile, one can imagine it going very well into Scots (as in Robert Garioch's splendid versions of the Roman poet Belli); but that would not be doing much of a service to most readers of an Oxford World's Classic. In the long run, the translator can only do his best to catch the tone of the Italian text while recognizing the need to sacrifice some stylistic nuances in order to provide the clarity and narrative pace that the modern English reader has come to expect.

It is not always easy to be consistent with names. My own practice has been to translate the names of popes and kings, but to leave other Italian names as they appear in the original. Thus, Duke Niccolò d'Este does not become Nicholas while Lazzero and Gabriello are not Lazarus and Gabriel. More controversially, perhaps, I have allowed Da Porto's Giulietta and Fra Lorenzo to re-emerge from Shakespeare's Juliet and Friar Lawrence.

Most *novellieri* introduce their stories with a brief plot summary, but give no titles. With the exceptions of Machiavelli's *Fable*, Manetti's *Fat Woodworker*, and Da Porto's *Story of Two Noble Lovers*, which are free-standing tales and thus given in italics, the titles used here have no authorial warrant but have been added for the convenience of readers.

The translations are based upon the following editions:

Boccaccio: *Decameron*, ed. Vittore Branca (Milan: Mondadori, 1985);
Bandello: *Novelle*, ed. Delmo Maestri, 4 vols (Alessandria: Dell'Orso, 1992–7);

[1] Erich Auerbach, *Mimesis*, trans. Willard Trask (Princeton: Princeton University Press, 1968), 216–19.

Basile: *Lo cunto de li cunti*, ed. Michele Rak (Milan: Garzanti, 1998)

For other authors I have relied upon the texts in the ongoing series of *Novellieri italiani* under the general editorship of Enrico Malato (Rome: Salerno) and on the relevant volumes in the Garzanti series of *Novelle italiane* (Milan: Garzanti, 1982).

SELECT BIBLIOGRAPHY

In keeping with the general policy of Oxford World's Classics, this bibliography is restricted to works in English. I should, however, like to acknowledge my debt to Italian scholarship and especially to Lucia Battaglia Ricci, Renzo Bragantini, Gioachino Chiarini, Marcello Ciccuto, Enrico Malato, Luigi Marfè, Giancarlo Mazzacurati, Elisabetta Menetti, Michelangelo Picone, and Bruno Porcelli.

Translations

An Italian Renaissance Sextet, commentary by Lauro Martines, trans. Murtha Baca (Toronto: University of Toronto Press, 2004).

Italian Novelists, trans. Thomas Roscoe, 4 vols (London: Prowett, 1825).

Italian Renaissance Tales, ed. and trans. Janet Smarr (Rochester, MI: Solaris, 1983).

Narrative and Dramatic Sources of Shakespeare, ed. Geoffrey Bullough, 8 vols (London: Routledge, 1957–75).

Romeo and Juliet before Shakespeare: Four Early Stories of Star-Crossed Love, ed. and trans. Nicole Prunsky (Toronto: Centre for Reformation and Renaissance Studies, 2000).

Basile, Giambattista, *The Tale of Tales*, ed. and trans. Nancy L. Canepa (New York: Penguin, 2007).

Boccaccio, Giovanni, *The Decameron*, trans. Guido Waldman, introd. and notes by Jonathan Usher (Oxford: Oxford University Press, 1993).

Boccaccio, Giovanni, *The Decameron*, trans. J. G. Nichols (Richmond: Oneworld Classics, 2008).

Boccaccio, Giovanni, *Tales from the Decameron*, trans. Peter Hainsworth (London: Penguin, 2015).

Criticism

Allaire, Gloria (ed.), *The Italian Novella* (London: Routledge, 2013).

Almansi, Guido, *The Writer as Liar: Narrative Technique in the* Decameron (London: Routledge, 1975).

Armstrong, Guyda, Daniels, Rhiannon, and Milner, Stephen J. (eds), *The Cambridge Companion to Boccaccio* (Cambridge: Cambridge University Press, 2015).

Branca, Vittore, *Boccaccio, The Man and His Works*, trans. Richard Monges (New York: New York University Press, 1984).

Caporello-Sykman, Corradina, *The Boccaccian Novella: The Creation and Waning of a Genre* (New York: Peter Lang, 1990).

Clements, Robert J., and Gibaldi, Joseph, *Anatomy of the Novella* (New York: New York University Press, 1977).

Glending, Olson, *Literature as Recreation in the Later Middle Ages* (Ithaca, NY: Cornell University Press, 1982).

Griffith, T. Gwynfor, *Bandello's Fiction: An Examination of the* Novelle (Oxford: Blackwell, 1955).

Kirkpatrick, Robin, *English and Italian Literature from Dante to Shakespeare* (London: Longman, 1995).

Marrapodi, Michele (ed.), *The Italian World of English Renaissance Drama: Cultural Exchange and Intertextuality* (Newark, DE: University of Delaware Press, 1998).

Marrapodi, Michele (ed.), *Shakespeare and the Italian Renaissance* (London: Routledge, 2010).

Mazzotta, Giuseppe, *The World at Play in Boccaccio's* Decameron (Princeton: Princeton University Press, 1986).

Migiel, Marilyn, *A Rhetoric of the* Decameron (Toronto: University Press of Toronto, 2003).

Nelson, William, *Fact or Fiction: The Dilemma of the Renaissance Storyteller* (Cambridge, MA: Harvard University Press, 1973).

Papio, Michael, *Keen and Violent Remedies: Social Satire and the Grotesque in Masuccio Salenitarno's* Novellino (New York: Peter Lang, 2000).

Pruvost, René, *Matteo Bandello and Elizabethan Fiction* (Paris: Champion, 1937).

Rodax, Yvonne, *The Real and the Ideal in the Novella of Italy, France and England: Four Centuries of Change in the Boccaccian Tale* (Chapel Hill, NC: University of North Carolina Press, 1968).

Rodini, R. J., *A. F. Grazzini, Poet, Dramatist and* Novelliere (Madison: Wisconsin University Press, 1970).

Russell, Sara E., *Courtship, Violence and the Formation of Marriage in the Early Modern Italian Novella Tradition* (UC Berkeley Electronic Theses and Dissertations, 2010).

Smarr, Janet, *Renaissance Story-Teller* (Cambridge, MA: Harvard University Press, 1973).

BIOGRAPHICAL NOTES

CRISTOFORO ARMENO (*fl.* 1557). *The Pilgrimage of the Three Sons of the Emperor of Serendip* was published in Venice in 1557 by Michele Tramezzino. Nothing is known of Armeno (the Armenian) who is credited with having translated the text from Persian into Italian, and the real author may well be Tramezzino himself. The structure of the book recalls the old Persian *Book of the Seven Sages* which was already well known in Europe and also the Persian legend of King Bahram. The fashion for oriental tales spread throughout Europe and continued in Venice down to the eighteenth century in the theatre of Carlo Gozzi (1720–1806).

MATTEO BANDELLO (1485–1561). Born in the Piedmontese province of Alexandria, Bandello followed his influential uncle into the Dominican order, but spent most of his life as courtier, literary counsellor, and diplomat, first at the Sforza court of Milan and later with the Gonzaga rulers of Mantua where he enjoyed the important patronage of Isabella d'Este. Firmly attached to the French interest during the wars of the century, Bandello was particularly close to the military leader Cesare Fregoso. When Fregoso was assassinated (1541), he accompanied the widow to Agen in France, where he served as bishop for five years (1550–5) before resigning in favour of the young Ettore Fregoso. Bandello is a competent minor poet and translator, but his literary reputation depends almost entirely on his *Novelle*, of which three parts (186 tales) were published in 1554, with a fourth (twenty-eight tales) appearing posthumously in 1573. By far the most important author of *novelle* since Boccaccio, Bandello departs from the much-imitated *Decameron* model in both style and structure. His prose lacks Boccaccio's formal elegance and he abandons the overall frame in favour of a scheme which gives to the telling of each tale its own particular context with illuminating (if idealized) pictures of courtly life in Renaissance Italy. Bandello's *Novelle* enjoyed a huge European success and were widely translated (in France by Boaistuau and Belleforest; in England by Painter, Fenton, and Whetstone).

GIAMBATTISTA BASILE (*c.*1570–1632). Neapolitan courtier and administrator who published widely in many genres: pastorals, lyric poetry, libretti, etc. His masterpiece is *Lo cunto de li cunti* (*The Tale of Tales*), a collection of tales, supposedly for children, written in Neapolitan dialect and published posthumously (1634–6). Basile's book marks an important stage in the story of European folklore and leads on to the famous collections of Perrault and the Brothers Grimm. It is here that we find the first published versions of such stories as Cinderella, Puss-in-Boots, Beauty and the Beast, and The Sleeping Beauty. Basile's versions are, however, more brutal and unsentimental than we would expect in tales for children. The content is matched by the style: ribald, aphoristic, proverbial, and splendidly inventive in metaphor, *The Tale of Tales* is one of the great triumphs of Italy's rich dialect literatures.

GIOVANNI BOCCACCIO (1313–75). Born in Florence or possibly in nearby Certaldo, the illegitimate son of Boccaccio di Chellino, an agent of the powerful Bardi banking family. As a youth of 14 or 15 he was sent to learn the banking business in Naples where the Bardi family managed the finances of the Angevin monarchy. In that refined and courtly atmosphere, he began to produce a series of vernacular literary works in verse and prose, following the early narrative poems (*Caccia di Diana*, *Filostrato*) with texts that reflect his own amorous passions (*Filocolo*, *Teseida*, *Ameto*, *Amorosa visione*, *Elegia di Madonna Fiammetta*). In 1340 a crisis in the affairs of the Bardi brought Boccaccio reluctantly back to Florence and to a less comfortable lifestyle; but it was the renewed contact with a mercantile as opposed to a courtly society that combined with his previous narrative experiments to produce the *Decameron*, composed between 1349 and 1351 in the aftermath of a catastrophic outbreak of the plague. In his later years (1351–75), with his literary reputation assured and with the encouragement of Petrarch, Boccaccio followed the new humanist trend by writing in Latin and by adopting a more moralistic and religious attitude. To this period belong the *Genealogiae deorum gentilium* with its celebrated discussion of poetry, the pastoral poems of *Bucolicum carmem*, and the brief lives of famous men and women in *De casibus vivorum illustrium* and *De mulieribus claris*. At the same time he made a vital contribution to the Dante cult with his commentary on the *Divine*

Comedy (*Esposizioni*) and his short biography of the poet (*Trattatello in laude di Dante*). Boccaccio's range and versatility have no parallel in Italian literature. In the sixteenth century Bembo established him as the unrivalled model for Italian prose, and the tradition of the *novella* is unthinkable without him. Boccaccio plays a pivotal role in the development of Italian literature, giving the urban culture of the late Middle Ages its most complete expression and also furthering the Latin humanism that was to characterize the Renaissance.

GIOVANNI BREVIO (*fl.* early 16th cent.). Little is known of Brevio's life beyond the fact that he led an ecclesiastical career and was in contact with such prominent literary figures as Bembo, Della Casa, and Aretino. All that survives of his work is to be found in *Rime e prose vulgari* (1545) which contains some predictable Petrarchist love poetry, a couple of moral treatises, and six *novelle*. Brevio has a marked interest in abnormal sexual situations like the complex incest story of Lisabetta with its surprisingly uncensorious happy end.

GIOVAMBATTISTA GIRALDI CINZIO (1504–73). Born in Ferrara where he taught for much of his life, Cinzio was prominent as a dramatist and literary theorist, especially interesting for his defence of tragi-comedy— drama that exploits traditionally tragic themes, but gives them a happy end, thus reconciling classical tragedy with Christian poetic justice. The hundred stories that make up his *Hecatommithi* (1565) have a frame that obviously recalls Boccaccio. Just as the *Decameron* opens with a description of the Plague, so the *Hecatommithi* is prefaced by a terrifying account of the Sack of Rome (1527). But Cinzio has none of Boccaccio's instinctive optimism; his narrators are effectively refugees, fleeing from a world in chaos. Italian critics have reacted negatively to Giraldi's taste for Senecan horrors and the moral fixity of his characters has often been associated with the repressive atmosphere of the Counter-Reformation. The *Hecatommithi* had a European influence second only to that of Bandello's *Novelle*.

LUIGI DA PORTO (1485–1529). Educated at the cultured court of Urbino celebrated in Castiglione's *The Courtier*, he was a friend of Bandello and of the influential poet and literary theorist Pietro

Bembo. Seriously wounded while fighting in the service of Venice (1511), he devoted the rest of his life to literature, writing poetry and a series of letters dealing with the wars of the League of Cambrai. He is now known above all for his *Story of Two Noble Lovers* (published 1530–1) which develops a tale ultimately derived from Ovid (Pyramus and Thisbe in *Metamorphoses* 4) and more closely reliant on Masuccio's Sienese story of Mariotto and Ganozza. It is Da Porto who moves the setting to Verona, names the lovers as Romeo and Giulietta, and gives the story the dramatic structure and much of the psychological depth that we find in Shakespeare's play.

GIOVANNI GHERARDI DA PRATO (*c.*1367–*c.*1446). Born in Prato, he studied law in Padua and worked as notary and architect in Florence, where he also lectured on Dante. He promoted the vernacular in opposition to the Latin turn of the humanists. Presumed author of the incomplete *Paradiso degli Alberti* (*c.*1420) which contains nine stories and takes its title from the setting of its Boccaccio-like frame in the villa and gardens of the Alberti family.

GIOVANNI FIORENTINO. Apart from the name, nothing is known of the author of the late fourteenth-century *Pecorone*—a self-deprecatory title meaning 'big sheep'. In the proem we are told that the work was begun in 1378 in Dovadola near Forlì. The frame of this collection of fifty stories is a series of twenty-five meetings between a friar and a nun who alternate as narrators. Many of the tales are lifted almost verbatim from well-known sources such as the *Decameron* and Giovanni Villani's *Nuova cronica*. The story of Giannetto and the Lady of Belmont is famous as a source of *The Merchant of Venice*.

PIETRO FORTINI (*c.* 1500–62). Composed during the years (1555–61) that saw the final defeat of Fortini's native Siena by the Florentines and its incorporation into the Grand Duchy of Tuscany, the eighty-one stories of *Le giornate delle novelle de' novizi* and *Le piacevoli ed amorose notti de' novizi* (*Tales for Beginners*) remained unpublished for over two centuries, largely on account of their erotic and sometimes obscene content. The frame is provided by a Sienese garden in which five women and two men exchange tales, most of which seem designed to open the eyes of the supposedly naïve young audience to the harsh realities of social and sexual negotiations.

ANTON FRANCESCO GRAZZINI (Il Lasca) (1503–84). A prominent and combative figure in Florentine literary circles, Grazzini was a founding member of the Accademia degli Umidi (1540), taking the literary name of *Il Lasca* (the Roach). His opposition to what he perceived as the stultifying conventions of conservative humanism led to his expulsion from the Umidi in 1547. Readmitted in 1566, he lived long enough to become a founding member of the famous Accademia della Crusca in 1582. Grazzini disliked the increased codification of Italian literary language and argued in favour of a more popular and colloquial style—a stance made clear in his harsh criticism of the new 'purified' edition of the *Decameron* (1573). A prolific author of comedies and burlesque poetry, he is now best known for *Le cene* (*The Suppers*), twenty-two stories of a planned thirty, explicitly presented as inspired by the example of Boccaccio and introduced by a famously charming account of a snowballing contest.

NICCOLÒ MACHIAVELLI (1469–1527). Generally regarded as the most important political thinker of the Italian Renaissance, author of *Il principe* and the *Discorsi*, both published after his death. The hard-nosed pragmatism of these major works gave rise to the popular caricature of Machiavelli as a prophet of duplicity and treachery, but they are more usefully seen as reflecting a turbulent period of foreign invasions when it seemed that only a radical realpolitik could offer any hope of continued independence for the divided Italian states. Machiavelli's strictly literary production includes two comedies (*La Mandragola* and *Clizia*), some comic and satirical poetry, and the single *novella* entitled *Favola* (*A Fable*), better known as the story of Belphagor.

ANTONIO MANETTI (1423–97). Florentine politician, architect, and man of letters, associated with the Neoplatonic circle of Marsilio Ficino. A significant Dante scholar, he also produced a volume of short biographies of famous Florentines. To his life of Filippo Brunelleschi he attached the *novella* of *The Fat Woodworker* which is the most satisfactory version of the huge prank played by the great architect on the unfortunate woodworker Manetto Ammannatini in 1409. Manetti's text concludes with an account of the multiple sources, both oral and written, that inform his narrative.

FRANCESCO PONA (1595–1655). A Veronese doctor and member of many academies, Pona was a prolific writer, producing medical and scientific texts, historiography, literary translation, drama, lyric poetry, prose romances, and tales. He is best known for the horrific and macabre stories of *La lucerna* (*The Lamp*, 1625). *Ormondo* (1635), with its five insert-stories, offers an interesting blend of romance and *novella* traditions.

GIOVANNI SABBADINO DEGLI ARIENTI (*c.* 1445–1510). Born in Bologna where he served the reigning Bentivoglio family as notary, in later life he moved first to the Este court in Ferrara and then to Mantua where he acted as literary adviser to the marchioness Isabella d'Este Gonzaga. Best known for *Le Porrettane* (1483), a collection of sixty-one stories supposedly told by young courtiers from Bologna over a five-day period at the spa of Porretta. At his best, Sabbadino blends a light touch with considerable narrative verve.

FRANCO SACCHETTI (*c.* 1332–1400). Born in Ragusa (now Dubrovnik, Croatia) into a family of Florentine Guelfs, he travelled widely as a merchant before devoting himself to a career in politics and diplomacy in the service of Florence. His insistence on negotiation as a means of resolving disputes was strengthened by the massacres that occurred during the so-called War of Eight Saints (1375–8) in which Florence and the cities of central Italy countered the territorial ambitions of the Papacy. His early work is that of a lyric poet in a wide variety of forms and genres, but his major achievement is the *Trecentonovelle* (1392–7), 300 tales of which 222 survive. The collection has no framing device, but its vivid picture of Florentine society is held together by the narrator's own robust moralizing.

MASUCCIO SALERNITANO (Tommaso Guardati) (1410–75). Born into a noble family of Salerno, he was employed at the court of Naples where he came into contact with the new humanism of Antonio Beccadelli and Giovanni Pontano. The first non-Tuscan to imitate Boccaccio, he composed his tales in a recognizably

Neapolitan idiom. The *Novellino* has fifty stories arranged in groups of ten; there is no overall frame, but each story is prefaced by a dedication and concluded with an authorial comment. Though the themes are largely conventional, Masuccio has a special taste for the sensational and the grotesque, and his anticlerical satire is particularly violent. The story of Mariotto and Ganozza (*Novellino* 33, not included here) would be reworked as Romeo and Juliet by Luigi Da Porto and Matteo Bandello.

GENTILE SERMINI (*fl.* early 15th cent.). Not much is known of Sermini's life beyond the obvious connection with Siena. His forty *novelle* were written *c.*1424. There is no frame, but an undated letter suggests that they may have been designed to entertain his brother who was visiting the local baths. Many of the tales are of a scabrous nature.

GIOVAN FRANCESCO STRAPAROLA (*c.*1480–*c.*1557). Born in Caravaggio near Bergamo, he published a volume of conventional Petrarchist verse (1508), but is remembered only for his *Piacevoli notti* (*Pleasant Nights*) which came out in two volumes (1550 and 1553) and was an immediate success. The frame presents the seventy-five *novelle* as being narrated on the Venetian island of Murano by the elegant guests of the bishop of Lodi during the thirteen nights of Carnival. The originality of Straparola lies in the way he challenges both the courtly atmosphere and the realistic tradition of the *novella* by introducing popular folklore elements that foreshadow the work of Giambattista Basile.

A CHRONOLOGY OF THE ITALIAN RENAISSANCE

1304   Birth of Petrarch (Francesco Petrarca), poet and humanist, author of love poems in Italian (*Canzoniere*) and vast and varied poetry and prose in Latin.

c.1305   Giotto's frescoes for the Scrovegni Chapel in Padua.

1308   Duccio altarpiece (the *Maestà*) for cathedral of Siena.

1309   Clement V moves papacy to Avignon.

1321   Dante Alighieri dies in Ravenna after completing *The Divine Comedy.*

1341   Petrarch crowned Poet Laureate on the Campidoglio in Rome.

1345   Ruin of the great Florentine banks of Bardi and Peruzzi when Edward III of England defaults on debts accumulated during the Hundred Years War.

1347   Cola di Rienzo appointed tribune of Rome, raising hopes (shared by Petrarch) of restoring the city to its old imperial glory and universal mission; his popularity soon wanes and he is killed during a riot in 1354.

1348   The Black Death strikes Florence.

1349–53   Boccaccio's *Decameron*.

1374   Death of Petrarch.

1377   Papal curia returns to Rome, but in 1378 the Great Schism begins when French cardinals refuse to recognize Urban VI and elect their own candidate as Clement VII.

1378–81   The Chioggia War between Venice and Genoa; Venice establishes its dominance over eastern Mediteranean trade, while Genoa turns from trade to banking.

1378–82   Popular revolt of the Ciompi (woolworkers) in Florence is followed by the restoration of government by a mercantile oligarchy.

1378–1402   Under Gian Galeazzo Visconti, the duchy of Milan becomes the richest and most powerful state in Italy with control over the whole of Lombardy and parts of Emilia.

1392–7   Franco Sacchetti, *Trecentonovelle*.

1397   Medici bank founded in Florence.

1417   Council of Constance ends the Great Schism with the election of Pope Martin V.

1417 Poggio Bracciolini discovers Lucretius' *De Rerum Natura* (*On the Nature of Things*).

1423 Masaccio's frescoes in the Brancacci Chapel of Santa Maria del Carmine (Florence).

1424 Lorenzo Ghiberti completes the sculptures for the bronze doors of the Baptistery in Florence.

1433 Cosimo de' Medici is exiled but is recalled the following year. The Medici become the de facto rulers of Florence.

1435 Leon Battista Alberti, *De pictura* (*On Painting*).

1436 Completion of Filippo Brunelleschi's great dome for the cathedral of Florence (Santa Maria del Fiore).

1440 Lorenzo Valla uses philological evidence to prove that the Donation of Constantine, granting temporal power to the Church, is in fact an eighth-century forgery.

1442 Sicily and Naples united under Aragonese rule.

1450 After the death of Filippo Maria Visconti, Francesco Sforza becomes duke of Milan and ends the war of succession with the Peace of Lodi (1454) between Milan, Venice, and Florence.

1452 Birth of Leonardo da Vinci.

1453 Fall of Constantinople strengthens Ottoman power in the Mediterranean and increases the exodus of Greek scholars towards Italy.

1462 Founding of Florentine Neoplatonic Academy; prominent members included Marsilio Ficino, Pico della Mirandola, and Poliziano.

1464 Lorenzo de' Medici (Lorenzo the Magnificent) governs Florence after the death of Cosimo.

1475 Birth of Michelangelo.

1475–1500 Painters Mantegna in Mantua and Giovanni Bellini in Venice.

1478 Pazzi conspiracy against the Medici family.

1482–99 Leonardo works for Lodovico Sforza in Milan.

1482–5 Botticelli paints *Primavera* and *The Birth of Venus*.

1487 Boiardo, *Orlando Innamorato* (*Orlando in Love*).

1492 Death of Lorenzo the Magnificent.

1494 The Medici are driven out of Florence.

1494 Charles VIII of France invades Italy to claim the throne of Naples; he occupies the city for a few months, but is forced to retreat.

1495 Aldine Press founded by Aldo Manuzio in Venice.

1497 Florentine reformer Savonarola, Dominican prior of San Marco, organizes Bonfire of Vanities.

1498 Execution of Savonarola.

1499 Michelangelo's *Pietà*.

1499 Louis XII renews French intervention in Italy; after initial success he is defeated by the Holy League.

1501 Michelangelo begins work on anti-Medicean *David*.

1508 Michelangelo called to Rome by Pope Julius II; begins work on the Sistine Chapel.

1509 Raphael paints frescoes in the Vatican (*Le Stanze*).

1510 Titian and Giorgione at work in Venice.

1512 Fall of the Florentine Republic; restoration of Medici rule.

1513 Machiavelli, *The Prince*.

1515 French king Francis I invades Lombardy, wins battle of Marignano, and occupies Milan.

1516 Ludovico Ariosto, *Orlando Furioso* (*The Madness of Orlando*).

1519 Death of Leonardo in France.

1525 Francis I defeated by imperial and Spanish forces of Emperor Charles V at Pavia.

1525 Pietro Bembo establishes the Tuscan of Boccaccio and Petrarch as a stylistic and linguistic model for vernacular prose and poetry.

1527 Sack of Rome by German mercenaries serving in the imperial army.

1528 Castiglione, *Book of the Courtier*.

1554 Bandello, *Novelle*, parts 1, 2, 3.

1545–63 Council of Trent marks beginning of Counter-Reformation.

1559 Treaty of Cateau-Cambrésis puts an end to the Italian Wars, leaving most of the peninsula under the direct or indirect control of Spain.

1564 Death of Michelangelo.

1565 Giovambattista Giraldi Cinzio, *Hecatommithi*.

1570 Palladio, *I quattro libri dell'architettura* (*Four Books of Architecture*).

1581 Torquato Tasso, *Gerusalemme Liberata* (*Jerusalem Delivered*).

1590 Dome of St Peter's completed.

1619 Paolo Sarpi's anti-papal *History of the Council of Trent*.

1634–6 Basile, *Lo cunto de li cunti* (*The Tale of Tales*).

ITALIAN RENAISSANCE TALES

GIOVANNI BOCCACCIO

PROEM
Decameron

This is the beginning of the Decameron, *a book also called* Prince Galahalt,* *consisting of one hundred tales told over a period of ten days by seven ladies and three young men.*

IT is natural for human beings to feel compassion for those who suffer. This is commendable in everyone, but it is especially required of those who, when they needed comfort, have found it in others. I am one of these, for if anyone ever needed comfort, cherished it, or found relief in it, then that is me. The fact is that from my earliest youth until very recently I burned beyond all measure with an exalted and noble love,* more inflamed perhaps than might be expected from someone of my lowly condition. And although I was praised by discerning people who heard about this and thought the better of me, yet still I could hardly bear it—not indeed because of any cruelty on the part of the lady I loved, but because of the excessive ardour born of an unrestrained appetite which left me dissatisfied with reasonable limits and subjected me to much unnecessary distress. My suffering, however, was greatly relieved by the pleasant conversation and laudable sympathy of certain friends, without which I am certain I should have died. But it has pleased Him who is Himself infinite to make it an immutable law that all earthly things should have an end. My love was so uniquely fervent that no resolve, no advice, no fear of shame or potential danger had the power to destroy or divert it. And yet, as time went by, it waned of its own accord so now all that it has left in the memory is the pleasant feeling that love usually grants to those who do not venture too far out upon its dark waters. As all my troubles have been removed, what used to be a heavy burden now remains only as a delight.

But although my pains are ended, this does not mean that I have forgotten the kindnesses I received from those whose affection towards me led them to feel for my suffering; only death, I believe, will cancel that memory. I am convinced that gratitude stands among those virtues that are to be most highly commended, just as its contrary is to be most blamed. That is why, so as not to appear ungrateful, now that I may say I am free, I mean to offer what little comfort I can in return for the comfort I received. If this does not concern those who actually did help me and who, through their own good sense or good fortune, require no such help themselves, it may at least bring some alleviation to those who are truly in need. They may well feel that my support or comfort, as we might call it, does not add up to much, but I still think that I must try to offer it where the need seems greatest, for that is where it will do most good and be most welcome.

And who on earth will deny that this help, for what it is worth, should be offered to fair ladies far more than to men? Through fear and shame they hide the flames of love within their tender breasts and those who have had that experience know how much stronger than an open blaze is that hidden fire. Moreover, constrained as they are by the wishes, the whims, and the orders of fathers, mothers, brothers, and husbands, they spend most of the time sitting almost idle, cramped up in their rooms, wishing one thing and its opposite in the same moment and brooding over thoughts that cannot possibly be always cheerful. And if their burning desire should give rise to a fit of melancholy, they will continue to be burdened by that distress, unless it is banished by some new concern. Besides this, ladies in love are far less resilient than men who, as we can plainly see, are not disturbed in the same way. When men are afflicted by melancholy or by heavy thoughts, they have many ways of alleviating or overcoming their troubles, for if they feel like it, nothing stops them going out and about to see and hear all kinds of things; they can go hawking, hunting, fishing, riding, gaming, or trading. These are all ways for a man to pull himself together, in part if not completely, distracting him from oppressive thoughts at least for a while. After which, in one way or another, he will find some consolation, or the pain will simply begin to fade.

My intention, therefore, is to provide some compensation for the wrongs done by Fortune which is always so sparing in her support to those who have least strength, as we see in the case of delicate ladies. And it is only to those who are in love that I mean to offer help and distraction, for the rest can get by with needle, spindle, and reel.

I intend to tell a hundred tales or fables or parables or histories,* or whatever we choose to call them, recounted over a period of ten days by an honourable group of seven ladies and three young men who came together during the recent deadly plague.* And I shall add some songs that those ladies sang for the delight of the whole group. The tales will include a variety of love stories, both sweet and bitter, and other events that have been the fruits of Fortune in modern and ancient times. When the ladies I speak of come to read them they will find in equal measure both pleasure in the entertaining subject matter and useful advice in that they may see what actions are to be shunned and what to be pursued. Such things, I believe, cannot occur without the disappearance of all their troubles. If this happens (and may it be God's will!), let them thank Love who, by freeing me from his bonds, has granted me the power to attend to their pleasures.

THE CONVERSION OF ABRAHAM
Decameron 1. 2

Having heard the arguments of Jeannot de Chevigny, Abraham, a Jew, goes to the papal court in Rome. When he sees the wickedness of the clergy, he returns to Paris and becomes a Christian.

THE ladies had listened to Panfilo's story* with great attention; parts of it had made them laugh and the whole tale won their praise. When it had come to an end, the queen* commanded Neifile, who was sitting next to Panfilo, to continue the entertainment by telling another tale. And Neifile, no less courteous than lovely, gladly consented and began as follows:

Panfilo's story has already shown that God in his loving kindness does not regard our errors when they result from causes that are beyond our ken: and in my story I intend to show how this same loving kindness bears patiently with the shortcomings of those who should give true witness to it in word and deed, but in fact do the opposite. Thus God gives proof of his own infallible truth so that we may follow what we believe with greater persistence.

As I once heard, gracious ladies, there lived in Paris a great and good merchant named Jeannot de Chevigny, a loyal and upright man with a considerable trade in cloth. He was particularly friendly with a wealthy Jew called Abraham, a merchant like himself and also loyal and upright. And it was because he saw these qualities in Abraham that Jeannot began to grieve that such a good, wise, and worthy man should go down to perdition because he lacked the true faith. In a friendly way, therefore, he set about exhorting him to abandon the errors of the Jewish faith and convert to the truth of Christianity, which, as he could see for himself, grew and prospered, whereas his own religion, on the contrary, was dwindling away to nothing.

The Jew replied that he believed no faith to be holy and true except the Jewish faith in which he had been born and in which he meant to live and die; nor would anything ever persuade him to change. This was not enough to discourage Jeannot who, after a few days, returned to the argument, outlining in the rough unvarnished way of merchants the reasons that make our faith better than that of the Jews. Now though Abraham was something of a specialist in Jewish doctrine, he may have been influenced by the great friendship that bound him to Jeannot, or perhaps he was moved by the words which the Holy Spirit had placed in the mouth of an unlettered man. The fact is that the Jew began to appreciate the arguments of Jeannot. But still obstinate in his belief, he could not be persuaded to convert.

Despite such obstinacy, Jeannot went on and on with his exhortations, until at last, overcome by such persistence, Abraham declared: 'Listen, Jeannot, you'd like me to become a Christian, and I'm ready to do so on one condition: that first I go to Rome to see the man whom you say is the Vicar of God on earth, so that I can study his way of life and behaviour and likewise that of his brother cardinals, and if what I see bears out what you've told me and convinces me that your faith is better than mine, as you keep trying to prove, then I'll do as I've just said. Otherwise I shall remain the Jew that I am.'

When Jeannot heard this he was deeply distressed and said to himself: 'All that wasted effort! I really thought I'd managed to convert him. Now, if he goes to the papal court in Rome, he'll see the immoral and filthy life of the clerics: that won't convert a Jew to Christianity—but if he were already a Christian he'd surely come back a Jew.' And turning to Abraham, he said: 'Look, my friend, why should you want to travel from here to Rome, with all that trouble and expense?—to say nothing of the dangers that a journey by land and sea would involve for a rich man like you. Do you think you can't find someone to baptize you here? And if you have any doubts about the faith as I've presented it, where can you find better teachers* than here where we have men who can answer all your questions and give you proper explanations? That's why I think this journey of yours serves no purpose. Remember that the prelates down there are just the same as those you see here—and even better because they are nearer to the chief pastor. So my advice is that you should save the effort for some other occasion—perhaps a pilgrimage; and then, who knows, I might be able to come with you.'

To this the Jew replied: 'Jeannot, I believe that things are as you say; but to put it in a nutshell, if you really want me to do what you keep asking, then I simply must go to Rome. Otherwise, I shall drop the matter—for good and all.'

Seeing that he was determined, Jeannot said: 'So go then, and the best of luck,' though inwardly he was convinced that the Jew would never become a Christian once he had seen the Roman court; but he decided not to waste his breath and said no more.

The Jew mounted his horse and rode off as quickly as he could to Rome where he was welcomed as an honoured guest by his fellow Jews. Then, while he stayed there, without telling anyone why he had come, he cautiously began to examine the behaviour of the Pope and the cardinals and the other prelates and all the courtiers; and adding what he learned from others to what he himself saw as a shrewd observer, he found that from top to bottom of the scale, they were all steeped in the sin of lechery, not only in its natural version, but with sodomy into the bargain, unchecked by remorse or shame, so that whores and rent boys were able to obtain all the favours they looked for. And as if this were not enough, he saw that all of them were gluttons, tosspots, drunkards, slaves to their bellies like the brute beasts. And on a closer look, he saw that they were also money-grubbers, so avaricious that they bought and sold human lives—the lives of Christians!—and all kinds of sacred objects used for the Mass or attached to benefices. They did more business and employed more brokers than the cloth trade or any other trade in Paris. And this fla-grant simony they called 'procurement' and their gluttony they called 'subsistence', as if God, like men, could be deceived by mere names and did not know their evil intentions, let alone the meaning of words. All these things—and many others which are better left unsaid—were abhorrent to a sober, modest man like the Jew, so he reckoned he had seen enough and decided to go back to Paris, which he did.

When Jeannot heard that his friend was back home, the last thing he expected was that he had become a Christian. Still he went to meet him and they celebrated the occasion together. Only when Abraham had had a few days of rest did Jeannot ask what he thought of the Holy Father and the cardinals and the other courtiers.

The Jew lost no time in answering: 'I think God should punish the whole lot; and I say this because, as far as I could see, there was no holiness, no devotion, no good works, no example of a virtuous life in any of the clergy; instead I saw them wallowing in lechery, avarice and gluttony, fraud and envy and pride, and vices of the same kind or even worse, if anything could be worse. It seemed a hotbed of works that were more devilish than divine. As far as I can see, your pastor, and hence the rest of them too, with all their craft and with all their wits, are doing everything they can to annihilate the Christian religion and banish it from the world—and this when they ought to be its foundation and support. And yet, when I see that what they seek simply doesn't happen, but that on the contrary your religion continues to prosper and become ever more luminous and bright, then I conclude that the Holy Spirit is deservedly its foundation and support as a faith more holy and true than any other. That is why, though I was once so stout and stubborn against your attempts to make me a Christian, I now tell you frankly that nothing could prevent my conversion. So let us go to church, and there have me baptized according to the rites of your holy faith.'

Jeannot, who had expected exactly the opposite conclusion, was overjoyed to hear this, and went with Abraham to Notre-Dame in Paris where he asked the priests to baptize his friend, which they did without delay; and Jeannot was his godfather at the sacred font and gave him the name of Jean. He then arranged for some very learned men to give him full instruction in the faith, and Abraham proved to be a quick learner. He was a good and worthy man and went on to live a holy life.

ALIBECH AND RUSTICO
Decameron 3. 10

*Alibech becomes a hermit and Rustico teaches her how to put the Devil
back into Hell. Taken back home, she is married to Neerbale.*

DIONEO had listened carefully to the queen's story, and when he
realized that it was finished and that he was the only one who had still
not spoken, he did not wait to be asked but smiled and began:

Gracious ladies, you may never have heard how to put the Devil back
into Hell, and so, without departing from the subject that you have
been discussing all day, I think I should inform you. Perhaps the
knowledge will help you to save your souls; and you may also learn
that Love, though he prefers joyous palaces and comfortable bed-
rooms to the hovels of the poor, can still sometimes make himself felt
in thick woods, jagged mountains, and desert caves—which goes to
show how all things are subject to his power.

Coming then to our story, there once lived in the city of Capsa*
in Barbary a very wealthy man who, among his other children, had
a sweet and lovely young daughter called Alibech. Though she was
not a Christian, she had heard many Christians in the city speak in
praise of their faith and of service to God; and so one day she asked
one of them how she could render such service with the least
impediment. He answered that the best way to serve God was to flee
the things of this world, like those who had once gone out into the
unpeopled Theban deserts.* The girl was very simple, about fourteen years of age, and not moved by any seriously pondered resolution
but rather by a childish impulse. The next morning, without telling
anybody, she set out secretly and all alone for the Theban desert
where she arrived in a few days after a very tough journey, but with
her enthusiasm still intact. From far off she spied a simple cabin and
there she went and found a holy man standing in the doorway.
Startled to see her, he asked what she was looking for, and she
answered that she had been inspired by God to seek out His service
and was also looking for someone who could teach her the way of that
service.

The worthy man, seeing how young and beautiful she was, feared
some subtle device of the Devil if he allowed her to remain with him;

and so he praised her good intentions, gave her water to drink and some roots, wild apples, and dates to eat, and then said: 'My daughter, not far from here lives a holy man who is a much better teacher than I am for what you wish to know. You should go to him.' And with that he sent her on her way.

When she reached this second teacher he said exactly the same thing, and so she went on until she came to the cell of a young hermit, a virtuous and devout man called Rustico; and to him she made the same request as to the other two. Unlike the others, he did not send her away or pass her on, but, in order to try his resistance to temptation, kept her with him in his cell; and when night fell he made her a rough bed of palm leaves in a corner of his cell and told her to rest on that.

Once that was done, it was not long before he was assaulted by the forces of temptation; he found that he had greatly overestimated his own powers and after a few initial skirmishes he turned tail and accepted defeat. Setting aside holy thoughts, prayers, and penitential discipline, he began picturing to himself the youth and beauty of the girl; then, taking things a step further, he began to wonder how he should go about getting what he wanted without her recognizing him as the lecher he was. He started by sounding her out with a few questions and soon discovered that she had never been with a man and was indeed as simple as she seemed; and with this in mind, he saw a way of getting her to pleasure him by convincing her that she would be serving the Lord. First, therefore, he explained at great length that the Devil was the enemy of Lord God, and then he gave her to understand that the most pleasing service she could render God was to put the Devil back into Hell, which was where the Lord had condemned him in the first place.

The girl asked him how this could be done, and Rustico answered: 'You'll soon find out: just do what you see me do'; and he began to take off the few clothes that he was wearing until he was stark naked. The girl did the same. Then he knelt down as if about to pray and made the girl do the same facing him. In that position, more aroused than ever by the sight of her beauty, Rustico experienced a resurrection of the flesh. Alibech looked on in amazement.

'What's that thing I see sticking out in front of you—something I don't have?'

'That, my daughter,' said Rustico, 'is the Devil I was telling you about; and, as you can see, he's giving me so much trouble that I can hardly bear it.'

'Praised be the Lord, for now I see that I'm better off than you are, because I don't have that Devil to put up with.'

'That's true, but instead you do have something that I don't.'

'What's that?'

'What you've got', said Rustico, 'is Hell, and I must tell you that I believe God has sent you here for the salvation of my soul. This Devil keeps giving me trouble, but if you have enough compassion to let me put him back into Hell, you'll bring me immense relief and also give great pleasure and service to God—I'm assuming, of course, that you did come here for that purpose, as you say.'

In all simplicity, the girl answered: 'Father, since I have Hell, it can be whenever you please.'

'Blessed art thou, my daughter,' said Rustico, 'let's go and put him back where he belongs so he can leave me in peace.' So saying, he led the girl over to one of the beds and gave her a practical demonstration of how to imprison that cursed enemy of God. The girl, who had never put any devil into Hell before, found the first time rather painful and said to Rustico: 'My father, this Devil really must be a bad person and an enemy of God, because he doesn't just harm people; he makes Hell itself hurt when he gets put back there.'

'It won't always feel like that,' said Rustico. And to make sure that it did not they repeated the operation six times before quitting the bed, so for the time being at least the Devil's pride was crestfallen and he was glad to be left in peace.

But in the days that followed the Devil's pride revived rather often, and each time the obedient girl was ready to draw it out of him until at last she began to enjoy the game and said to Rustico: 'Now I see that those worthy men of Capsa were telling the truth when they said that serving God was such a sweet thing, because I certainly can't remember anything that has given me such delight and pleasure as putting the Devil back into Hell. I reckon that only an ignoramus would bother to do anything but serve God.' It was in this spirit that she now kept coming up to Rustico and saying: 'Father, I came here to serve God and not to lie idle; let's go and put the Devil back into Hell.' And sometimes, while they were on the job, she would say: 'Rustico, I don't understand why the Devil wants to get out of Hell; if he were as happy to be in Hell as Hell is happy to receive him, he'd never leave.'

What with all these exhortations and invitations to come and serve God, the girl had more or less knocked the stuffing out of Rustico so that sometimes he cooled down just when other men would have been hot and sweating. So he began telling her that there was no need to punish the Devil or to put him back in Hell, except when he raised his proud head, 'and by God's grace we've tamed him so well that he's praying the Lord to be left in peace'. This was enough to silence the girl for the time being.

But when she saw that Rustico had stopped asking her to put the Devil back into Hell, she said one day: 'Rustico, though your Devil has been punished and no longer bothers you, my Hell never lets up. You'd be doing a good deed if you used your Devil to calm the raging of my Hell, just as I used my Hell to humble the pride of your Devil.'

Poor Rustico, who lived on a diet of roots and spring water, was in no state to satisfy her request and told her that it would take too many devils to calm the fury of her Hell, but he would do the best he could. Sometimes, indeed, he did manage to satisfy her, but these occasions were so rare that it was like throwing a bean in the mouth of a lion, and more often than not the girl grumbled that she was not serving God as much as she wanted.

But while Alibech's Hell and Rustico's Devil were at odds, with an excess desire on the one hand and a growing impotence on the other, something had happened back in Capsa. A fire had broken out in the house of Alibech's father and he had been burned to death together with all his other children and kinsfolk, and thus Alibech was left as his sole heir. This fact attracted the attention of Neerbale, a young man who had squandered all his wealth by living beyond his means. Hearing that Alibech was alive, he set out to find her and succeeded in doing so before the authorities could confiscate the estate of her father on the grounds that he had left no heir. Then, to Rustico's great relief, but against the will of Alibech herself, he took her back to Capsa where he married her and shared her immense inheritance.

Now before Neerbale had slept with her, some of the ladies asked Alibech how she had served God in the desert; and she answered that she had done so by putting the Devil back into Hell and that Neerbale had committed a grave sin by taking her away from such service. 'But how do you put the Devil back into Hell?' asked the ladies, and when Alibech explained with a mixture of words and gestures, they could hardly stop laughing: 'Don't you worry, girl,' they said, 'we do those things here as well. With your help, Neerbale will do the Lord God some good service.'

The story spread all over the city and it became proverbial to say that the best way to serve God was by putting the Devil back into Hell. That proverb crossed the sea and is still in use today. And therefore, you young ladies, who need the grace of God, learn to put the Devil back into Hell; it is highly pleasing to God and pleasurable also to the parties involved, and it may be the cause of much good.

TANCREDI AND GHISMONDA
Decameron 4. 1

Tancredi, prince of Salerno, kills his daughter's lover and sends her the heart in a golden cup. Over it she pours water with poison in it which she then drinks, and so dies.

IT is a grim subject that our king has proposed for us today. He thinks that though we have come here to cheer ourselves up, we should tell stories about the distress of others, the kind of stories that cannot be told without both teller and hearer being moved to compassion. Perhaps he has done this to temper the jollity of the last few days; but whatever the reason, it is not for me to go against his wishes, and so I shall tell of a pitiful event—indeed, a tragedy that is well worth our tears.

Tancredi, prince of Salerno* was a most humane ruler and could be seen as having a kindly disposition, had he not, in his old age, stained his hands with the blood of lovers. In all his life he had only one child, a daughter, and he would have been a happier man if she had not been born. He loved her more tenderly than any daughter was ever loved by her father, and because he loved her so much, he kept her with him many years beyond the age when she should have had a husband. At last he gave her in marriage to a son of the Duke of Capua, but it was not long before she was left a widow and returned to live with her father.

She was as beautiful in face and figure as any woman ever was, youthful, high-spirited, and perhaps more knowing than a lady should be. Living with her tender father, in the lap of luxury like a great lady, she saw that because of the love he bore her he did little to find her a new husband. And since she thought it hardly decent to go and ask him directly, she resolved to find, if possible, some worthy man as a secret lover. Her father's court, like any other court, was frequented by some men who were nobly born and by some who were not. Among the many courtiers whose manners and behaviour she studied, there was one who pleased her more than all the others: this was Guiscardo, a young valet of her father, of humble birth, but noble in his virtues and graces. Seeing him so often, she became inflamed with a secret passion and admired him more and more as time went on. And the young man, who was by no means slow on the uptake, became aware of her interest and received her into his heart with such love that he had practically no mind for anything else.

So they loved each other in secret, and the young woman longed for nothing so much as to be alone with the youth, but could not bring herself to confide in anyone else. At last she hit on a clever device for telling him how they could meet. She wrote a letter explaining what he needed to do in order to be with her the following day: this she inserted into a hollow reed which she gave to Guiscardo with this jocular advice: 'Get your servant girl to stir up the fire by blowing in this tonight.'

Realizing that she would not have given it to him and spoken like that without some good reason, Guiscardo took the reed back home with him. There he examined it, saw that it was split, opened it and found the letter. Once he had read it and understood the instructions, he was overjoyed and immediately got ready to go and meet her in the way she had outlined.

Next to the prince's palace there was a cave that had been hollowed out of the mountain in days long gone by. What light there was came down from a shaft that had been hewn through the mountainside but was now almost completely blocked by the weeds and brambles that had grown up since the cave had fallen out of use. The cave could, however, still be entered by a secret stairway that led from one of the lady's rooms on the ground floor of the palace and was closed off by a massive thick door. It was so long since the stairway had been used that most people had forgotten its very existence; but Love, from whose sharp eyes no secrets are hidden, had recalled it to the memory of the lovestruck lady. Taking care not to attract attention, she laboured for several days with a variety of tools until at last she managed to prise open the door and go down into the cave. There she saw the shaft above her, and it was then that she had sent the message to Guiscardo telling him to find a way of getting down into the cave through the shaft and giving him an idea of how great the drop was from the shaft to the ground. Setting about the task without delay, Guiscardo got himself a rope with knots and loops so that he could climb up and down and also a leather outfit as a protection against the brambles. Then, the next night, without telling anyone, he went off to the shaft, tied one end of the rope to a sturdy bush that grew near the vent, and lowered himself into the cave to wait for his lady.

The next day the lady pretended that she needed to sleep, dismissed her maids, and locked herself in her room. She then opened the old door and went down into the cave where she found Guiscardo. The two lovers exchanged rapturous greetings and went up to the lady's room where they spent the best part of the day in mutual pleasure. After which, when they had taken every precaution to keep their love a secret, Guiscardo went back down into the cave while she locked the door behind him and went out to join her maids. At nightfall Guiscardo climbed up the rope, came out through the shaft by which he had entered, and returned home. Now he knew the way, and as time went on he did not fail to repeat the journey.

But Fortune, begrudging the two lovers such lasting and supreme delight, devised a catastrophe that would turn their joy to bitter tears. It was Tancredi's habit, from time to time, to come alone to his daughter's room, where he would stay to talk to her for a while and then go away. One day, after dining, he came down while Ghismonda (for that was the lady's name) was out in the garden with her maids; and, not wishing to interrupt his daughter's pleasure, he entered the room unseen and unheard. Finding the windows closed and the curtains drawn back around the bed, he sat down on a stool at one of the corners, rested his head against the bed, and drew the curtain over himself almost as if he were hiding. There he fell asleep. Unfortunately, Ghismonda had arranged for Guiscardo to come that day; and so, while her father was sleeping, she left her maids in the garden, went quietly to her room, and locked herself in, with no idea that someone else might be there. Then she opened the door to the waiting Guiscardo. They got into bed and were making love and sporting around as they usually did when Tancredi suddenly awoke and saw and heard what Guiscardo and his daughter were doing. He was horribly distressed and was about to cry out, but then he decided to stay silent and to remain hidden so that later on, with greater discretion and less scandal, he could carry out the plan that was already taking shape in his mind. The two lovers kept at it, as usual, for quite some time, completely unaware of Tancredi's presence. At last, when they felt it was time to get up, they climbed out of bed; Guiscardo went back down to the cave and Ghismonda left the room. Tancredi, old though he was, climbed out of a window, let himself down into the garden and returned unseen to his room, with death in his heart.

That night, at about bedtime, Guiscardo, still hampered by his leather jerkin, was seized by two of Tancredi's men as he emerged from the shaft. He was secretly led before Tancredi who almost broke into tears: 'Guiscardo,' he said, 'my kindness towards you did not deserve the outrage and the shame that you have brought upon what is mine, as I have seen today with my own eyes.'

Guiscardo answered only: 'Love is more powerful than either you or me.'

Tancredi then ordered that Guiscardo should be taken secretly to one of the inner rooms and kept under guard—and this was done.

The next day Ghismonda still knew nothing of all this while Tancredi's mind was filled with strange and terrible thoughts. After eating, he went, as was his custom, to his daughter's room; and when he called for her and locked himself in with her, he began to speak through his tears: 'Ghismonda, I thought I knew your virtue and your chastity: whatever I might be told, if I hadn't seen it with my own eyes, I would never have believed that you could give yourself to a man who is not your husband. I couldn't imagine you would ever think of it, let alone do it. The memory of it will torment me for what little life remains to my old age. And if you had to indulge in such immorality, I wish to God you had taken a man suited to your own high rank. But of all the men at my court you chose Guiscardo, a lowborn youth, brought up in our court since he was a child, more or less out of charity. You have put my mind into such a turmoil that I don't know what to do with you. I had Guiscardo seized last night as he came out of the shaft; he is in prison now, and I have made up my mind about him; but as for you, God alone knows, because I don't. On the one hand, I am moved by the love I have always borne you, a love greater than any father ever had for his daughter. On the other hand, there is my righteous anger at your huge folly. Love says I should forgive you; anger urges me to go against my nature and inflict some cruel punishment. But before I make up my mind, I want to hear what you yourself have to say to all this.' So saying, he bowed his head and wept loudly like a beaten child.

When Ghismonda heard her father and learned not only that her secret love had been discovered but also that Guiscardo had been taken, she was seized by an unspeakable sorrow that more than once she came near to expressing with womanly cries and tears. But her proud spirit overcame such cowardice and she composed her features with extraordinary self-control. Convinced that Guiscardo was already dead, she resolved to die, rather than to seek any mercy for herself.

It was not, therefore, like some wretched woman being reproached for a fault, but bravely impassive, dry-eyed, and unperturbed that she replied to her father: 'Tancredi, I shall neither deny the facts nor beg for mercy. The former would be useless and I have no wish for the latter. Moreover, I have no intention of doing anything to appeal to your tender heart and your love for me. Instead, confessing the plain truth, I shall first defend my good name with good reasons and then act in a way that confirms my bold spirit. It is true that I have loved and still love Guiscardo; and I shall go on loving him for the rest of my life, which will not be long. And if there is love after death, then I shall never stop loving him. It was not feminine weakness that brought me to this, but the manly virtues of Guiscardo and your negligence in failing to find me a husband. As a creature of flesh and blood yourself, Tancredi, you should have understood that the daughter you fathered is also flesh and blood—not stone or iron. Though you are now an old man, you should have remembered the laws that govern youth and how strong they are. You spent your best years under arms, but all the same you could still have imagined the effects of idleness and luxury on old and young alike. Consider then that you fathered me as a creature of flesh and blood and that I am still a young woman: on both counts I feel the power of carnal desire—all the more strongly because I have been married and know the pleasure that comes with the satisfaction of such desire. Young and a woman as I am, I was unable to resist that impulse and chose to follow where it led; and so I fell in love. I certainly did everything I could to avoid bringing shame on you and on myself through what is a natural instinct, however sinful it may be. At last, Love had pity on me and Fortune proved kind, both combining to show me a secret way of satisfying my desires without anyone knowing. I do not know who told you of this or how you found it out, but

I will not deny the fact. Unlike many women, I left nothing to chance. Indeed, I thought things over carefully before choosing Guiscardo above all others and deliberately attracting him to my side. And it is because we have both been so wise and cautious that I have been able to satisfy my desires for so long. But it seems that you follow common prejudice rather than the truth and that if you reproach me so bitterly, it is not for the sin of loving, but for loving a man of low class, as if you would not be upset if I had chosen a nobleman. You do not understand that what you are really blaming is not my sin but Fortune which often exalts the unworthy and leaves the most worthy far below.

'But let us drop these details and pass to basic principles. You see that we are all of one flesh and have souls created by the one same Creator, with the same faculties, the same powers, the same virtues. We are all born equal and always have been; and it was virtue that originally created distinctions in that those who possessed and manifested more virtue were called noble and the rest were not. And although long custom later obscured this law, yet nature and good conduct show that it has still not been uprooted or destroyed. For the man who acts virtuously proves that he is noble, and if there be any fault, it lies not with him but with those who would deny him that title. Look round at all your noblemen and consider their lives, their bearing, their behaviour, and then compare them with Guiscardo. If you judge impartially, you will say that he is most noble and that your noblemen are a bunch of peasants. My belief in Guiscardo's virtues and worth came from the evidence of my own eyes and from no other other opinion but your own. Who praised him as much as you did for all those qualities that make a good man deserving of praise? And surely you were not wrong: for unless my eyes deceived me, there was not one of those praiseworthy qualities that I did not see in action, even more admirably than your words could express; and if I was deceived in anything, it was you who deceived me. Will you say then, that I have embraced a man of low class? You would not be speaking the truth. But if, perhaps, you said a poor man, that might be granted, but only to your shame in that you have done so little to raise a worthy servant. Poverty is no impediment to true nobility, though riches may be. Many kings, many great princes were once poor, and many of those who till the soil and keep sheep were once very wealthy. As for your last problem, which is what to do with me, you can put it from your mind: if now, in your extreme old age, you want to be more cruel than you ever were when you were young, then inflict that cruelty on me. I shall beg nothing of you—you, the first cause of my sin, if sin it be. Be sure of this: unless you do to me what you have already done— or will do—to Guiscardo, I shall do it to myself with my own hands. Now go! Go and weep among the women. Be cruel, and if you think we deserve it, strike one single blow to kill us both!'

The prince knew his daughter's proud soul, but did not believe she would go as far as her words had suggested. He left her and, having given up the idea of any kind of physical punishment for her, decided to cool her ardour by the cruelty inflicted upon the other guilty party. So he gave orders that the two men who were guarding Guiscardo should strangle him quietly that night and then cut out his heart and bring it to him. And his orders were carried out.

The next morning the prince placed Guiscardo's heart in a fine great golden cup and had it carried to his daughter by one of his most discreet servants with orders that when he delivered it he should say: 'Your father sends you this to console you for the loss of what you love most, just as you have consoled him for the loss of what he loved most.'

Ghismonda, whose fierce resolve remained unshaken, had sent for poisonous herbs and roots as soon as her father had left. These she distilled into a liquid ready for use if what she feared should come about. When the servant came with the prince's gift and his message, she took the cup with no sign of emotion and lifted the lid; and when she saw the heart she understood her father's words and knew for certain that it was the heart of Guiscardo. At which, looking up towards the messenger, she said: 'Nothing less precious than gold could be a fitting tomb for a heart such as this: my father has acted wisely.'

She then lifted the cup to her lips, kissed it, and said: 'In all things, always, down to these last moments of my life, I have known the tenderness of my father's love; but now more than ever. You will convey to him my final words of thanks, the thanks I owe him for so great a gift.'

Then, turning to the cup that she clasped to herself and looking at the heart within, she said: 'Ah, sweetest dwelling of all my joys, cursed be the cruelty of that man who forces my two eyes to see you thus! It was enough for me to see you always with the eyes of the mind. You have run your course and departed in the way allotted to you by Fortune; you have reached the end that all men run towards; you have left the toils and troubles of this world, and even from your enemy received the tomb that your excellence deserved. There was nothing lacking in your funeral rites save the tears of the woman you loved so much in life. But so that you should have these also, God put it into my pitiless father's mind to send you to me: and now I shall shed them for you, although I had determined to die with dry eyes and no fear in my face. That done, with your aid, I shall hasten to join my soul with the soul that you, dear heart, once enclosed and cherished.* With what other company could I more happily or more safely travel toward lands unknown? I am sure that your soul is still here among us, looking at the places where we shared our joys; and I am sure it still loves me and is waiting for my soul that loves it so supremely.'

After these words, without any womanish complaints, she bent over the cup and began to weep as if she had a fountain in her head, shedding so many tears that it was a wonder to behold, kissing the dead heart over and over again. Her handmaids gathered around her and, though they knew not whose heart it was or what her words meant, they were moved to pity and wept with her, asking in vain the reason for her grief and striving to comfort her as best they could.

When she thought she had wept enough, she raised her head and dried her eyes. 'O much-loved heart,' she said, 'here ends all my duty towards you, and nothing is left for me to do but to bring my soul to yours and keep it company.'

Then she bade them give her the phial with the liquid that she had prepared the day before and she poured it into the cup where the heart had been washed with so many tears. She then raised it fearlessly to her lips; and when she had drunk the liquid down, still holding the cup, she climbed up onto the bed and lay down with all due decorum, placing her dead lover's heart next to her own. In silence she waited for death.

Her maids, who did not know what the liquid was that she had drunk, had sent to tell Tancredi everything that they had seen and heard; and he, fearing what might occur, came down quickly to his daughter's room, arriving in the very moment when she laid herself on the bed. Bending down, he sought to comfort her with sweet words, but it was too late; and seeing the state that she was in, he began to weep bitterly. As he did so, the lady spoke: 'Tancredi, save your tears for a sadder destiny than mine, and do not shed them for me for I do not want them. Who but you has been seen weeping for what he himself desired? And yet, if any of the love you once bore me still lives in you, grant me this last request: since you would not let me live quietly and secretly with Guiscardo, let my body be laid out in public with his, wherever you have had it thrown.'

The prince could not reply for he was choked with tears, and the young woman, feeling that her end was near, clasped the dead heart to her breast, saying: 'God be with you all, for now I take my leave.' Her eyes grew dim and her senses failed and she departed this life of pain.

This was the unhappy end of the love of Guiscardo and Ghismonda, as you have heard. Tancredi wept at length and repented of his cruelty too late; and it was amid the general grief of the people of Salerno that he had the lovers buried honourably together in a single tomb.

THE POT OF BASIL
Decameron 4. 5

The brothers of Lisabetta kill her lover, who then appears to her in a dream and tells her where he is buried. She secretly unearths the head and puts it in a pot of basil and weeps over it for hours on end day after day. Her brothers take it from her and soon after she dies of grief.

WHEN Elissa's tale was over and had been praised by the king, it was the turn of Filomena who, with a sigh of compassion for poor Gerbino* and his lady, began:

My story, gracious ladies, will not be about people of such high rank as those in Elissa's tale, but it may be no less pitiful; and it was the mention of Messina a little while ago that reminded me of it, for that was where the events took place.

Now there once lived in Messina three young merchants, brothers who had been left very wealthy on the death of their father, who came originally from San Gimignano.* They had a sister called Lisabetta, a charming and beautiful girl who, for some odd reason, had still not found a husband. In one of their warehouses, however, the three brothers had a young Pisan manager called Lorenzo who handled all their business for them. He was very handsome and engaging, and Lisabetta, who had marked him out more than once, began to find him unusually attractive. Likewise Lorenzo, who had noticed her behaviour on a number of occasions, began to turn his attention away from his old loves and fix his mind on her.

And so, since the attraction was mutual and they were sure of their feelings, it was not long before the two lovers did what they were both longing to do.

They carried on like this for some time, taking pleasure together and enjoying themselves; but they were not secretive enough to avoid discovery. One night, when Lisabetta was going to the room where Lorenzo slept, she was observed by the eldest brother, though she noticed nothing at the time. This brother was a sensible young man and, though he was greatly distressed by what he had learned of his sister, he decided to act cautiously. For the moment he said nothing to anybody, but kept thinking matters over until morning came. Once it was daylight, he told his brothers what he had learned about Lisabetta and Lorenzo that night; and, after much discussion, they decided to avoid involving themselves or their sister in any kind of scandal by keeping silent about the whole thing and behaving as if they knew nothing and had seen nothing until such time as, without too much fuss and bother, they could wipe out this disgrace and prevent the matter from going any further.

They stuck to this plan for some time, chatting and joking with Lorenzo as they always had done; but then one day the three brothers pretended they were going out into the country on a pleasure trip. They took Lorenzo along with them and when they reached a very remote and lonely spot, they seized the opportunity to catch him off guard and kill him. Then they buried him on the spot so that nobody would know what they had done. When they got back to Messina they told people that Lorenzo was travelling in their service; and this was readily believed because they had sent him out on such business trips often enough in the past.

When Lorenzo failed to return, Lisabetta grew anxious about the delay and kept asking her brothers about him. One day, when she was particularly insistent, one of the brothers snapped: 'What's all this about? What have you got to do with Lorenzo that makes you ask about him all the time? If you keep bothering us, we'll give you the answer you deserve.' After this, the dejected girl asked no further questions, but became ever more fearful without knowing why.

Often at night she would call Lorenzo and implore him to come back; and sometimes she would lament his long delay with copious tears. She had no joy in life, and all she could do was wait.

One night when she had been weeping over Lorenzo's absence and had fallen asleep at last as the tears still fell, Lorenzo appeared to her in a dream, pale and dishevelled, with his clothes all sodden and torn; and he seemed to say: 'O Lisabetta, you keep calling me and mourning my long absence, and you accuse me harshly with your tears; know, therefore, that I can no longer return, for on the day when you saw me for the last time your brothers murdered me.' Then he told her exactly where they had buried him, repeated that she should no longer call him or wait for him, and disappeared.

The girl awoke, fully convinced by the vision, and wept bitterly. When she got up in the morning, though she dared not say anything to her brothers, she decided to go to the place Lorenzo had described to see if what had appeared in her dream was actually true. She obtained permission to go for a stroll outside the city walls and set out as soon as possible, taking with her a woman who had once been in their service and knew all about the affair. When she arrived, she swept away the dead leaves that covered the spot and dug down where the earth seemed less hard. She had not gone very deep before she found the body of her poor lover, not yet rotting or decayed, which proved the truth of her vision. She was the unhappiest of women, but she knew that this was no place or time for weeping. She would have liked to take the whole corpse away for a proper burial, but seeing that this was not possible, she took a knife and, as best she could, severed the head from the trunk, wrapped it in a towel, and gave it to the servant to carry in her lap. Then she piled the earth back over the rest of the corpse and went home unobserved.

Once closeted in her room, she wept long and bitterly over the head, washing it with her tears and kissing it all over. Then she took a good large pot of the kind used to plant marjoram or basil and put the head inside, wrapped in a fine cloth. She covered the head with earth and planted several shoots of the best Salerno basil which she watered only with essence of roses or orange blossom or her own tears. She made a habit of sitting near the pot and of gazing at it with intense longing, since it was where her dear Lorenzo lay hidden. And when she had gazed her fill, she would go and weep over it until at last all the basil was drenched with her tears.

It may have been the result of this long and constant care or it may have been that the soil was enriched by the rotting head inside, but the fact was that the basil flourished and became a strong and wonderfully fragrant plant. But the neighbours often noticed the girl's strange unchanging behaviour and commented on it to her brothers who were already shocked by her fading beauty and sunken eyes: 'We've noticed', they said, 'that she goes through the same strange routine every day.' When the brothers heard this and saw it for themselves they tried scolding the girl, but their reproaches had no effect and so they secretly had the pot removed. Seeing that the pot was missing, the girl kept asking for it, insisting over and over again. When she did not get it back, her sobs and tears redoubled and she fell ill. And even in her illness, the pot was the only thing she asked for. The young men were so puzzled by these repeated requests that they decided to look into the pot to see what was there; and when they had emptied out the earth, they found the cloth with the head inside, still not so decayed as not to be recognized by its curly hair as that of Lorenzo. Dismayed at the sight and fearing that now the whole story would come out, they buried the head and, without telling anyone, left Messina very quietly; after which they closed down their business and moved to Naples.

As for Lisabetta, she continued to weep and ask for her pot of basil until at last she died of weeping, and that was the end of her unhappy love. But later the story became widely known and someone composed the song that is still sung today:

> Who was the evil man who came
> And stole away my pot, etc.

MADONNA FILIPPA'S DEFENCE
Decameron 6. 7

Madonna Filippa's husband catches her with a lover. She is taken before a magistrate, but with a prompt and witty reply she manages to free herself and have the law changed.

FIAMMETTA had fallen silent and everyone was still laughing about the clever argument Scalza had used to prove the superior nobility of the Baronci family* when the queen ordered Filostrato to tell his story; and he began thus:

Worthy ladies, being able to speak well in a variety of situations is always a fine thing, but I consider it particularly fine when it responds to a necessity; and this was the case with the noble lady I intend to tell you about, who spoke so well that she not only amused and enter- tained all those who heard her but also managed to free herself from the bonds of a shameful death, as you shall hear.

In the city of Prato there was once a law as truly disgraceful as it was harsh. It stipulated that any woman caught by her husband in the act of adultery with a lover should be burned alive, making no distinc- tion between such wives and those women who were found to have sold themselves to all and sundry for money. While this law was still in force it happened that a beautiful, noble, and passionate lady called Madonna Filippa was caught out by her husband, Rinaldo de' Pugliesi, who discovered her in her own bedroom, lying in the arms of Lazzarino de' Guazzaliotri,* a noble and handsome youth of that city, whom she loved as much as she loved herself. Rinaldo was enraged by what he saw and could hardly keep from rushing at them and killing them on the spot—and indeed, his anger was such that he would have done so, but that he feared the trouble it might cause for himself. Yet although he managed to hold back, he still wanted the law of Prato to do what he could not legally do for himself; that is, put his wife to death.

And so, at daybreak, having all the evidence that he needed to prove the guilt of his wife, without any further thought, he lodged an accus- ation against her and had her summoned before the court. Now the lady was as courageous as those who are truly in love usually are, and despite the advice of many friends and relatives, she was determined to appear before the court. She preferred to confess the truth and die bravely rather than to run away and live in cowardly contumacious exile and thus prove herself unworthy of such a lover as the man in whose arms she had spent the night. And so, well escorted by ladies and gentlemen, all urging her to deny the charge, she came before the magistrate and, with an impassive face and in a firm voice, asked what he wanted of her. When the magistrate looked at her, he saw that she was beautiful and gracious, while her words demonstrated that she had a bold spirit; and as he began to pity her, he feared that she might make a confession that would, given his honour as a magistrate, oblige him to condemn her to death.

But since he could not avoid asking her about the charge laid against her, he said: 'Lady, as you see, here is your husband Rinaldo whose accusation is that he caught you committing adultery with another man; and so he asks me to punish you with death, according to the law that is in force here in Prato. But I cannot do this unless first you confess; so be careful what you answer, and tell me if your husband's accusation is true.'

Not in the least abashed, the lady replied in a pleasant voice: 'Sir, it is true that Rinaldo is my husband and that last night he discovered me in the arms of Lazzarino where, for the true and perfect love I bear him, I have been many times before. This is something I shall never deny. But as I am sure you know, the laws should be the same for all and made with the consent of those concerned by them. This is not the case with the present law which is binding only on us poor women who, when it comes to satisfying the sexual desires of others, can do it on a much larger scale than men. Moreover, not only did no woman give her consent when this law was made, but no woman was ever asked. That is why it deserves to be called a bad law. And if you decide to observe this law, to the ruin of my body and your soul, that's your affair; but before you pass judgement on anything, I beg you to grant me one small favour: ask my husband whether or not I gave myself to him without reserve each and every time, as often as he pleased, without ever saying no.'

To this, without waiting for the magistrate to ask, Rinaldo promptly answered that the lady had certainly allowed him to enjoy her every time he asked.

'Well then,' continued the lady, 'I ask you, sir magistrate, if he always took from me whatever he needed and whatever he pleased, what was I supposed to do then or now with what was left over? Should I throw it to the dogs? Rather than letting it spoil or go to waste, isn't it better used for the pleasure of a gentleman who loves me more than he loves himself?'

Almost all the citizens of Prato had come to hear the examination of such a famous lady and as soon as they had stopped laughing at her witty request, they cried out with one voice that the lady was right and had spoken well. And before they left, with the agreement of the magistrate, they modified that cruel law so that it applied only to those women who betrayed their husbands by selling themselves for money. Rinaldo left the court feeling completely baffled by the result of his absurd venture: as for the lady, now happy and free, having been, as it were, saved from the fire and restored to life, she returned home in glory.

PERONELLA AND THE JAR
Decameron 7. 2

*Peronella hides her lover in a jar when her husband comes home unex-
pectedly. Her husband says he has sold the jar, she tells him she has
already found a buyer who is now inside the jar checking to see whether
it is sound. The man jumps out and gets the husband to scour the jar
and carry it home for him.*

EMILIA'S story was received with much laughter and the final prayer*
was approved by everyone as good and holy. When she had finished,
the king ordered Filostrato to speak next, and he began:

My dearest ladies, men—and especially husbands—play so many
tricks on you that when, as occasionally occurs, a woman does the
same to her husband you should not simply be glad that it has happened and happy to hear about it: you should go out yourselves and
spread the story to teach men that women can be as smart as they are.
This cannot fail to serve your cause, because when a man knows that
others are as smart as he is, he doesn't go in for tricks quite so easily.
Who can doubt, therefore, that when men hear what we have to say on
this topic, they will find good reason to stop and think before they try
anything on, since they know that you, ladies, can play the same game?
I therefore intend to tell you what a young woman, low-born though
she was, did to her husband on the spur of the moment to get herself
out of an awkward situation.

Not so long ago in Naples a poor man married a lively and pretty
young girl called Peronella; and what with his work as a mason and
her spinning they just about managed to make ends meet. Now one of
the smart young lads about town happened to see Peronella, found
her very attractive, and became besotted with her; and he courted her
so assiduously in one way or another that finally they became lovers.
This was the system they hit upon so that they could be together:
every morning, when the husband got up early either to go to work or
to find work, the young man would be standing in some place where
he could see him leaving; and since there are never many people
around in the Avorio district,* he could nip into the house as soon as
the husband was gone. They did this very often.

But one morning, when the good man had gone out and Giannello

Scrignario (that was the young man's name) had slipped in and was with Peronella, things went wrong. The husband, who nearly always stayed out all day, suddenly came back home and finding the door locked began to knock; and as he knocked, he thought to himself: 'All praise be ever yours, O Lord, for though you made me poor, you consoled me with a young wife who is virtuous and chaste! See how she locked the door as soon as I went out, so that nobody could come in and pester her.'

Peronella knew it was her husband from the way he knocked: 'Oh no! Giannel darling, I'm done for. That's my husband back again, God blast him! Don't ask me what it's all about; he never comes home at this time; maybe he saw you coming in. Anyway, since that's how things are, for God's sake get into that big storage jar over there, and I'll go and open to him and find out why on earth he's come home so early this morning.'

Giannello hurriedly clambered into the jar and Peronella went to the door and opened to her husband: 'What's all this about?' she said, with a scowling face, 'what do you mean by coming home so soon this morning? It looks as if you don't feel like doing anything today, since I see you standing there with your tools in your hands. What are we going to live on if you carry on like this? How shall we get our bread? Do you think I'll let you pawn my best skirt and petticoats? What's my life day and night but spinning, spinning, until my fingernails fall off? And all so we can have enough oil to keep our lamp alight! Husband, husband, all the wives round here are shocked; and what's more they make fun of me for putting up with it. And now you come home with your hands dangling down when you should be out working.'

After a bout of weeping, she started up again: 'That's my fate, that is! It was in those rotten stars from the hour I was born! I could have had a nice decent chap, and I ditched him for this fellow who doesn't know how lucky he was to take home someone like me. These other women have a good time with their lovers—and there's not one of them who doesn't have two or three. They have fun and persuade their husbands that black's white. And me, I have to suffer and have all the bad luck, just because I'm a decent woman who doesn't go in for that sort of thing. I don't know why I don't pick up a few lovers myself, just like the others do. Now you just listen to me, husband, because if I wanted to go wrong I'd have no trouble finding someone who'd do it with me. There are some fine lively lads who've taken a fancy to me and offered me stacks of money, or jewels or dresses, if that was what I wanted. But my heart would never let me do it, because that's not the kind of stock I come from. And now you come back home when you should be out working!'

Her husband answered: 'For God's sake, woman, there's no need to be so upset. I did go out to work, but it's obvious that what you didn't know and what I didn't know myself is that today's the feast of Saint Galeone* when nobody works, and that's why I've come home so early. But all the same, I found a way of making sure we'll have bread for a month or more. You see this man who's here with me. Well, I've sold him that big jar: you know, the one that's been cluttering up the house for so long. He's giving me five silver florins for it.'

'That only makes things worse,' said Peronella. 'You're a man and you go out and about, so you ought to know how such things work, and you've sold the jar for five florins. And here am I, a simple woman who hardly ever puts her nose outside the door. But I saw how that jar was in the way and I sold it to an honest man for seven florins. When you came back, he'd just climbed inside to check whether it's sound.'

When her husband heard this, he was delighted and said to the man who had come with him: 'Off you go, mate. You heard what my wife said. She's sold it for seven and you only offered me five.' 'So much the better for you then!' said the man as he left.

'Come on up,' said Peronella to her husband, 'since you're here, you may as well deal with him yourself.'

Giannello had been listening with ears pricked to find out if there was anything he needed to do to save his skin. Now, when he heard what Peronella was saying, he promptly jumped out of the jar: 'Where are you, good lady?' he asked, as if he had no idea that her husband had come back.

The husband was already coming upstairs: 'Here I am, what do you want?'

'And who are you? I want to talk with the lady who agreed to sell me this jar.'

'Don't worry, you can deal with me. I'm her husband.'

'Well, the jar seems sound enough, but you must have left the lees of wine inside because it's all encrusted with something so dry that I can't scrape it off with my fingernails. So I'm not going to take it unless it's cleaned up first.'

'Oh no,' said Peronella, 'we won't let that spoil the deal; my husband will scour the whole thing.'

'All right then,' said her husband, putting down his tools and taking off his jacket; and when they'd lighted a candle and given him a scraper, he clambered into the jar and started scraping. Peronella meanwhile acted as if she wanted to see what he was doing. She put her head, her arm, and her shoulder into the mouth of the jar which wasn't very wide, and started to bombard him with 'Scrape here, and there, and over there too' and 'look, you've missed that bit'.

While she was in that position, telling her husband what to do and reminding him of this and that, Giannello had an idea. He had not managed to get full satisfaction before being interrupted by the husband's return that morning, so now, since he could not have things exactly the way he wanted, he decided to make do with the best on offer and came up behind Peronella who was covering the mouth of the jar. Just as wild stallions mount their mares in the broad plains of Parthia,* even so did Giannello's youthful ardour produce its natural effects. And in that same perfect moment, the cleaning of the jar was completed: Giannello backed away, Peronella lifted her head, and her husband climbed out of the jar.

'Take this candle, good man,' said Peronella, 'look inside and see if it's clean enough for you.' Giannello looked inside the jar and said that everything was fine and he was happy with it. Then he paid out the seven florins and had the husband carry it round to his house.

PATIENT GRISELDA

Decameron 10. 10

Urged to marry by his subjects, the marquis of Saluzzo does so in his own way by choosing the daughter of a peasant. She bears him two children and he makes her believe that he has killed them. Then he pretends that he has grown tired of her, drives her out dressed only in her shift, and brings his own daughter home as if she were to be his new wife. Finding that his true wife bears all this with perfect patience, he takes her back and cherishes her more dearly than ever; he shows her the two children who are now grown up, honours her as his lady, and ensures that others do the same.

THE king's long story came to an end and everyone seemed to have enjoyed it. Dioneo laughed and said: 'The good man who waited till the following night to see the ghost's tail go down wouldn't have given tuppence for all the praise you lavish on Messer Torello,'* and then, knowing that he was to be the last one to speak, he began:

Gentle ladies, it seems to me that all the stories today have been devoted to kings and sultans and the like; and so, not to stray too far from that direction, I will tell you of a marquis; yet it will not be a story of noble behaviour but of bestial cruelty, and even though it ended happily for him, I would not advise anyone to follow his example, for it is a real sin that he came out of it so well.

A long time ago, as the eldest son of the family, a young man called Gualtieri became marquis of Saluzzo.* Being unmarried and child-less, he spent all his time hunting and bird-catching, with no thought of wife and children—a very wise attitude, one might think. His sub-jects, however, did not see it that way, and time and time again they begged him to take a wife so that he would not be left without an heir or they without a lord. They offered to find him someone with the right kind of father and mother, a bride who would give them hope and make him very happy.

'My friends,' replied Gualtieri, 'you are trying to force me into something that I had absolutely decided never to do, considering how difficult it is to find a wife whose ways would suit me and how many possible wives are completely unsuitable. And how wretched life can be for a man who ends up with a wife who doesn't suit him! You say you can tell the character of a daughter by observing her father and her mother and that's how you'll find a wife who pleases me. Well, that's sheer nonsense, because I don't see how you can know the secrets of the mothers or what the fathers are really like. And even if you could, daughters can be very different from their fathers and mothers. But since you insist on shackling me with these chains, I shall give way; and to avoid blaming anyone but myself if it turns out badly, I have decided to go and look for a wife by myself. But let me tell you this: whoever she is, if you do not honour her as your lady, you shall learn to your cost how much harm you did me by forcing me to marry against my will.' The worthy gentlemen replied that they were per-fectly happy, just so long as he agreed to take a wife.

Now for some time already Gualtieri had been attracted by the behaviour of a poor young woman from a village near his estate; and since she was also very beautiful, he judged that with her he could lead a perfectly comfortable life. Therefore, without looking any further, he decided to marry her. He summoned her father, who was indeed very poor, and made arrangements with him to take the girl as his wife.

The next thing Gualtieri did was to gather together all the friends who lived in his domain: 'My friends,' he said, 'you wanted me to think about taking a wife, and I have arranged to do so, more to please you than out of any personal desire to get married. You know what you promised, which is that you would agree to honour as your lady any woman I happened to choose. Now the time has come when I have kept my promise and I expect you to keep yours. I have found a young woman after my own heart not far from here, and I mean to take her as my wife and to bring her home in the next few days. Therefore, you should think how best to celebrate the wedding-feast and how to receive her with all due honours, so that I can be happy to say that you have kept your promise and you can say that I have kept mine.'

Those worthy subjects were delighted and replied that they would be happy to accept her as their lady, whoever she might be, and to honour her as such in every way; they then set about preparing a joyous and splendid wedding-feast. Gualtieri did likewise, making his own arrangements for a magnificent wedding by inviting a host of friends, relatives, great noblemen, and other local guests. He also ordered lovely expensive dresses and had them fitted on a girl whose figure resembled that of the young woman he was about to marry. And then there were girdles, rings, a fine precious tiara, and everything that a bride could wish for.

Early in the morning on the day he had chosen for the wedding, Gualtieri mounted his horse and all those who had come to honour him did the same. Now everything was ready and he declared: 'Gentlemen, it is time to go and meet the bride,' and so they set out and came to the hut where her father lived. There they found her coming home with water from the well, and she was hurrying so that she could go with the other women to catch a glimpse of Gualtieri's bride. When Gualtieri saw her, he called her by her name, Griselda, and asked where her father was. She answered shyly: 'My lord, he's at home.'

Then Gualtieri dismounted and, telling everyone to wait, went alone into the hovel and found the girl's father who was called Giannucolo. 'I have come to marry Griselda,' he said, 'but first I want her to answer a few questions in your presence.' Then he asked her whether, if he were to marry her, she would always do everything to please him, and never be upset by anything he might do or say, and whether she would always be obedient, and many other questions in the same vein. And she answered yes to everything.

Then Gualtieri took her by the hand, led her outside, and, in the presence of his retinue and everyone else who was there, had her stripped naked. Then he quickly had her clothed and shod in the garments that he had prepared; and on her hair, dishevelled though it was, he placed a coronet. Everyone was amazed to see this, and he said: 'Gentlemen, this is the woman I mean to have as my wife, if she will have me as her husband.' Then, turning to Griselda who was standing there, bashful and uncertain, he asked: 'Griselda, will you take me as your husband?' She replied: 'Yes, my lord.'

'And I take you as my wife,' he said; and before all those who had gathered there, he married her. Then he set her upon a palfrey and, with a fitting retinue to do her honour, led her to his home where the wedding-feast was as splendid and spectacular as if he had married the daughter of the king of France.

The young wife seemed to have changed her character and her manners along with her clothes. As we have already said, she was beautiful both in face and figure, and not only was she beautiful, but also so charming, so pleasant, and so courteous that she seemed to be the daughter of some noble lord rather than a poor shepherdess, the child of Giannucolo. Indeed, those who had known her before were astonished by the change. Moreover, she was so obedient to her husband and so obliging that he thought himself the happiest and most satisfied man in the world. Likewise, she was so gracious and so kind towards her husband's subjects that everyone loved her, gladly honouring her and praying for her health, prosperity, and good fortune. Whereas they had once censured Gualtieri as imprudent for taking such a wife, they now proclaimed that he was the wisest and most farsighted man on earth, for no one else could have discerned the great virtues hidden beneath her humble dress and peasant cloak. In short, she lived up to her role so well that before long people were praising her worth and her good deeds, not only in the marquisate but throughout the land; and those who had carped about her husband's marriage completely changed their tune.

She had not been married long when she became pregnant and in due time gave birth to a daughter, to Gualtieri's great delight. But a little later a strange idea came into his head: he decided to test her patience by subjecting her to long-drawn-out and intolerable trials.

He began with sharp words as if he were angry, saying that his gentle-men were dissatisfied with her because of her lowly origin—all the more because she was now having children. In particular, he said, they kept complaining about the daughter she had borne.

The lady heard these words with great composure, determined not to stray from the virtuous course she had chosen. 'My lord,' she said, 'do with me whatever may turn to your greater honour or happiness, and I shall be content, for I know that I stand below them and that I was not worthy of this honour that you have kindly conferred upon me.' This reply was very pleasing to Gualtieri since it showed that she had not been made proud by any honour received from him or from others.

Shortly after, having hinted to his wife yet again that his subjects could not put up with her newborn daughter, he called up one of his trusted servants and despatched him to her with a message. 'My lady,' said the servant, looking deeply distressed, 'on pain of death, I am obliged to do what my master commands. He has ordered me to take this daughter of yours and to . . .', there he broke off.

Hearing these words and seeing the face of the servant, she remem-bered what her husband had said and deduced that he had ordered his servant to kill the child. So she quickly took the baby from the cradle, kissed her, and blessed her; and despite the great pain in her heart, she kept her composure and placed the little girl in the arms of the servant, saying: 'Take her, and do exactly what your lord and mine has commanded, but do not leave her to be devoured by wild beasts or birds, unless he has ordered that as well.' The servant took the child and repeated these words to Gualtieri who was amazed at his wife's fortitude. He then sent the servant off to a female relative in Bologna with a request that she should bring the child up and educate her with great care, but without telling anyone whose daughter she was.

Now the lady became pregnant again and in due course gave birth to a son, which was a great joy to Gualtieri. But what he had already done to his wife was not enough for him and he decided to wound her still more deeply. One day, with an angry look, he said to her: 'Lady, since you gave birth to this male child, my subjects have become impos-sible to deal with, so bitterly do they resent the idea that a grandson of Giannucolo should rule over them after my death. If I don't want to be driven out, I'm afraid I shall have to do what I did last time and in the end leave you and take another wife.' The lady listened to him patiently and answered simply this: 'My lord, think only of your own happiness and pleasure and have no care for me, for nothing pleases me but what I see pleases you.'

A few days later Gualtieri sent for the son just as he had sent for the daughter. And again he let it be thought that he had given orders for the child to be killed, but in fact sent him also to be brought up in Bologna. And through all this the lady said nothing and showed no more emotion than she had for the little girl. Gualtieri was astonished and said to himself that no other woman could have behaved in the same way; and if he had not seen how dearly she cherished her children when he allowed her to do so, he would have thought that she acted like that because she was glad to be rid of them; but he knew that in fact it was wisdom that inspired her. His subjects, thinking that he had had his children killed, were loud in their condemnation of his cruelty and full of compassion for his wife; but when other ladies expressed their sympathy with her over the loss of her children, she said only that what pleased her was whatever pleased the man who had fathered them.

When some years had passed since the birth of his daughter, Gualtieri thought that the time had come to put his wife's powers of endurance to the ultimate test. He told many of his subjects that he could no longer put up with Griselda as his wife and that he realized his marriage to her had been a youthful folly; and this was why he was doing everything in his power to get a dispensation from the Pope so that he could take another wife and leave Griselda. Several worthy men rebuked him, but he answered simply that this was how it had to be. When the lady heard this, she understood that she might now be forced to return to her father and perhaps watch over the sheep as she had done in the past—all this while seeing another woman possess the man to whom she had given her whole heart. She was deeply distressed; but just as she had endured all the other blows of Fortune, she was now calm and resolute in facing up to this one.

A little later Gualtieri arranged for fake letters to come from Rome. These he showed to his subjects as proof that the Pope had given him a dispensation to leave Griselda and take another wife. Then, summoning her before a large assembly, he said: 'Lady, the Pope has given me permission to leave you and to take another wife; and because my ancestors were great nobles and lords in this land whereas yours have always been mere labourers, I have resolved that you should no longer be my wife but go back home to Giannucolo with the dowry you brought me. After which I shall take another wife, one I have already found and who is more suited to my rank.'

When she heard these words, the lady had to make a huge effort, well beyond the natural powers of women, to hold back her tears. 'My lord,' she said, 'I have always known that my lowly station was unsuited to your nobility. I regarded my privileged position as something granted by God and by you, but always as a loan, never as a gift. Now that it pleases you to take back that position, I must be pleased to restore it to you; I am happy to do so. Here is the ring with which you wedded me: take it. You tell me to take with me the dowry I brought you. You won't need a banker for that, and I shan't need bag or pack-horse, for I have not forgotten that you took me in naked. If you think it decent that this body which has borne your children should be seen by all and sundry, then I shall go naked; but I beg you, as a reward for the virginity that I brought here and do not take away, that over and above my dowry you grant me a single shift to wear.'

Gualtieri felt like bursting into tears, but he put on a stern face and said: 'Then go with a shift.'

All those present implored him to grant her a robe of some kind so that the woman who had been his wife for thirteen years or more should not be seen leaving his house in such a poor and shameful state as to be wearing nothing but a shift. But their prayers were in vain, and the lady, commending him to God, left her husband's house and went home to her father in her shift, barefoot and with nothing on her head, amid the tears and lamentations of all who saw her. Giannucolo had never really believed that Gualtieri would keep his daughter as his wife and was expecting something like this to happen one day or other. So he had kept the clothes that she had taken off on the morning of her marriage. Now he gave them back to her, and she put them on and busied herself as she had done in the past with humble menial tasks in her father's house, bravely enduring the fierce assault of adverse Fortune.

The next thing Gualtieri did was to make his subjects believe that he had chosen a daughter of one of the counts of Panago,* and as he was preparing for a grandiose wedding ceremony, he sent for Griselda. When she arrived, he said: 'I shall soon be bringing here the lady I have decided to marry and I mean to receive her with all fitting honours on her first visit. You know that here in the house I don't have women who know how to smarten up the rooms and fix all the things that such a festive occasion calls for. Since you know more about this than anyone else, just work out what needs to be done. As for the welcome party, invite any ladies you think suitable, and receive them as if you were still the lady of the house. Then, when the wedding is over and done with, you can go back home.'

These words were like daggers in Griselda's heart, for she could not renounce the love she bore him as easily as she had given up the gifts of her good fortune: And yet she replied: 'My lord, I am ready and willing.' And so in her rough hodden clothes she re-entered the house that not long before she had left clad only in a shift. She set about sweeping the rooms and tidying them up; she hung new drapes and tapestries in the halls; she prepared the kitchen for the feast—all this with her own hands as if she were a simple housemaid. Nor did she stop until everything was ready for the great occasion. Then, having invited the ladies of the region in Gualtieri's name, she stayed on to wait for the festivities. On the day of the wedding, despite her peasant dress, she welcomed the ladies with the smiling grace and courtesy of a noblewoman.

Gualtieri had taken care to have his son and daughter fittingly brought up in Bologna by a female relative who had married into the family of the counts of Panago. The boy was six and the girl was twelve and the loveliest creature ever seen. Gualtieri now sent to Bologna with a request that his relative's husband should bring the children to Saluzzo, escorted by a splendid retinue: he was to tell everyone that he was bringing the girl to be Gualtieri's wife and he should give absolutely no hint of her real identity. The gentleman did what the marquis had asked and set off with the girl and her brother and a gallant company. A few days later they arrived in Saluzzo just in time for the feast and found all the local people and folk from round about waiting for Gualtieri's new bride. When the ladies had greeted her and escorted her into the hall where the tables were laid out, Griselda, still in her rustic clothes, came cheerfully forward and said: 'Welcome, my lady.' The ladies had begged Gualtieri that he should either let Griselda stay in a room apart or else lend her one of the robes that had once been hers so that she should not have to appear before the guests so poorly dressed; but it was all in vain, and now they were seated at table and served. Everyone took a good look at the girl and the company was unanimous in declaring that Gualtieri had made a good exchange; and Griselda was among those who bestowed the most lavish praise on the girl and on her little brother.

Gualtieri felt that he had seen all the proof he needed of his lady's patience. He saw that there were no circumstances, however strange or outrageous, that could change her. And, since he knew how wise she was, he was certain that her behaviour was no sign of insensitivity. He decided it was time to put an end to the distress which he felt she must be hiding behind those calm composed features. As everyone looked on, he called her forward and asked with a smile: 'What do you think of our bride?'

'My lord,' she replied, 'I think very well of her, and if she is as wise as she is beautiful—which is surely the case—then I have no doubt that life with her will make you the happiest lord on earth. But let me beg of you with all my heart: do not wound her in the same way as you have wounded the woman who used to be your wife, for I do not think she could bear it. She is younger and has had a refined upbringing, whereas your first wife had to work hard ever since she was a child.'

Gualtieri saw that Griselda firmly believed that the girl was to be his wife and yet she had nothing but good to say of her. He made her sit down beside him and said: 'Griselda, the time has come for you to reap the reward of your long patience and for those who have condemned me as cruel, unjust, and savage to understand that I have acted with a deliberate end in view. I wanted to teach you how to be a wife and to show them how to choose and treat a wife; and for myself I wished to ensure an enduring peace for as long as my life with you might last.

'When I decided to take a wife, I feared it would not turn out that way, and that is why I put you to the test with all the injuries and torments that you know too well. Yet I never saw you counter my wishes either in word or deed, and since I am now sure that you will give me the happiness I long for, I mean to restore in one moment everything that I have taken from you for so long and to heal with the sweetest balm the wounds I inflicted. With joy in your heart, therefore, embrace this girl that you thought was my bride, and also her brother, for they are our children—the children that you and many others long thought I had cruelly put to death. I am your husband who loves you above all else, for I think I can boast that no other man can be so happy in his wife.'

With this, he embraced and kissed her. She wept for joy as they rose and went together to where their daughter was sitting, astonished at what she had just heard. Tenderly they embraced the sister and brother, and thus not only the girl but all those who were present learned the truth. The ladies were delighted and, getting up from the table, they led Griselda aside into a room where they removed her rough clothes and dressed her in a splendid robe; and remembering how they had done this once before, they wished her better luck this time. Then they led her back into the hall dressed as the noble lady she was and had always appeared to be, even in her rags. What followed was a marvellous celebration with the children, and there was such general rejoicing at the way things had turned out that the merriment and feasting kept increasing and went on for several days. People thought Gualtieri had been very wise, though they considered that the trials of his wife had been so harsh as to be intolerable. But wisest of all, they decided, was Griselda.

After a few days the count of Panago returned to Bologna, and Gualtieri took Giannucolo away from his labour and installed him as his father-in-law to live out a respected and comfortable old age. Finally, after finding a good match for his daughter, Gualtieri lived a long and happy life with Griselda whom he always treated with the utmost honour.

What more can be said except that divine spirits sometimes descend from Heaven into humble dwellings, just as royal palaces may house spirits more suited to be swineherds than lords of men? Who but Griselda could have suffered the cruel unheard-of trials inflicted on her by Gualtieri—not simply without tears, but with apparent cheerfulness? Perhaps it would have served him right if his choice had fallen on a different kind of woman—one who would have reacted to being driven out in her shift by finding another man to jiggle her muff* and maybe give her a new dress as part of the deal.

SER GIOVANNI FIORENTINO

GIANNETTO AND THE LADY OF BELMONT
Il Pecorone (The Big Sheep) 4. 1

THERE was once in Florence, in the house of the Scali,* a merchant called Bindo who had often travelled to Tanais* and Alexandria and made all the usual long trading voyages. This Bindo was very rich and had three fine sons; so, being near to death, he called the eldest and the second son and made his will in their presence, leaving them the heirs of everything he had in the world. And to the youngest son he left nothing.

Hearing the will that his father had made, the youngest son, who was called Giannetto, went to his bedside and said: 'Father, I'm shocked by what you've done and that you haven't remembered me in your will.'

The father answered: 'Giannetto, there's nobody in the world that I love more than you; that's why I don't want you to stay here after my death. Instead, I want you to go to Venice, to your godfather Ansaldo who has no sons and has often written, asking me to send you to him. And I can tell you that he's the richest merchant in Christendom. Therefore, when I'm dead, I want you to go to him and give him this letter; and if you know how to behave, you'll become a rich man.'

The son said: 'Father, I am ready and willing to do as you command.'

The father blessed him, and died a few days later. All three sons were deeply grieved and paid fitting honours to the corpse. Some days passed and then the two brothers called Giannetto and said: 'Brother, it's true that our father made a will that has left us as his sole heirs and that of you he made no mention; nevertheless, you are still our brother and so whatever is ours is also yours for as long as it lasts.' Giannetto answered: 'Brothers, I thank you for your offer, but for my part, I mean to seek my fortune elsewhere. I am determined to do so, and you can keep the inheritance that has been blessed and assigned to you.'

Then the brothers, seeing that his mind was made up, gave him a horse and some money for the journey, and Giannetto took his leave and set off for Venice. When he arrived at the counting-house of Ansaldo, he handed over his father's deathbed letter, from which Ansaldo learned that this was indeed the son of his dearest friend Bindo. After reading it through, he embraced the young man, saying: 'Welcome, my godson. I've been hoping to see you for so long.' Then he asked after Bindo and when Giannetto replied that he was dead Ansaldo broke into tears and embraced and kissed him, saying: 'I am, indeed, sorely grieved by the death of Bindo because he helped me to gain much of what I now possess; but seeing you gives me such joy that it calms the sorrow.' And he took him home and gave orders to his clerks and assistants and grooms and all his household that Giannetto was to be obeyed and served better and more promptly than he was himself. And he handed over the keys of his cash-boxes and said: 'My son, whatever is there is yours: spend it today on clothes and footwear, just as you like; invite people to dine with you and make yourself known. This is the thought I leave you with: I shall like you all the more for the impression you make on others.'

So Giannetto began to frequent the gentlemen of Venice, to give dinners and suppers, to bestow gifts and employ servants, to buy fine horses, to joust and bear a lance, always at ease and skilled in such matters, magnanimous and courteous in everything; and he well knew where it was fitting to show due honour and respect and always honoured Messer Ansaldo as being more than a hundred times his father. So properly did he behave with all kinds and conditions of people that almost everyone in Venice loved him when they saw him so sensible, so pleasant, and so extraordinarily courteous. Both men and women adored him, and Ansaldo had no eyes for anyone else, so pleased was he with the youth's manners and behaviour. And there was hardly a feast to which Giannetto was not invited, so well liked was he by all and sundry.

Now it happened that two of his best friends had chartered two ships to go to Alexandria on a trading expedition as they usually did every year, and they asked Giannetto whether he would enjoy going with them to see something of the world, and especially Damascus and the surrounding region. Giannetto answered: 'Truly, I would be very glad to go with you, if my father Ansaldo gives me his permission.' And they said: 'We shall see to it that he does, and gladly too.' So off they went to Messer Ansaldo: 'We beg you to give Giannetto your permission to come with us to Alexandria in spring, and to charter a ship for him so that he can see something of the world.' Ansaldo replied: 'I am content, if that's his pleasure.' And they said: 'Yes, sir, it is.'

Then Messer Ansaldo had a fine ship prepared, laden with merchandise and equipped with all the necessary banners and arms. And when it was ready, Ansaldo ordered the captain and the crew to do whatever Giannetto commanded and to take good care of him: 'For I'm not sending him out for any profit he might make, but only so that he can enjoy seeing something of the world.'

When Giannetto was about to embark, the whole city hastened to see him off, for no ship so splendid or so well equipped had set sail from Venice in a very long time; and everyone was sad to see him go. Then, when he had taken leave of Messer Ansaldo and all his friends, the ships put to sea and hoisted sail, making for Alexandria in the name of God and good fortune.

The three friends in their three ships had been sailing together for several days when, one morning before daybreak, Giannetto looked out and saw an inlet with a fine port. He asked the captain what the port was called and the captain answered: 'Sir, that port belongs to a noble lady, a widow who has ruined many a gentleman.' 'How so?' 'Master, she is truly a lovely lady and most enchanting; but she has this law: that any man who arrives must sleep with her, and if he succeeds in enjoying her he must take her as his wife and become lord of all that land; but if he fails, then he loses everything he has in the world.' Giannetto thought it over for a while and then said: 'Do whatever you can to get me into that port.' And the captain insisted: 'Mind what you say, sir, for many gentlemen have gone there and have ended up ruined for life.' 'Don't worry about that,' said Giannetto, 'just do as I say.'

And so it was done. They quickly changed direction and slipped into the port unnoticed by the other two ships. When morning came, the news spread that this splendid ship had entered the port and all the people flocked to see it; and when the news was brought to the lady, she sent for Giannetto who went straight to her and greeted her with all proper respect. She took him by the hand and asked who he was and where he came from and whether he knew the custom of her country. Giannetto replied that indeed he did, and that he had come there for no other reason; and she replied: 'Then you are a hundred thousand times welcome.'

So all that day she paid him great honour, and to keep him company she invited a host of counts, barons, and knights who were her subjects. All those noblemen were delighted with the bearing of the young man who was so courteous, so affable, and so easy in conversation that almost everyone fell in love with him; and all that day there was dancing and singing and feasting in his honour, and everyone would have been happy to have him as their lord.

Now when evening came the lady took Giannetto by the hand and led him to her chamber, and said: 'I think it's time to go to bed,' and he answered: 'Lady, I'm all yours.' Once they were in the bedchamber, two handmaids came in, one with wine and the other with sweetmeats. Then the lady said: 'I know that you must be thirsty, so have something to drink.' Giannetto took the sweetmeats and drank some of the wine which, unknown to him, had been drugged to make him sleep; and, finding it to his taste, he drank a good half-cup before undressing quickly and lying down to rest. And no sooner had he touched the bed than he fell fast asleep. The lady lay down beside him, but he did not wake up until it was morning and past the third hour. The lady, however, arose at daybreak and began to have the ship unloaded, finding it full of rich and valuable merchandise. And when it was the third hour of the day,* the lady's chambermaid came to Giannetto's bed and woke him up, bidding him to go with God, since he had lost his ship and all that was in it; and he was ashamed when he understood how foolish he had been. The lady provided him with a horse and some money for the journey, and he rode off towards Venice, wretched and downcast.

When he came to Venice he felt too ashamed to go straight home to Messer Ansaldo; instead, when night came, he went to the house of a friend, who was amazed to see him and said: 'Giannetto, what on earth has happened?' Giannetto answered: 'My ship struck a rock by night and broke up and was dashed to pieces. I managed to hold onto a piece of wood which cast me ashore, and so I came back here by land.'

Giannetto remained secluded in that house for some time, until one day his friend went to visit Messer Ansaldo whom he found plunged in melancholy. 'What makes you so sad?' he asked. Messer Ansaldo answered: 'I'm so afraid that my son may be dead or has come to some harm at sea that I can find no rest and shall have no peace until I see him. Such is the great love I bear him.' Then the young man said: 'Messer, I have news for you: he has been shipwrecked and lost everything, but he himself is safe.' 'God be praised,' said Ansaldo, 'so long as he is safe, that's enough for me: and for what has been lost I care nothing.' Immediately he set off to see Giannetto, and when he came there he ran to embrace him, saying: 'My son, there's no need to feel ashamed when you see me; there's nothing strange about ships being wrecked at sea; and therefore, my son, don't be so downcast; as long as you have come to no harm, that's all I care about.' Thus, comforting him all the way, Ansaldo took him home. The news soon spread throughout Venice, and everyone felt sorry for Giannetto's loss.

Now shortly after this Giannetto's two companions returned from Alexandria laden with riches. And on their arrival they asked about him and were told everything that had happened.

They hurried to embrace him, saying: 'How did you leave us and where did you go, for we never had any news of you? All that day we turned back to look for you and yet there was no way of seeing or knowing where you had gone. And we were so distressed that we had no more joy in our voyage, believing you were dead.' Giannetto answered: 'A contrary wind got up in a gulf of the sea and the ship was driven straight against a rock near the shore: everything was smashed and scattered, and I was lucky to escape.' This was the story that Giannetto told in order to hide his folly. Then they all made a great feast, thanking God that he had been saved and saying: 'Next spring, with God's grace, our profits will make up for what you lost; in the meantime let's have a good time and banish sad thoughts.' So indeed they set about having a good time, just as they had done in the past.

But still Giannetto could think of nothing but returning to that lady, brooding and saying to himself: 'Surely I must have her for my wife or I will die.' He seemed so dispirited that Ansaldo often told him: 'My son, don't be so cast down, for we still possess so much that we can live very comfortably.' Giannetto answered: 'Sir, I shall never be happy unless I make that journey again.' Seeing his resolve, Messer Ansaldo set about providing him with a more valuable ship laden with even more merchandise than before. He began early, so that when the time came to leave, the ship was fully furnished and ready; and in it he had invested almost everything that he possessed in the world. Giannetto's two friends, when they had equipped their own ships with all that was necessary, put to sea, hoisted sail, and set forth with him on their voyage.

They sailed on for many days, and Giannetto was always on the lookout for the port of that lady, which was called the Port of the Lady of Belmont. Coming one night to the mouth of the inlet, he immediately recognized it, and, setting sails and rudder for a new course, slipped inside so stealthily that the other two ships failed to notice.

The lady, when she got up in the morning, looked down into the port and saw the flags of the ship waving in the breeze. She immediately recognized them and, calling her maidservant, asked: 'Do you know those flags?' The maidservant answered: 'My lady, I think they belong to the young man who came here a year ago and brought us such riches with his merchandise.' 'You must be right,' said the lady, 'and this means that he must be truly in love with me, for I never saw anyone come here a second time.' And the maid added: 'I never saw a more courteous and pleasant man.'

The lady then sent many young pages and squires who went joyfully to meet him; and he was gay and gracious with them all, and so he came up into the lady's presence. And when she saw him, she embraced him with great joy and pleasure and he returned her embrace with all due respect. And so they spent the whole day in revels and jollity, for she had invited many noblemen and ladies who came to court and joined in the festivities for love of Giannetto. He was so pleasant and courteous that almost all the nobles regretted that he was not their lord; and almost all the ladies fell in love with him when they saw how gracefully he danced; and always his countenance was so amiable that everyone assumed he must be the son of some great lord.

At last, when it was time to sleep, the lady took Giannetto by the hand and said: 'Let's go and lie down.' So they went into her chamber, and as soon as they sat down two handmaids appeared with wine and sweetmeats. Then they ate and drank and went to bed, where Giannetto immediately fell sound asleep. And the lady undressed and lay down beside him, and, in short, the whole night passed and still he did not awake. When morning came, the lady got up and gave orders to unload the ship. And when the third hour of the day was past, Giannetto awoke and reached out to touch the lady; and not finding her, he raised his head and saw that it was already late in the morning. Then he got out of bed as the shame began to sink in. He was given a horse and enough money for the journey and told to be off. And so he promptly rode away, distressed and downcast for shame, not stopping for many days, until finally he reached Venice. And when night came, he went to the house of the same friend as before who was astounded to see him and exclaimed: 'What's all this?' 'Something very bad for me,' replied Giannetto, 'cursed be the fate that ever brought me to this land.' 'You may well curse,' said the friend, 'for you have ruined Messer Ansaldo who was the greatest and richest merchant in Christendom; and the shame of it is worse than the loss.'

So for several days Giannetto stayed hidden in his friend's house, not knowing what to do or say; and he was almost tempted to return to Florence without saying a word to Messer Ansaldo. At last, however, he resolved to go to him. And when Ansaldo saw him, he rose up and ran to embrace him, saying: 'Welcome home, my son'; and Giannetto embraced him and wept. Then Ansaldo comforted him: 'You know how it is. You shouldn't be so downcast. As long as I have you back, that's all I want; and we still have enough left to live at ease. After all, that is the old way of the sea which gives to some and takes from others.'

The news of the event soon spread throughout Venice and everyone talked about Messer Ansaldo and grieved for the losses he had suffered—the more so because now he had to sell many of his possessions in order to pay the creditors who had supplied him with the merchandise. Now at that time Giannetto's two companions were returning from their journey, having made a great profit; and when they arrived in Venice they were told how he had been shipwrecked and lost everything. They were astonished and exclaimed: 'This is the strangest thing ever.' And they went off to see Ansaldo and, amid much feasting, said: 'Don't you worry, Messer, for next year we intend to trade on your behalf; for, in a way, we were the cause of your loss because we persuaded Giannetto to come with us that first time. So have no fear; as long as we have anything ourselves, use it as if it were your own.' Ansaldo thanked them and said that he still had enough to manage fairly well.

But Giannetto continued to brood from morn to eve and could not shake off his gloom. Messer Ansaldo kept asking him what was the matter, and he answered: 'I shall never be happy until I get back what I lost.' Ansaldo said: 'My son, I don't want you to go away again, for it's better that we should live here quietly on what little we have rather than that you should risk it all again.' But Giannetto insisted: 'I'm determined to do what I said, for I think it would be shameful to remain here like this.'

When Ansaldo saw that his mind was made up, he arranged to sell everything he possessed and provide him with another ship. And so, leaving nothing for himself, he sold up and purchased merchandise to fill a very fine ship. But because he was still ten thousand florins short, he went to a Jew at Mestre* and arranged a loan on the following terms and conditions: namely, that unless he reimbursed the loan before Saint John's day next June, the said Jew could take a pound of his flesh from whatever part of the body he chose. To this Messer Ansaldo agreed, and the Jew had a written bond drawn up before witnesses, with all the proper formal guarantees; and then the Jew counted out ten thousand gold florins. With these Ansaldo supplied the ship with whatever was lacking; and if the first two ships had been very fine, the third was was even more splendid and better equipped. His friends had also equipped their own ships, intending to transfer their own profits to Giannetto. When the time came for them to leave and they were about to embark, Ansaldo said to Giannetto: 'My son, now you are leaving, and you know the terms of my bond; I ask you one favour: that even if some misfortune should befall you, yet still you will come to me, so that I may see you before I die; and then I shall depart in peace.' Giannetto promised: 'Messer Ansaldo, I shall do everything that I think will please you,' and Ansaldo gave him his blessing. The three friends took their leave and set off on their journey.

His two companions kept careful watch over Giannetto's ship, while Giannetto himself was always on the lookout, wondering how he might slip off into the port of Belmont; until, at last, he managed to persuade one of his steersmen to take the ship by night into the port of that lady. When morning came and it was light, the others looked around but could find no trace of Giannetto's ship. 'This can only be his bad luck,' they thought, and decided to go their way, completely bewildered by what had happened.

Now when the ship had berthed in port, the whole city came out to see it, hearing that Giannetto had returned. They were astonished to see him again and said: 'He must surely be the son of some very great man, since he comes here every year with so much merchandise and such splendid ships; would to God he were our lord.' And so he was visited by all the citizens, knights, and noblemen of the city.

When the lady was told that Giannetto had arrived, she went to the window and saw the splendid ship and recognized its flags. She crossed herself and said: 'How extraordinary! It's the man who left all his riches in this country.' So she sent for him and Giannetto went up to her and they greeted each other with many embraces and with great respect. And the whole day was spent in revelling and festivities; and there was a tournament in honour of Giannetto and many knights and nobles jousted that day. Giannetto himself decided to enter the lists and did wonders with arms and horse, bearing himself so well that he won the admiration of all the noblemen, who longed to have him as their lord.

Night came, and since it was time to sleep, the lady took Giannetto by the hand and said: 'Let's go and lie down.' And as they came to the chamber door, one of the lady's maids, feeling sorry for Giannetto, leant down and whispered in his ear: 'Pretend to drink, but don't drink tonight.' Giannetto understood her words and went into the bedchamber.

The lady said: 'I know you must be feeling thirsty, so I think you should drink something before you go to sleep.' And there and then two angelic-looking handmaids came in to offer him the usual wine and sweetmeats. Giannetto said: 'Who could refuse to drink when he sees two such lovely damsels?' The lady laughed. Giannetto took the cup and pretended to drink, but instead poured it down his chest. The lady thought that he had drunk the wine and said to herself: 'You will have to bring us another ship, for you've certainly lost this one.' Giannetto went to bed with a perfectly clear head and in high spirits so that it seemed an age before the lady came to join him; and he thought to himself: 'Surely, this time I've caught her; now the boot's on the other foot.' And to make the lady come to bed more quickly, he began to snore and pretended to be asleep. Then the lady said: 'You're fine like that,' and quickly undressed and lay down beside him. Giannetto did not waste a moment and as soon as she was in bed he turned towards her and embraced her, saying: 'Now I hold what I have desired for so long.' And with this he gave her the peace that comes from performing the holy rites of wedlock, and all night long she never left his arms.

Now the lady was delighted, and the following morning she arose before daybreak and sent for all her nobles and knights and many other citizens and told them: 'Giannetto is now your lord; let the celebrations begin.' And as the news spread, the whole country raised a great shout: 'Long live our lord'; and the bells rang and the trumpets sounded, calling the barons and counts from town and country to come and see their new lord. So began a great and magnificent feast; and when Giannetto came out of the bedchamber, he was dubbed a knight, seated on a throne, and given a sceptre to hold; then he was hailed as lord for life with great pomp and splendour. And when all the barons and their ladies had come in, Giannetto married this noble lady with more joy and feasting than can be described or imagined. All the nobles and gentlemen of the country came to the city to join in the feast, with feats of arms, jousting, dancing, singing, playing music, and all things fitting for a great feast. As for Giannetto, generous as he was, he began to give away the silken cloths and other precious things that he had brought with him; he also assumed a more awe-inspiring and masterful bearing as he upheld right and justice for people of all ranks and conditions. So he continued to live in joy and gladness, with no thought or care for poor Ansaldo who had given his bond to the Jew for ten thousand florins.

One day, however, as Messer Giannetto was standing at the window with his lady, he looked down into the square and saw a group of men with torches in their hands on their way to make a votive offering. Giannetto asked: 'What does this mean?' and his lady answered: 'That's a guild of craftsmen going to make an offering at the church of Saint John, whose feast is today.' Then Giannetto remembered Ansaldo and moved away from the window with a deep sigh; and his expression changed as he walked up and down, thinking about the situation. His lady asked him what was the matter, and he replied: 'It's nothing.' But she began to insist, saying: 'I'm sure you're worried about something, but you don't want to tell me what it is.' And she went on so long that finally Giannetto told her the whole story of how Messer Ansaldo had given his bond for ten thousand florins. 'The term of the bond is today,' he said, 'and I greatly fear that my father will die for my sake, for if he cannot pay he must lose a pound of his own flesh.' Then the lady said: 'To horse at once! Go by land which is quicker than by sea, and take as many men with you as you need. Carry a hundred thousand ducats and don't stop until you reach Venice; and if he's not dead, bring him back here.' So he had the trumpet sounded and mounted his horse; and then with more than a hundred companions and with all the money needed, he took his leave and galloped off towards Venice.

Now when the term of the bond expired, the Jew had Ansaldo arrested and demanded his pound of flesh. Messer Ansaldo begged him to postpone the deadly event by a few days so that if his Giannetto came, he might at least see him. The Jew answered, 'I agree to the postponement since that's what you want, but even if he comes a hundred times, I still intend to have a pound of your flesh, accord-ing to the bond.' Messer Ansaldo replied that he was satisfied with that. All Venice was talking about the affair and people were so dis-tressed that a group of merchants combined to raise enough money to pay off the debt; but the Jew would never accept it. In fact, he wanted to commit that homicide so that he could boast that he had caused the death of the greatest merchant in Christendom.

Now while Giannetto was hurrying towards Venice, his lady, with two servants, followed close behind, dressed like a lawyer. Giannetto, as soon as he arrived in Venice, had gone straight to the house of the Jew where he embraced Messer Ansaldo with great joy. Then he told the Jew that he would pay off the debt and as much more as he asked; but the Jew answered that he would not take the money since it had not been paid at the appointed time; instead he wanted his pound of flesh. This provoked a great debate. Everybody blamed the Jew, but at the same time they considered that Venice was a city that respected the rule of law and that the Jew had his rights attested in perfectly legal form; so nobody dared to oppose him and all they could do was beg him to show mercy. So all the merchants of Venice came up to plead for Ansaldo, but the Jew was more inflexible than ever. Giannetto offered him twenty thousand, and he refused; he went up to thirty, then forty, then fifty thousand, until in the end he reached a hundred thousand. The Jew said: 'Let me tell you this: if you gave me more than this whole city is worth, it still wouldn't give me any satisfaction; I will do what is written in my bond.'

This was the situation when the lady, dressed as a lawyer, arrived in Venice and dismounted at an inn. The innkeeper asked one of her servants: 'Who is this gentleman?' and was told: 'The gentleman is a lawyer who has been studying in Bologna and is returning home.' Hearing this, the innkeeper treated his guest with great respect, and when they were at supper the supposed lawyer asked: 'How is the law in this city?' The innkeeper answered: 'Too strict.' 'How so?' 'I shall tell you,' said the innkeeper: 'There was a young man called Giannetto who came here from Florence to see his godfather who is Messer Ansaldo; and he was so gracious and courteous that both men and women fell in love with him. Nobody quite so charming had ever come to this city before. Then his godfather provided him with three ships, all of great value, and one after the other they were all wrecked. There wasn't enough money left for the last ship, so Master Ansaldo borrowed ten thousand florins from a Jew on these terms: that if the debt were not paid by the feast of Saint John the following June, then the Jew would take a pound of flesh from whatever part of Ansaldo's body he should choose. Now this fine young man has returned and wants to pay back the ten thousand florins, but the wicked Jew will have none of it. And the best men in the city have gone to plead with him, but all in vain.' 'But this problem is easy to solve,' said the lawyer, and the innkeeper replied: 'If you're ready to go to all the trouble of settling it so that this good man won't die, you'll earn the favour and the love of the most upright youth that was ever born, and then that of everybody in this city.'

So this lawyer made it publicly known throughout the city that anyone who had a problem with the law should come to him; and Messer Giannetto was told that a lawyer had come from Bologna who could settle any legal problem whatsoever. So Giannetto said to the Jew: 'Let's go to this lawyer.' And the Jew said: 'Let's go; but no matter who comes, I mean to have my legal rights according to the bond.' And when they came before the lawyer and paid their respects, the lawyer recognized Giannetto, but Giannetto did not recognize her because she had transformed her face with the juice of certain herbs. So Messer Giannetto presented his case, as did the Jew, in orderly fashion. The lawyer took the bond and read it, and then said to the Jew: 'I advise you to accept these hundred thousand ducats and free this good man, who will be obliged to you forever.' But the Jew answered: 'I shall do nothing of the kind.' 'It would be better for you,' said the lawyer; but the Jew absolutely refused to give way.

They agreed, however, to go before the proper court for such cases, and the lawyer spoke for Messer Ansaldo and said: 'Let the Jew come forward,' and when he did so, the lawyer continued: 'There now, settle your claim and take a pound of his flesh from wherever you choose.' Then the Jew had Ansaldo stripped naked and picked up a razor which he had brought for his purpose. Messer Giannetto turned to the lawyer and said: 'Sir, this is not what I asked of you,' but the lawyer answered: 'Don't worry; he still hasn't taken his pound of flesh.' The Jew was now about to start, but the lawyer intervened: 'Be careful how you go about it, for if you take anything more or less than a pound, I shall have you beheaded. And another thing: if you shed one little drop of blood, I shall have you put to death. For your bond says nothing about shedding blood and, moreover, it says only that you should take a pound of flesh, neither more nor less. And therefore, if you are wise, you'd better think carefully how best to go about it.' Then the lawyer sent for the executioner and had him bring the axe and the block, saying: 'As soon as I see a drop of blood, I shall have your head cut off.'

The Jew now began to feel afraid, and Giannetto's spirits revived. At last, after much discussion, the Jew said: 'Sir lawyer, you've been too clever for me; but just give me those hundred thousand ducats and I shall be satisfied.' But the lawyer replied: 'I want you to take your pound of flesh according to the bond, and therefore I won't give you a penny; you should have taken the money when I offered it to you.' The Jew came down to ninety thousand and then to eighty thousand, and the lawyer would not budge. Then Giannetto said: 'Give him what he wants, provided he releases Ansaldo.' The lawyer answered: 'I tell you, leave this to me.' Then the Jew: 'Give me fifty thousand'; and the lawyer: 'I wouldn't give you the most worthless copper you've ever seen.' Finally, the Jew said: 'Give me at least my ten thousand ducats, and damned be your earth and air,' and the lawyer said: 'Didn't you understand me? I shall give you nothing. If you want your pound of flesh, go and take it. If not I shall have your bond declared null and void.'

This delighted all those who were present, and everyone mocked the Jew, saying: 'He's been caught in the snare he laid for others.' At which, the Jew, furious that he could not get what he wanted, seized the bond and tore it into shreds. And so Ansaldo was released. Giannetto led him home amid great rejoicing and then took the hundred thousand ducats and hurried to see the lawyer who was in his room getting ready to leave. Giannetto said to him: 'Sir, you've done me the greatest service I have ever known, and therefore I would like you to take this money home with you, for you have certainly earned it.' The lawyer replied: 'My dear Messer Giannetto, I thank you, but I have no need of it. Keep it for yourself, lest your wife should say you've been a spendthrift.' 'Now, by my faith,' said Giannetto, 'my lady is so generous and so gracious that she wouldn't object if I spent four times this amount, for indeed she wanted me to come here with a much larger sum.' 'And are you pleased with her?' asked the lawyer. Giannetto answered: 'There is no creature in the world that I cherish more, for she is so wise and so lovely that Nature could not make anything better. And if you do me the favour of coming to see her, you'll be astonished by the honours she pays you and see for yourself whether she doesn't exceed all that I say of her.' 'I can't come with you', said the lawyer, 'because I'm busy with other matters; but since you speak so well of her, do give her my greetings when you see her again.' 'It shall be done', replied Giannetto, 'but I still wish you would take some of this money.' While he was speaking, the lawyer spied a ring on his finger and said: 'I won't take any money, but I would like to have that ring.' 'Very well', said Master Giannetto, 'but I give it to you with great reluctance, for it was a gift from my lady who told me to wear it always for her love; and if she doesn't see it, she'll think I have given it to some other woman; and then she'll be furious with me and believe that I've given my heart elsewhere, although I love her more than I love myself.' The lawyer replied: 'I'm sure she loves you so much that she'll believe you when you tell her you've given it to me. But perhaps you really wanted to give it to one of your old flames here in Venice?' Giannetto exclaimed: 'Such is the love and the faith that I bear her that I would not change her for any other woman in the world, for she is perfectly beautiful in every way.' Then he took the ring from his finger and gave it to the lawyer, and they embraced with all mutual respect. The lawyer said: 'May I ask you one favour?' 'Ask it,' said Giannetto. 'It is that you should not stay here, but hurry home to see your wife.' And Giannetto answered: 'It feels like an age until I see her again.'

So they took their leave. The lawyer embarked and set out with God's grace. Messer Giannetto remained for a while, making merry and holding court, with banquets and dinners and gifts of horses and money to his friends. Then, bidding farewell to the Venetians and taking Ansaldo with him, he went away, accompanied by many of his old companions; and both men and women shed tender tears to see him go, for he had borne himself so graciously with everyone during his time in Venice. And so he returned to Belmont. Now his lady had arrived before him, pretending to have been at the baths; and, dressed once more in her womanly clothes, she prepared a great reception, hanging silk tapestries in the streets and assembling men at arms for a tournament. When Giannetto arrived with Ansaldo the whole court and all the nobles greeted him with cries of 'Long live our lord! Long live our lord!' And as soon as they reached the city, the lady ran to embrace Ansaldo, but pretended to be rather annoyed with Giannetto, although she loved him more than she loved herself. Then there was a great feast, with jousting, tilting, dancing, and singing for all the nobles and ladies and damsels who were present.

Messer Giannetto, however, seeing that his wife did not greet him as warmly as usual, went into his chamber and called her, saying: 'What's the matter with you?' He tried to embrace her, but she said: 'You don't need to come on to me like this, for I know very well that you've been looking up your old flames in Venice.' Giannetto was beginning to protest when she suddenly asked: 'Where's the ring I gave you?' He answered: 'That's what I knew would happen; indeed, I said that you'd blame me for it. But I swear by the faith I bear to God and to you that I gave that ring to the lawyer who won the case for me.' His wife said: 'And I swear by the faith I bear to God and to you that you gave it to a woman. I know this for sure, so don't disgrace yourself by swearing the contrary.' 'May God destroy me', retorted Giannetto, 'if I'm not telling the truth—and I told the lawyer this would happen when he asked me for the ring.' And his wife: 'You should have stayed in Venice and sent Messer Ansaldo here; then you could have enjoyed your old flames, since I'm told they were all in tears when you left.' Then Giannetto began to weep and show all the signs of deep distress, saying: 'You're swearing what's not true and couldn't be true.'

His tears were like a knife in the heart to his wife, who ran to embrace him; and laughing heartily, she showed him the ring and told him everything—what he had said to the lawyer, how she was that lawyer, and how he had given her the ring. Messer Giannetto was absolutely amazed, but when he understood that it was all true, he began to enjoy the jest and went out of the room to share it with his nobles and companions. Thus these events increased and multiplied the love between Giannetto and his lady. To conclude, Giannetto called the maidservant who had warned him not to drink that night and gave her as wife to Messer Ansaldo. And so they spent the rest of their long lives in joy and happiness.

FRANCO SACCHETTI

PIERO BRANDANI'S SON
Trecentonovelle (Three Hundred Tales) 17

*Piero Brandani of Florence files a lawsuit and gives some documents
to his son who loses them, runs away, and catches a wolf for which
he receives fifty lire in Pistoia.* He then returns home and buys new
documents.*

IN the city of Florence there once lived a citizen called Piero Brandani
who was forever going to law. One morning, when he was due at the
Magistrate's Court* to file a lawsuit, he gave his son, a lad of eighteen, some legal documents with instructions to go ahead and wait for
him by the Abbey Church.* The youth did as he was told, went to the
meeting place and stood there to wait for his father. And this was in
the month of May.

Now it so happened that as the lad was waiting it began to rain
heavily, and a peasant woman who was passing by dropped the basket
of cherries that she carried on her head so that the fruit was scattered
all over the street where the gutter turns into a river every time it rains.
Eager to help, as such lads often are, the youth joined other folk who
were helping to pick up the cherries here and there, even in the gutter
where they were being carried away by the water. But when the cherries had been collected and he went back to where he had been standing, he discovered that the documents were no longer under his arm
because they had fallen into the water and been flushed away towards
the Arno without him noticing. And as he rushed up and down, asking
here and there, he heard someone say that the documents were already
on their way to Pisa. The lad was very upset and decided to run away
for fear of his father; and that very day he got as far as Prato* which is
where Florentine outlaws and runaways usually go. There he came to
an inn where, just after sunset, a number of merchants arrived—not to
stay the night, but simply to stop on their onward journey towards the
Agliana bridge.* When these merchants saw the lad so quiet and cowed,

they asked what was the matter and where he was from; and after hearing his answer, they asked if he would like to go along with them.

He was quick to accept and set out with them. Two hours later they reached the Agliana bridge and knocked at the door of an inn. The innkeeper, who had already gone to bed, came to the window: 'Who's there?'—'Open up, we want to stay the night.'

The innkeeper grumbled: 'What! Don't you know that this place is swarming with robbers? I'm surprised you haven't been attacked.' And in fact, the innkeeper was telling the truth, for the place was indeed plagued by a gang of bandits.

After some pleading from the merchants, the innkeeper opened up; and when they had gone inside and stabled their horses, they asked for something to eat. The landlord answered: 'There's not a bit of bread in the house.'—'So what shall we do?'—'I can only see one solution. Get this boy of yours to put on some rags so that he looks like a pauper and send him up that path where he'll find a church: he should call Ser Cione (that's the priest), say I sent him, and ask him to lend me twelve loaves of bread. I say do it like this, because if those evildoers come across a poor ragged urchin, they won't bother with him.'

When they had shown him the path, the lad set out, but unwillingly because it was night and hard to see anything. He was scared stiff, as you can imagine, and made a tortuous job of it, turning this way and that, without finding the church. After entering a thicket, he seemed to see a faint light shining on a wall and decided to go towards it, thinking it must be the church; and when he came into a big yard, he supposed it must be the church square. The light, in fact, came from a farmer's house, but the youth went up to it and knocked on the door.

The farmer heard him and shouted down: 'Who's there?'—'Open up for me, Ser Cione; I've been sent by the innkeeper at the Agliana bridge to see if you can lend him twelve loaves.'—'What loaves? A sneaky little thief, that's what you are, a spy for that bunch of brigands. If I come out there, I'll get you sent to Pistoia and hanged.'

When the lad heard this, he did not know what to do, and stood there almost stunned, turning round to see if he could find his way to some safer place. Just then he heard a wolf howling near the edge of the wood; and looking back, he saw a barrel on one side of the yard, upright and with the lid bashed in. In a flash he ran and jumped inside; and there, with his heart in his mouth, he waited to see what Fortune would do to him next.

Up then comes the wolf, who was probably old and itchy, and begins to scratch himself against the barrel, and as he rubbed and rubbed, his lifted tail somehow entered the bunghole.

When the youth felt the tail touching him, he took fright; but for all his fear, given the situation, he grabbed the tail, determined to hold onto it with all his strength and see what might happen. The wolf, feeling himself caught by the tail, began to pull; the youth held on and began to pull as well. And as they both pulled, the barrel fell over on its side and began to roll away. The boy held on and the wolf kept pulling; and the more he pulled the more knocks he received from the rolling barrel. This rolling lasted for two hours and the wolf was so knocked about that he died. As for the youth, he was more or less done in; but he had his share of luck, for the more firmly he hung onto that tail the more he protected himself and harmed the wolf. Yet even when he had killed the wolf, he dared not come out of the barrel or let go of the tail.

In the morning the farmer who had been woken by the youth's knocking was out doing the rounds of his land when he suddenly saw the barrel at the bottom of a ravine. This set him thinking and he said to himself: 'These devils who go about at night do nothing but harm, and if they can't find anything else, they take my barrel that was up in the yard and roll it down here.' Then, coming nearer, he saw the wolf lying beside the barrel, and since it did not seem to be dead, he began to shout: 'Wolf, wolf, wolf!' Then some of the villagers came running up and saw the dead wolf and the boy in the barrel.

'Who are you? What's all this about?' they asked, making the sign of the cross. The boy, more dead than alive, could hardly get his breath back and said: 'Help me for the love of God! Hear me out and do me no harm.'

The peasants listened, eager to hear the cause of such a strange case, and he told them the whole story, from the loss of the documents down to that moment when they saw him; and the peasants felt very sorry for him, and said: 'Well, son, you've been very unlucky, but things won't turn out as badly as you think: there's a law in Pistoia that anyone who kills a wolf and shows it to the Commune gets paid fifty lire.'

The boy's low spirits began to rise as he accepted their offer to go along with him and help with carrying the wolf. And all together, taking the wolf with them, they came to the inn at the Agliana bridge which was where the lad had started out the night before. The innkeeper was astonished by what had happened, as you can imagine, and told them that the merchants had gone on their way, and that both he and they were convinced the youth had been devoured by wolves or captured by the brigands. At last, the lad presented the wolf to the Commune of Pistoia who heard what had happened and gave him fifty lire. He spent five of these entertaining the villagers who had come with him; then he took his leave and took the remaining forty-five back home. There he told his father everything that had happened to him, begged forgiveness, and handed over the forty-five lire. His father, like the poor man he was, took the money with pleasure and forgave his son. With some of the money he paid for the documents to be copied out again, and the rest he spent happily on his lawsuits.

And so one should never despair, because just as Fortune takes away, so she gives; and even as she gives, she takes away. Who could have imagined that the documents that had been washed away would be recopied thanks to a wolf who shoved his tail through the bunghole of a barrel and was so strangely caught. There is surely a lesson here: not only should we never despair, but whatever happens to us, it should not be the cause of dejection or melancholy.

A SERMON ON USURY
Trecentonovelle (Three Hundred Tales) 32

A preaching friar arrives to give Lenten sermons in a Tuscan town; finding that nobody comes to hear him, he succeeds in attracting the crowd away from other preachers by announcing that he will show how moneylending is not a sin.

THE friar that I shall tell of in this chapter was better at making up a good story than the ambassadors of Casentino.* This friar went around preaching in Lent, as the custom is, and in one of the largest cities in Tuscany he saw that, as often happens, great numbers went to hear other preachers, but practically nobody came to him. So one Wednesday morning he mounted the pulpit and said:

'Good sirs, for a long time now I've seen that the theologians and preachers are making a big mistake; which is that they say moneylending is usury and therefore a great sin, and that all moneylenders are heading for damnation.* But from what I understand and from what

I've read, I've learned that moneylending is not a sin. Don't believe that I'm joking or bamboozling you with subtle arguments, because I can tell you that the truth is the opposite of what the preachers keep saying. Now this is a big topic and I don't want you to think I'm making things up, so if I have time I shall preach here on Sunday morning; and if I don't have time, I'll find some other day. Anyway, you'll be convinced and freed from error.'

As the congregation heard this, some mumbled here and others grumbled there; but when the sermon was over and they came out of church, the news spread around and everyone was thinking 'What does this mean?' The moneylenders were happy and the borrowers were sad, and people who had never lent money before began to do so now. Some said: 'He must be a very clever man,' and others said: 'He must be a fool, whoever heard of such a thing!'

People are always eager to hear something new and soon the whole city was waiting for Sunday morning; and when it came, they all rushed to find a place in the church, while the other preachers were left looking at empty benches. Whereas shortly before the friar's hearers had been so sparse that the distance between one and another could have been measured in yards, now they were so packed in as to be suffocating—which, of course, was just what he wanted.

The friar climbed up into the pulpit, said a Hail Mary, and then, following the usual order of such occasions, took a passage from the Gospel as his text, and said: 'First, I shall give some moral advice, then I shall comment on the Gospel and draw from it the lessons that it contains, and then finally I shall talk about usury, as I promised.' Then the worthy friar preached a lengthy sermon, spending a particularly long time on the Gospel passage, so that when he came to the question of usury, it was already late in the morning; and this he did deliberately to check their impatience. Then he concluded: 'Good sirs, I was wrong this morning when I chose this passage because it is particularly complex and profound, as you've heard, and I've spent so long on it that now there's no time left for what I promised. But just be patient, and in these coming mornings I'll keep my sermons shorter, and when I see that the time is ripe I'll preach about moneylending because that's a topic where I simply can't wait to put you right.'

And so he kept putting them off from one day to the next until the following Sunday when there was an even bigger crowd than before. Once again he went into the pulpit and at the end of his sermon he said: 'Good people, I know that if there are so many of you here today, it's only because of what I've promised more than once: you want to hear what I have to say about moneylending. Unfortunately I'm still suffering from a touch of fever and so you'll have to excuse me this morning. But you come on the day I name and with God's grace I'll give you the sermon you're waiting for.'

So it went on, and what with one excuse and another, he had crowds coming to hear him throughout Lent, keeping them in suspense until Palm Sunday when he said: 'I've promised to speak on this matter so many times that I don't want to let this morning pass without keeping my word. You know, good sirs, that charity is as pleasing to God as any other virtue, and perhaps more so. And charity is nothing other than helping our neighbour, and moneylending is just such a help. Therefore, I say, moneylending is permissible and legitimate; and more than that, the lender earns grace. So where's the sin? The sin lies in calling in the debt; and so the moneylending in itself, far from being sinful, is actually an act of kindness most acceptable to God. And I will go further and say that one can call in the debt in a way that is not a sin, but a great work of charity. Let me give you an example: one man lends another a hundred florins and on a given day is reimbursed with a hundred florins and no more; this moneylending and this reimbursement is allowable and pleasing to God; and it would be even more pleasing to God if, out of charity and love, the man gave up the idea of being paid back and left the money to the debtor. This means that usury consists in being paid back more than is really due because the sin lies not in the hundred florins, but in the amount that has been added to the real debt; and this small amount cancels out all the charity in the original hundred florins and all the service and the good done to the honest borrower: it becomes illicit and in itself something that should be paid back. To conclude, my dear brethren, I say that moneylending is not a sin, but that recovering more than the real debt is a great sin. With this you may go happily about your business, for you may surely lend money in the way I have preached; just beware of how you are reimbursed and you will all be the sons of your Father *qui in coelis est.*'*

Then he recited the Credo, which was neither heard nor understood because of the great muttering and grumbling that went on. And some folk laughed out loud, saying: 'He's really put one over on us. We've been coming to hear this sermon all Lent, and today we were here before daybreak. What a trickster! A knife in his guts, that's what he deserves.'

There was a lot of shouting and fuss here and there, and for several days the city talked of nothing else. But this friar was a worthy man because he showed (or sought to show) people how unthinking they were to run after foolish fancies and newfangled ideas rather than following Holy Scripture. The fact is that they were eager to hear what suited their own appetites. Thus moneylenders or those who wanted to lend money hurried to hear that sermon and were made fools of, just as they deserved, even though they have already gained so much ground that they seem to think God can neither see nor hear them. And they baptize usury with all kinds of names, such as compensation for loss of income, interest, credit, equity release, exchange, public utility, venture capital, creative investment, and so on. But this is a grave error, for usury lies in the work itself and not in the name.*

GIOVANNI GHERARDI DA PRATO

THE TALE OF CATELLINA
Il paradiso degli Alberti (The Paradise of the Alberti)

IN Naples, one of Italy's finest cities with its wealthy and noble citizens, there lived a beautiful young woman called Catellina, married to an upstanding young man Filippello Barile. Now among the companions and friends of Filippello there was one whom he loved so much that he spent almost all his time with him, day and night, so that it seemed as if he could not live without him; and this friend's name was Aniello Stramazzafigli, as handsome and graceful a youth as any in Naples; virtuous too, but above all very affectionate. Nor did Aniello, in Filippello's house or elsewhere, behave towards Catellina otherwise than as if she were his sister, without thinking or imagining anything that was not proper and decent.

This easy familiarity had not lasted for very long before Catellina, seeing and considering the lively and lovely graces of Aniello, fell so passionately in love with him that her only pleasure lay in contemplating and watching him. And, as her love increased from day to day, she began to suffer greatly for she had no thought of revealing her passion, believing that Aniello's affection for Filippello would render such a venture both useless and dangerous; and thus she fell into a deep melancholy. Sometimes she would show him some sign of great and loving tenderness, but the chaste and faithful young man saw nothing in it but pure and honest affection, so that she became even more reluctant to reveal anything of her feelings. Thus she went on from day to day, with little hope and with melancholy heaped on melancholy. She became ever more pale and thin, and as solitary as a nun, for she was rarely seen to be cheerful—she who once had been gay and joyful by nature, more talkative and witty than any other girl in Naples. It was a change that shocked all those who knew her.

It happened that one day, as she was alone in her room, lamenting silently and unable to hold back her tears, she was interrupted by the old nurse who had suckled her. Seeing her weeping and sighing so deeply, the nurse exclaimed: 'O my dear girl, what's up with you? Come on, you don't want to kill yourself like this, wasting your youth and spoiling your beauty. Are you worried about Filippello? I'm sure that you're all he cares about, and I reckon that your strange ways are making him very sad. Now you just tell me what's the matter; and have no fear, because there's nothing you need that I wouldn't do for you, by myself or with others, however or whatever it is, great or small. Come on now, don't hide your wishes from me! Don't be like that! If you can't trust me, who can you trust, you silly girl? Don't you know that you're all I have? Look up then, and tell me right now.'

Encouraged by these affectionate words and feeling she could speak freely, overcome with grief and sighing, Catellina answered: 'O my dear old mother, I'm dying and I long to die, for I'm in love with the most cruel and unfeeling man alive: that's how it is, and I can't live without loving and thinking of him. I'm like someone who's in love with a star in Heaven and has no consolation but looking at it. That's how things are with me and that's why I've decided to die and to live no longer. Ask me nothing more.' And she fell silent. At these words, the nurse, putting on a bolder look and nodding her head, answered: 'O my sweet silly girl, what's all this? There's a remedy for everything but death. Now what would you say if a friend of mine could make him love you even more than you love him? If you can manage to give him a bite to eat, that's all it takes. So now tell me: who's the man that's making you pine like this?' At these words, Catellina began to see a glimmer of hope: 'I'll tell you,' she said, 'there's nothing that I need to hide since I've lost all hope and only long to die. The man I'm so mad for is Aniello Stramazzafigli, who loves Filippello and is loved by him in return, as you well know. And this is too much for me to bear, since it means that he can never ease my pain. So you see, dear mother, what a state I'm in.'

'Now don't be so upset,' the nurse said promptly, 'cheer up, because tomorrow I'll bring you Madonna Fiondina of Pozzuoli* who is such a good and loving friend of mine that she'll do whatever we want; you should know that there's no hatred between two people so bitter that she can't remove it in less than a week with her potions and spells, and then make them burn with love for each other. You want the proof? Don't you remember that Boffillo Caraccio couldn't see or hear his wife Damiana? He used to make her life a real way of the cross. Well, now she's so fresh and gay there's not her like in Naples or Capua; and today Boffillo cares for no one but her, and he's scared that the birds of the air will fly off with her, and he's so jealous that he never leaves the house. And that cure was worked with nothing but a spell and the heart of a mole. And, you know, for that sort of thing she has the most blessed hands of any living creature; and what she did for that woman she's done for many, many more I could tell you of; but nobody knows about these things because they're done in secret; and don't you say anything to anybody about this because you'll spoil things for yourself and bring trouble and shame on her. So come on, my silly girl, cheer up, because I promise you by God's cross that Aniello will go mad for you before the week's out, and then you'll have the time of your life.'

When the nurse had left, Catellina thought over what she had said, and her hopes began to rise so high that every hour felt like a year as she waited for the nurse to return with Madonna Fiondina. The next day, just as she had promised, the nurse brought Madonna Fiondina who was given a warm and happy welcome by Catellina; and after some hesitation the nurse spoke: 'Madonna Fiondina, listen to my Catellina who needs something and has placed all her trust in you. For her love and mine, I'm begging you to do what you can, because it's really urgent.' Hearing this, Madonna Fiondina spoke directly to Catellina: 'Listen, my girl, have no fear and put your mind at rest, because I promise that soon you'll enjoy just what you desire, because your nurse Damiata has told me that you've fallen in love with Aniello, but that he's cold and shows no sign of loving you. Now if you want him to share your passion, you must get him to eat, on a Friday, the things that I tell you. You'll need two hearts, one of a live mole and the other of a monkey, then the navels of two men, and add two myrtle leaves. Get him to eat this as best you can and for each of the three ingredients recite three times the spell that I've written on this paper. And when you've given him to eat, make sure he doesn't see you again for twelve hours. Then show yourself to him, look at him, and greet him on the spot; he'll tremble as he gazes at you and he'll say something that will give you the courage to speak out. And even if he says nothing, you'll see the change in him, how deeply he sighs to show his ardour; and in the end he won't be able to live without putting his passion into practice. Now go and get those things and be quick about it if you want to save yourself more torment.' Catellina had carefully noted everything down on a piece of parchment and continued to discuss the matter for over an hour as they dined together; then, when she was alone at last, she began to think about all the ingredients, and it was the navels of two men that seemed most difficult to get hold of.

But the day before these considerations, the executioner had carried out the death sentence on four robbers, and Catellina, having seen them led to the gallows, thought that they might serve her purpose. So, without telling anyone, she decided to go and get those navels and immediately prepared herself for the task. And when night came, since Filippello Barile had gone to inspect one of his properties in the country, she left the house and went to the place of execution which is by the sea near the city boundary and walled in except for the part facing the sea. When she had got into the place, Catellina used a ladder that was there to climb up and start cutting away the navel of one of the men, and when she had done so, she put it into a bag that she had with her; then she turned to the next man, and while she was working, the moon came out, and whereas before it had been the darkest night, now it seemed as clear as day, so that everything could be seen from quite far off. Just then a sturdy and gallant young man, profiting from the fresh night air to return from some business with a house in Naples, came riding by on a powerful horse. And drawing near the place of execution, as so often happens, he turned his eyes towards those dreadful sights; and seeing not only the hanged men, but also a form that seemed alive, he was astonished and began to wonder who it could be that was shaking or moving the corpses. As he came nearer, eager to see more, as if his hair were not already standing on end, he said to himself: 'This must be either a devil or a man; if it's a devil, I want to stay and see the end; if it's a man I shall surely find out what profit or pleasure leads him to do such a terrible thing as going among hanged men at night.' And with this, he spurred forward.

The young woman, who had seen and heard everything and feared discovery, promptly decided to scare him off; and, coming down from the ladder with dishevelled hair like some infernal fury, she made for the entrance towards which the eager young man was spurring his horse. And getting there before him, now almost throwing herself on the ground and now jumping up in the air, she raised such horrible howls and fearsome screams that the horse, alarmed by the hanged men or the woman's wild ways, refused to go forward and began to back away. But the young man strove again and again to force it towards the woman until at last the horse could no longer resist. Bowing its head, it made one jump and went straight towards her; and at this she fled towards the seashore and leaped into the water, determined to drown herself. But the man followed her and, as she was sinking, he seized her by the hair. Then with a suffering voice the woman said: 'Why do you torture me? Ah, let me drown myself for pity's sake and for the love of whoever it is you love most.' The young man replied: 'First I must know who you are and then you can do as you like.' Then he started to pull her up and she tried to dive down again; but at last, seeing that she could not free herself from his grasp, she said: 'Since you want to know who I am, I'll tell you, but only on condition that you promise me on your honour never to say a word to anyone.' The youth gave his solemn promise and Catellina pulled herself up out of the water and, putting her hair in order, said: 'Now see if you know me.' As he examined her and looked her in the face, he was astounded to recognize her: 'What does this mean, Madonna Catellina? What need or what impulse has led you here, and why? I think I'm dreaming: I beg you to tell me; and I ask your pardon if I've caused you any pain for I could never have guessed who you were.'

'O my Efremo, it's love not hate that has brought me to this,' and when, finally, she had told him everything, Efremo was amazed at the terrible enterprise of the woman, especially because he was a close friend of her husband. 'Quickly now, mount this horse with me,' he said, 'and I shall take you back home lest you meet with some misadventure that would bring you harm and shame.' Immediately she mounted the horse and they set off for the city.

Since the young man was tall and handsome in his silk tunic and with skin so milky white that it conquered the shades of night, they made an almost miraculous sight. And the young men who were in the streets taking the air recognized Efremo straightaway as he rode by with the woman on the horse's back. They whistled and he answered, but they dared not do or say more than that to the noble youth, though they were very eager to know who the young woman might be, for she seemed extraordinarily beautiful. And so, turning to their own affairs, they went their ways; and the woman, having reached her home, dismounted and went in.

The next morning was a holiday in honour of Charles II (known as Charles the Lame),* and all the noblemen and youth of the city were assembled in the place reserved for the festivities. Among them was the worthy young Efremo, and all those who had seen him the night before implored him at length and with ardent prayers to say who was with him on the horse's back last night, for they swore they had never seen so lovely and so noble a lady.

But he stubbornly eluded the question and refused to answer. Then, suddenly, the king himself came up and enquired: 'What are you quarrelling about?' 'My lord,' said one of them, 'there is no quarrel, and we ask nothing of Efremo but that he should tell us who was that lady, the loveliest lady ever seen, on the horse with him last night; but he doesn't want to say.' The king, who was of a jovial nature and loved to hear about women, turned to Efremo: 'And why won't you say? Are you afraid that she'll be taken from you, handsome as you are? I wish you'd stop refusing to tell us.' Efremo answered: 'My lord, what they say is true, she certainly is a lovely creature and I would be happy to tell you who she is; but I have made a solemn promise on my honour to say nothing; and truly, if I could tell you without breaking my promise, you would hear the strangest and the grimmest story that ever was.' These words made the king even more keen to know and taking Efremo by the hand, he led him apart and said: 'You must know that you cannot and should not refuse my requests on account of your promises, and therefore I command you to tell me, and you can do this with a good conscience. So tell me without delay.'

The young man, feeling compelled by the king's command, decided to speak; and in fact he was very eager to do so. He recounted in detail everything that had happened and how the affair had begun, and the advice and assistance of Madonna Fiondina—all of which astounded the king. And since he felt that it would be wrong to let such a witch live, the king had Madonna Fiondina burned by his executioner, but without any disgrace to Catellina. Thus there was an end to the witch-craft that she advised and practised.

GENTILE SERMINI

ANSELMO SALIMBENI AND ANGELICA MONTANINI
Novelle (Tales) 14

Anselmo loves Angelica and does a great and courteous favour to her brother Carlo; not wishing to be ungrateful, Carlo and Angelica do a similar favour to him, and Anselmo then shows them such courtesy that it is hard to say which of the three is the most generous; which is why the reader is asked to decide.

IN the splendid city of Siena there lived a noble young man of the Salimbeni family whose name was Anselmo, son of Messer Salimbeni. Handsome, charming, and rich, he fell deeply in love with an honest noble girl of the Montanini* family, whose name was Angelica. She had lost her father and mother and had nobody apart from her brother who was called Carlo. The two of them lived a decent respectable life, but were rather poor, despite their noble birth, for they possessed only one small property and a house. That property was coveted by a rich citizen who kept trying to get hold of it and more than once offered them over a thousand florins. But Carlo refused to sell because it had been in the family for centuries; and for this the citizen held a secret grudge against him.

Now it happened that Carlo got involved in a lawsuit after wounding another wealthy citizen, and his enemy seized this opportunity to force him to sell by urging that he be condemned to a heavy fine. Carlo was then arrested, imprisoned, and condemned to pay a thousand florins within a fortnight or have his right hand cut off. As Carlo languished in prison, he decided that to save his hand he would have to sell the property. The citizen, however, now imposed tougher conditions by reducing his original offer from a thousand florins to eight hundred and no more. At the same time he sought to cheat Carlo by acting to prevent anyone else from buying the property. Partly because he did not want to dispossess his sister and partly because he hated to be cheated, Carlo decided to resign himself to the will of God.

Anselmo, in the meantime, had returned from his travels and was very distressed when he heard what had happened. Knowing himself to be rich enough and eager to gain the favour of Angelica and her brother, he intervened in the case, paid the thousand-florin fine without Carlo knowing anything about it, and finally had him released from prison. Carlo thanked both God and Anselmo and asked how he had managed it. 'Don't think about that,' said Anselmo, 'what matters is that you're free.' But Carlo asked around, and when he discovered that Anselmo had paid the fine for him, he sought him out and said: 'The way you've helped me makes me more obliged to you than to any man alive. So go and find a notary, for I wish to transfer our property to you in payment of what we owe.' But Anselmo wanted nothing, and it was in vain that Carlo begged to be allowed to pay the debt. And so, seeing how things stood, Carlo went home to Angelica and told her the whole story, explaining that Anselmo wanted his service to be seen as a gift and not as something to be bought and sold. Then the two of them discussed Anselmo's truly regal courtesy at length, and both agreed that ingratitude could never be a good thing. Carlo, noble-minded as he was, could have no peace until he found some way or other of showing how grateful he was. At last, seeing that Anselmo was so much in love with Angelica and realizing that it was for her sake that Anselmo had done him such a great service, he said to himself: 'O Carlo, are you so ungrateful towards the man who saved your hand from being cut off, who paid your fine of a thousand florins, and who had you released from prison without being even asked to do so? Are you so ungrateful that when you can do him a service you wait to be asked? Don't you see that you and Angelica are obliged to serve him in every way you can? Truly, if he doesn't want money or anything else that we possess, what can we pay him with except our bodies? I know that this is what he wants.' And when he hinted at this to Angelica, he gathered that she took it wisely and was not offended by the idea of such a service.

So when he had thought it over, he went to Anselmo and said: 'Noble youth, you have saved me from ruin and preserved the honour of myself and my sister. If there's nothing that we can do for you that would be a fitting return for such a favour, choose at least something that is in our power, for we're ready to do anything that will please you, rather than seem ungrateful for your kindness.' Softly and sweetly

Anselmo answered: 'But this is nothing compared to what I would like to do for you and your sister. It's enough for me to be thought of as a friend.' Since Anselmo would say no more than this, Carlo went on: 'Anselmo, I know that you love my sister; and, being a gentleman, you have always behaved in a perfectly decent way and respected her honour and mine. And indeed I know that what you did for me was done out of love for her. For this we are bound to serve you with all that we have, including our bodies. You don't want your money, so take the bodies. My body you already have, but I know that's not enough to pay such a debt. So I shall see to it that Angelica be the one who pays. Therefore, wait for her tonight, and she will come to pay you with a full purse never opened before;* but for your honour and hers, I shall bring her discreetly to your study at the third hour. And you too should make sure that she can come to you in secret.'

Anselmo's joy at this proposal was so great that he almost fainted and was lost for words, and stood staring Carlo in the face. At last, when he came to himself, he managed to stutter out: 'Brother, do as you please.' Then they went off to make their respective arrangements—Anselmo to ensure that Angelica could come without being seen, and Carlo to convince Angelica—which he did with such effective arguments that she soon gave way and agreed to carry out the promise he had made. And so, at the third hour, with all due precautions, he led Angelica to Anselmo's study, saying: 'Take your time and pay off the whole debt.' Then he left her there and went back home.

It would take me too long to describe the kind and courteous welcome that the noble Anselmo gave to Angelica and her wise, dignified, and gracious bearing. These things were beyond words and therefore I leave you, my reader, to picture them for yourself, though I doubt if you will be able to imagine more than a fraction of what they were. And let my pen refrain from relating the happiness of Anselmo when, by mutual consent, they went to bed.

But when, at last, the moment came that he had desired for so long, seeing that she lost nothing of her courteous and dignified attitude, the noble youth was immediately conquered by her sage conduct. For a while he remained silent and lost in thought, and then with a sigh he said: 'Noblest of women, gracious and gentle maid whom I love and long for, how far beyond praise is the high courtesy that has brought you here in this way, regardless of your worldly honour or your virginal fame, and only for my satisfaction. Freely and entirely, you grant me your most

worthy body, graciously consenting that all unworthily I should take carnal possession of that rich treasure. Here you show that you place my
happiness above your own honour. What then should I do? Should I not
place your honour above my happiness? Yes, indeed; for justly would
I be called ungrateful if I should satisfy my own appetite with your
shame. Therefore I have resolved to control my unbridled lust with the
reins of righteous and prudent reason. And so, if your brother Carlo and
your kinsfolk consent, I now with all my heart ask you to accept me,
unworthy as I am, as your bridegroom and husband. Moreover, in asking this, I agree that you must come to your husband as a virgin bride,
and this I desire more than that you should now become a harlot. For
even if you said: "Nobody but us will ever know," you would still feel
ashamed of yourself ever after. I have no wish to cause you such suffering. So put your clothes on, and I will take you back to your gracious
brother a virgin as you came.' To which the wise and courteous maiden
replied: 'O noble youth, now I see that when you speak of me loving you
more than myself, these are words that should be applied to you and not
to me; for you well know that I don't deserve to be your wife. You, scion
of one the first and noblest families of Italy, son of a famous knight,
endowed with great wealth, replete with knowledge, handsome in form
and feature, gracious and courteous—in you are all those praiseworthy
qualities that a young man could possess. You would deserve a bride of
royal blood or noble lineage, and not a pauper like me. Take of me then
what you will, but do not lower yourself to honour me. And yet I know
I shall not err if I trust your judgement.'

Many were the sweet words they exchanged until at last, in perfect
concord, they went to Carlo and explained everything they had agreed
together. Carlo was overjoyed and thanked Anselmo as best he could;
after which they secretly set about preparing the alliance, for Anselmo
remarked: 'We do not want this marriage to look like a prearranged
affair. People know that I love Angelica, and so nobody will be surprised that I have asked for her hand. And so, for the honour of all
concerned, I shall speak to Messer Cino Berarducci, my neighbour
and a relative too, and he will be my go-between and ask you to give
me Angelica as my wife; and you will answer as you should, and we
shall seal the alliance in a perfectly honourable fashion.' So it was
agreed and they went their separate ways.

The following morning Anselmo went to see Messer Berarducci
and very respectfully said: 'You know that I love Angelica Montanini;

would you please help me to get her as my wife?' Messer Cino, as a good wise kinsman, took him to task, raising a number of objections and offering him the best matches in Siena: 'Take your pick, Anselmo, so long as it's honourable; just leave it all to me.' But Anselmo interrupted him: 'I shall never have any wife but her,' and he added, 'and don't be too greedy about the dowry; I've got enough to keep her in style, thank God, without taking her money. I shall be satisfied with the essential. If you want to help me, I beg you, by all means, do so, and I shall be very grateful; if not, I shall choose a go-between who doesn't raise so many objections.' And he concluded: 'I shall never have any wife but her; and if, by chance, she marries someone else, I will make the kind of trouble that my relatives won't appreciate. So don't raise any more objections because my mind is made up.' Finally, Messer Cino saw that there was no way of stopping him; and since, after all, the woman was noble and well born, he decided to do as he was asked. To this end he found time to speak to Carlo who proved so agreeable to his proposition that in a few days the alliance was sealed and the marriage took place publicly in the church of San Donato. On that occasion the noble Anselmo spoke as follows:

'I thank Almighty God for granting me such grace, in that Carlo and all his kinsmen have agreed to give me the noble Angelica as my wife. This is something I have always desired since first I heard of her countless virtues. And therefore, deeming myself unworthy to possess such a treasure, I have not sought and nor do I wish for any kind of dowry. She alone is all I want, and all I need for my happiness. And since she is far more worthy than I am, I hereby endow her with all that I possess in the world. Put that down, Ser Giuliano, in the marriage contract. And as for Carlo, her brother, whose virtue and gentle bearing I cherish: if he consent, I shall receive him not as my brother-in-law, but quite simply as my brother. And if he wants to share a home with his sister and myself, then I grant him half of all I have.' Then, turning to him, he asked: 'Is this to your liking?' Carlo consented and ran to embrace him, saying: 'Ser Giuliano, put this in the contract, that I agree to whatever Anselmo wishes,' and adding that he also divided all he had with Anselmo: 'And since he contributes to this bargain a hundred times more than I do, I count it my duty to serve as his steward while he leads a life of leisure.'

So, after much talk on both sides, the agreement was made, and freely they became brothers. With everything settled, there were great and fitting festivities when, at the end of the month, Anselmo led Angelica to her new home as his lady; and that very morning the pact of brotherhood between Anselmo and Carlo came into effect, and the celebrations, added to those of the wedding, lasted for a whole month. Thus, in love and concord, the three of them lived for the rest of their lives.

Now, if you consider all the acts of courtesy that passed between them and that I have related here, it remains to be decided which of them was the greatest and most praiseworthy.

ANTONIO MANETTI

THE FAT WOODWORKER
Il grasso legnaiuolo

THE city of Florence has had many pleasant and entertaining men in the past, and especially in more recent times. Thus, in the year 1409, one Sunday evening, as was their custom, a lively group of respectable citizens gathered to dine in the house of Tomaso Pecori,* a thoroughly decent and witty fellow who took great pleasure in their company which was made up of government officials, and masters of the more creative crafts such as painters, goldsmiths, sculptors, woodworkers, and the like. They had dined cheerfully and, as they were sitting round the fire because it was winter, they talked either in small groups or all together about many things, but chiefly about the crafts or professions that they practised. In the middle of this conversation, one of them asked: 'How comes it that Manetto* the woodworker isn't here tonight?' (for Manetto was the name of a colleague they called Grasso, 'the Fat Man'); and from the answers it appeared that one of them had told him about the meeting but for some unknown reason had been unable to bring him along.

This woodworker had his workshop in Piazza di San Giovanni* and was one of the best masters of his craft in Florence at the time; and among other things he was famed for his skill with pediments and altarpieces and suchlike which not every woodworker could handle. He was about twenty-eight years of age, very amiable, as most fat people are, and usually known as Grasso because of his corpulent build. He was a bit on the simple side, but so far from being a complete fool that it would have taken a shrewd mind to notice this. Now since he was usually part of the group, they began to imagine all sorts of reasons for his absence until, for lack of any other explanation, they concluded that what kept him must be one of those strange caprices by which he was occasionally affected. Since almost all of them belonged to a higher rank and station than the woodworker, they felt somewhat offended by this behaviour and began to amuse themselves thinking of how they might be revenged. Then the man who had spoken first, said: 'And what if we could play some kind of trick on him, something that would make him a bit wiser next time?' One of the others answered: 'What could we do, unless we could trick him into paying for a dinner that he wouldn't be there to eat?' Among the group was Filippo di Ser Brunellesco,* whom most people still remember as a man of wonderful talent and intelligence. At that time he was about thirty-two and had known Grasso long enough to weigh him up and take a secret pleasure in his foolishness. Now, after a pause for thought, he said: 'I heartily wish we could find some prank to take revenge on him for not coming here this evening, something that would amuse us all. If you go along with me, I'd love to do it. Just now it struck me that we could make him believe that he is someone else,* and no longer Grasso the Woodworker.' All this with a certain self-confident grin that was typical of him.

The whole group knew that Filippo was supremely clever at whatever he turned his hand to (it is only the blind who cannot see the sun), nor were they entirely ignorant of Grasso's simplicity; yet still they all thought the thing was quite impossible. But Filippo, who knew perfectly well what he was about, explained his plan with such subtle arguments and careful reasoning that he finally convinced them. At last, having all agreed about how to behave in order to keep the matter secret, they resolved to take their revenge by leading Grasso to believe that he had become someone called Matteo, a fellow already known to some of them, including Grasso himself, but not one of the inner circle who met to eat together. And some who stood a little aside from the others, aroused much laughter by declaring the sooner the better.

This pleasant story got got under way with no waste of time; indeed it began the following evening in this way. Filippo was familiar with all the victim's habits and knew them as well as Grasso himself precisely because the woodworker, with his good nature, confided in him completely (otherwise, Filippo could not have carried out his plan). And so, at the hour when craftsmen of that kind usually lock their doors and work by lamplight inside, he went to Grasso's workshop, just as he had done a thousand times at the same hour. As the two stood talking, there came, as arranged, a boy all breathless who asked: 'Is Filippo di Ser Brunellesco round here?' To which Filippo, coming forward, answered: 'Here I am; what do you want?' And the boy: 'If you're Filippo, you'd better come home immediately.' 'God help us!' said Filippo, 'what's happened?' The boy replied: 'I was sent running to you and it's because your mother had an attack about two hours ago, and she's at death's door, so you'd better come quickly.' Filippo feigned surprise, commended himself to God again, and took his leave, but Grasso said to his friend: 'I'll come with you, in case there's something that needs doing; you need all the help you can get at a time like this: I'll just shut up shop and come along.' Filippo thanked him and said: 'I'd rather you didn't come just yet; I'm sure it's not as important as all that; but if I do need something, I'll let you know. Do me a favour and stay here in your shop, and don't leave for whatever reason because I may need you after all. Then, if I don't send for you, you can go about your business.' So, having made sure that Grasso stayed in his shop, and pretending to make his way home, he turned off under an archway and went to Grasso's house which was near Santa Maria del Fiore.* There, with a practised hand, he used a knife to prise open the door, entered the house, and bolted the door behind him so that nobody could get in. Grasso's mother was away at Polverosa* in the country, doing the laundry, curing meat, and seeing to other odd jobs, and he was expecting her back any day. That was why the door had been left on the latch rather than locked, as Filippo well knew.

Grasso waited for a while in his shop before locking up; then, to make double sure of keeping his promise to Filippo, he walked up and down several times outside the shop until at last he said to himself: 'Things can't be going all that badly with Filippo; he won't be needing me'; and with that, he set off home. When he arrived before the door which was up two flights of stairs, he went to open it as he usually did, but after trying and failing several times, he realized that it was bolted from inside. So he knocked loudly, shouting: 'Who's there? Open up!', assuming that his mother had returned and locked herself in for some strange reason or by mistake. Filippo came to the top of the stairs and imitated the voice of Grasso to perfection, saying: 'Who's down there?' Although the voice did not sound much like his mother's, Grasso answered: 'It's me, Grasso.' Filippo now pretended that the voice he was hearing was that of Matteo (the man they wanted to convince Grasso that he had become), and so he replied: 'O Matteo, go with God, I've got such a world of things to do; Filippo di Ser Brunellesco was in my shop when he got news that his mother had been on her deathbed for a couple of hours. Which makes it a bad evening for me.' Then, turning back, as if he were speaking to the mother, he said: 'Get my supper ready. You should have come back two days ago, and now you turn up at night!', following it up with other grumbles. When Grasso heard whoever was inside grumbling at his mother, not just with his own voice, but with all his quirks and mannerisms, he said to himself: 'What's the meaning of this? That fellow up there seems to be me myself, telling how Filippo was in his shop and how they came to say his mother was sick: and what's more, shouting at Monna Giovanna with a voice exactly like mine! Am I losing my mind?'

Grasso hurried down the stairs and as he stepped back to call up at the windows, who should arrive, as planned, but his friend Donatello,* the famous sculptor, who had been at the dinner that evening and now approached him in the twilight, saying: 'Good evening, Matteo, are you looking for Grasso? He went home not so long ago.' Then, without stopping, he went about his business. If Grasso had been amazed before, he was now even more astonished to hear Donatello call him Matteo. Stunned and almost senseless, with yes and no contending in his head, he set off towards Piazza San Giovanni, saying to himself: 'I shall stay here until someone comes by who knows me and says who I am. Am I like Calandrino* and have I turned into someone else so quickly that I didn't even realize it?' As Grasso stood there, half out of his mind, up came (always as planned) six guards from the Merchants' Court* and a bailiff, and among them was a man who pretended to be a creditor of that Matteo whom Grasso was almost beginning to believe he had become. Coming up to Grasso and turning to the bailiff and the guards, he said: 'Take away this Matteo here. He's my debtor. You see, it's taken me a long time to track you down, and now I've caught you.' The bailiff and the guards seized Grasso and began to lead him away, but he turned to the man who was having him arrested and dug in his heels with 'What have I got to do with you and why do you want me arrested? Tell them to let me go. You're mixing me up with someone else. I'm not who you think, and it's a crying shame to disgrace me like this when I've got absolutely nothing to do with you. I'm Grasso the woodworker and I'm not Matteo and I don't even know what Matteo you're on about.' Then he began to lay about him with all his strength, for he was a big man; but they managed to grab him by the arms and the creditor came forward and looked him carefully in the face and said: 'What! So you've got nothing to do with me? And I don't know the difference between my debtor Matteo and Grasso the woodworker! I've got you written down in my little book, and what's more there's this judgement against you that I've had for a year or more. So you've got nothing to do with me? And the scoundrel says he's not Matteo. Take him away. This time you'll have to pay up before you've done with it. We'll soon see if you're Matteo or not.' And while the two were still arguing the toss, they led him off to the jail at the Merchants' Court, and because it was about half an hour before supper time and already rather dark, they met nobody either there or on the way who knew the woodworker.

When they arrived at the Merchants' Court the clerk pretended to write the name of Matteo in the register and had him put in jail, for he had been told everything in advance by Tomaso Pecori who was a close friend. The other prisoners who were there, having heard the racket when he arrived and how he was repeatedly called Matteo, received him as if that were his name and asked no questions since, as it happened, none of them knew him except by sight. And hearing himself called Matteo all the time and by everyone, even the woodworker was like a man possessed, feeling almost certain that he had become someone else. So when someone asked him why he had been arrested, he was totally confused and replied: 'I owe quite a bit of money, that's why I'm here; but I'll get it all settled first thing tomorrow morning.' And the other prisoners said: 'Look, we're just about to have supper; eat with us and you can settle everything tomorrow morning; but we'd better warn you: this is a place where men stay longer than people think: God grant that it doesn't happen to you.' Grasso accepted the invitation but ate little and when they had finished supper one of them lent him part of his wretched pallet, saying: 'Matteo, try and manage with this for tonight: if you get out tomorrow, all well and good; if not, you can always send home for some bedding of your own.' Grasso thanked him and settled down to sleep as best he could.

Once the youth who had acted as the creditor had arranged everything that seemed necessary at the Merchants' Court, he met with Filippo di Ser Brunellesco who did not leave him until he had heard all the details of the arrest and imprisonment. Grasso, meanwhile, was lying on the edge of that pallet and brooding over his situation: 'What shall I do if I really have become Matteo? For as far as I can see all the evidence points that way and everyone agrees about it. But which Matteo is it? And what if I send a message home to my mother and

Grasso happens to be there—where I heard him? They'll make me
a laughing stock!' Beset by such thoughts and seeing himself as Grasso
one moment and Matteo the next, he suffered until morning, getting
practically no sleep and plagued by a host of strange imaginings.
When he got up with the others, he went to stand at the small window
in the prison door, supposing that someone would surely turn up who
could recognize him and resolve the doubts that had troubled him
during the night. Then along to the Merchants' Court came Giovanni
di Messer Francesco Rucellai* who was one of the company who had
dined together and was part of the merry plot. Grasso knew him very
well and happened at that time to be working for him on the pediment
for a Madonna. Indeed, he had spent quite some time in Grasso's
workshop the day before, nagging him about the job which the woodworker had promised to finish in four days' time. When Giovanni
arrived at the Merchants' Court, he poked his head into the entrance
on the ground floor where the prison window was in those days, and
where Grasso was standing. When the woodworker saw Giovanni he
began to look him in the face and grin, but Giovanni, as if he were
wondering who this might be, looked at him as if he had never seen
him before, for he did not know Matteo or pretended that he did not.
'What's so funny, my friend?' said he, and Grasso answered: 'Nothing,
really,' and as he saw that Giovanni did not recognize him, he asked:
'Tell me, good sir, do you know someone called Grasso whose workshop is in Piazza di Santo Giovanni hereabouts and who does inlaying?' 'Are you talking to me?' said Giovanni, and went on: 'Of course,
I know him very well. He's one of my men, and soon I need to see him
about a little job he's doing for me. Is he the man who's had you
arrested?' 'No, by Saint Mary,' said Grasso, 'but forgive me if I ask
you a favour, just between ourselves; since you have to go and see
him, could you please tell him: "A friend of yours is being held at the
Merchants' Court and he'd take it kindly if you dropped in to have
a word with him."' Trying hard not to laugh, Giovanni stared at him
and asked: 'And who are you? Who shall I say is asking for him?' This
was so he would admit to being Matteo and be mocked for it later.
Grasso said: 'Don't worry about that; just tell him what I said.' And
Giovanni: 'Well, if that's all, I'll do it gladly,' and off he went; and
when he came across Filippo he laughed and told him everything that
had happened.

Left standing at the prison window, Grasso thought to himself: 'Now

I can be sure that I'm no longer Grasso. Giovanni Rucellai never took his eyes off me, and yet he didn't recognize me even though he's in and out of my shop every day. And surely he can't be out of his mind! The fact is that I'm no longer Grasso and that I've become Matteo. Damn and blast my rotten luck! If people get to know of this, I'll be shamed and mocked; they'll think I've gone mad and the children will run after me in the street and I'll be in all kinds of danger. And come to that, what have I got to do with another man's debts or with the troubles he's got himself into? Just the kind of bother I've always avoided, along with a thousand other dangerous doings? There's no one I can consult about this, no one who can give me good advice, though God knows I need it! I'm in a fix, whichever way you look at it. But let's see if Grasso comes, and if he does, maybe I'll understand what all this means. Could he possibly have become me?' Lost in such thoughts, he waited in vain for Grasso, but finally left his place at the window to another prisoner while he sat with his hands clasped, looking up and down at the ceiling and the floor.

In those days, a judge,* whose name is better not said, was being held in the jail for debt. He was a genuinely gifted man and no less famed for his literary merits than for his knowledge of the law. He had already settled his own case and was soon to be released; and so when he saw Grasso so obviously downcast and distressed, he assumed that this also must be a matter of debt. Although he did not know Grasso and had indeed never heard of him, moved by charity as one sometimes is, he set out to comfort him: 'Come now, Matteo, you're as wretched as if you were near to death or in danger of some terrible disgrace; yet from what you say the debt seems pretty small. You don't have to give up simply because you've had a bit of bad luck. Why don't you send for some friend or relative? Don't you have anybody? See if you can't pay up or make some kind of deal so that you can get out of jail; and don't let this business get you down.' Finding himself comforted with such compassion and with such kind words, Grasso did not say, as he might have done to someone else: 'Why don't you mind your own business?' Instead, knowing the judge to be a worthy man, even though he was in prison, he decided to speak to him with all due respect and to tell him the whole story. Drawing him away into a corner, he said to him: 'Sir, although you don't know me, I know you well as a talented man, and that's why your kindness moves me to tell you what makes me so miserable; for I wouldn't want you or anyone else to think that I'm distraught because of some small debt, even if I'm only a humble craftsman. The truth is that I'm upset by something quite different, something that may never have happened to anyone else in the world.' The judge was astonished to hear this and listened with great attention.

Grasso recounted what had happened to him from beginning to end, striving to hold back his tears and begging two things: first, that for his honour's sake the judge should never speak about this to anyone else; second, that he should give him some advice and assistance, adding: 'For I know how much time you've spent reading of many things, ancient and modern stories and men who've written about all kinds of events: did you ever come across something like this?' Having heard this and given the matter prompt consideration, the worthy man concluded that it had to be one of two things: either the timorous fellow had lost his mind through some excess of melancholy caused by his present predicament or by some other trouble, or else he was the victim of some prank—as in fact he was. And to get a better understanding of things, he replied that he had often read of one man becoming someone else, and that this case was far from new. Indeed, it could be worse for there were examples of men becoming brutish beasts, like Apuleius* who became an ass and Actaeon* who was transformed into a stag 'and plenty of others you can read about, though I don't remember them right now'—saying this simply to keep himself amused. To which Grasso answered: 'Oh, I would never have believed it,' and he took it all as being quite literally true. Then he went on: 'Now tell me, if I who was Grasso have become Matteo, what has happened to Matteo?' And the judge answered: 'He must have become Grasso because this is an exchange of identities, and that's how it usually happens, from all I've read and from the odd cases I've seen up to now. It can't be any other way. I'd love to have a look at that fellow; this is really worth a good laugh.' 'Especially when the joke's not on you!' said Grasso. 'That's true,' said the judge, 'these are terrible disasters, and may God protect us all; we're none of us safe. The very same thing happened to a worker I once had.' Grasso sighed deeply, not knowing what to say since that was how things were. The judge continued: 'It's just the same as what you read about the companions of Ulysses and the rest who were transformed by Circe.* It's true that from what I've heard and read, if I remember well, that there have been some rare cases where a man came back to his old self; but

if the transformation lasts a bit too long that's not likely to happen.'
This was said to increase Grasso's confusion and left the woodworker
completely bewildered.

He was still in this state at about three o'clock and had not yet eaten
when the two brothers of this Matteo came to the Merchants' Court
and asked the bursar if their brother Matteo was being held there and
how much was his debt because they wanted to get him released from
jail. The bursar said yes and pretended to look him up in the book by
turning a few pages: 'Here's the sum,' he said, 'and this is the creditor.'
'Too much,' said one of the brothers, and then: 'We'd like to have
a few words with him and then we'll make an order of payment for
him.' When they came to the prison, they said to a man who was
standing behind the bars: 'Tell Matteo over there that his two brothers are here and that he should come this way,' and as they peered in
they immediately recognized the judge who happened to be talking
with Grasso. Grasso was just asking how that worker of his had ended
up, and hearing that he was never himself again, he became even
more downcast. When he received the message of his brothers, he
went up to the prison bars and greeted them; then one of them looked
him in the face and started up: 'The same old story, Matteo; how
many times have we warned you about your bad behaviour, and how
many times have we bailed you out of this prison or others? And nothing we say does any good because you go from bad to worse. How little
we have left to help you with God alone knows, for you've already
swallowed up a fortune. And what good did you ever get for all you
spent. Nothing! You just squandered it, threw it away. Not to speak of
your gambling where everyone cheats you: haven't you been twisted
out of half your cash? And we're the ones who suffer for it; all the
shame is ours because you simply don't care. In fact, I reckon you go
out of your way to shame your friends. And then you think you can
explain everything by saying: "You've mistaken me for someone
else." Are you a child? It's about time you grew up. But you can be
sure of one thing: you've done this to us so often that we'd have left
you to fend for yourself if it weren't for our family honour and the
fact that our mother keeps pleading for you—she's old and frail and
we worry about her more than about you. But we're telling you once
and for all, come what may, that if you ever mess up again, you'll stay
in jail a lot longer than you'd like. That'll do for now.' After pausing
for a few moments, he concluded: 'And so as not to be seen doing this

kind of business, we'll come for you this evening when they ring for the Angelus* and there'll be fewer people around, so we won't have everyone knowing our troubles and putting us to shame on your account.'

Grasso turned to them and did his best to sound contrite, for he was now absolutely sure that he was Matteo since they had paid up for him and looked him steadily in the face when it was not dark. He promised them that they would have no more trouble from him, that he would surely mend his ways, and that if he ever behaved badly again, they should close their ears to him and to his mother and to any excuses he might make. Now determined to be Matteo, he begged them, for God's love, to come for him at the appointed time. They promised they would and went away; and Grasso, turning back and going up to the judge, said: 'Now we're in a bigger fix: two brothers of this Matteo came here to see me—I mean the Matteo I've been exchanged with; how can I say this?'—looking the judge in the eyes— 'and they both spoke to me face to face and in the light, as you could see for yourself—all just as if I were Matteo. After giving me a long telling-off, they promised to come back at Angelus time and get me out of jail. Until now I would never have believed it, but now I see that what you tell me is true.' Then he asked: 'So that worker of yours never became himself again?' 'Never, poor fellow,' replied the judge. Grasso sighed deeply: 'So now they'll get me out of here; where am I to go? Go back where? Not to my house. And which is my house?— that's the question. Think of it'—and he looked at the judge—'because if Grasso's there (which he surely will be since I heard him with my own ears) what can I say that won't make me look like a madman or a fool? You get the picture: if Grasso happens to be there he'll say: "Has this fellow gone mad?", and if he's not there and he comes home and finds me, what will happen then? Who stays and who has to go? You see, if I hadn't been at home when my mother returned from the country, wouldn't she have looked for me and found me, even if I were up in the stars? But because she saw *him* there, she has no idea of what's going on.' The judge was having tremendous fun and could hardly keep from laughing: 'No, don't go home; go with these two who say they're your brothers, see where they take you and what they do with you; what have you got to lose? Anyway, they're paying for you.' 'That's true,' said Grasso, and the judge added: 'You'll get out of jail, and since they're sure you're their brother, who knows, you might be better off. Perhaps they're richer than you.'

They were still talking things over as night came on; and the judge, who could hardly contain himself, was dying to get away and start laughing. Grasso's supposed brothers were there at the Merchants' Court waiting for their moment and laughing all the time. The judge's case was settled and they saw him emerging from the jail and departing as calmly as if he had been consulting a magistrate about some client's case, the way lawyers do. Then they came forward and pretended to settle accounts with the creditor and the bursar; after which the bursar got up, took the prison keys, went over to the jail and said: 'Which of you is Matteo?' Grasso stepped up and answered: 'Here I am, sir,' not doubting that he had indeed become Matteo. The bursar looked at him: 'Your brothers here have paid your debt and everything else, so now you're free: come this way,' and with that he opened the door.

Outside it was already quite dark and Grasso was more than pleased to be out of jail without being out of pocket. Since he had not eaten anything all day, his first thought when the door opened for him was to go home; but then, remembering that he had heard Grasso there the night before, he changed his mind and decided to follow the advice of the judge and go with the two brothers who lived near the church of Santa Felicità* at the beginning of the Costa San Giorgio. As they went along together they accused him of upsetting his mother and reminded him of how many times he had promised to change his ways—but they did so gently and without the harshness they had shown in the prison. They asked where he had got the idea of saying he was Grasso—whether he really believed it to be the case or whether he had simply invented it so that he could plead mistaken identity and be released. Grasso did not know what to answer, and as he thought it over he began to regret going with them, for he hated to admit that he was Matteo; but on the other hand, he reflected: 'If I go back to saying I'm Grasso, maybe they won't want me, and then I'll have lost both their house and my own.'

So he promised he would mend his ways and put off answering the question about why he claimed to be Grasso.

They had now arrived home where they took him to a room on the ground floor, saying: 'Stay there until supper time,' as if they did not want their mother to be upset by his sudden reappearance. Since a fire had been lit and the table was already laid, one of them stayed behind with him while the other went to Santa Felicità to see their parish priest who was a good man. 'I come to you', he said, 'in all confidence, as one neighbour to another and also because you are our spiritual father. To give you some idea of the situation so that you will know what's best to do, let me just say that we are three brothers and your near neighbours, as you may already know.' 'Yes,' said the priest, who knew them vaguely. And the brother went on: 'Well, there's one of us, called Matteo, who has been held for debt at the Merchants' Court. And because it's not the first time we've had to bail him out, he's so upset that he seems to have gone half crazy as if he were obsessed by it, though in every other way he's the same old Matteo, or almost. What's new is that he's got it into his head that he's become someone else, and that he's not Matteo. You never heard such an absurd story! He says he's a certain Grasso the woodworker, someone he actually knows, who has his workshop behind San Giovanni and his house by Santa Maria del Fiore. And we've tried everything to get the idea out of his mind, but nothing works. That's why we got him out of prison, took him home, and put him in a room so that nobody outside learns about his antics; because you know that once a man starts giving signs like that, he'll always be treated like a fool, even if he becomes perfectly sane later on. What's more, if Mother sees him before he's recovered, it could do her some real harm. Who knows? Women are frail, and she's old and ill. So, to cut a long story short, we're begging you, for pity's sake, come home with us and see if you can't get this crazy idea out of his head. We're asking you rather than anybody else because we know you're too wise and good to tell other people about our disgrace. We shall always be obliged to you and you'll have merit in the sight of God; and, in any case, it's your job to seek his salvation since he's one of your flock and you'll have to ren-der an account of him; because if he's gone mad in a state of mortal sin and then dies without recovering, he might well be damned.'

The priest agreed that it was indeed his duty, he would be happy to spare no pains in helping them out. And in fact, quite apart from his duties, he was a very obliging man. After a pause for thought, he added: 'And maybe our pains will not be wasted; take me to him . . . unless he's dangerous.' 'No, by Saint Mary,' said the brother. 'Oh, I see, you mean if he were in some violent frenzy.' 'Well,' said the priest, 'you know what people in that state are like: they wouldn't recognize their own father, let alone a priest, for they don't see any-thing the way it really is.' 'Reverend sir, I do understand you,' said the brother, 'and you're right to ask me about it; but as I say, it's more like something that comes over him than real raving madness, and to see him neither you nor anyone would notice anything amiss. And indeed, if he were really raving mad, we'd have no hope and we wouldn't be going to all this trouble, because people in that state almost never recover. You could say that he's strayed from the path rather than completely lost his way, and we don't want his mother to know anything about it. It's because we have some hope that we're doing this.' 'If that's how it is, then I want to see him,' answered the priest, 'and I'll try everything I can, for in a case like this everybody should do their best to help; and I realize that your mother is in danger, as you say, and that we should keep her out of this trouble, if we can.' So then the brother brought him home and into the room where Grasso was.

Grasso was sitting lost in thought, but got up as soon as he saw the priest's cassock. The priest said, 'Good evening, Matteo,' and Grasso replied, 'Good evening and happy New Year.' 'It is, since you say so,' said the priest who thought he sounded already cured. Then he took him by the hand: 'Matteo, I've come to stay with you for a little while,' said he; and seating himself by the fire he drew up a small chair for Grasso who showed none of that stubborn insistence on being the woodworker that the priest had been told of. This gave some hope of a successful outcome, and the priest made signs to the brother who had brought him there that so far everything was going swimmingly and that he should stay out of the room, which he did. Then the priest began to speak as follows: 'You must know, Matteo, that I am your parish priest and your spiritual father, and as such my duty is to care for all my parishioners, in soul and in body, to the best of my ability. I hear things that distress me: it seems you've been in prison for debt. Well, you know there's nothing very extraordinary about that, and you shouldn't think there is, either for you or for anyone else. That's the way the world goes, bringing its load of misfortunes, great or small, from day to day. All you can do is arm yourself with patience and put up with them. I say this because I've heard that you've become so depressed that you were on the verge of madness. Men of real worth don't react like this: when the need arises, they strive to take the shield of patience and trust in providence to put everything right. And that's good sense. Now what's this folly, among all the others I keep hearing of—that you say you're no longer Matteo and insist that you're someone else called Grasso who's a woodworker? This fixed idea brings shame on you and makes you look ridiculous. You really are to blame, Matteo! To take a small misfortune so much to heart that you seem to have lost your wits! For six florins! Is that such a big deal? Especially now they've been paid.

'My dear Matteo,' continued the priest, squeezing his hand, 'I don't want you to carry on like this. For my sake—and for your own honour and that of your family, who strike me as such decent people—I want you to promise me that from now on you'll give up this silly fantasy and look to your own affairs like a decent sensible man; and commend yourself to God because hope in Him is never in vain. That's the way you'll do yourself some good, with honour for you and your brothers here and for everyone who loves you, including me. Now look! Is this Grasso such a great master and so rich that you'd rather be him than yourself? What do you think you'll get out of behaving like that? And let's suppose that he's a worthy fellow and richer than you are (though from what your people tell me, it's a bit the other way round): saying that you're him won't get you his reputation, nor his wealth, if he has any. Do what I tell you, because I'm saying it for your own good. Along with everything else, if you brought down such a disgrace upon yourself, you'd risk having the children mock you in the street and you'd live in shame and trouble for the rest of your days. That's all you'd have gained. But I promise to speak well of you to your brothers so that they'll always love you and help you as a good brother. Come on now, Matteo, act like a man not an animal, and drop all this silliness about Grasso or not Grasso. Do as I say, for it's good advice.' And he gave him a gentle earnest look.

Hearing how much love and eloquence went into these words and not doubting that he was indeed Matteo, Grasso replied immediately that he'd do everything he could to follow the priest's advice. And because he realized it was all for his own good, he promised that from then on he'd do his best and give up for good trying to convince people that he was Grasso—unless, of course, he became Grasso again. But he still wanted one favour from the woodworker, if at all possible. He needed to have a little chat with him, and for one very good reason: because speaking with him would end all his doubts. Whereas if he didn't meet and speak with Grasso, he feared he'd be unable to keep any promise he might make. At this the priest frowned and said: 'My dear Matteo, all this is against your own best interests, and I see that you've still got that idea stuck in your head. What do you mean by "unless I become Grasso again"? I don't understand it. Why do you

need to talk with Grasso? What have you got to do with him? Because
the more you talk about him, and the more people you talk with, the
more you'll let the world know about this business. And the worse
things will get and the more harm you'll do yourself.' The priest went
on like this until at last Grasso agreed not to speak to the woodworker,
though with some reluctance. Before he left, the priest reported the
whole conversation to the two brothers, with all that Grasso had
answered and what he had promised at last, though with great difficulty. And indeed, there was something he had said—something the
priest did not quite grasp—that made him suspect he might not keep
that promise. Anyway, he had done what he could. One of the brothers put a silver coin in his hand to make the thing look more credible,
then thanked him for his good offices and begged him to pray God
that Matteo be restored to them in his senses. The priest opened his
hand, grasped the coin, took his leave, and returned to his church.

While the priest had been with Grasso, Filippo di Ser Brunellesco
had arrived. Amid great laughter, but at a safe distance from the room,
he had one of the brothers tell him the whole story: how they had got
him out of prison and what they had said to him on the way home and
later; and they also told Filippo about the judge they had seen speaking
with Grasso in prison and how they had seen him released. Filippo
paid careful attention so that he could remember all this in addition
to what he had been told by the supposed creditor responsible for
Grasso's arrest. And showing the brother a potion that he had brought
in a little phial, he said: 'When you're having supper, make sure you
give him this, in wine or any way you like, provided he doesn't notice.
It's an opiate that will make him sleep so soundly that even if you gave
him a beating he wouldn't feel it for quite some time.' With that settled, he went away.

The brothers went back to the room and sat down to supper with
Grasso, for it was already getting on for ten o'clock; and as they dined
they gave him the potion without him noticing for it was neither
unpleasant nor bitter. When they had finished, they remained for
a while around the fire, still talking about their brother's bad behaviour and begging him to mend his ways; and especially for their sake
and for the love of their mother to give up this madness of believing
he had become someone else: it was really too much and he should
not be surprised if they implored him to stop, for it harmed them
almost as much as it harmed him. That very day, in fact, when they

were walking through the Mercato Nuovo* on their way to procure the money for his release, they had heard someone behind them say: 'Look, that's the man who's lost his wits; he's forgotten who he is and he thinks he's become someone else'—though another man said: 'No, that's not him; it's his brother.' While they were talking like this, the opiate potion began to take effect so that Grasso could hardly keep his eyes open, and they said: 'Matteo, you look ready to drop; you can't have had much sleep last night.' And they were right. Grasso answered: 'I can tell you this: I've never been so sleepy in all my life.' 'Off to bed!', they exclaimed, and he only just managed to undress and get into bed before he fell asleep so soundly that, as Filippo had said, he could have been beaten without feeling it; and he snored like a pig.

Filippo came back at the agreed time, bringing six friends with him because the woodworker was big and fat. All six had been at the supper given by Tomaso Pecori and were lively young sparks who wanted to join in the prank after hearing Filippo give a hilarious account of the whole affair. They entered the room where Grasso was and, finding him in such a deep sleep, they lifted him up, put him in a basket along with all his clothes, and carried him off to his home, where, by a lucky chance, his mother had not yet returned from the country (they knew all this because they were keeping an eye on everything); then they put him to bed and placed the clothes in their usual place. But him they put the wrong way round, with his head where his feet should have been. After which, they went off to the workshop which they entered with the key that they had taken from his belt. Once inside, they set about moving all his tools around from one place to another: they took his planes and turned the blades upside down; they did the same with the handles of the hammers; they put the saws with the teeth pointing inward. They did this kind of thing wherever they could until the whole workshop looked as if it had been invaded by a horde of demons. Then, leaving everything in a right old mess, they locked up and took the key back to Grasso's house where they hung it in its proper place. Closing the door behind them, they went off to sleep in their own homes.

Drugged by the potion, Grasso slept soundly all night. But in the morning, when the effect had worn off and it was already morning, he woke to the sound of the Angelus from Santa Maria del Fiore, recognized the bell, opened his eyes, and, thanks to some shafts of light in the room, realized that he was back in his own house. His heart swelled with joy for it seemed clear that he was Grasso once again and in full possession of everything that he had feared might be lost. He could hardly contain himself and almost wept with happiness. And yet he was disturbed and surprised to find himself lying with his head where his feet should be. Then he began to remember what had happened to him and the place where he had gone to sleep the night before; and immediately he fell into a state of dazed bewilderment, uncertain whether he had dreamed all that or whether he was dreaming now. First he thought one thing and then he thought the other, and then he looked around the room and said: 'This is surely the room that was mine when I was Grasso, but when did I get here?' And he started touching one arm and then the other and then his chest to make sure that he was really Grasso. Then he said to himself: 'But if that's the way it is, how come that I was arrested as Matteo? For I still remember that I was in prison and that nobody took me for anybody but Matteo; and I was bailed out by those two brothers, and I went to Santa Felicità where I had a long talk with the priest and there I dined and went to bed because I was so sleepy.' So once again he was at a loss as to whether he was dreaming then or now. Yet anxious though he was, he still felt some glimmer of joy when he remembered what the judge had said to him in the jail, for he believed that, on the whole, it was more than likely that he had returned to being Grasso; and although he remembered everything that had happened, from his arrest up to where he had slept the night before, it did not distress him for, after all, since he had become Grasso again, things seemed to be turning out the way they should. But then, as he looked back on what had happened, he returned to his old doubts. 'Who knows whether I dreamed all that or whether I'm dreaming now,' he said, sighing deeply, 'may God help me!' At last, he got out of bed in his usual way, dressed, took the key for his workshop, and set off. When he arrived and unlocked the door, he saw the whole shop turned upside down and every tool out of place; and, since he was still confused about how he had come back to his own room, he was promptly assailed by new thoughts that cancelled out the old ones.

Now, while he was pondering these matters, unsure whether he was waking or dreaming, but still happy to be Grasso again and in possession of what was his, along came Matteo's two brothers who, finding him thus absorbed, pretended not to know him; and one of them said: 'Good day, master.' Grasso turned round and recognized them, but did not return their greeting. With no time to think things over and decide on a reply, he simply said: 'What do you want?' One of them answered: 'The fact is that we have a brother called Matteo who was arrested for debt a few days ago and it's affected him so badly that he's gone a bit crazy. It's a shame on our family, but that's the way he is; and among other things, he says he's not Matteo (which is his name), but the master of this workshop who seems to be someone called Grasso. And though we've given him a good telling-off and had him properly warned, we still can't manage to cure him of this folly or stupidity or whatever it is. Yesterday evening we even brought in the priest of Santa Felicità (that's our parish, and he's a good man) and our brother promised him that he would drop this crazy idea. Then he dined with us quite agreeably and fell asleep there in front of us. But this morning, without anyone hearing him, and maybe long before daybreak, he went out leaving the door open behind him. And where he went we don't know. That's why we've come to see if he might have turned up here or if you know anything about him.'

The fact that these men, who had paid to bail him out and who had taken him home and fed him and given him a bed, did not recognize him as their brother—all this seemed to Grasso a proof that he had indeed become himself again; especially because he had just come from his own home. Almost bursting his breeches for sheer joy, he thought for a moment that he might have a laugh at their expense, and said: 'If he's a child, I'd look for him at the Foundlings' Hospital.' But he soon gave up the idea. He had been busy mending the blade of a plane and grasping it firmly in his hand (a very big hand), he looked them straight in the face. Seeing that he was not in the mood they expected, they feared that he might throw it at them and decided to beat a hasty retreat.

The truth was that Grasso had no such intention; nevertheless, when they had left, he still could not work out what had happened, and so he decided to leave his shop for a while and walk as far as Santa Maria del Fiore. This would give him time to think things over and find out whether he was Grasso or Matteo by meeting other men—even though the fact that he had slept in his own house and that the two brothers had not recognized him as Matteo made the matter almost certain. Then again, mulling over the old questions of whether it had been dream or reality and who he really was, he kept going to get his cloak, then forgetting it and turning to something else, and then coming back for the cloak until he was totally confused. Yet, at last, he did manage to take the cloak, close the shutters of his shop, and set off for the church, behaving exactly as he had done with the cloak, taking four steps forward and three steps back. Finally he got there, saying to himself, 'This is a strange case: the judge can say what he likes, but I still don't know how it happened.' Then he thought: 'It wasn't just one person who mistook me for Matteo, it was everybody: so there must be something in it.' He tried to clear his head of such ideas and concentrate on the question of whether he had truly become Grasso again, but he could not free himself of the fear that he might go back to being Matteo or be transformed into someone else. With these thoughts jostling in his mind, he suddenly decided to find out what had been happening to Matteo in the meantime so that he could learn whether what the judge had told him was true or not. And since he did not think anyone was watching him, he kept pacing back and forth like a wounded lion—that, at least, is what those who saw him reported later.

It was a workday and there were few people about and nobody was watching him, so he felt that the church was a place where he could give vent to his feelings in this way. It was in this state that he came across Filippo and Donatello who were talking together as they usually did. This time, however, they were there on purpose and had been watching out to see Grasso come in. Filippo knew that Grasso had no idea that the whole thing had been a joke, and he could hardly have suspected them, for they were sure they had made a good job of covering their tracks. Filippo put on a cheerful face and went on a bit longer than usual to make his greeting more convincing: 'Things actually turned out quite well for my mother; the attack was almost over by the time I got home, and that's why I didn't send for you. It's happened to her before; that's what old folk are like. So I didn't see you after that. What were you doing last night? Have you heard this story about Matteo Mannini?' Grasso stared at the two of them, turning from one to the other, in bewilderment. 'What's it all about?' asked Donatello, and Filippo answered: 'Don't you know?' Then, turning to Grasso, he said: 'That evening when we were all together, sometime between eight and nine, it seems that he was arrested here near the piazza; and with the bailiffs was the man who had him arrested—I've no idea who he was, but it's irrelevant, anyway. And Matteo kept saying to the bailiffs and the guards: "What do you want? You're mistaking me for someone else; I'm not in debt to anyone, I'm Grasso the wood-worker. Is it me you want?"' Grasso found all this perfectly convincing and had no idea that Filippo was directly involved in the affair. Filippo went on: 'The man who was having him arrested was a debt-collector for a draper's shop and had been warned by the bailiff: "Mind what you're about, because it's your responsibility: if this isn't the man, you'll have to pay the costs, because we want to be paid; and besides, even though it's not our fault, we could still be in trouble ourselves." So he went up to Matteo, looked him in the face, and said: "He's try-ing to look like someone else, the scoundrel!" And then, after inspect-ing him again: "It's Matteo, all right, take him away; this time he'll have to pay up." As they led him away, Matteo kept repeating that he was Grasso the woodworker and insisting: "Here's the proof that I've just come from closing my shop," and he showed them a key.'

All this was indeed exactly what Grasso had done, and it was the young man who had reported it so precisely to Filippo, who now went on: 'And I hear it was just as much fun at the Merchants' Court. And you've really heard nothing about it? It was the funniest thing in the world.' Donatello pretended to know nothing about it: 'I remember they were talking about it yesterday in my workshop, but I was busy and had other things to think about, so I paid no attention. Now I remember that I did hear those names Matteo and Grasso and some-thing about "getting arrested", but it didn't strike me to ask about it because I didn't have Grasso in mind at the time. Come on, Filippo, give us the story, since you know all about it. Him being arrested and then claiming to be Grasso—that's a real laugh! How did it end up?' Filippo said: 'It's impossible that Grasso doesn't know about it. Where were you yesterday evening? Didn't anyone come to your shop and tell you? They say it's all over Florence,' and then, putting the knife in: 'Three or four times yesterday I meant to come to your shop for a talk, and then for some odd reason I didn't make it.' Grasso's gaze went back and forth between Filippo and Donatello as he wondered which to answer first, choking on his words and turning from one to the other like a man possessed, uncertain whether they were telling the truth or having him on. At last, with a deep sigh, he said: 'Filippo, these are surely strange things!' Filippo immediately grasped what he meant and could hardly keep from grinning: 'You said you'd heard nothing about it. How was that?' Then they wanted Grasso to sit down with them so that they could listen to him at their ease. Grasso regretted having spoken and, having no idea what to do, remained tongue-tied with embarrassment, because sometimes he thought they were speaking seriously and sometimes it seemed quite the contrary.

Right then, without any of them noticing, who should come along but Matteo himself, for he too had been on the lookout, as instructed by Filippo. And as luck would have it, he could not have arrived at a better time. Matteo greeted them, and Grasso, in his confusion, was about to say: 'Your brothers were in my shop just now, looking for you,' but then he stopped short. Filippo asked: 'Where have you come from, Matteo? We want to know; we were just talking about you, and now we're all here.' Then Donatello chipped in: 'Were you arrested one of these past nights? Tell me the truth, because Filippo says . . .' 'So what's new about someone getting arrested?' said Matteo; and then to Filippo who was looking him in the eye: 'I've come from home.' 'Oh,' said Filippo, 'people were saying you'd been arrested.' 'Well, I *was* arrested, and my debt was paid, and I got out, and here I am. What the devil's going on? Don't they have anything to talk about but my affairs? My mother's been nagging me all morning, from the minute I got home; and ever since I came back to town my brothers have had long faces and they look at me as if I were growing horns; and when they met me here they kept on asking: "What time did you go out this morning, and did you leave the door open?" I reckon they've gone crazy, and my mother too; I don't understand them. And then they say something about me being arrested and them paying my debt—crazy stuff!' Filippo said: 'So where have you been? I haven't seen you for several days.' Matteo answered: 'Look, Filippo, I'll tell you the plain truth. It's true that I was in debt to a draper's shop for six mint florins, and I kept them waiting for a while, because there was someone in Empoli* who owed me eight florins and I should have had them days ago because he'd promised me and I thought I could pay off my debt and still have some left over. On Saturday I promised my creditor he'd be paid on Tuesday without fail, because I was counting on the fellow from Empoli. Then the draper got this judgement against me—the fact is that I've been owing him for quite a while, but I was really short of money—and so, before he could do me some harm, I cleared off to our place near the Charterhouse.* I stayed there for two days and that's why you haven't seen me, because I only got back less than an hour ago.

'Now I went into the country on Tuesday after dinner and what happened to me there was the strangest thing you ever heard. I had nothing much to do and it was years and years since I'd been out there (we have the wine sent to us at vintage time and everything else in season). Well, I idled along the road, killing time, and stopped for a couple of drinks at Galluzzo so as not to bother our worker about supper—which meant that when I arrived it was night. I asked him for a light and went straight to bed. What I'm going to tell you now is a real laugh. I've said it once and I'll say it again: I reckon everybody's gone crazy, and maybe me more than the rest. I was getting dressed this morning down there in our country place, and I'd opened the window—to be honest, I don't know whether I'm dreaming now or whether I dreamed what I'm going to tell you—I feel like someone different this morning. It's a funny business, Filippo, but let it go. Our worker—the one who'd given me the lamp—he says: "Where were you yesterday?" And I say: "Didn't you see me yesterday night?" And he says: "Not me, when?" And I say: "Talk about forgetful! Didn't you light the lamp for me when it wouldn't burn?" And he says: "Yes, the night before last, but I didn't see you last night, nor all day neither; I thought you'd gone off to Florence and I was surprised you hadn't told me anything because I figured you must have come here for some reason." So I must have slept all day yesterday, and I asked the worker: "What day is it today?" and he told me it's Thursday. So there it is, Filippo, I must have slept one whole day and two whole nights without waking up—just one big sleep.'

Filippo and Donatello were all ears and pretended to be surprised. Filippo said: 'Whatever you ate last night must be pretty well digested by now,' and Matteo answered: 'I'm so hungry I can almost see the food.' 'Better not share a meal with you then,' said Donatello. But Grasso, thinking of all the things that had happened to him, was amazed to hear that Matteo had been sleeping for exactly that time, and he said to himself: 'There's no help for me, I must be going mad; I wouldn't have believed it three days ago, but now . . .' Matteo continued: 'But I dreamed the craziest things you've ever heard.' 'You're light-headed because your belly's empty,' said Filippo. Matteo went on: 'I just ran into a man from the draper's where I owe the six florins: he apologized and said it wasn't him who had got me arrested—he's the one who usually comes to ask for the money and he's a decent chap. Then he says: "Sorry about all the expenses you had." So as far as I can see, the debt's been paid off. That's how I understood what my mother and brothers were on about when I thought they'd gone crazy. As I was just saying, they paid the debt; but I still don't know how. I wanted to find out from the draper's man. Anyway, however it happened, it looks as if I was in prison all the time I thought I was sleeping. Filippo, you work it out for yourself because I have no idea. But I couldn't wait to tell you the tale and have a good laugh.' Then, turning to Grasso: 'I've spent most of this time between your house and your workshop. This will make you laugh. I find that I've paid a debt of several florins, and all the time I was sleeping I thought I was a different person—as sure as I'm standing here among you. But who knows whether I'm dreaming now or was dreaming then?' Donatello said: 'I don't quite understand; tell me again because I was thinking about something else. You're driving me crazy. You just said that you were out in the country.' Matteo replied: 'I know very well what I did.' 'He means in a dream,' added Filippo. 'Filippo understands me,' said Matteo.

Grasso did not say a word, but stood there bewildered, listening carefully to see whether Matteo had been him during that time. Filippo was as happy as a piglet having a scratch. While Grasso seemed totally lost, some of the group couldn't contain the odd giggle and people were now beginning to gather round. So Filippo took Grasso by the hand and said: 'Let's go up into the choir stalls for a while so that we won't have this crowd round us, for this is the best story I've heard in my whole life. This is one I want to hear. You tell me your story, Matteo, and you'll hear another from me later on, one that the whole town is telling—because you make me suspect that these two stories are one and the same.'

They all sat down in a corner of the choir stalls where they could easily see each other (in those days the choir was between two big pillars just before you come to the apse),* and there was a brief silence because Filippo seemed to be waiting for Matteo to speak and Matteo was waiting for Filippo. Filippo was the first to speak and, turning to Matteo (who was playing his part very well), rather than upsetting Grasso, he laughed and said: 'Hear what they're talking about all over Florence; I've already told it to these friends; and then we'll hear your story, since you want me to speak first. They're saying you were arrested on Monday.' 'Me, arrested?' said Matteo. 'Yes, for that debt you mentioned,' and Filippo turned to Donatello: 'You see, there was some truth in it.' Donatello said to Matteo: 'It must have been when I found you knocking at Grasso's door the other night.' 'When? I don't remember ever knocking at his door.' 'What? You never knocked at his door? Didn't I speak to you there?'

Matteo feigned surprise and Filippo carried on: 'And they say that on the way to the prison you kept protesting to the bailiffs and to the fellow who had you arrested, "You've mistaken me for someone else; I'm not the man you want, I'm not in debt to anybody", and you defended yourself by insisting that you were Grasso here. And now you claim you were out in the country and, by your own account, sleeping in your bed at that very hour. How could that be?' 'They can say what they like,' replied Matteo, 'but you must be joking: I was down in the country, as I told you, precisely to avoid getting arrested, for the truth is I was dead scared. And as for what Donatello was just saying, I'll swear on the altar that neither then nor ever did I knock at Grasso's door. Now listen to what really happened which is a world away from what you've heard. I asked a notary friend of mine who works for the authorities at the Signoria to get me a guarantee against arrest for debt and to send it to me in the country. I expected to receive it by yesterday. Early this morning the notary sent a messenger with a letter saying that the Counsellors* had not assembled yet because they were all down in the country and since there was no other business the Priors didn't want to bring them back just for guarantees against debt. He added that if I wanted to avoid arrest I could stay away from the city for a few more days. But I came back and kept a sharp lookout; now, since the debt's been paid, everything's all right. Filippo and Donatello, that's the honest truth. But what I dreamed in the meantime, that's a real laugh, Filippo, and I'm not making it up. I never dreamed anything that felt more real. I thought I was in this fellow's house'—and he touched Grasso—'and that his mother was my mother and I was chatting with her just like with my own mother; I was eating and talking about my own business and she was answering me so that I can still remember a thousand things she said. Then I went to bed in that house and when I got up I went to Grasso's workshop, feeling as if I wanted to work just the way I've seen him do a thousand times when I've been with him there; but there wasn't a single tool in its proper place, so I put everything back in order.'

Grasso was staring at him like a madman, for those very tools had just been in his hands. Matteo went on: 'Then, when I tried to use those tools, none of them worked for me and they were all the same;

I put some back in the wrong places, meaning to put them in order when I had time, and I picked up others; but it made no difference. And I seemed to be answering people who came to ask me something just as if I were Grasso, for honestly that's the way it felt. And I went to eat and then came back to the shop, and in the evening I locked up and went home to bed, as I said; and the house looked just the way it is and as I've seen it myself when I've been there with Grasso, as he knows.'

Grasso had been silent for an hour and he did not think there was anything he could say that would be of any help with Filippo who was quick to catch people out, but Matteo's story had convinced him that he was now snarled up in a hopeless tangle. That dream of one day and two nights seemed to have lasted exactly the same time as his own troubles. Filippo and Donatello put on a great show of astonishment as they heard it, and then Filippo said: 'So it seems that you weren't the one who was arrested, and yet you say that the debt was paid off while you were down in the country: this is a skein that Aristotle himself couldn't unwind.'

Pursing his lips and shaking his head, Grasso may have been thinking over Matteo's story about becoming him and also about what the judge had told him at the Merchants' Court, for he said: 'These are strange things, Filippo, and from what I hear they've happened before. Matteo has spoken and you two have had your say, and I'd have something to add myself, but it would probably make you think I'm crazy, so I'm going to keep my mouth shut. That's enough, Filippo, let's just stop talking about it.' At that moment he really thought that what the judge had told him was a manifest truth, since there was so much evidence to support it; and he certainly believed that he had been Matteo and Matteo had been him—though Matteo, having been asleep, had been plagued with fewer troubles and suffered less than the man he had become.

But now he truly believed that he was Grasso once again, since it was clear from the story he had heard that Matteo was no longer Grasso. And as his mother had not yet returned from Polverosa, he was impatient to see her and ask whether she had been in Florence during that time, and who it was that was with her in the house that evening when he had knocked on the door, and who had opened his shop in the meantime. Then he took his leave of his friends who tried in vain to make him stay—although their urgings were gentle and courteous, partly because they did not want to upset him again and partly because they needed to give vent to a laughter they could no longer control. But Filippo did say this much: 'We must have supper together one of these evenings,' and Grasso left without replying.

Need you ask if Filippo, Donatello, and Matteo burst into laughter? To those who saw and heard them they seemed even crazier than Grasso, especially Donatello and Matteo who simply could not contain themselves. Filippo kept grinning and looking from one to the other.

Grasso meanwhile decided to shut the shop and go out to Polverosa; there he found his mother who told him that she had not been to Florence and explained why she had stayed away. Grasso thought this over and, as he returned to his senses and to Florence, concluded that it had been a practical joke, though he could not understand how it had worked out. But that was how it appeared to him since in all that time his mother had been away from Florence and the house had remained empty. He did not want to expose himself to ridicule or defend himself if someone asked him about the prank; and above all he was worried that he would not be able to face up to Filippo.

That is why the woodworker decided to go to Hungary.* He remembered that he had already been asked to go and he set about finding the man who had invited him, an old colleague from the days when they had studied inlaying together under Master Pellegrino in Via delle Terme. This young man had left for Hungary a few years before and had done very well with the help of Filippo Scolari, better known as our fellow citizen Pippo Spano* who was then captain–general of Sigismund's army. This Sigismund* was the king of Hungary and son of King Charles of Bohemia: a wise and prudent king, he was later elected emperor in the time of Pope Gregory XII and was crowned Caesar by Pope Eugene IV. Pippo Spano welcomed all Florentines who possessed some intellectual or manual skill, for he was a most worthy lord who loved his countrymen most sincerely and was loved by them in return for all the assistance he provided. Now about this time Master Pellegrino had come to Florence to see if he could recruit some masters of his craft since he had so many commissions in Hungary, and more than once he had tried to persuade Grasso to go with him, promising that he would become rich in no time. Grasso ran across him by chance, went up to him, and said: 'You've often tried to convince me to go to Hungary with you, and I've always said no. But now something awkward has happened and I've fallen out with my mother; so if you still want me, I've decided to go with you. But if you agree, let it be tomorrow, because if I hang around any longer, I won't be able to leave.' Master Pellegrino answered that he would be delighted to have him, but that he couldn't leave the following morning because he had business still to finish; but Grasso could leave whenever he liked and wait for him in Bologna where he would join him in a few days. Grasso was satisfied with that. After they had reached agreement on everything, Grasso returned to his workshop and picked up some of his tools and a few trinkets, together with some money that he kept there; after which, he went to Borgo San Lorenzo and hired a horse to take him as far as Bologna. The next morning he climbed into the saddle and went off down the Bologna road as if he were being hunted, without a word to his relatives or anyone else. But he did leave at home a letter addressed to his mother, telling her to use whatever was left behind in the workshop as guarantee for a regular income because he was going to Hungary and intended to stay there for some years.

In the short time before he mounted his horse and left Florence, he showed himself as little as possible, but he could not entirely avoid walking in the street, and as he passed by he could hear people discussing what had happened to him, and everyone was laughing and joking about it. And he overheard someone saying that it had been a great prank. The first to leak the story had been the fellow who had him arrested, and the second was the judge who had been with him in jail. In a hilarious meeting with this judge, Filippo had asked what Grasso had been saying in jail and then revealed the whole plot; and amid fits of laughter the judge had told him everything. All over Florence people were saying that the author of the prank was Filippo Brunelleschi, which confirmed what Grasso already suspected because he knew all too well what Filippo was like. He saw that he had been made a fool of and knew that it was Filippo's idea. All this strengthened his determination. And this is how Grasso came to leave Florence and go with his friend to Hungary.

The friends of the supper party continued to get together from time to time; and the next time they met, it was in the same old place, Tomaso Pecori's house. And meaning to have a good laugh about the prank, they invited the judge who had been detained in the Merchants' Court. When he learned who they were, he was happy to accept, partly because he already knew some of them, partly to find out more about the whole business, and partly to tell them his side of the story because he could see they were eager to hear it. They also called the draper's man who was with the bailiff, and Matteo and the two brothers who had led the dance from the prison to their fireside at home. They would have liked to have the bursar from the Merchants' Court, but he could not come. The judge heard the whole story with pleasure and then told them about the questions Grasso had asked and how he had answered them by bringing in Apuleius and Circe and Actaeon and his own worker to make it seem more plausible: 'And if anything else had struck my mind, I would have used that too.' Laughing all the time, they switched from one episode to another, just as it occurred to them.

And looking back on how the affair had turned out, they saw how lucky they had been with the judge and the priest and everything else. Then the judge gave them a little speech, saying that in all his life he had never been at a banquet where the food had been better or more abundant, and most of it was so good that rarely if ever could such delicacies be found on the tables of emperors or kings, let alone minor princes or private men like themselves. And he doubted whether anyone could have seen through the trick, given the foresight and subtlety of Filippo.

When Grasso and his colleague arrived in Hungary, they set to work and proved so fortunate that in a few years they became very wealthy for men of their class and profession. They were helped by Pippo Spano, who appointed Grasso as master engineer so that he was now called Master Manetto of Florence and enjoyed a high reputation. Spano took Grasso with him in the field when he went on military manoeuvres, paid him well, and found many occasions to reward him with rich gifts. Spano was, indeed, as magnanimous as if he had been born a king, generous with everybody, but especially with Florentines—and this, apart from his other qualities, was something that had attracted Grasso to Hungary. When he was not in the field, Grasso was able to look after the many commissions that he worked on both with his colleague and by himself.

Later on, over a period of several years, Grasso often came back to Florence for a few months at a time. And the first time he was back, when Filippo asked him why he had left Florence in such a hurry and without consulting his friends, he told him the whole story, laughing all the while, with a thousand comical details that only he could know about, such as being and not being Grasso and wondering whether it had been a dream or whether he was dreaming when he remembered it, so that Filippo laughed more than he had ever done in all his life. Then Grasso looked him in the eye and said: 'But you know all this better than I do, for you really made a fool of me that day in Santa Maria del Fiore.' 'Never you mind,' answered Filippo. 'This will make you more famous than anything you did with Pippo Spano or King Sigismund: people will still be talking about you a hundred years from now.' Grasso laughed, and so did Filippo, no less than before. For all that, Grasso never wanted to be with anybody but Filippo when he had a bit of spare time, although he knew full well that Filippo had set up the whole affair; and Filippo would joke with Grasso, saying: 'I knew from the start that I would make you rich; there are plenty of people who wish they were Grasso and been fooled like you were. You really have got rich out of it, and hobnobbed with the emperor of the world and Pippo Spano and so many other princes and barons.' And in fact, this visit of Grasso and those that followed gave Filippo ample opportunity to question him more often and at greater length, and to ask in minute detail about what the judge and the young draper's man had said to him, for most of the truly funny things had happened, so to speak, in Grasso's mind. This then is how it was that the story came to be written down in detail and with full knowledge of the facts, for Filippo repeated it several times and the present version is derived from those who heard him, who declare that it would be impossible to recount all the details without leaving out some amusing parts, whether they belong to Filippo's version or to the story of what really occurred. Therefore, after the death of Filippo, the story was taken down from people who had heard him tell it several times: from a man called Antonio di Matteo dalle Porte, from Michelozzo and his heir and disciple Andreino da San Gimignano, from Scheggia, Feo Belcari, and Luca della Robbia, from Antonio di Migliore Guidotti and Domenico Michelino, and from many others.* Although something was written about it in Filippo's time, it accounted for less than a third of what happened and was fragmentary and defective in many places. But perhaps it did some good in that it saved the story from being completely lost. Thanks be to God. Amen.

MASUCCIO SALERNITANO

SAINT GRIFFIN'S DRAWERS
Il Novellino (The Book of Tales) 3

*Fra Niccolò da Narni consummates his love for Agata. When they
are interrupted by her husband she tells him that the friar has cured
her sickness with certain relics. The husband is upset when he finds the
friar's drawers at the bedhead, but she manages to convince him that
they once belonged to Saint Griffin. The friar then takes the drawers
back to church in a solemn procession.*

To the famous poet Giovanni Pontano*

Exordium

IF from true friends as from oneself, my most excellent Pontano, one
seeks honour and ease, then I, although counted among your most
humble friends, am obliged and duty-bound to seek the same for you.
I know you to be endowed with such singular virtues that we may
rightly call you the light of orators and the mirror of poetry, to say
nothing of your many other talents; and thus, when I see all these
qualities soiled by one single stain which is easy to efface, I cannot
remain silent. I refer to your constant and close association with monks
and friars of every kind, for you yourself may judge that in a man of
your integrity this is a greater and more reprehensible fault than plotting with heretics; for we see that those who consort with them are
none other than usurers, fornicators, and ruffians who use this hypocritical behaviour to deceive their fellow men. Therefore, not being
a wolf yourself, you should not line your cloak with a wolfskin. I beg
you, leave this shameful and damned path and resolve not only to give
up such a bad habit, but also to ban such people from your house with
an eternal decree as if they were infected with the plague. Thus you
will avoid suspicion in the future and prevent them from following
their usual practice and using your friendship as a way of corrupting
your household. And to make sure that you do not run towards the

precipice, in addition to these arguments I offer you the following tale. By the authority of my discourse and as a guide to your future conduct, I shall show what profit the friendship of a holy friar brought to a doctor of Catania who was a devoted follower of that order, although he was a very jealous man; and how, by the subtle craft of his wife and the friar, the poor man was betrayed and made a fool.

The Narrative

Catania, famed and noble as we all know, is counted among the most notable cities of the island of Sicily; there, not so long ago, lived a doctor of medicine called Rogero Campisciano. Though well advanced in years, he had taken to wife a young girl called Agata, from a highly honourable family in that city, who was, according to the general opinion, the most lovely and gracious lady in the whole island, so that her husband loved her no less than his own life. And since love rarely if ever comes without jealousy, he very quickly became so unreasonably jealous that he forbade her to converse not only with strangers but even with her own friends and family. And although he was very involved with the Friars Minor* as guardian of their finances, procurator of the order, and their servant in all things, yet still, to be on the safe side, he had insisted that she should avoid their company no less than that of dishonest laymen.

Now shortly after, it so happened that a friar called Fra Niccolò da Narni arrived in Catania. He seemed a pious soul, with his heavy clogs like shackles and with leather on the front of his cloak, going around with hypocrisy up to his twisted neck; and yet he was young, handsome, and well built. Not only had he studied in Perugia and become a master in the doctrine taught there, but he was also a famous preacher and it was well known that he had been a companion of Saint Bernardino,* some of whose relics he claimed to possess; and God had shown their power by many miracles. For this reason and because they were devoted to the order, large numbers of the faithful came to hear his sermons. One morning, as he was preaching, among the assembled women he saw Madonna Agata who seemed to shine like a precious ruby surrounded by white pearls; and casting sidelong glances at her without interrupting his sermon, he kept thinking how happy a man would be if he proved worthy of the love of such a fair young woman. Agata, as people do when they listen to a sermon, was looking steadily at him; she found him exceptionally good-looking and, without any unfitting sensuality, began to wish that her husband were as handsome as the preacher; and at the same time she determined that the friar should hear her confession. With this in mind, as soon as she saw him come down from the pulpit, she went towards him and begged him to give her audience. The friar was inwardly delighted, but in order to hide his sinful thoughts he replied that it was not his office to hear confessions. To which the woman said: 'Don't I have any privileges with you for the love of my husband Master Rogero?' The friar answered: 'Since you're the wife of our procurator, you may follow me, and for his sake I shall hear you.'

And when they had withdrawn to where the friar usually heard confessions, she knelt before him and began to make her formal confession. When she had told some of her sins, she turned to the excessive jealousy of her husband and asked the friar if, with his skills, he could find some way to get that sick fantasy out of the doctor's head, thinking perhaps that such an infirmity could be cured by herbs or poultices, just as her husband cured his patients.

Delighted by this request and convinced that good fortune was opening the path he sought, the friar comforted her with many fine words and then continued as follows: 'My daughter, it's hardly surprising that your husband should be so very jealous; if he were not, I would consider him distinctly unwise, and so would everyone else. And you shouldn't blame him, since it proceeds simply from Nature which has endowed you with such angelic beauties that they can't possibly be possessed without jealousy.'

The woman laughed at this and, after a few more jests, seeing that it was time to rejoin her companions, she asked the friar to give her the absolution; but, heaving a sigh, he turned to her with a pitiful look: 'My daughter, a man who is bound himself cannot set others free; and since, in this short time, you have bound me, I cannot absolve you or myself without your help.'

The young woman, who was a Sicilian, immediately knew the score and was highly pleased to find him so handsome and so enamoured of her; yet still she was surprised that friars should bother about such things. It was not just that, since her earliest years and by the solemn injunction of her husband, she had never had any converse with monks and friars; she was firmly convinced that, compared to other men, friars were like chickens who had been castrated. But since it was clear that he was a cock not a capon, she was stirred by a desire she had never felt before and decided to give him all her love: 'Dear Father, leave the pain to me for I came here as a free woman and I return a slave to love and you.' The friar, glorying in his triumph as never before, replied: 'Since our desires are the same, why not find a way to escape this harsh prison and enjoy our flowering youth together?' To which she replied that she would gladly do so if she could: 'And now I come to think of it,' she added, 'for all his jealousy, there is still a way for us to satisfy our desires. Almost every month I have a burning pain in my heart, so sharp that I practically lose my senses. So far no medical treatment has had the slightest effect, but older women have told me that it comes from the uterus. Now since I'm young and would be perfectly able to have children but for the age of my husband, I suggest that one of these days, when he goes into the country on business, I should pretend to be troubled with the usual pain; I shall send for you and ask you to lend me a relic of Saint Griffin.* You will have made yourself ready on the sly, and so, with the help of my trusty maidservant, we shall be together just the way we like.'

The friar was overjoyed: 'My dear daughter, may God bless you for having such a good idea. I think we should carry out your plan; and what's more, I shall bring one of my brethren so that your trusty maidservant won't feel neglected.'

With that decision and with burning amorous sighs, they parted. When the woman got home, she told her maid all about the plan she had made with the friar for their mutual pleasure and satisfaction; and, very happy at the news, the maid answered that she was always ready to do whatever was asked of her. Now as good fortune would have it and as his wife had predicted, Master Rogero went out of town the following morning; and so, without wasting any time, she pretended to have the usual pains and began to invoke Saint Griffin. The maid advised her: 'Why don't you send for his holy relics, since everyone believes they are so miraculous?' The woman, as they had agreed beforehand, answered as if she could hardly speak: 'Yes indeed, go and send someone to get them.' 'I'll go for them myself,' said the maid with a pitying voice. Then she hurried off and delivered the message to the friar who promptly set out, accompanied, as he had promised, by one of his brethren, a young man perfectly fitted for the work in hand. When they came into the bedroom, Fra Niccolò respectfully approached the bed where the woman, who lay eagerly waiting, greeted him with great humility: 'Father, pray for me to God and glorious Saint Griffin.' To which the friar replied: 'God make us worthy of his aid! But there must be sincere devotion on your part; if you want to receive God's grace through the powers of the relics I have brought with me, you must first show contrition in holy confession, for with the soul once healed we may more easily cure the body.' 'That is all I think of and all I long for; let us do it straightaway, I beg you.'

And with this, having very properly dismissed everyone else from the room except for the maidservant and the friar's young companion, they locked the door so that nothing could disturb them and were soon locked in wild embraces. Fra Niccolò, having climbed into bed, eager to get a leg over without anything in the way and perhaps feeling perfectly safe, took off his drawers and threw them to the bedhead. Then he and the lovely woman in his arms began the sweet and long-desired chase where his well-trained hound, which had been kept on a leash for so long, was soon bold enough to bring two hares out of the same form; and he was calling up his dog for a third when they heard the clatter of horse's hoofs from the street outside. It was Master Rogero, already home from his business in the country. The friar leaped out of bed and, overcome as he was with fear and pain, completely forgot to take the drawers that he had put at the bedhead. The maidservant, no less displeased at being taken from the task in hand, threw open the door and called the people who were waiting in the next room, announcing that her mistress had been perfectly cured by the grace of God; and they all trooped in freely, giving praise and thanks to God and Saint Griffin.

Meanwhile Master Rogero had made his way into the room and seeing all this commotion, he was upset to see his beloved wife in pain once again and even more to find friars coming to frequent his house. But Agata, recognizing the change in his face, said: 'My dear husband, honestly I would be dead by now, if our father the preacher had not come to my aid with the relics of Saint Griffin; he placed them near my heart and immediately, like a little fire doused out by a bucket of water, all my pains disappeared.'

The husband believed her and was more than happy to hear what a salutary remedy had been found for such a chronic illness; not only did he thank God and Saint Griffin, but turning at last to the friar, he expressed his infinite gratitude for all the good he had done. Then, after some holy and devout conversation, the friar and his companion took their proper leave. But on the way, feeling his good hound* swinging freely to and fro, the friar remembered with dismay that he had left the leash at the bedhead. His companion, however, having heard the whole story, managed to put his mind at rest, since surely the maidservant would be the first to find the leash and would hide it. And with a laugh he added: 'Master, you show that you're not used to feeling uncomfortable, since you like to give your hound a long leash all of a sudden wherever you are; but perhaps you're copying the Dominicans whose dogs always go without any leash at all and catch plenty of game. But still, dogs who've been kept on a leash are fiercer and bite more firmly when they are set free to hunt.'

And the friar: 'That's true enough, and God forbid that my mistake should cause any scandal! But how did you manage with the prey I left in your claws? I know that my sparrowhawk caught two partridges in one flight and was ready for a third when Master Rogero turned up—if only he'd broken his neck first!' 'I may not be a blacksmith, but I did my best to forge two nails in one fire; and I had finished one and was just about to put the head on the other when the maid started cursing the day she was born and saying: "That's my master at the door!" So I went along with you, leaving my work unfinished.' 'May God grant that I return to the hunt,' said the friar, 'and so you can make nails by the hundred, since that's what you want.' 'I don't deny it' came the answer, 'but one feather of your two partridges is worth all the nails in Milan.' The friar laughed and they went on with their jests, secretly enjoying the witty contest.

Now as soon as the friars had left, Master Rogero began to cuddle his wife, touching her throat and her breasts and asking if the pain had been very severe; and as he went on talking, he reached towards the pillow to settle it under her head and caught the ribbon of the drawers left by the friar. Pulling them out and recognizing them immediately as what friars wear, his look darkened: 'What the devil does this mean, Agata? What are these friar's drawers doing here?' The young woman was quick on the uptake and her natural intelligence had been awakened and sharpened by love; without hesitation she answered: 'After everything I've told you, husband, what could they be if not the miraculous drawers once worn by the glorious Saint Griffin—one of his famous relics that the preaching father brought here? Through their power God has had mercy on me and I know that I've been freed from all pain. And to be absolutely sure and for my own devotion, when he wanted to take them away, I begged him to leave them with me until vespers; and afterwards he could come by himself or send someone else for them.'

This explanation was so prompt and reasonable that the husband either believed it or pretended to believe it; but being jealous by nature, the episode had put his mind in turmoil, constantly blown this way and that by opposing winds. Still, having heard his wife's reply, he calmed down and said nothing more. The woman, however, being wise enough to see that he was still worried, thought up a new way of removing all suspicion from his breast, and turning to the maidservant she said: 'Go straight to the convent and tell the preacher that he should send for the relics he left me because, thanks be to God, as things stand, I no longer need them.'

The trusty maid understood exactly what her mistress really wanted and hurried off to the convent where she asked them to call the preacher. Coming to the entrance and thinking perhaps that she had brought back the souvenir he had left behind, he greeted her with a smiling face: 'What news?' She answered sharply: 'Not good, thanks to your carelessness; and things could have been much worse if my mistress hadn't been so smart.' 'What's wrong?' said the friar. Then the maid told him what had happened, adding that she thought he should waste no time about coming to retrieve the relic in ceremonial fashion. 'In the morning,' said the friar and dismissed her with a promise to put everything right that had gone wrong. Then he went straight to the Father Guardian and spoke as follows: 'Father, I've just made a grave mistake, but since it's something you can punish later, I beg you to help me without delay, for the matter is so urgent that it needs to be put right *in promptu*.'* When the friar had told the whole story as briefly as he could, the Father Guardian was more than a little troubled and reproached him bitterly for his imprudence: 'What a great feat, what a fine fellow you are! So you really thought you were safe? If you couldn't manage without taking them off, shouldn't you at least have found a better place to hide them— next to your chest or up your sleeve or anywhere else about you? But you're so used to provoking these scandals that you never think of the burden you place on our consciences or of the damage to our reputation. Honestly, I don't know what keeps me from locking you up as you deserve, without mercy. But that can wait for another time; what matters now is the honour of the order; and we need an immediate solution, not a sermon from me.'

He had the bell rung to call the chapter, and when the friars were all assembled, he told them how that day, in the house of Master Rogero, through the power of their own Saint Griffin's drawers, God had worked a most conspicuous miracle. After this summary of events, he persuaded them to go immediately to the house of the said Master Rogero, whence, with honour and glory to God and for the increase of Saint Griffin's miraculous works, they would bring back the relics in a solemn procession.

Thus, two by two, with the cross carried ahead and with the Father Guardian, dressed in a rich cope, bearing the tabernacle from the altar in his arms, they proceeded amid great silence to the doctor's house. And when Master Rogero came forward to greet the Guardian and ask the reason for this unusual ceremony, the smiling Guardian had his answer ready:

'My dear Master, the rules of our order stipulate that when we bring the relics of our saints to the house of someone who has requested them, we should do so in secret so that if the invalid, through some fault of his own, fails to receive the desired grace, they can be taken back no less quietly without the least prejudice to their miraculous fame. But when, through these same relics, God has shown us a conspicuous miracle, then we must conduct them back to the church with all possible ceremony and solemnity, thus making manifest that miracle and giving it public recognition. And since, as you know, your wife has been freed from a most dangerous sickness by the power of our relics, we have come in this solemn manner to take them home.'

The doctor, seeing the whole chapter so piously united, judged that they could never have come in such numbers for an evil purpose. With perfect faith in the Guardian's false explanations, banishing all his suspicions and saying 'You are most welcome,' he took the Guardian by the hand and led him and the preacher into the room where his wife lay. She was not sleeping and had used the time to wrap the drawers in a fragrant white cloth. This the Guardian opened and when he had kissed the drawers with great reverence, he made the doctor and his wife and finally all who were in the room devoutly to do the same. Then, placing the drawers in the tabernacle he had brought for that purpose, he gave a sign to his brethren who in unison began to sing the *Veni Creator Spiritus*.* And thus, proceeding through the city, accompanied by a huge crowd, they brought them to the church and placed them upon the high altar where for several days they left them exposed for the devotion of the people who by then had already heard of the miraculous event.

Master Rogero was eager to increase popular reverence for the order, and so, as he went about his business, both in and out of the city, wherever he happened to be, he told everybody of the solemn miracle that God had worked in his house through the power of Saint Griffin's drawers. And while he was thus occupied, Fra Niccolò and his companion did not forget to go on with their profitable hunt, to the considerable pleasure of Madonna Agata and her maidservant. And indeed, deep down, quite apart from any sensual pleasure, she really did think that this activity was the only remedy for her painful condition since it took place so close to the cause of her suffering. Moreover, being the wife of a doctor, she remembered hearing some-one cite that text of Avicenna* where he says that remedies applied often will help and that those applied continually will cure. Therefore, enjoying both one and the other, she knew that she had been freed from an incurable sickness of the uterus by the timely remedy of the holy friar.

Masuccio

Although all parts of this tale are full of pleasing material and fit to be reread and heard over again, I would, nonetheless, like them to be read in the presence of those who constantly stand ready to attack me, with biting reproaches, because I write against these tricksters, not only by showing the deception and adultery committed by the lecherous friar, but also by demonstrating clearly that his actions were like those of a notorious heretic and despiser of Christ's faith, works, and doctrine. This can be seen not just in what he actually did, but in the very idea of putting a pair of stinking drawers, swarming with fleas and full of a thousand other kinds of filth, in the chosen vessel and true receptacle of the sacred body of the Son of God. Read the terrible Passion of Christ and you will find that not even the perfidious Jews, for all the iniquity and shame of that murder, ever showed him such monstrous contempt as this. So let the earth gape and swallow alive the whole crew, both the leaders and their idle followers—and not just for the punishment of the living but also as a fearful and eternal example to their fellows in the future. Moreover, to prove that the slanders of my enemies have no power to alter my decision to tell the truth about these soldiers of Satan, I intend next, whether they like it or not, to recount the cunning stratagem thought up by two other damned friars to collect money and make themselves prelates, as you shall hear when I tell of their false miracles which no power could prevent.

THE CASTILIAN STUDENT
Il Novellino (*The Book of Tales*) 45

A Castilian student, on his way to Bologna, falls in love with a woman in Avignon and agrees to pay a thousand ducats for her favours; then, full of regret for what he has done, he takes his leave. He happens to meet her husband and, not knowing who he is, tells him the whole story. Realizing that the woman in question is his wife, the husband takes the student back to Avignon where he forces his wife to repay the money, kills her, and loads the student with honours and gifts.

To the illustrious lord Don Enrico of Aragon*

Exordium

THE common folk, my lord, often cite the proverb 'Every promise is a debt'; and if this is true, as it obviously is, then all reason and honesty dictate that, as soon as he can, every debtor should satisfy those to whom he has made a promise. Therefore, remembering that I have made myself a debtor by promising you a tale, I have decided to free my tired shoulders from that heavy burden with the following story, in which you shall hear of the exceptional high-souled generosity shown by a French knight to a noble young Castilian. And although this virtuous behaviour will, no doubt, be highly commended by many people, I am convinced that there are some who, in a similar situation, would find it easier to preach than to practise.

The Narrative

Attracted by the ancient and illustrious reputation of its university, a noble young Castilian law student was determined to go to Bologna* and study there for his doctorate. His name was Messer Alonso da Toledo and he was not only young and endowed with many good qualities, but also very rich. And so, on the death of his father, a respected knight, he wasted no time before putting his good intentions into effect. Equipped with precious books, elegant clothes, good horses, and a fitting number of servants, accompanied by a baggage train and with a thousand florins in his purse, he set off for Italy. After many days, having left the kingdom of Castile and crossed that of Catalonia, he entered France and arrived at Avignon. There, whether to rest his horses or for some other reason, he chose to remain for a few days and took up lodgings at an inn.

The next day, attended by his servants, he went for a walk in the city and, as he crossed from one street to another, as chance would have it, he caught sight of a lady at a window. She was young and quite good-looking, but he thought he had never seen any woman whose beauty could be compared with hers; and indeed he found her so attractive that before he left that street he was so much in love that no amount of argument could have cured him. Thus, forgetting the path of virtue, he vowed not to leave Avignon before he had obtained all or the greater part of her favours. He began to walk up and down in front of her house, and the lady, who knew how to put on an act, soon understood that the poor youth was so infatuated with her that he could hardly tear himself away. Seeing that he was still young and beardless, and judging from his clothes and his retinue that he must be rich and noble, she decided to use all her wiles to fleece him as thoroughly as she could. To get him to the stage where he would try and speak to her, she behaved like a becalmed ship that sends a skiff ashore to collect wood. In other words, she turned to an old servant who was well versed in such affairs and gave her work to do at the window where the young man could get to know her—which, of course, he was eager to do. They began to talk together and without much difficulty they soon exchanged confidences. The old servant reported everything to her mistress and carried messages back and forth until, at last, there was a clear agreement that the following night the lady would be waiting to give the youth her love, and he would bring her a thousand gold florins, which was all he had.

The long-desired hour came and the ill-advised young man went with his thousand florins to the house of Laura (for that was her name) who received him joyfully and flattered him outrageously. She received the promised money with great delight, and then, after some preliminary celebrations, they were off to bed. Messer Alonso was already in such a state that he hardly knew the difference between the beginning and the end of his task, and you can imagine that he spent the rest of the night satisfying his lust. When morning came, he got out of bed and, after arranging everything for a return to the venture so well begun, joined his servants who had been waiting wearily at the door and went back to the inn, feeling sleepy and vaguely repentant.

The lady was delighted to see how quickly she had won the jackpot, and she knew that the youth was so firmly hooked that Bologna and the law had gone clean out of his mind. Yet still, even before he left her, she had decided not to receive him again if he should think of enjoying her a second time. Messer Alonso, meanwhile, was happy with the arrangement they had made, and expected the lady to give him an even warmer welcome the following night.

So when the day was done and night came, he went as before to Laura's door; there his repeated knocking received no answer but silence, and at last he realized that in one fell swoop he had lost the lady, his honour, and his whole fortune. With death in his heart, he returned to the inn and that night there was not a moment free from troubled and anxious thoughts. When morning came, seeking a final proof that he had been rejected, he went back to walk around the lady's house and found the doors and windows locked along with many other signs that he had indeed been cunningly betrayed and made a fool of by that wicked woman; after which, he went back to his men, so distressed and desperate that more than once he was about to plunge a dagger into his breast; but then, holding back for fear of the worst, he decided to be off. And since he had not a single coin left in his purse, he decided to sell one of his best mules. This enabled him to pay the landlord and with the little that was left, he proceeded through Provence on his way to Italy, weeping and sighing, and tormented above all by the thought that whereas he had intended to study in a manner befitting his noble rank, he now had to go bartering and borrowing from inn to inn on the road to Bologna, and once there get by somehow as poor students do.

Thus he journeyed on, needy and anxious, until he came to an inn at Trayques* where, by a strange coincidence, the husband of Madonna Laura had taken lodgings that very evening. He was an accomplished and gracious knight, very eloquent and of great authority, who was returning from a mission to the Pope in the service of the king of France. As he sat at table, he asked the landlord if there was any other gentleman staying at the inn, because if so he would like to have his company, this being the courteous custom of French knights on their travels. The landlord replied that there was a Spanish student who, from what his servants said, was on his way to Bologna and who had become so melancholy that he had gone two days without eating. At this the knight, moved by natural kindness, insisted that the student come and dine with him, and went himself to fetch him. And finding him sad and depressed in his room, the knight took his hand in familiar fashion and, without any further greeting, announced: 'You must absolutely come and dine with me.' Since the knight's appearance showed him to be of high rank, the youth made no reply but followed him to table. And when the meal was over and the servants had been dismissed, the knight asked Messer Alonso who he was, what was the purpose of his journey, and finally, if he might be so bold, what was the cause of his melancholy. Messer Alonso, who could hardly speak a word without deep sighing, answered the first two questions as briefly as he could; but as to the last, he begged the knight not to insist. But having learned who the youth was and why he had left home, the knight remembered that he had already heard of the Castilian's noble father, and all this increased his desire to know what exactly had caused him such extraordinary suffering on his journey. Despite the young man's reluctance, the knight kept on nagging him until at last, without further ado, he told the whole story from beginning to end—including not only the pleasure he had taken with the lady, but all the details down to the name of her husband. And he added that he had often been close to taking his own life, distressed as he was by the shame of being so deceived and by the loss of so much money.

By persisting with his questions, the knight had found what he never expected and even less hoped to hear. Only those who have had the same experience can truly judge how deeply he was grieved by the news, how stunned he was, and, given that his honour was at stake, how far his anguish exceeded that of the student. Nevertheless, with remarkable wisdom, he managed to control his anguish. There was a pause as he let the pain of it sink in, but then he had an idea about how he should handle the matter and turned to the young man: 'My son,' he said, 'your own reason and experience will tell you how badly you've behaved and how childishly simple you've been to let yourself be deceived by that vile whore. And truly, if I thought that my reproaches would do you any good or if I thought that we were going to be together forever, then you would never see me tire of condemning your immense folly. But since I see that you need practical help more than rebuke, I think that this time the painful recognition of your fault will be punishment enough. So be of good heart, and banish all those mad ideas of harming yourself, because you'll find that I mean to treat you as if you were my own son. As you see, I'm a traveller and a stranger here and in no position to do as I want, so would you mind coming with me for a few days until I get back home? Then you can complete your journey properly equipped in the way you first intended. When I think of your famous forefathers and your own noble bearing, I simply cannot let you go to your studies in Bologna in a state of such strange and stubborn despair that poverty would prevent virtue from going hand in hand with nobility.'

Amazed at such kindness, the young man offered him all the thanks that his past sufferings and renewed youthful happiness allowed him to express, and after some further conversation they both went to rest. Early the following morning the whole party rode on towards France and, taking the shortcuts that knights are skilled in, they reached Avignon and entered the city late that evening. The knight then took Alonso by the hand and led him to his house which the youth immediately recognized—and not only the house, for there too was the lady of the house, coming to meet her husband with lighted candles and great celebration. As soon as he saw what the situation was, Alonso concluded that this was where his life would end, and he was so dizzy with fear that he could hardly dismount. But dismount he did at the urging of the knight, who took him by the arm and led him into the very room where, not so long before, he had been welcomed for his brief pleasure and to his lasting shame. The lady, in her turn, had recognized the student and guessed the trouble she was in with a terror and foreboding that is not hard to imagine. Supper was served and they all sat down to eat—the two men and the frightened woman—all three racked with anguish, but for different reasons. When the meal was over and they were alone, the knight turned to his wife and said: 'Laura, bring here the thousand gold florins that this man gave you and for which you sold your body and my honour and that of all our kin.'

At these words, the lady felt as if the roof had caved in and fallen on her head; and she seemed too dumbstruck to reply. But the knight, with a sudden severity, seized his dagger and threatened: 'You evil woman, do as I say without delay, unless you want to die.'

Seeing him so fierce and angry and realizing that there was no point in resisting, she went off, tearful and terrified, and came back with the florins and threw them on the table. The knight examined them and then took one and handed it to the youth, who was still so frightened that at every moment he expected to be killed along with the lady. But the knight said: 'Messer Alonso, it is only right that everyone involved in this troublesome affair should receive proper payment. From my wife here you received some pleasure along with an outrageous act of trickery, and for the dishonest price she charged you for this, she deserves to be numbered among the whores. Well now, a whore, however good-looking, cannot and should not earn more than a ducat for one single night; so I suggest that now you should pay her the proper price for the goods you bought.'

The wife was forced to take the one ducat and immediately did so. The knight now saw that the young man was too shamefaced and frightened to look him in the face and that he needed reassurance rather than anything else; so he said: 'My son, take back the money that you guarded so badly and spent even worse; and in future be warned not to buy such foul goods at so high a price. And since you left your home in search of honour, fame, and glory, do not waste your time and talents in lechery and lust. For this evening I shall no longer bother you with my words, so go and take your rest. And be reassured, for I promise, on my honour as a knight, that I would rather harm myself than even think of doing any harm to you or what is yours.'

Then, summoning his servants, he installed the young man, together with the money he had recuperated, in a luxurious bedroom that had been specially prepared for him. That done, before he went to bed himself, he gave his wife her last supper with a cunning poison. When morning came, he presented his guest with a gallant steed, along with many other rich and noble gifts; and after a light breakfast, he mounted and rode together with the young man and his party until they were ten miles outside the city. And as he took his leave, he said: 'Dear son, I may have given you back your property as well as your life, but this is not enough to fulfil my intentions towards you. Take, therefore, these small gifts, since I have no time to give you greater ones; and also this horse in exchange for the mule you sold. And as you make use of these gifts, remember your father, for it is as a true father that I want you to think of me from now on; bear that in mind at every moment and in every deed; and I will do the same, taking you as my only son for the rest of my life.'

He then embraced Alonso, who could hardly open his mouth to express his gratitude, overwhelmed as he was with tears of joy at such magnanimity and generosity. The knight bade him be silent for he himself was weeping; and so, without formal leave-taking, they kissed tenderly and went their separate ways. The knight returned to the city and in due time Messer Alonso reached Bologna; but since I have no further notice either of them or of their precious friendship, I shall write no more.

Masuccio

In my humble opinion, the knight of Avignon is to be praised no less for the way he punished his wicked wife than for his generosity to the noble Castilian, even though he was driven to the former by his sense of honour and duty, whereas to the latter he came of his own free and virtuous will. Moreover, I am not inclined to blame the gentle student as much as others might do, given that his noble character was such that when he was truly in the throes of passion he was not afraid to risk his wealth and his life in the service of his generous spirit. But enough has been said; and so, giving my pen a rest from these two men but not from the subject of magnanimity, I shall speak next of how three people of different ranks performed three singularly virtuous deeds*—so extraordinary, in fact, that it would be hard to praise one more than another.

SABBADINO DEGLI ARIENTI

THE PRIEST AND THE FRIAR
Le Porrettane (Tales from Porretta) 12

Some young men of Arezzo take a companion dressed up as a woman to dance at Monte San Savino;* the prior of the friars of Saint Augustine falls in love with him and is ridiculed.

HONOURABLE gentlemen, we were a group of fine lively young fellows from Arezzo and often used to go out to local feasts in the countryside to cool off and amuse ourselves. So it was that in mid-August we left Arezzo and went up to Monte San Savino where they celebrate the feast of the Queen of Heaven and hold a horse race; and after supper the local lads and lasses come and dance until sunset in the splendid castle square. With us we took a friend of ours, a priest of about sixteen years of age, a pleasant, witty, upstanding youth called Francesco di Ludomero to whom God had granted such features that whosoever looked him in the face might have thought he was seeing a beautiful young maiden. We decided to dress him up as a Florentine gentlewoman with a silk skirt, blouse, stockings, and a typically Florentine headdress, so that, with his costume and his feminine way of speaking, he really seemed a maiden sent down from Heaven. When we reached the place where they were dancing he gave a courteous greeting to all who there and was immediately seated in a place of honour among the ladies. And since, as you have heard, his beauty was so great as to seem miraculous, all the men and women at the feast turned their eyes towards him as if they could never have enough of gazing on his angelic face and contemplating the grace and dignity of his bearing. Some youths had already fallen in love with him and began to fight for the right to dance with him—the more so because he excelled all the ladies in his graceful Tuscan way of dancing.

Now in the square there was a convent of Augustinian friars whose prior, a most convivial friar called Fra Puccio, had come out to watch the dancing. Seeing our friend so elegantly dressed and so lovely, and believing that he was a woman, he immediately fell head over heels in love and thought that in all his life he had never seen so fair a creature. So when he heard that the young lady had come from Arezzo with a group of friends, he came up to one of us whom he knew already and asked: 'Who's that young Florentine lady who dances so gracefully?' And our friend answered: 'Why do you want to know?' 'Because she's a lovely creature, and I really admire her style.' From the friar's question and from the way he kept watching the dance, our friend guessed that he had lost his head and replied: 'She came with us; we brought her from Arezzo to join in the feast.' And when the friar went on to ask if the girl was a relative, he said: 'Enough! No more questions; if there's anything to do with her that I help you with, just ask me as if I were your son.' Then said the friar: 'I thank you, and since I've always loved and trusted you, I'll speak to you as a faithful old friend. The beauty of that girl delights me so much that I'm burning with love; and what makes it worse is that this habit forces me to hide it like a sudden consuming flame confined in a furnace. So I don't know what to do. On the one hand, my conscience tells me it's wrong; on the other hand, the deadly arrows of Cupid spur me on to seek relief for my racked heart by giving way to this sweet and burning passion. I'm only a weak friar and I can't compare myself with great men like Samson the Strong or David the Holy or Solomon the Wise;* yet even they couldn't resist the force of love. So don't be scandalized, dear brother, if I reveal my fate in all confidence. Help me! Alas, I'm dying, I burn, I languish! Could you be my go-between and make the girl understand how much I love her? Since you offered to help, put in a good word for me and give her a letter. Do this, and I shall be your eternal servant for the rest of my life.'

When our friend heard this, he rejoiced inwardly at the prospect of yet more amusement and replied: 'Sir, I shall do it. Go quickly and write your letter because we shall soon be leaving. Remember that she can read and write perfectly well, and I shall bring you back her answer.' Delighted with this offer, the friar left the feast and hurried off to write the following letter:*

'Most fair young maid, whom I love more than anything else in the world, if I have any debt to Heaven, it is only because it has deemed me worthy to contemplate your beauties which are indeed more celestial than human, and which please me as much as anything that I have ever seen on earth or that could, I believe, be found in Heaven.

Neither you nor anyone else should be surprised that, although I am a friar and in holy orders, I burn and am consumed in the fire of my great love for you. For when first I saw you appear among the other ladies at the feast, I seemed to see a second sun rising in your face to eclipse the first. It was a vision of sweetness and bliss that immediately invaded all my spirits, and both my soul and my heart were lost in thoughts of you, so that in you and all your gentle virtues, for the very sweetness of my heart I trust to remain forever. And to comfort my loving soul I have penned this little letter, expressing the fervent and heartfelt love I bear you, with the firm hope that you will receive it graciously through the goodness that shines in your benign countenance. Therefore, I pray you, be content to accept my love, since I have chosen you as the queen of my heart; for by acting to the contrary you alone would shortly cause my death—the which (since you are human and not made of stone) would grieve you ever after, even though, perhaps, you think me a lover unworthy of your worth. Thus, dear young lady, since I am unable to resist love's arrows, for God's sake do not disdain my infinite love, but grant me, I pray, the favourable answer that so desirously I await. And to you, from whom all my well-being and every good proceeds, I give myself, imploring God on high to keep you always and move you with pity towards me.'

Having written this letter and sealed it with a golden thread, he gave it to our young friend, saying: 'Be careful with this because I'm pinning all my hopes on you.' Promising to do the best he could, our friend went back to the feast where he found the rest of us and, to our great amusement and his own, told us how the friar had fallen in love. So then, in our desire to complete the prank, we took our damsel out of the feast and led her with honour to the house of a good friend. Once there, our priest was delighted when we told him about the prank and showed him the love letter: 'This is the greatest fun we've ever had', he said, 'but what shall we do now?' We answered, laughing: 'You should reply to his letter, showing that you're not too young to be in love and that already you have nothing against being loved by him, so he won't despair: indeed, by giving him a bit of hope, we shall add to the joke by making him wear Cupid's garland on his friar's hood.' And so, after much more talk and laughter, we composed the reply and the priest wrote it out in his own hand as follows:

'Were it not, dear sir, that a man of your age and respected virtues might think badly of me, given my age and my condition as a woman,

I could well feel offended and complain that for those of your profession there can be nothing good or praiseworthy about falling in love and tempting honest young women to forfeit things that they should hold dearer than life itself. But since I ought to appreciate the human feelings in the letter I have received from you, I shall take everything in good part, with a warning, however, that I am not the kind of light-headed girl that perhaps you think I am. It is true that one should always be glad to be cherished by men of virtue like you, because good may come of it, although I have neither intelligence nor courage nor even the beauties that you call celestial, for in that you are certainly deceived by your excess of love. But be that as it may, if your health and happiness depend only on me, then I am very happy to be loved by you and to be the chosen queen of your heart, provided always that my honour is safe. The which I recommend to you above all else; and may the merciful God preserve you from all evil and guide both of us always in the way of virtue.'

When the letter was finished, our friend took it to the friar who was enraptured, reading and rereading and kissing it a thousand times over. And not knowing what to do, he kept asking whether there was any hope that the woman he loved would yield to his love. Our go-between answered yes and no, with words that did not exactly commit him one way or the other, though he still said enough to convince the friar to persist. Finally, he said: 'Sir Prior, without wasting any more words, I'm your friend and I think it's a work of mercy to help someone who lies burning in the fire of love; so when you decide, I'm ready and willing to come here with my friends and bring her along to dine with you; and then I shall find a way to leave you alone with her.' Hearing this, the happy friar hugged him, saying: 'You would be my god.' Our go-between offered to serve him with all his heart: 'Dear friend, feel free to make use of me; just tell me how I should bring her to you.' The friar answered: 'Come tomorrow and go into the church, pretending that you are there to look at the frescos, and you'll soon find a room where everything will be ready for a meal, and there'll be a present of some lovely veils for the young lady, and some money too.' Then our friend left and, knowing what he had to do, returned to us and told us the whole story. We were delighted and could hardly wait to see how things would turn out. And the following day, with the priest dressed up as a woman, we set out for the meal.

There were eight of us, all lads from Arezzo, and when we arrived at the church, after pretending to admire the frescoes, we entered the friar's room. He was waiting in a high good humour, greeted us with all courtesy, and regaled us with a fine elegant meal. When the meal was over, we all slipped quietly out, leaving the young woman with the friar who, seeing us leave, softly closed the door of the room, saying: 'Fair maiden, these veils are for you. Forgive me if they are not as lovely as your kindness deserves for, as I told you in my letter, I would willingly give you my soul with them,' and then he tried to kiss her. But the priest, finding himself alone and subjected to this assault, was well prepared with all the necessary skills to resist. Not wanting to be kissed, he began to protest: 'O wretched me! What am I doing here? Who brought me to this? Woe the day that I was born! Alas! poor me! Is this how you seduce a young maid? Has my brother-in-law left me here to be disgraced like this?' The friar tried to calm her: 'My dear love, don't be so upset; cheer up, unless you want me to die; there's nothing to be afraid of; you're in good hands. Here, take this money, or whatever you like.' And he took her by the hand and tried to touch her breasts, but she objected and carried on protesting: 'Alas, good sir, keep your hands to yourself; if my mother knew, or my brothers, they'd kill me. Is this how I must lose the honour that my letter insisted on?' Then the friar: 'What's this I hear, my dear girl, sweet hope of my loving soul? You're not with a pack of wolves or in a dark wood with wild beasts. No, you're in a calm safe place with me who loves you more than life itself. What would you say if you saw someone who hated you, if you put such a frown on your sweet little angel face for someone whose love knows no limits? Yours must be an ungrateful breast to harbour such a senseless complaint. You have such a gracious aspect; to complete your glorious beauties all you need to do is show some pity for the love I bear you now and forever.'

So saying, he opened his arms to embrace her, but the young priest, pulling back, cried piteously: 'For God's sake, sir, leave me alone! I cherish my own honour too much for this; and you would cherish it too if you truly loved me. If I cannot restrain your lustful wishes, then I would prefer to be devoured by wild beasts in a wood—anything rather than stay here and lose my honour. And so I humbly beg you, respect that honour if you desire my love.' But the friar persisted, pleading his love and begging for satisfaction, which the priest continued to refuse until the friar, inflamed with passion and gaining nothing from gifts, prayers, and promises, finally seized him and threw him down on the bed.

Now flat on his back and feeling that it was time to reveal himself, the priest dropped his assumed Florentine accent and spoke in his native Aretine: 'My good sir, don't strain yourself, because there's more manhood on me than there is on you.' And when the astonished friar tried to clear up the mystery, his hand encountered a very sizeable proof of virility. But seeing how handsome the priest was and still burning with love, he pursued his perverted appetite, saying: 'Well, so what? Man or woman, I love you just the same.' Then the priest, not without some real fear, gave a violent kick to the friar's immodest breast and jumped down from the bed: 'O friar, go and hang yourself by the neck! The unbridled lust, the perverted appetite of a friar, how deserving of eternal disgrace! Who would ever have thought that under that holy habit, the glory of the Christian religion, you could give way to such villainy? Who could have expected this of you, the master and teacher in this place?

'Rather than repenting of your first appetite, you then sought to taste the infamous sin for which Sodom and Gomorrah* were miraculously burned to ashes. O diabolical spirit, O profane breast, how could you bear to break your sacred vows? Why doesn't Heaven punish your sacrilege in a way that would make you a mirror of suffering and an example of pain to all other evil and villainous friars? But you can be sure that, as far as I can, I shall bring shame and disgrace on you, by letting the world know of your stinking appetite.'

Not far off, the rest of us were still listening, and when we heard the friar scorned and denounced by the priest disguised as a woman, we ran into the room, laughing and saying: 'What's all this, Sir Prior? What's wrong with you?' Overcome with shame, he answered: 'Since you've tricked me like this, I beg you, for God's sake, don't say anything, and if there's anything you want from me, just ask.' We said that we would gladly do as he asked; but as soon as we were out of there we would have died rather than keep the prank to ourselves, and so we told it openly to everyone in the neighbourhood. And as a result, the friar was immediately thrown out of the convent in shame and disgrace. We returned to Arezzo, brimming with joy and laughter, and with happy memories of Monte San Savino and the prank we had played there together with the priest—who, by the way, is still alive, an excellent witty priest and a perfect choirmaster.

NICCOLÒ MACHIAVELLI

A FABLE
Favola

BOTH oral tradition and the old chronicles of Florentine affairs report the vision of a holy man whose life was universally celebrated by the people of that time. One day while he was rapt in prayer he saw a vast host of souls descending to Hell. These were those wretched mortals who had died without the grace of God; and all of them or the great majority complained that they had been led to this unhappy end only because they had taken a wife.

All this was very surprising to Minos and Rhadamanthus* and the other infernal judges. They could hardly believe that these slanders against the female sex were true and since the complaints grew more frequent every day, they made a full report of the matter to Pluto,* who decided that all the infernal judges should examine the question very thoroughly and then take whatever measures were most apt to discover the falsehood of those assertions or establish the whole truth.

Having summoned them, therefore, to a council, Pluto addressed them as follows: 'My dear subjects, although I possess this kingdom by heavenly disposition and fatal irrevocable destiny so that my heavenly and earthly judgements are not open to objection, yet still for those who hold power the greater wisdom is to submit to the laws and heed the opinion of others. That is why, in a case that could bring discredit upon our empire, I have decided to seek your advice as to how I should act. Every man whose soul comes down to our kingdom says that the fault lies with his wife, and since this seems to us impossible, we fear that if we base our judgements on this report, we shall be condemned as too credulous; and if we do not, we shall appear as lax and regardless of justice. Since the former is the vice of light-minded men, and the latter that of the unjust, we have sought to avoid both accusations; but finding no way of doing so, we have called you together to help us with your good counsel and ensure that this kingdom will continue to live without scandal in the future as it has done in the past.'

All the infernal leaders thought the matter was very important and deserving of great consideration; but though they were unanimous about the need to discover the truth, they disagreed about the manner of doing so. Some thought they should send one or two emissaries to earth in human form to find out the facts through personal experience; many others reckoned they could save themselves all that trouble by applying various tortures to selected souls. In the end, however, the majority rallied to the idea of sending someone to earth; and since they could find no volunteer for this enterprise, they decided to cast lots. The lot fell on Belphagor,* an archdevil, but one who had been an archangel before he fell from Heaven. Although he was very reluctant to undertake the task, he felt obliged by the command of Pluto to carry out the instructions of the council and to accept the conditions that they had solemnly laid down, which were as follows: that whoever received the commission should be given a hundred thousand ducats to take with him into the world, and that there, in the shape of a man, he should take a wife and live with her for ten years; after which, feigning death, he should return and, on the basis of his experience, testify before his superiors to the toils and troubles of marriage. Also that during the allotted time he should be subject to all the ills and afflictions of mortal men such as poverty, prison, sickness, and every other kind of misfortune, unless he managed to escape them by his own deceit and cunning.

With his human form and his money, therefore, Belphagor entered the world and, having chosen horses and companions from his infernal retinue, made a splendid entry into Florence, the city that he chose above all others for his residence as being most suitable for someone who hoped to employ his money in the practice of usury. Then, calling himself Roderigo of Castile, he rented a house in the district of Ognissanti,* and to head off any attempt to trace his origins, he said he had recently left Spain for Syria and made all his money in Aleppo;* after which he had come to Italy in order to take a wife in regions kinder, more civilized, and more suited to his temperament. This Roderigo was a most handsome man and seemed about thirty years of age. Within a few days he had already given proof of his great riches and shown himself so generous and open-handed that many noblemen who were rich in daughters but poor in cash offered to give him a wife. Among all the candidates, Roderigo chose a very beautiful girl called Onesta, the child of Amerigo Donati who had three other marriageable daughters and three grown-up sons; and though he was of noble stock and highly regarded in Florence, yet he was poor, considering the large family he had to support.

Roderigo arranged a spectacular and magnificent wedding-feast, leaving out nothing that could be desired on such an occasion. And since, according to the law that had been given to him when he left Hell, he was subject to all human passions, he soon began to take pleasure in worldly pomp and circumstance and to bask in the praise of men—all of which involved no mean expense. Moreover, he had not been long with his Monna Onesta before he fell hopelessly in love with her, so that he could not bear to see her sad or displeased in any way.

Together with her beauty and her noble rank, Monna Onesta had brought into the house more pride than Lucifer himself ever had. So, at least, thought Roderigo who had experience of both and gave the prize to his wife. Moreover, her pride became greater than ever when she realized how much her husband loved her; and thinking she could command wherever and whenever she wished, she ordered him about without mercy or respect, not stopping short of foul insulting language if ever he denied her anything. This was immensely annoying for Roderigo, but still he managed to put up with it, partly for the sake of his in-laws and his new brothers and relatives and partly out of respect for the bonds of marriage; but above all because of the love he bore his wife. I shall pass over the huge expense of dressing her according to the latest fashions and satisfying her taste for the new styles that our city has the innate habit of creating. More important was the fact that he could not live in peace with her without helping his father-in-law to find husbands for her sisters, a task that involved considerable sums of money. And then the next thing was sending one of her brothers to the east as a cloth merchant and another to the north with textiles, and to set up yet another as a goldsmith in Florence—all in the interests of domestic harmony. In these things he spent most of his fortune. But that was not all. At Carnival time or on the feast of Saint John the Baptist,* when the rich and noble citizens honour themselves and tradition by providing splendid banquets, Monna Onesta could not lose face among the other ladies and insisted that her Roderigo should give entertainments that outshone all the rest.

Roderigo bore with these things for the reasons I have already given; nor, serious though they were, would he have found them too burdensome if they had given him peace at home and some calm while he awaited his ruin. But what happened was the opposite. Because along with the intolerable expenses, it was his wife's irascible character that caused him endless trouble. There was no manservant or maid who who could stand her for longer than a few days, so that Roderigo suffered the serious inconvenience of not having any faithful servant to attend to his business. And even those devils whom he had brought with him as supposed members of his household preferred to go back and suffer the fire of Hell rather than live on earth subjected to her command.

With this turbulent and restless way of life and its unchecked expenses, Roderigo had already spent the cash he had brought with him and was now living on the profits that he hoped to get from the western and eastern ventures; and since his credit was good, he thought to avoid losing status by borrowing. Soon there were so many of his promissory notes in circulation that he was well known to every moneylender in the market. Just when his situation was beginning to look serious, bad news came from the west and the east. One of Monna Onesta's brothers had gambled away all the money he had received from Roderigo, and the other was drowned when his ship went down, laden with merchandise and completely uninsured. No sooner was this made known than Roderigo's creditors gathered together and came to the conclusion that he was ruined. They could not, however, take any measures immediately because the payments were not yet due; and so they decided that it would be wise to keep a close watch on him lest he slip away in secret. Roderigo, for his part, seeing no solution to his problems and aware of the infernal laws that bound him, was looking for some way to escape, and one morning, he took to horse and galloped out of the Prato Gate which was not far from where he lived. As soon as they realized that he had left, the creditors raised a hue and cry, first informing the magistrates and then sending their agents after him along with a rowdy mob.

Roderigo was not more than a mile from the city when he heard the noise behind him; and seeing that things were going badly, he decided to put them off the scent by leaving the highway and trying his luck across the fields. This, however, was made difficult by the many ditches that cross the countryside and make riding impossible, so he was forced to leave his horse by the roadside and go on foot. Crossing field after field, covered with the vines and reed-beds that abound in that region, as he neared Peretola,* he came to the house of Gianmatteo del Brico who worked for Giovanni del Bene; and there by chance he found Gianmatteo himself who was just bringing the oxen home to be fed. Roderigo begged Gianmatteo to save him from the enemies who were at his heels and who wanted him to die in prison. In return he promised that he would make him rich, and before he left he would give him a convincing proof that he could do so; and if he failed then Gianmatteo could turn him over to his enemies.

Now although he was a peasant, Gianmatteo was a shrewd fellow and reckoned he had nothing to lose by helping the fugitive. So he gave his promise and shoved Roderigo under a heap of manure that stood in front of his house and covered the whole thing with straw and other rubbish that he had gathered to burn. Roderigo had hardly finished hiding himself when his pursuers arrived, but for all their attempts to scare Gianmatteo they could not get him to admit that he had ever seen the man they were looking for. In the end, they went on their way and, after searching in vain all that day and the next, they returned wearily to Florence.

When they had left and the noise died down, Gianmatteo pulled his guest out and reminded him of his promise. Roderigo answered: 'Brother, I owe you a great debt and I'm determined to pay it off; and to convince you that I can do what I promised I shall begin by telling you who I am.' Then he explained what kind of being he was and by what laws he was bound when he left Hell and how he had taken a wife. He went on to describe the manner in which he intended to make him rich which was this: whenever Gianmatteo heard of a woman possessed by a devil, he should know that he, Roderigo, was the devil involved and that he would never come out unless commanded to do so by Gianmatteo who would then be well paid by her family. With that all settled, Roderigo took himself off.

Not many days passed before the news spread throughout Florence that Messer Ambrogio Amidei's daughter, who had married Bonaiuto Tebalducci, was possessed by a devil. Her relatives had not failed to try all the remedies that are usual in these cases—such as crowning her with the head of Saint Zenobius and the cloak of Saint John Gualberto*—all of which were treated with contempt by Roderigo. And to prove to everyone that this really was a case of demonic possession and not the fruit of some wild imagination, he spoke in Latin, discussed philosophical problems, and amazed his hearers by revealing the hidden sins of many people—among them a monk who had kept a woman in his cell for four years disguised as a novice. Messer Ambrogio meanwhile was leading a most unhappy life. He had tried every remedy in vain and had lost all hope of curing his daughter when Gianmatteo came and promised to restore the girl's health in exchange for the sum of five hundred florins that he needed to buy a farm at Peretola. Messer Ambrogio accepted the deal and after arranging for a couple of Masses and a few ceremonies to make the whole thing look legitimate, Gianmatteo went up to the girl and whispered in her ear: 'Roderigo, I've come here to see you keep your promise.' To which Roderigo replied: 'That's fine with me, but it's not enough to make you rich. So as soon as I've left here I shall enter into the daughter of King Charles of Naples,* and I won't leave her unless you tell me. So make sure that you get a proper fee, and from then on just leave me alone.' After which he came out of the girl amid the joy and admiration of all Florence.

It was not long before the whole of Italy learned of the terrible misfortune that had befallen the daughter of King Charles. The king had heard of Gianmatteo and since no other remedy could be found, he sent a message to Florence calling him down to Naples. Gianmatteo came and, after a few fake ceremonies, cured the girl. But before leaving Roderigo said: 'You see, Gianmatteo, I've made you rich as I promised. So now, having paid off my debt, I have no further obligations toward you. So make up your mind to stay away from me from now on, because just as I've been good to you in the past, I can do you harm in the future.'

Gianmatteo went back to Florence a very rich man for the king had given him more than fifty thousand ducats, and he thought that now he could enjoy his wealth in peace, even if he did not really believe that Roderigo meant to harm him. But his good intentions were suddenly challenged by the news that the daughter of Louis VII,* king of France, was possessed by a devil. This event seriously disturbed Gianmatteo's mind as he balanced the authority of the king against Roderigo's parting words. The king could find no remedy for his daughter's condition and, since he had heard of Gianmatteo's powers, he first sent a simple messenger asking him to come. But when Gianmatteo pleaded illness as an excuse for refusing, the king felt obliged to appeal to the Signoria,* who forced him to obey. So off he went dejectedly to Paris where he explained to the king that though he had certainly performed some successful exorcisms in the past, this did not mean he could always do so, for there were some devils of such an evil nature that they feared neither threats nor incantations nor the power of religion. He would try to do his duty, but begged pardon in advance if he should fail. The king was furious and vowed to hang him unless he succeeded in curing his daughter. Gianmatteo was terrified, but plucking up courage he sent for the girl; and when she came he whispered in her ear, pleading with Roderigo and reminding him of how he had once helped him and how ungrateful it would be to abandon him now in his hour of need. 'You rotten traitor,' answered Roderigo, 'you dare to come before me like this! You think you can go around boasting about how I've made you rich? I'll show you and everyone else that I can give and take whenever and whatever I please; and before I leave here, I'll have you hanged, that's for sure.'

Seeing that it was no use looking to Roderigo for a solution, Gianmatteo decided to try his luck another way. Sending the possessed girl away, he said to the king: 'Sire, as I told you, there are many spirits who are so malevolent that they are impossible to deal with, and this is one of them. Nevertheless, I want to have one last try. If it works, Your Majesty will have got what he wished for, and so shall I. If it fails, then I'm in your hands and I hope I'll get the compassion that my innocence deserves. What I propose is this: in the square before Notre-Dame, have a great stage erected, big enough to hold all the nobles and clergy of the city; have it covered with cloths of silk and gold; and in the middle of this stage build an altar. Next Sunday morning hold an assembly there with the clergy and the princes and the barons. Do so with full royal pomp and let them be arrayed in rich and splendid robes. Then, after a solemn High Mass, bring forth the possessed girl. Moreover, on one side of the square I want at least twenty musicians with trumpets, horns, drums, bagpipes, bells, cymbals, and anything else that makes a noise; and when I raise my hat, let them start playing those instruments as they move towards the stage. With all that noise, plus a few secret remedies of my own, I reckon they'll drive that devil out.'

The king gave orders immediately and when Sunday morning came the stage was packed with notables and the square crowded with the common folk; and after the solemn High Mass, the possessed girl was led onto the stage by two bishops and a group of nobles. When Roderigo saw such a vast gathering and such formal proceedings, he was almost stunned and said to himself: 'What does this stupid lout think he's doing? Does he think he can scare me with all this show? Doesn't he know that I've seen all the pomp and show of Heaven and the furies of Hell as well? I'll see him punished for this.' And when Gianmatteo drew near and asked him to come out of the girl, he exclaimed: 'Now this was a bright idea! Where do you think you're going with all this fuss? Do you really hope to escape my power and the king's anger? You scurvy wretch, I'll have you hanged before we're done.' They went on like this for some time, one pleading and the other swearing at him, until Gianmatteo felt that he could not waste any more time. He raised his hat and all those fellows who had been hired to make a noise started playing their instruments and moving towards the stage with a racket that shook the skies. Roderigo pricked up his ears when he heard the noise; not knowing what it was, taken by surprise and dazed, he asked Gianmatteo what was going on. And Gianmatteo, with a distressed air, replied: 'O Roderigo, my friend! I'm afraid it's your wife who's come to find you.'

One can hardly imagine how upset Roderigo was when he heard the name of his wife. The shock to his mind was so great that he said nothing more and without thinking whether it was possible or reasonable for her to be there, he took fright and fled, leaving the girl free. For indeed he preferred to go back to Hell and account for his actions rather than submit once again to the yoke of marriage with all its hassles, squabbles, and dangers.

So it was that Belphagor returned to Hell and bore witness to the ills that a wife brings into the house. And Gianmatteo, who had proved smarter than the devil, went home a happy man.

GIOVAN FRANCESCO STRAPAROLA

FORTUNIO
Le piacevoli notti (The Pleasant Nights) 3. 4

*Offended by his adoptive mother and father, Fortunio leaves home.
Wandering in a wood, he meets with three animals who reward him
for a wise judgement. He then goes to Poland where he jousts and wins
the hand of the king's daughter, Doralice.*

THERE is a proverb that the common folk often use in conversation:
'Don't joke with grief or jest with truth,' meaning that the man who
hears and sees and holds his tongue harms nobody and lives in peace.

Now there lived in the remotest parts of Lombardy a man called
Bernio who, though not rich in Fortune's gifts, considered himself no
less bold and high-spirited than other men. He took for wife a worthy
and gracious woman called Alchia who, despite her low birth, possessed
a sharp mind and dignified manners; and she loved her husband as
much as any woman ever has. The couple longed to have children, but
God withheld that grace, since most often men ask without knowing
what is truly good for them. Persisting in this desire and finding it
inexorably thwarted by Fortune, they eventually resolved to adopt
a child and to keep him and bring him up as their own legitimate son.
So early one morning they went to a place where they look after children
abandoned by their parents; and when they spied one who seemed
lovelier and more charming than the rest, they took him and brought
him up with all proper diligence and discipline.

Now, as it pleased the Ruler of the Universe who tempers and
moderates all things, Alchia became pregnant, and when her time
came, she gave birth to a son who was the image of his father. The
couple were overjoyed and gave him the name Valentino. Well nour-
ished and cared for, the child grew up strong in virtue and courtesy;
and he loved his brother Fortunio so much that when they were apart
he felt he would die with sorrow. But Discord, the enemy of every
good, seeing their warm and fervent friendship and unable to bear

such affection, intervened to give them a first taste of his bitter fruits. Thus one day, as they were playing together as children do and were heated in the game, Valentino, unable to accept that Fortunio was winning, became so angry and enraged that several times he called his brother a bastard, born of some wretched whore. Fortunio, in surprise and distress, turned to him and said: 'What! Am I a bastard?' And Valentino, with sharp words, almost against his will, boldly confirmed the fact. At this, Fortunio, sick at heart, left the game and went straight to his stepmother and quietly asked if she and Bernio were truly his parents. Alchia answered yes, and realizing that Valentino had insulted him with offensive words, swore that she would punish him severely. But Fortunio doubted the words of Alchia, and felt certain that he was not her legitimate child. Determined to find out the truth, he asked her repeatedly whether he was in fact her son, until Alchia, seeing how stubborn he was and unable to dissuade him from asking such questions, finally confirmed that he was not her real son, but had been brought up in her home for the love of God and in penance for her sins and those of her husband. These words were so many daggers in Fortunio's heart and new pain added to the old. Yet though he was overwhelmed by anguish, his heart would not allow him to take his own life; and so he resolved to leave the house of Bernio and travel the world to see if Fortune might one day show him favour.

Alchia, finding Fortunio more firmly determined with every hour that passed and seeing no way to deter him from his fixed purpose, was inflamed with anger and indignation; she gave him her curse, praying to God that if he should ever sail the sea, he might be swallowed up by the Siren even as ships are by the swelling stormy waves of the sea. Fortunio, urged on by his own impetuous wind of scorn and anger, did not hear this maternal curse and, without taking any further leave of his parents, set out towards the north.

Fortunio made his way by lake and stream, over hill and dale, through wild and mountainous places until at last one morning, between nine and twelve o'clock, he reached a dense and tangled wood. And entering there, he found a wolf, an eagle, and an ant who were quarrelling violently over the body of a deer, unable to reach any agreement as to how it should be divided among them. Locked in this bitter conflict and each unwilling to give way to the other, the three animals finally agreed that young Fortunio who had just arrived should put an end to their dispute by giving to each of them the part that he deemed most appropriate.

And to this they all consented, promising that they would calm down and in no way challenge the definitive judgement, even if it should be unjust. Fortunio willingly accepted the task and, after considering at length the different conditions of three animals, divided the prey as follows: to the wolf, as a voracious and well-toothed animal, in reward for his hard work, he assigned all the bones and the lean meat; to the eagle, a bird of prey without teeth, he offered the innards with the fat that surrounds the flesh and bones; to the busy grain-bearing ant, as lacking the strength that Nature has given to the wolf and the eagle, he gave the tender brain as the prize for his unstinting toil.

They were all happy with this wise and well-founded judgement, and gave him the most hearty thanks for his courtesy. And since ingratitude is the most reprehensible of vices, all three agreed that the youth should not leave before each of them had given him the best possible reward for the service he had rendered. The wolf, therefore, in recognition of the judgement, said: 'Brother, I give you this power: that whenever you wish to become a wolf and say "if only I were a wolf", you will be transformed into a wolf—returning, however, to your original shape whenever you wish.' And similar powers were bestowed upon him by the eagle and the ant.

Fortunio was delighted with these gifts and, after thanking the animals as profusely as he could, took his leave and went on his way; and so far did he travel that at last he reached the noble and populous city of Poland* which was governed by the mighty and worthy King Odescalco who had a daughter called Doralice. And since he wished her to be honourably married, the king announced a great tournament in his realm, for only to the winner of the jousting would he join her in matrimony. And many dukes and counts and other mighty lords came from all parts in the hope of obtaining the precious prize. Now the first day of jousting was already over, and a Saracen, swarthy and horrible to see, ill-shapen and as black as pitch, seemed to be the most successful thus far. The daughter of the king, as she looked on the darkness and deformity of the Saracen, was seized by anguish at the thought that he might be the winner of the honourable jousts; and leaning her damask cheek on her tender and delicate hand, in her grief and affliction, she cursed her harsh and evil fate, craving death rather than marriage with such a misshapen Saracen.

Fortunio entered the city and noted all the pomp and circumstance and the great number of jousters; and when he learned the cause of such a glorious occasion, he burned with an ardent desire to prove his valour in the tournament. Bitterly, however, he realized that he possessed none of those things that every jouster needs. And standing sadly there and looking upward, he saw Doralice, the daughter of the king, leaning against a stately window where, surrounded as she was by graceful and gracious matrons, she seemed no less than a bright and living sun amid the myriad tiny stars. And when the dark night came and everyone had retired to rest, Doralice withdrew to a well-furnished and elegant chamber and as she stood alone and sad, with the window open, there was Fortunio! For on seeing the maiden he had said to himself: 'Ah, why am I not an eagle?' and no sooner had he said these words than he became an eagle and flew through the open window. Then, regaining human shape, he appeared before her beaming with happiness and joy. At the sight of him the maid took fright and, as if she were being torn apart by hungry dogs, began to cry out loud. The king, who was not very far off, heard the screams and ran to his daughter; and when he heard that there was a young man in the chamber, he searched the whole room. But at last he returned to his rest, having found nothing, because the youth, transformed into an eagle once again, had flown out of the window. And no sooner had Doralice's father settled down to rest than yet again the maiden began to scream out loud because the youth had appeared before her once more. But Fortunio, hearing the shouts and fearing for his life, changed into an ant and hid himself in the golden tresses of the lovely girl. Odescalco came running when he heard his daughter scream and, finding nothing, lost his temper with her, harshly threatening that if she started screaming again, it would be his turn to play a joke that she would not find so funny. Then off he went in a rage, thinking that her imagination must have conjured up one of the men who had been killed in the tournament for love of her.

Now when the youth heard what the father said and saw him leave, he left off his antlike shape and resumed his true form. And Doralice immediately wanted to jump out of her bed and scream, but she could not do so because Fortunio closed her mouth with his hand and said: 'My lady, I haven't come here to take your honour or your goods, but to help you and to be your humble servant. If you scream again, one of two things will happen: either your good name and fair fame will be spoiled, or you will be the cause of my death and your own. And therefore, lady of my heart, do not stain your honour and, at the same time, endanger both our lives.' While Fortunio was speaking, Doralice wept and complained bitterly, unable to bear such a fearsome assault. But the youth saw how upset she was, and with sweet words that would have split a rocky mountain, he continued to plead until at last he succeeded in softening the lady's stubborn will, so that she made her peace with him, conquered by his grace and courtesy. The sight of such a handsome young man, shapely and strong, brought back to her mind the ugliness of the Saracen and she grieved that he should be both the victor of the tournament and the possessor of her person. And as she was lost in these thoughts, the youth said to her: 'Damsel, if I could find some way to join the jousting, I would willingly do so, for my heart tells me that I would win the tournament.' The maiden answered: 'And if this should be the case, then no one but you would be my lord and master.' Then, seeing him so eager and ready for the enterprise, she furnished him with money and with abundant jewels. And when he had happily taken the money and the jewels, the youth asked her what she would like him to wear. To which she answered: 'White silk.' And he did as she desired.

The next day, therefore, equipped with shining arms, and wearing a surcoat of white silk finely encrusted and embroidered with gold, Fortunio mounted a powerful and spirited horse caparisoned with his rider's colours. Nobody recognized him as he made his way to the square; but when the crowd of spectators saw the bold unknown knight with the lance in his hand ready to joust, they began to gaze as if lost in amazement; and one said to the other: 'Who can this be? Coming to joust, so handsome and resplendent; and yet nobody knows him!' Fortunio now entered the lists and made sign to his rival to do the same; and, lowering their sturdy lances, they clashed like frenzied lions. The youth gave his adversary such a violent blow to the head that the Saracen was thrown from his horse and, like glass smashed against a wall, lay dead on the bare earth. And all those who jousted against Fortunio that day were overthrown as well. The damsel was delighted and looked on him with an intense admiring gaze, inwardly thanking God who had delivered her from the Saracen and praying that He would give Fortunio the palm of victory.

When night came and Doralice was called to supper, she chose not to go; instead she had fine delicacies and precious wines sent up, pretending that she had no appetite, but might eat alone if she grew hungry later on. Then, locking herself in her chamber and opening the window, she awaited her devoted lover with fervent desire. And, when he returned as on the night before, they dined joyfully together. Afterwards, Fortunio asked how he should be dressed the next day, and she replied: 'In green silk, embroidered with silver and fine gold; and likewise the horse.' All this was promptly done the following morning. The youth presented himself in the square and entered the lists once again, giving even greater proof of his valour than he had done the day before. And everyone declared out loud that the delicate damsel should be his by right.

When evening came, the damsel, inwardly rejoicing, blithe and happy, used the same pretext as the night before and locked herself in her room with the window open to await the bold young man; and again they dined together at their ease. Then once again he asked her how he should be arrayed the following day, and she replied: 'In crimson silk, all embroidered with gold and pearls; and likewise shall your horse be caparisoned, for I also shall be dressed in the same way.' 'Lady,' said Fortunio, 'if tomorrow I come to the tournament somewhat later than usual, do not be surprised, for my lateness will not be without cause.'

When the third day came and it was time for the jousting to begin, all the people were happily awaiting the end of the tournament; but no jousters dared to appear, for fear of the measureless strength of the bold unknown knight. And the knight himself was so late that it began to worry not only the crowd, but also the damsel, although she had been warned of the delay. Overcome by her anguish and seeing nobody arrive, she fell down senseless; but when she heard Fortunio drawing near to the square, her vital spirits began to revive. He was dressed in a splendid rich cloak and the caparison of his horse was of fine gold studded with glittering rubies, emeralds, sapphires, and great pearls which, by general consent, were worth a whole state. When the brave Fortunio entered the square, they all shouted with one voice: 'Long live, long live the unknown knight!', acclaiming him with festive hand-clapping and whistles. And when he had entered the lists he bore himself so bravely that all his adversaries were stretched on the bare earth and the tournament ended with his glorious triumph. Dismounted from his sturdy steed, he was lifted onto the shoulders of the town's most prominent citizens and, to the sound of trumpets and assorted instruments and shouts that rose to Heaven, carried straight before the king. And the king removed the helmet and the shining armour to reveal a handsome youth. So he called his daughter and, in the presence of all the people, gave her in marriage, with celebrations at court that lasted for a whole month.

When Fortunio had been living with his beloved wife for a certain time, he began to feel that it was a low and unfitting thing to dwell in idleness, counting the hours like a witless fool. So he decided to leave and go to places where his valour might be openly known. With the consent of his wife and his father-in-law, he embarked in a galley laden with the many treasures that the king had given him; and, sailing with fair and prosperous winds, reached the Atlantic Sea. He had not ventured more than ten miles into that sea before the biggest Siren that was ever seen swam up beside the galley and began to sing a sweet song. Fortunio, who was leaning over the side of the galley and looking down into the water, fell asleep, and in his sleep he was swallowed by the Siren who then dived beneath the waves and fled away. Unable to help him, the sailors were overwhelmed by sorrow. Sad and disheartened, they covered the ship with dark cloth and returned to the unhappy and unfortunate King Odescalco; and when they had told him of the horrifying and piteous tragedy that had occurred at sea, the king and Doralice and the whole city were plunged in grief and dressed themselves in black.

Doralice's time was near and she gave birth to a lovely boy whom she nurtured tenderly and carefully until he was two years of age. But she was still sad and grieving for her beloved husband and had no hope of seeing him again. She decided, therefore, in her noble and virile spirit, to try her luck and test her fortune at sea, even without the consent of the king. And when she had prepared a galley, fully armed and perfectly equipped, she took with her three metal apples, all wonderfully wrought—the first of brass, the second of silver, and the third of the finest gold. Then, bidding farewell to her father, she embarked with her son and, aided by a fair and prosperous wind, set out on the high seas. And as they sailed on in calm weather, the grieving lady ordered the sailors to take her to the place where her husband had been swallowed by the Siren. This was done; and when the ship had reached the spot, the child burst into a flood of tears; and since his mother could find no other way of quieting him, she took the brass apple and gave it to him. But as he played with it, he was seen by the Siren who swam up beside the ship, raised her head above the foamy waves, and said to the lady: 'Lady, give me that apple, for I desire it so much.' To this the lady replied that she would not do so because it was the plaything of her little son. 'Let me have it, if you please,' said the Siren, 'and I will show you your husband as far as the chest.' The lady longed to see her husband and when she heard this she gave her the apple. And the Siren, in return for the precious gift, showed her husband as far as the chest, just as she had promised. Then, diving back under the waves, she disappeared from sight. The lady, who had watched everything with the utmost attention, grew even more eager to see him completely. Not knowing what to do or say, she turned for solace to her child who once again began to cry until his mother sought to quiet him with the silver apple. Now, as chance would have it, the Siren saw this and asked the lady to give it to her. But seeing that it was the plaything of her child, the lady refused with a shrug of her shoulders. So the Siren said: 'If you give me that apple, which is far more beautiful than the other, I promise to show you your husband as far as the knees.' Poor Doralice, eager to see more of her husband, set aside her love for her son and happily gave it to her; and the Siren kept her promise and then dived beneath the waves.

The lady looked on, silent and tense, but could think of no way to save her husband from death; and so she picked up her son who was still crying and again sought solace with him. The child, however, remembered the apple that he loved to play with and burst into such a flood of tears that his mother was obliged to give him the golden apple. This was observed by the greedy fish who saw that it was far more beautiful than the other two and once again asked for it as a gift. And so well she pleaded that the mother let her have it, much against the will of the child. Now because the Siren had promised to show Doralice her husband from head to foot and did not want to break her word, she drew near to the galley and lifted up her back to present him quite openly. Fortunio, finding himself above the waves and perched in liberty upon the Siren's back, wasted no time and happily exclaimed: 'If only I were an eagle!' Immediately he became an eagle and soared up onto the pennant of the galley's lateen sail; and from there, watched by all the sailors, he came down and regained his real form. And first his wife and child and then the whole crew hugged and kissed him.

Thus, all delighted to have recovered the lost husband, they returned to their homeland where, as they entered the port, they announced their arrival with trumpets, castanets, drums, and other instruments, so that it came to the ears of the king who listened intently and wondered what it might mean. But he had not long to wait before a messenger came and informed him that his son-in-law Fortunio and his beloved daughter had arrived. And when they had disembarked from the galley, they all went up to the palace where they were received with great and triumphant festivities.

A few days later Fortunio went back to his old home where he transformed himself into a wolf and devoured his stepmother Alchia and his brother Valentino in revenge for the way they had insulted him. Then, returning to his true shape, he mounted his horse and returned to the kingdom of his father-in-law. There he found his dear and beloved wife Doralice, and together for many years they lived in peace and in the enjoyment of great and mutual pleasure.

MARGHERITA SPOLATINA
Le piacevoli notti (*The Pleasant Nights*) 7. 2

Margherita Spolatina* falls in love with Teodoro Calogero and swims across to his island in order to be with him. Discovered by her brothers and led astray by a lamp, she is tragically drowned in the sea.

LOVE, as I find it wisely described by learned authors, is nothing but an irrational impulse caused by a passion that lustful thoughts provoke in the heart. Its evil effects are the dissipation of earthly riches, the wasting of bodily strength, the perversion of the intellect, and the loss of freedom. It knows no reason, it knows no order, it knows no stability whatsoever. It is the father of vices, the enemy of youth, and the death of old age; and seldom if ever is it allowed a happy and glorious end. And this may be seen in the case of a lady of the Spolatina family whose subjection to love led to the tragic end of her life.

Ragusa,* worthy ladies, is a famous city of Dalmatia by the sea, and not far off there is a little island which is commonly called the Middle Island* and where there is a strong and firmly based castle. Between Ragusa and this island is a rock where there is nothing but a small chapel and a sort of cabin half covered with tiles. The place was so barren and the air so bad that nobody lived there except an orthodox monk called Teodoro, who devoutly served the chapel as a penance for his sins. Having no means of subsistence, he used to go begging, sometimes in Ragusa and sometimes on the Middle Island. Now one day, when Teodoro was on the Middle Island, begging his bread as he usually did, something happened that he could never have imagined. A graceful and charming young lady called Margherita came towards him and, seeing that he was of a fine and handsome build, thought to herself that he was better equipped for human pleasures than for monastic solitude, and indeed she held him so firmly in her heart that she thought of nothing else day and night. The monk, meantime, unaware of what had happened, continued to go about his begging and often went to seek alms at the house of Margherita. Burning with love, she gave him the alms without daring to reveal her passion. But love, who protects all those who follow his precepts and never fails to teach the way to the desired end, finally gave her the necessary courage. Coming up to him she spoke as follows: 'Teodoro, brother and sole comfort of my heart, so great is the torment of my passion that unless you help me I shall soon lose my life. I burn with love for you and can no longer resist the fire. So help me, lest you cause my death.' And with this, she burst into tears.

The monk, who until then had no idea that she was in love with him, was struck dumb at first; but then, feeling more sure of himself, began to talk things over with her. And the upshot of their conversation was that they set aside celestial subjects and entered upon matters of love. Nothing remained but for them to find out how to be together and satisfy their mutual passion. The young woman, who was very acute, said: 'My love, don't worry, I'll show you how we can manage. It will be like this. This evening, at ten o'clock, put a lighted lamp in the window of your cabin; and as soon as I see it, I shall come to you.' Teodoro said: 'Ah, my dear girl, but how will you cross the sea? You know that neither of us has a boat, and to ask others to ferry you over would be very dangerous for the honour and life of us both.' 'Have no fear,' she replied, 'leave it all to me for I know how to come to you without any danger to honour or life. When I see the lamp, I shall swim across to you; and nobody will know about what is our own business.' To which Teodoro objected: 'But you risk being drowned; it's a long way and you are young and frail; you could easily run out of breath and go under.' 'No,' the young woman answered, 'I'm not afraid of being short of breath, for I swim like a fish.' The monk, seeing how determined she was, at last gave way.

When the dark night came, he lit the lamp as they had planned and, with a white towel ready for her, waited joyously for the beloved young lady. She was overjoyed when she saw the light and then, bare-foot and wearing nothing but her shift, she went down to the seashore. Then, taking off the shift and wrapping it round her head after the fashion of those parts, she plunged into the sea; and so vigorously did she move her arms and her legs that in less than a quarter of an hour she had swum over to the cabin where the monk was waiting. As soon as he saw her, he took her by the hand and led her into his leaky cabin where he took the snow-white towel and dried every part of her with his own hands. Then, taking her into his cell, he set her upon a little bed and, lying down himself, plucked with her the ultimate fruits of love. The lovers spent two long hours in sweet conversation and close embracings; after which the young woman, happily sated with her monk, took her leave—but not without promising to return.

Addicted by now to the sweet food provided by the monk, Margherita went swimming across to him every time she saw the lamp burning. But hostile blind Fortune, the enemy to all happiness and the bringer of revolution to states and change to worldly things, would not allow her to enjoy her precious lover for long, but, as if envious of others' good, intervened to disrupt all her plans. Thus it was that one night of foul all-enveloping fog, when the woman had seen the lamp and plunged into the sea, she was spotted by some men who were fishing not far off. At first, the fishermen took her for a fish, but when they looked more closely they saw that she was a woman and that she came ashore at the monk's cabin. Amazed by this, they seized their oars, rowed to the shore, hid near the cabin, and waited until she came out again and swam off towards the Middle Island. But the wanton girl was not stealthy enough to prevent the fishermen from recognizing her.

So now the fishermen had seen and recognized her and when they had watched her make the dangerous crossing several times and understood the meaning of the burning lamp, they discussed what to do and at first decided to keep the matter secret. But then, consider-ing the dishonour that might come to a respectable family and the fact that the woman was risking her life, they changed their mind and decided to reveal everything to Margherita's brothers. So they went to the house where the brothers lived and told them the whole story in every detail.

When the brothers heard the bad news, they refused to believe it until they had seen the facts with their own eyes. But when they had

done so, they resolved that she should die; and after carefully considering what to do, they put their plan into action. When dusk came
down in the evening, the younger brother climbed into a boat and
quietly went across to the monk's cabin. There he begged to be given
lodging for the night because something had happened to put him in
great danger of being captured and executed. The monk, who knew
him as Margherita's brother, made him welcome and treated him
kindly; and all that night he remained with him, discoursing on the
wretchedness of worldly things and on the grave sins that afflict the
soul and make it the servant of the Devil. While the younger brother
was with the monk, the other brothers secretly left their house and,
taking a long pole and a lamp, set out in a boat for the monk's cabin.
And when they arrived there, they raised the pole upright with the
burning lamp on top, and waited to see what would happen. The
woman, seeing the lamp, plunged into the sea as usual and started
swimming strongly towards the cabin. The brothers kept perfectly
silent, but as soon as they heard the motion of Margherita in the
water, they took up their oars and quietly moved away from the cabin,
taking their lamp with them.

Unheard by Margherita and unseen in that dark night, they slowly
began to row away without making the slightest sound. The woman
followed the lamp because, in all that darkness, she could see nothing
else. But the brothers went on ahead until they had led her into the
open sea; and then they hauled down the pole and put out the lamp.
The wretched girl was already tired from her long swim; and now,
with no light to show her where she was, she lost heart; and knowing
that she was far from any human help, she gave up altogether and was
swallowed by the sea like a wrecked ship. The brothers, seeing that
there was now no way in which she could escape her fate, left their
unfortunate sister amid the waves and returned home. The younger
brother, as soon as it was day, gave due thanks to the monk for his
welcome and took his leave.

The castle town was already full of the sad news that Margherita
Spolatina was nowhere to be found. The brothers pretended to be
overcome with grief, but rejoiced in their heart of hearts. Before the
third day was done, the dead body of the unhappy woman was washed
up on the shore by the monk's cabin and when he saw and recognized
her, he almost expired with the shock. But then, being unobserved, he
took her by the arm, pulled her out of the water, and carried her into

the cabin; and there, casting himself down, he wept long over her dead face and bathed with a flood of tears her snow-white breast, calling and calling in vain upon her name. But when he had finished weeping, he thought of how he might give her worthy burial and help her soul with prayers and fasts and other good offices. And taking the spade he used to work in his little garden, he dug a grave in his chapel and closed her eyes and her mouth with many tears. With roses and violets he made a garland and placed it on her head. Then, having blessed her and kissed her, he placed her in the grave and covered her with earth. And thus was preserved the honour of the brothers and of the lady, and nobody ever knew what had become of her.

LUIGI DA PORTO

THE STORY OF TWO NOBLE LOVERS
Storia da due nobili amanti

In the days when Bartolomeo della Scala,* that benevolent and courteous lord, governed my fair homeland with bit and bridle, there
were in that city, as my father heard tell, two noble families who were
bitter enemies, either because they belonged to different factions or
because they had some private motives for their hatred. One family
was called Montecchi and the other Cappelletti. It seems certain that
the former family now lives in Udine where, after some disastrous
events in Verona, Messer Nicolò and Messer Giovanni (now known as
Monticoli) came to live, bringing nothing of what their ancestors had
possessed beyond their kind and courtly manner. And although in
some old documents I have read how the two families united to drive
out Azzo d'Este,* the ruler of Verona (who later returned with the
help of the San Bonifacio faction), nevertheless I shall limit myself to
telling you the story as I heard it, without any modification.

There were then, as I have said, at the time of the above-mentioned
lord, these two families in Verona, both equally endowed by Heaven
and Fortune with worthy men and wealth. And between them, as so
often happens with such great houses, whatever the cause, there
reigned a most cruel enmity. Many were killed on both sides until,
at last, they renounced further violence, partly because they had
grown tired of it and partly because they were threatened by the lord
of the city who looked on their quarrel with the greatest displeasure.
And as time went on, without any formal peace, they were so far
reconciled that most retainers of the two houses could at least talk to
each other.

With the old enemies now almost at peace, Antonio Cappelletti,
a jovial and pleasant man and the head of his family, held a series of
Carnival feasts, lasting night and day and attracting the whole city.
Now it is the custom of lovers to follow their ladies wherever they go
as closely as they can, not only with their hearts, but with their bodies

too; and thus it was that a youth of the Montecchi faction turned up in pursuit of his cruel mistress. He was very young, tall and beautiful, graceful and charming; and since he was dressed as a woman and had put on a mask as they all did, there was not an eye that did not turn towards him—both because his beauty rivalled that of any of the fair ladies who were there and because they were surprised to see him come to that house, especially at night. But nobody observed him with more attention than the only daughter of Messer Antonio who was herself most graceful, spirited, and lovely. When she saw the youth, his beauty struck her with such force that as soon as their eyes met, she felt that she was no longer in command of herself. He was standing apart from the feast with a listless air, all alone, rarely dancing or engaging in conversation, like a man led there by Love and wary of what might happen; but the girl was distressed to see him like this since she had heard that he was a very pleasant and charming youth.

It was already past midnight and time for the dance that usually marks the end of the feast. This is what we call the dance of the torch or the hat, where the dancers form a circle and the men and women choose and change partners as they please. The handsome youth was drawn into the dance by one of the ladies and soon found himself placed by chance next to the enamoured girl. On her other side was a young nobleman known as Marcuccio the Squinter who, by some freak of nature, always had cold hands, winter and summer alike. Romeo Montecchi (for such was his name) came up on her left and took her lovely hand in his, according to the rules of the dance; and perhaps because she wanted to hear him speak, the girl exclaimed: 'Bless you for coming up next to me, Messer Romeo.' To which the youth, who was aware that she had been looking at him, replied with some surprise: 'Why should my coming be so blessed?' 'Your coming to my side is blessed', she answered, 'because at least you will keep my left hand warm while Marcuccio is freezing my right.' And Romeo, growing somewhat bolder: 'If I have warmed your hand with mine, you have inflamed my heart with your eyes.' The maiden sketched a smile and, fearful of being seen or heard talking with him, simply added: 'I swear to you, Romeo, that there is no lady in this room who seems to these eyes as beautiful as you.' And he, already burning with love: 'Whatever else I may be, if it please you, I shall always be the faithful servant of your beauty.'

Soon after, Romeo left the feast and went home. There he considered the cruelty of his first love who had left him to pine so long for so little reward and decided that from then on he would give himself entirely to Cappelletti's daughter, provided only that she consented—and this even though she happened to be the child of his enemies. The young girl, for her part, could think about little but him and after many sighs concluded that she would be happy forever if she could have him as a husband. But the enmity between their two houses gave her little hope of such a happy end, so that, torn as she was between contrasting thoughts, she often said to herself: 'What a fool I am! What strange passion draws me into this labyrinth where I have no guide and there is no way out? For Romeo Montecchi cannot love me. His hatred for my family can only mean that he seeks my disgrace. And even if he wishes to marry me, my father will never consent to give him my hand.' But then another thought came into her mind: 'Who knows? Perhaps the union that I long for might be seen as a way of reconciling the two houses who are already sated and weary with this long strife.' And trusting in this hope, she began to look kindly upon the youth.

The two lovers now burned with the same fire, both hearts engraved with the image of the other. They began to exchange longing looks, sometimes in church and sometimes from a window, for there was no joy for either of them unless they could see each other. Romeo, especially, was so enamoured of her sweet ways that he would often spend the whole night alone before the house of his beloved, at the risk of his life in case of discovery. And sometimes, unknown to her or to anyone else, he would climb up to the balcony of her room and listen to her speak, and at other times he would lie out in the street. Now it happened that one night, as Love would have it, the moon was shining more brightly than usual and Romeo was about to climb onto the balcony when the maiden came to open the window, either by chance or because she had some idea of what he had been doing. And as she leaned out, she saw him.

Not knowing that it was her, he tried to retreat into the shadow of an adjoining wall; but recognizing him and calling his name, she said: 'What are you doing here all alone at this hour of night?'

'What Love commands,' he answered, recognizing her voice.

'If you were caught, you could easily meet your death.'

'I could indeed meet my death here and I surely will do so one of these nights unless you come to help me. But since I am no less near to death everywhere else, I shall seek to die as close to you as possible;

for it is with you that I shall always long to live, with Heaven's consent and yours.'

'There will be no obstacle on my part to our living honestly together; the only obstacle will come from your side, or rather from the enmity that I see between your house and mine.'

'Believe me, no desire could be greater than my constant desire to be with you, and therefore if you consent to be mine as I long to be yours, so be it with all my heart; nor do I fear that anyone will take you from me.'

With this, they arranged to meet again some other night when they would have more leisure to speak. Then they went their separate ways.

They did indeed speak together like this several times until, one night, at their usual meeting place, as it was snowing heavily, Romeo said: 'Ah, why do you make me suffer like this? Have you no pity for me, when every night I wait for you in the street in weather like this?'

'Of course, I am sorry for you; but what can I do, except tell you to go back home?'

'You could let me into your bedroom. Then we could talk more easily.'

Then the maiden, almost angrily, answered: 'Romeo, I love you as much as any woman can virtuously love a man, and perhaps I allow you more freedoms than my virtue should permit. This I do because I love you as you deserve. But if you think that by long insistence or by some other method you can enjoy the fruits of that love, then put it out of your mind, for in the end you will be disappointed. But I see that you are putting your life in danger by coming this way every night, and so I vow that if you wish to take me as your wife, I am ready to give myself entirely to you and to go with you wherever you please.'

'That is all I desire,' said the youth, 'let us do it now.'

'Let us, indeed. But first let us repeat our vows before my confessor Fra Lorenzo if you wish me to be wholly and happily yours.'

'So Fra Lorenzo of Reggio knows all the secrets of your heart?'

'Yes, and it would make me happy if we made all our vows in his presence.'

And having discussed how this might be done with all due discretion, they parted.

This friar was a Franciscan, an accomplished philosopher, well versed in the natural sciences and the magic arts, and so closely linked in friendship with Romeo that in those days perhaps there were no two like them. He was eager to maintain his reputation with the ordinary simple folk and at the same time to enjoy some of the pleasures of life;* and for this reason he had found it useful to confide in some gentlemen of the city. Among these his choice fell upon Romeo who was lively and daring, but also prudent, and to him the friar had opened his heart, laying bare what he kept hidden from the others. Now it was Romeo who went to him and frankly told him how he desired to have his beloved lady as his wife and how they had both decided that the friar alone should be the secret witness to their marriage, in the hope that he might later persuade her father to give his consent.

The friar was happy with this, partly because he could not have denied any request of Romeo without danger to himself, and partly because he thought that he could bring this affair to a good end, which would bring him great honour with Lord Bartolomeo and with all those who wanted the two houses to live in peace.

It was now Lent and one day the maiden went to the monastery of San Francesco, pretending that she wished to confess. There she entered one of the confessionals that are still in use, especially among Conventual Friars, and asked for Fra Lorenzo who, at the sound of her voice, came from the convent with Romeo, locked the door of the confessional behind him and drew back the iron grate that separated them from the girl. 'I am always happy to see you,' he said, 'but now you are more dear to me than ever since you wish to take my Romeo as your husband.' 'There is nothing that I desire more', she answered, 'than to be his lawful wife, and that is why I have come before you, trusting that, together with God, you will bear witness to what love obliges me to do.' Then, in the presence of the friar who agreed to everything under the seal of confession, Romeo and the lovely maiden gave their word and were married. They exchanged a single kiss, arranged to spend the following night together, and took leave of the friar, who closed the grate and remained there to confess other women.

Having become man and wife in the manner you have heard, the two lovers spent several nights happily enjoying their love and hoping that with time they would find a way to pacify the girl's father whom they knew to be opposed to their wishes. And this was how things stood when Fortune, enemy of all earthly joys, sowing I know not what evil seed, revived the almost withered enmity between the two houses. The unrest had already lasted for many days when the Montecchi and Cappelletti factions met in the main street; and since neither side would give way, they began to fight. Thinking of his wife, Romeo did his best to avoid striking any of her family, but in the end, seeing so many of his own people wounded and almost all of them driven from the street, he was unable to control his anger. Rushing up to Tebaldo Cappelletti, who seemed the fiercest of his enemies, he struck him dead with a single blow and put all his henchmen to flight, dismayed as they were by the loss of their leader.

Too many people had seen Romeo wounding Tebaldo, so the homicide could not be hidden. When the case came before Lord Bartolomeo, all the Cappelletti accused Romeo alone and demanded a sentence of perpetual banishment from Verona. Any woman who has truly loved will easily imagine with what heart the poor young lady heard this news. She wept so long and so bitterly that no one could comfort her; and her suffering was all the greater because she dared not reveal its cause. As for her young husband, exile from his home-land was painful to him only insofar as it meant separation from his lady. He was determined not to go without taking leave of her, and since he could not venture to her house, he turned once again to the friar, who then charged one of the Cappelletti servants, a great friend of Romeo, to take a message to the lady, saying that she should come to see him—which she did. Once again the lovers met in the confessional and bewailed their misfortune until at last she said to him: 'What shall I do without you? I have no heart to go on living. It would be better for me to come with you, wherever you go. I shall trim these locks and follow you like a servant; and indeed you could not find a better or more faithful servant than I am.' 'God forbid', said Romeo, 'that you should ever come with me, dear soul, in any condition but that of my wife. But I am sure that things cannot remain like this for long and there will eventually be peace between our families; and then I shall beg our sovereign lord to grant me a pardon. That is why I think you should stay here for a time. And then, if things do not turn out as I hope, we shall find some other way of being together.' With this decided, they embraced and kissed over and over again and wept to think that they must now be separated; and the lady begged Romeo to stay as near to Verona as he could and not to go to Rome or Florence as he had planned. A few days later Romeo, who had been hidden in the monastery by Fra Lorenzo, went dejectedly off to Mantua; but before he left he gave instructions to one of the lady's servants that he should let Fra Lorenzo know if he heard any news of her in the Cappelletti household, adding that he should do whatever she asked with true faith if he wanted to have the rest of his promised reward.

Romeo had been gone for many days and the lady still wept so bitterly that it marred her beauty, and more than once her mother, who loved her tenderly, asked what was the cause of these tears: 'O daughter,' she said, 'I love you as I love my life. What has suddenly made you so sad? You used to be such a cheerful girl, and now you can hardly stop crying. If there is something that you want, just let me know, and as long as it is lawful, I shall make sure you are satisfied.' But when the girl gave only evasive answers, it struck her mother that she might be longing for a husband and that this was what made her weep, though she was too fearful and ashamed to say so. One day, therefore, fearing for her daughter's health and even for her life, she said to her husband: 'Messer Antonio, for some time now, I've seen how our daughter keeps weeping so that she no longer seems the girl she used to be. You must have seen it yourself. And when I ask what's the cause, I can't get anything out of her. And I really can't explain it myself unless it means that she wants to get married, and, like the decent girl she is, can't bring herself to admit it. So before she wastes away I say it would be a good idea to find her a husband; in any case, she was eighteen on Saint Euphemia's day and women don't get much older than that without losing some of their beauty. Besides, girls aren't the kind of goods you can keep at home for long. As for the dowry, I know you've had it ready for some time, so let's see if we can find a suitable husband.' Messer Antonio replied that it would indeed be a good thing to marry her off, and he praised his daughter for suffering her desire in silence rather than pleading with her father or mother. A few days later he began to negotiate a marriage with one of the counts of Lodrone,* and when the arrangements were almost complete, Giulietta's mother thought she would give her daughter great pleasure by announcing: 'Now cheer up, daughter, it won't be long before you're properly married to a gentleman and then you'll have no cause for crying. Because although you wouldn't tell me, I understood the cause with the help of God. And so your father and I have done what it takes to make you happy.'

At these words the lovely girl could not hold back her tears, and her mother said: 'Do you think I'm telling lies? In less than a week you'll be the wife of a fine gentleman from the house of Lodrone.' On hearing this, Juliet's tears redoubled, and her mother tried to comfort her:

'Come now, daughter, doesn't it make you happy?'

'No, mother, it will never make me happy.'

'What do you want then? Just tell me and I'll do whatever you want.'

'I want to die. Nothing else.'

Madonna Giovanna (for such was the mother's name) was a wise woman and now understood that her daughter must be in love, so after some vague comments she left her alone.

That evening she told her husband how their daughter had answered her with tears. Messer Antonio was far from happy at the news and decided that he had better not risk some disgrace by going ahead with the marriage contract until he had first consulted his daughter on the matter. And so one day he sent for her and said: 'Giulietta, I'm about to arrange a noble marriage for you: dearest daughter, doesn't that make you happy?' After a long silence, she replied:

'No, father, it won't make me happy.'

'So you prefer to become a nun?'

'I don't know, sir.' And she burst into a flood of tears.

'But I know. I know you don't want it. Well, you'd better make up your mind to it, because I'm going to have you married to one of the counts of Lodrone.'

'That will never be,' she answered, with even more tears.

Messer Antonio was so angry that he threatened to beat her if she dared to defy him again and if she refused to reveal the cause of her weeping. And since he could get nothing from her but tears, still ignorant of what was in her mind, he went off in a rage, leaving her with Madonna Giovanna.

Giulietta's father had a servant called Pietro, who knew of her love for Romeo, and to him she repeated everything that her mother had said; and in his presence she swore that she would willingly drink poison rather than have anyone but Romeo as husband, even if she were free to do so. And Pietro, as they had arranged, conveyed the news to Romeo via Fra Lorenzo. Romeo then wrote to Giulietta saying that on no account should she consent to the marriage or reveal the love between them, because within a week or ten days he would find a way to abduct her from her father's house.

Meanwhile Messer Antonio and Madonna Giovanna found that

neither by cajolery nor threats could they discover their daughter's reason for refusing the marriage; nor was there any way of finding out who her lover might be. Madonna Giovanna kept telling her: 'Now look, daughter, there's no need to cry; we'll find you the kind of husband you want, even if it turns out to be a Montecchi—though I know you wouldn't want that.' But Giulietta gave no answer but sighs and tears. This made them more anxious than ever and they resolved to go ahead with the Lodrone marriage as soon as possible.

When Giulietta heard this she became thoroughly dejected and kept calling on death to release her. She decided, however, to confide in Fra Lorenzo for she had greater hope in him than in anybody except Romeo, who had indeed told her of the wonderful things the friar could do. One day, therefore, she said to Madonna Giovanna: 'Dear mother, don't be surprised if I don't tell you the cause of my grief because I don't even know it myself; I only know that I always feel so depressed that it makes everything a burden, even life itself. And I cannot imagine where this comes from, let alone tell you or my father. Unless, perhaps it is the result of some sin I have committed but can't remember. My last confession helped me so much that with your permission I should like to go to confession again so that when Whitsun comes I can receive the sweet medicine of Our Saviour's body* as a remedy for my sickness.'

Madonna Giovanna gave her consent and two days later she took Giulietta to the monastery of San Francesco and left her with Fra Lorenzo, but only after insisting that he should use the girl's confession to find out the cause of her depression. As soon as her mother had left them together, the girl told the friar the whole story of her troubles and, in the name of the love and friendship that bound him to Romeo, begged him to help her in her hour of need. The friar replied: 'What can I do for you, my daughter, when there is such enmity between your husband's house and yours?' 'Father,' said she, 'I know that you can do many things and help me in a thousand ways, if you so wish; but if you do nothing else for me, do at least this. I hear that my wedding is being prepared in a manor of my father beyond the city bounds, about two miles on the road to Mantua. They think that once they've taken me there I won't have the courage to refuse this new husband who will already be waiting before I arrive. Give me enough poison to free myself from such suffering and Romeo from such shame. If not, we shall both suffer more, for I shall bathe a dagger in my own blood.' When Friar Lorenzo heard how determined she was, he remembered how much he still depended on the discretion of Romeo who would certainly become an enemy if he failed him on this occasion.

'Look, Giulietta,' he said, 'I admit that I confess about half the inhabitants of this city and that there's not a will or a pact that I don't have something to do with; and so for all the world I don't want to get involved in any kind of scandal or have it known that I was mixed up in this business. But since I love you and Romeo, I'm ready to do something that I've never done for anyone else, provided you keep it absolutely secret.' And she: 'Father, you can safely give me that poison; nobody else will ever know of it.' 'No, my daughter,' he replied, 'I shall not give you poison, for it would be too great a sin if you should die so young and so beautiful; but if you have the courage to do what I tell you, I can promise to bring you safely to your Romeo. You know that the crypt of your Cappelletti is in the graveyard of this monastery. I shall give you a powder to drink that will make you sleep for about forty-eight hours so deeply that no doctor, however learned, will doubt that you are dead. Just as if you had really departed this life, you will certainly be buried in the crypt; and then, when the time comes, I shall come to take you out of it and hide you in my cell until I go to Mantua for the general assembly of our order. This will be quite soon and I shall take you to your husband, disguised as one of our order. But tell me, won't you be afraid of the corpse of your cousin Tebaldo who was buried there so recently?' The answer was joyful: 'Father, if it were the way to Romeo, I would be ready to pass through Hell.' 'Well then,' said he, 'since that is how you feel, I shall be happy to help you. But before we do anything, I think you should write to Romeo and tell him everything; I know how much he loves you and if he believes you're dead he could do something desperate. I always have brethren who go to Mantua where, as you know, Romeo is waiting. Let me have that letter and I'll send it to him by some trusty messenger.'

As we have seen, no serious project could be brought to conclusion without the good friar, who now left the girl in the confessional, went to his cell, and came back with a little bottle. 'Take this powder,' he said, 'mix it with cold water and at the third or fourth hour of night, drink it without fear: it will begin to take effect at around six, and our plan is sure to succeed. But don't forget to send me that letter for

Romeo which is very important.' Giulietta took the powder and went happily back to her mother, saying: 'Truly, mother, Fra Lorenzo is the best confessor in the world. He has been so comforting that I've almost forgotten my old sorrows.' Madonna Giovanna was relieved to find her daughter so cheerful and said: 'One of these days, daughter, you should do something for him; give alms, perhaps, since friars are always poor.' And talking of such matters, they came home.

Seeing that Giulietta had become so cheerful after her confession, Messer Antonio and Madonna Giovanna dropped the idea that she might be in love and concluded that her weeping and melancholy must have been caused by some strange inexplicable accident; and they would have been happy to leave things as they were without giving her a husband. But the affair was already so far advanced that it could not be simply abandoned without serious consequences.

Now the count of Lodrone was eager that some of his relatives should see his future wife and since Madonna Giovanna's health was rather fragile, it was decided that two aunts should accompany the girl to the country manor that we have already mentioned. Giulietta raised no objection and went with them, but once there she was seized by fear that her father had sent her off so suddenly because he meant to give her a second husband without further delay. She had brought with her the powder given her by the friar and that night, at about the fourth hour, she called a maidservant who had been brought up with her and was almost like a sister. Saying that the food she had eaten that evening had made her thirsty, she asked for a cup of cold water, dissolved the potent powder, and drank it all down. Then she turned to the maid and to an aunt who was there, and said: 'My father certainly won't give me a husband against my will, if I can help it.' The two women heard these words but did not understand them for they were simple folk; and although they had seen her drink the powder which she said she took to refresh herself, they suspected nothing and went back to sleep.

With the light out and the maidservant departed, Giulietta found some natural pretext to get up, dressed herself from head to foot, and lay down again, her arms crossed upon her breast like someone about to die, waiting for the potion to work. In little more than two hours she appeared to be dead.

When morning came and the sun was already high in the sky, the girl was found lying on her bed in the way I have described. Unable to wake her, and finding her already growing cold, the aunt and the maidservant remembered what she had said and the powder and the water that she had drunk the night before. And when they saw her fully dressed, lying on the bed in that deliberate posture, they concluded that the powder must have been poison and that she was certainly dead. Both women burst out into loud cries, but it was especially the maidservant who wailed: 'O my lady, this is what you meant when you said "My father won't have me married against my will!" You tricked me into giving you the cold water that caused your death. Wretch that I am, should I blame death or should I first blame myself? I alone have killed you and myself and your father and your mother all at once. Oh, why did you reject in death the company of the servant you seemed to cherish in life? For as I was always happy to live with you, so I would have happily died with you.' And she threw herself on the bed and embraced the corpse-like body of the girl.

Messer Antonio, who was not far off, heard the noise and ran trembling to his daughter's room. And when he saw her lying on the bed and heard what she had drunk and what she had said, he was convinced that she was dead. Nevertheless, he still took the precaution of sending to Verona for the family doctor, who came and examined and touched her before declaring that the girl had passed away two hours earlier after drinking poison. The sad news soon reached the unfortunate mother who fell down in a cold swoon, drained of all vital warmth. Then, coming to herself, she gave a piercing scream, beating her breast like a madwoman, filling the heavens with her lament and calling her beloved daughter by name: 'Dead, dead, my daughter, you, the only support of my old age! How cruel to leave your poor mother like this, not even there to hear your last words, to close your lovely eyes! Dear ladies who attend me here, help me to die, and if there is any pity in your hearts, let your hands kill me before my sorrow does. And you, O God in Heaven, since I cannot die as soon as I wish, let your lightning take me from my hateful self.' Raised up by one of the women and helped onto her bed, she wept bitter tears and grieved without ceasing. Soon after, the body of the girl was transported to Verona where, after a solemn funeral and mourned by all her relatives and friends, she was placed, as if she were truly dead, in the family crypt in the cemetery of San Francesco.

Fra Lorenzo, meanwhile, was out of the city on monastery business and had given Giulietta's letter for Romeo to a friar who was going to

Mantua. The friar went to Romeo's lodgings two or three times, but, as ill luck would have it, could never find him at home; and so, reluctant as he was to deliver it to anyone but Romeo in person, he still had the letter in his hands. Back in Verona, the faithful servant Pietro, believing that Juliet was dead and desperate at not finding Fra Lorenzo in the city, took it on himself to bring Romeo the tragic news of his wife's death. Leaving his master's country manor at dusk, he set off for Mantua and arrived the following morning. When he found Romeo, who had still not received his wife's letter, he gave a tearful account of how he had seen Giulietta dead and buried and also related in detail all that she had said and done in the hours before her death.

When Romeo heard the news, he became as pale as death and drew his sword to kill himself. Restrained by Pietro, he burst out: 'My life can last no longer, since she who was my life is dead. O Giulietta, I alone am the cause of your death, for I wrote that I would come and take you away from your father, and then I failed to do so. You chose to die rather than abandon me, and shall I then live alone for fear of death? Never!' Then, turning to Pietro, he gave him the brown cloak that he was wearing, and said: 'Now go, Pietro, my friend.'

Left alone, Romeo locked himself away and, feeling that nothing could be sadder than this life, thought hard what he should now do with himself. At last, dressed as a peasant and hiding in his sleeve a small phial of poisoned water that he had reserved in case of need, he set out for Verona. He hoped he would either be caught by the authorities and lose his life (though he would have wished a more honourable death) or else go to the crypt, since he well knew where it was, to lock himself in with his wife and die there. Fortune favoured the latter project, for the following evening, hardly more than a day after Giulietta's funeral, he entered Verona without being recognized; and when night came and all was quiet he went to the cemetery of the Franciscans where the crypt was.

At that time the Conventual Friars in Verona did not yet occupy the site of San Fermo, and the Observants* had not yet separated from them to found the convent of San Bernardino. All the Franciscans assembled in the little church of San Francesco where the saint himself had stayed and which can still be seen inside the citadel; and there they followed faithfully the true rule of the order, so distorted nowadays by the scandalous lifestyle of their successors. Built up against the outer walls of this place, as with other churches, there used to be a number of monumental crypts. One of these was the ancient crypt of all the Cappelletti where the lovely girl now lay, and it was about the fourth hour when Romeo arrived. Being a strong young man, he was able to lift the heavy covering slab which he then propped open with poles that he had brought with him to prevent it from falling back until he chose. Then he slipped into the crypt, removed the props, and closed it up again. The unfortunate youth now opened a covered lantern that he had brought with him so that he could take a last look at his wife, and there he saw his fair Giulietta, lying as if dead on the heaped rags and bones of a mass of corpses. At this sight, over-come with tears, he broke into a passionate lament: 'O eyes that were the clear light of mine while it pleased Heaven! O mouth that I have sweetly kissed a thousand times and that always uttered such wise words! O that fair breast that sheltered my heart in such joy! Where do I find you now, blind, speechless, and cold? O most ill-fated lady, to what end have you been led by Love? To this narrow space, the death and refuge of two sad lovers! Alas, is this the promised end of all those hopes when first I burned with love for you? What still binds me to this miserable life?'

So saying, he kissed her eyes and mouth and breast, weeping ever more abundantly and calling to the stone slab above his head: 'Could you but fall upon me now and shorten my sad life! And yet all men are free to choose death; only a coward longs to lose his life and fails to take it.' Then he took the phial of poison from his sleeve and said: 'I do not know what fate condemns me to die in their tomb among the enemies that I killed; but yet it pleases me to die beside my lady, and die I shall.' Raising the poison to his mouth, he drank it to the last drop, and clasping the lovely girl in his arms, he cried out: 'O fair body, only end of all my desires, if any feeling remains in you when the soul has departed, or if you can see my cruel death, since I could not live with you happily in the sight of men, let me at least die with you sadly and in secret.' And still holding her close, he waited for death.

It was already time for Giulietta to awake as her natural warmth overcame the cold insensitivity brought on by the powder. Embraced and shaken in Romeo's arms, she came to herself and sighed: 'Where am I? Who is clasping me so tightly? Who's kissing me?' And think-ing that it must be Fra Lorenzo, she cried: 'Is this how you keep faith with Romeo? Is this how you bring me safely to him?' Romeo was astounded to hear his wife's living voice and, thinking perhaps of Pygmalion,* exclaimed: 'My sweet lady, do you not recognize me? I am your unhappy husband, come from Mantua, alone and in secret, to die here by your side.' Giulietta, finding herself in the crypt and in the arms of a man who claimed to be Romeo, at first hardly knew where she was; but when she freed herself from his grasp and looked into his face, she immediately knew him and embraced him with a thousand kisses, saying: 'What madness brought you here and into such danger? Surely you knew from my letters that with Fra Lorenzo's help I was going to feign death and that I would soon be with you?'

Then the ill-fated young man understood what a fatal mistake he had made, and broke out: 'O my wretched misfortune! O miserable Romeo! The most unlucky of all lovers! I never had your letters.' And then he told her how Pietro had taken her feigned death for real and given him the news, so that he had meant to keep her company in death by taking poison—the poison that he felt at that moment spreading death through all his limbs. On hearing this, the poor maiden was so overcome by grief that she could do nothing but tear her lovely tresses and beat her innocent breast, kissing Romeo who was already lying stretched on the ground and bathing him with a flood of tears. Trembling and paler than ashes, she said: 'Must you then die in my presence and by my fault? And will Heaven suffer that I should live after you, for however short a time? Wretch that I am, if only I could give you my life and be the only one to die!' To which Romeo, with fainting voice, replied: 'If my faith and love were ever dear to you, I beg you to live on after me—if only to think sometimes of one who lived for love of you and died for love before your eyes.' And Giulietta answered: 'If you will die because of my feigned death, what should I then do for your death unfeigned? I regret only that I can find no way of dying here before you, and I hate myself for being still alive. But as I was the cause of your death, so I hope soon to be your companion in dying.' She struggled to complete the phrase and then fell to the ground where she remained senseless until, with a painful effort, she went to catch the dying breath of her lover on her own sweet lips.

Fra Lorenzo in the meantime had heard how Giulietta had drunk the powder and been buried as if she were dead. And since he knew that the time had come when the effect of the powder would wear off, about an hour before daybreak he went with a trusted companion to take the girl out of the crypt. When he arrived he heard her weeping and moaning and, looking through a chink in the slab, he was surprised to see a light inside and supposed that the girl had somehow contrived to bring a lantern with her into the crypt and that she had now woken up and was weeping for fear of the dead or because she was afraid of being closed in there forever. With the help of his companion, he quickly opened the crypt and saw Giulietta sitting there, grieving and dishevelled, cradling her expiring lover in her lap. 'Were you afraid that I would leave you here to die?' said he. But when she saw him her tears redoubled as she answered: 'No indeed; my fear is that you will take me out alive. Ah, for God's sake, close up the tomb, go away and let me die. Or give me a dagger so that I can end my pains by stabbing myself to the heart. O Father, Father, you must have sent the letter! Soon I shall be truly married! Soon you will lead me to Romeo! You see him here, already dead in my lap.'

And then she told him everything that had happened. Fra Lorenzo heard the story and was lost in amazement, and as he looked on Romeo who was about to pass into the next life, he wept bitterly and called out: 'O Romeo, what disaster takes you from me? Say something; turn your eyes towards me. See how your dear Giulietta begs you to look on her! You are lying in her lap; say something to her at least.' At the sound of his wife's loved name, Romeo raised his fading eyes, already clouded by death, and saw her and closed them. Soon after, he heaved one brief sigh and died.

When the unhappy lover had died in the way I have described, the friar wept for some time; but then, as daybreak was near, he said to the girl: 'And you, Giulietta, what will you do?'

'I shall die in here.'

'Surely not, daughter: don't say that. Come out. I may not know how I can help you now, but you will surely find some convent where you can retire and pray for yourself and your dead husband, if he needs it.'

'Father, I ask you only one favour which you will grant me in memory of the love you bore to this man' —and she pointed to Romeo—'and that is never to reveal our death, so that our bodies may remain together in this tomb forever. And if by chance our death should be known, then, for that same love, beg our wretched fathers, in both our names, to leave those whom Love burned with a single flame to rest in a single tomb.'

She turned to Romeo whose head she had laid on a pillow that had been left with her in the tomb, and after reverently closing his eyes and bathing his cold face with her tears, she said: 'What could I do in life without you, my lord? and what else can I do for you now except follow you into death? No, nothing else, for though only death could separate me from you, that same death has no power to keep us apart.' With this, her spirit overwhelmed by her misfortune and by the loss of her beloved, she resolved to live no longer. She forced herself to hold her breath until at last she fell lifeless upon the body of her husband.

When he realized that the girl was dead, Fra Lorenzo was so stunned by grief that all he could do was weep over the dead lovers, together with his companion, and it was in this state that they were seen by some local people who had risen early and who recognized them by the light coming from the tomb. One of them immediately went to tell the Cappelletti who then hurried off to Lord Bartolomeo to insist that he find out, by torture if necessary, what the friar was doing in their crypt. And their anger was all the greater because they knew that the friar was a friend of their enemies. The lord, having placed guards to make sure that the friar could not escape, had him summoned and asked: 'What were you looking for this morning, reverend sir, in the crypt of the Cappelletti? Tell us, for we are determined to know.' But while the friar was trying to invent stories to excuse himself and hide the truth, his brethren from the monastery, who had heard the news, went to open the crypt and look inside to see if they could discover what the two friars had been doing there the night before. And when they saw the dead body of Romeo, they made a great noise and hurried to the lord who was still questioning the friar. There they announced that Romeo Montecchi was lying dead in the crypt of the Cappelletti where the friar had been caught that night. This struck everyone as something amazing and almost beyond belief; and Fra Lorenzo, seeing that he could no longer hide things as he wished, knelt before Lord Bartolomeo and said: 'Forgive me, my lord, if I told lies in answer to your questions. I did not do so out of malice or for personal gain, but to keep the promise that I made to two unfortunate lovers who are now dead.' And thus he was obliged to recount the whole story to a large audience.

When Bartolomeo della Scala had heard the tale, moved almost to tears, he went to see the dead bodies himself, and went to the crypt followed by a great crowd. He had the two lovers taken out and placed on two rich cloths in the church of San Francesco. At the same time the fathers of the lovers came to that church and wept over their dead children; and though they had long been enemies, they embraced, overcome by a double sorrow. Thus the enmity between them and their houses—an enmity that neither the prayers of their friends, nor the threats of Lord Bartolomeo, nor the harm they suffered, nor even the passage of time had ever been able to extinguish—was brought to an end by the tragic and pitiful death of these lovers. The two were given a fine monument on which was carved the cause of their death; and with a grand and solemn funeral, attended and mourned by the lord, by their relatives, and by the whole city, they were buried together.

GIOVANNI BREVIO

MADONNA LISABETTA
Rime e prose volgari (Vernacular Poetry and Prose)

Left a widow, Madonna Lisabetta falls in love with her son who is himself deeply in love with her maid. Thinking that he is with the maid, he lies with his mother who becomes pregnant and gives birth to a daughter. The son then becomes this girl's brother, father, and husband.

FAIR and loving ladies, there are certainly many unfortunate lovers, but no less great, I believe, is the number of strange events and wonderful effects that result from ever-deceptive love. And since the whole world today is full of such happenings, I do not think it unfitting to relate one of them which happened not so long ago. I am happy to do this, not only to raise your spirits, but also to offer some justification for you before those harsh and hypocritical men who look upon your actions with a stern face and condemn them far more severely than they deserve, as if you were not made of flesh and blood and created, moreover, with a nature more delicate and fragile than theirs. But if such men looked on themselves and their own actions with an impartial eye, they would surely be more gentle and compassionate judges and not hurry—or rather rush—to blame and shame your every action and motion, however insignificant. It is as if they alone were rightly privileged to say and do whatever they like, while you must behave like statues. I do not deny that immortal praise is due to those women, and men too, who quench the fiery and lustful carnal appetites with the pure water of morality and live decent, chaste, or at least prudent lives. But if we really consider the force of concupiscent love, the multitude of its impulses, and the fragility of human nature, then we shall conclude that those women who stumble when burning desire drives them into its snares are more deserving of compassion than of harsh condemnation. It is my pleasure, therefore, to tell you the story of how a worthy gentlewoman, possessed by excessive love, succeeded in satisfying her desire.

In our city,* where love causes more strange adventures than anywhere else in the world, there lived not so long ago a beautiful and
noble lady called Lisabetta. The death of her husband had left her
a widow, with only one son of about fifteen years of age, a youth as
handsome and charming as any in Venice. With this son the mother
fell passionately in love, with a carnal and lascivious desire so fierce
that she could have no joy except when watching or thinking of him.
And the noble lady found this love all the more difficult to bear in that
her great sense of decency forbade her to reveal it. Thus, from day to
day, as her son grew yet more handsome and gracious in his ways, so
the flames of love rose ever higher in the heart of his mother. Knowing
her desire to be not only unchaste, but contrary to every divine and
human law, she bore with it patiently as best she could, pining and
wasting away like snow in the sunshine; and often she lamented her
sad fate and blamed herself, saying: 'Ah, wretched Lisabetta, what is
it that your soul seeks so eagerly? Can it be fitting for you to love like
this? How often have you closed your ears to the sweet pleading of
a host of worthy lovers ready to serve you in honest and proper fashion! And now you indulge a carnal lust for your own son, an even
graver sin than hating your father and mother! Must you then give
way to such lechery? Open the eyes of your mind and see yourself for
what you are: what would the world say if this were ever known?
Wouldn't you be blamed and pointed at for the rest of your life?
Yes, indeed. Pull yourself together; drive out such harmful wicked
thoughts; make space for reason and temper those unhealthy desires.
Turn your mind elsewhere and govern yourself with the reins of reason, break the bonds and fetters of this disgraceful and abominable
passion so that you may love him chastely as the laws of nature
dictate.'

But on the other hand, assailed by passion and still thinking of her
son, she answered herself: 'Alas for my distress! How is this love my
fault? Did I choose to fall in love like this? No, never: the heavens
have forced me to love him in this way; and if this be the will of the
stars, what can I do? They are stronger than we are; everybody and
everything in this world is subject to them and their power is far
greater than that of mortals such as we. How then can I, a mere
woman, defend myself against their force? How is it possible that
I should not love my son and not yearn to hold him always in my
arms? Surely this can never happen? Why should the laws forbid me

to love him? Why, among us, should the mother be forbidden to marry her son, and the father to marry the daughter, as happens elsewhere? Why wasn't I born in one of those lands? Must I suffer simply because I was born in this place?' Then, accusing herself again, she would pray God to free her from that passion; yet still, whenever she saw her son, she burned with new and fiercer flames.

In this manner then, going over the same old ground, sometimes with the same old reasons and sometimes with new ones, the infatuated woman kept accusing and excusing herself, feeding on unceasing tears and laments, and living in the deepest distress, expecting nothing save that her own death or the work of all-consuming time might prove a healing remedy for her grievous and fatal wound. But not many days passed before Love, who rarely leaves his faithful to perish, showed how she could satisfy her desires in all secrecy. Madonna Lisabetta had a beautiful and seductive young maid whose sole task was to keep order in her mistress's chamber and assist her in dressing. Now Girolamo (for this was the name of Lisabetta's son) was burning with love for this maid and she for him; but their love could find no consummation, being restrained by fear of his mother who already nursed some suspicion of the affair and kept careful watch over them with jealous eyes. And so, with mere gestures and glances, and sometimes (though not often) with a few snatched kisses, their life went on as they waited for some benign fate to offer them a chance to fulfil their amorous desires. Now while these naughty young lovers spent their time yearning for each other, it happened that Girolamo resolved to speak with Elena (for that was the maid's name) and, knowing that she was in his mother's room, waited for her outside the door; and when she came out he went up to her in the dark and, without speaking, put his arm round her neck and tried to kiss her. Elena knew all too well who her assailant was and struggled to escape for fear of being caught in the act; Girolamo clasped her as tightly as he could and she continued to resist. In the midst of all this Madonna Lisabetta, alerted by the shuffling and scuffling, took off her slippers and came to the door where she heard her son imploring Elena that at six o'clock that very night she should wait for him in a room on the ground floor of the house. It did not take much pleading for Elena to agree, and after a sweet exchange of kisses, they went their separate ways.

To Madonna Lisabetta, who had heard everything, it seemed that Love and Fortune had finally shown her the way to get the one thing she wanted more than anything else. When the time was right, she called Elena and handed her a pair of sleeves that she had carefully torn in advance, telling her to stitch them up and, for her life's sake, not to go to bed or leave the room until she had finished the job. Then, feigning to go and say her customary evening prayers, she went into another room through a door that was in her chamber; and there, after closing the door and locking it with her key, she remained a while, deep in thought about what she intended to do. At last, overcome by love, against which no human force can avail, she went down the stairs that led to the room on the ground floor, and waited in the dark for her son. He soon arrived, and believing her to be his Elena, sweetly embraced her; and far more warmly was he received into the arms of his mother. And so in silence they shared that pleasure and sweetness than which, without doubt, nothing can be greater. Thus for a long time they remained, until at last, with whispered and broken speech, artfully employed so as not to be recognized by her son, Lisabetta arranged a meeting for the following night. Then they separated.

The relationship continued in this way until Madonna Lisabetta became pregnant; and when the time to give birth came near she went to her country house; there she gave birth to a lovely daughter whom she secretly confided to a wet nurse before returning home. Not long after this, she had her chambermaid married off to a servant of one of her relatives who was leaving to become consul in Corfu.* Thus was Elena sent on her way.

Two years later Madonna Lisabetta sent for her daughter under the pretence that she was taking in a child from the orphanage to be brought up in her own home for the love of God—the kind of charitable action that is a daily occurrence in our city, and indeed, she looked after the girl as carefully and lovingly as if she were her own daughter. So Giulia (for this was the girl's name), being properly fed, grew up with such beauty and such gracious manners that she was a wonder to behold; and when she reached marriageable age, Girolamo began to look at her often and attentively, and finding her extraordinarily attractive, he fell head over heels in love. This did not escape the notice of Madonna Lisabetta who kept a strict watch over her, to the great discontent of Girolamo. At last, almost despairing and knowing that his love could find no satisfaction as long as his mother maintained this tight control over Giulia, he resolved that, whatever the consequences, he would take her as his wife. One day, entering his mother's room when she was alone, he confessed his burning love for Giulia, revealing all his emotions and intentions; and in short, as fervently as he could, he begged her to consent to his wishes. His mother was stunned to hear this and pleaded with her son not to even think of such a thing. She told him that if he really wanted to get married, he could choose among the city's best matches, with ladies who were beautiful, noble, and rich—unlike Giulia who, she said, was not his equal and had neither property nor money nor family. She added that if he went ahead, he would bring great shame not only on himself, but also on her and on all her family; and, to conclude, she did everything in her power to persuade him to give it up.

But Girolamo, moved more by love than by good sense, went on pleading with his mother and, adding tears to his pleas, vowed that he would die of his passion if this thing were denied him. And his words and actions proved so effective that his mother began to fear that her son might really fall ill. Moreover, she knew all too well the power that love's flames can have in a noble sensitive soul. All told, she preferred to have her son alive and well—though with a touch of shame and a rather guilty conscience—rather than dead or sick with the most honourable of wives and a sinless soul; and so she consented to his marriage with Giulia.

Since Girolamo was bursting with impatience, it took only a few days for the relatives to be informed and to gather at the house, as is the custom in our city, and the marriage was celebrated in a most splendid and decorous way. All these people are still alive, and may God give them many years of pleasure.

This then, dear ladies, is what came of the passion of Madonna Lisabetta who, as I said at the start of my tale, is to be excused, given the power of love and the weakness of human nature. Nonetheless, considering how harmful to the soul and disgraceful to the body is intercourse with one's own blood, I believe that there is no one among you who would not blame such a relation and avoid it altogether. And for this I commend you all the more insofar as you lead your lives in simplicity and purity, seeking only those loves that Nature, kind mother and teacher of life, may bring before you.

MATTEO BANDELLO

THE COUNTESS OF CHALLANT
Novelle (Tales) 1. 4

From Bandello to the Most Illustrious and Excellent
Lady Isabella d'Este, Marchioness of Mantua*

OFTEN, my lady, since the pitiful death of the countess of Challant,*
I have remembered what you told me not so long ago in your pleasant
house in Diporto about when she was married to her first husband,
Lord Ermes Visconti,* whom God receive into glory. You said that he
was thought to be very jealous and that he was much blamed for this
in Milan. He did not allow her to go visiting, except to the home of
Lady Ippolita Sforza Bentivoglio,* where I often saw and talked with
her myself. She was still a girl, and, like most girls, she wanted to go
out and enjoy herself as freely as Milanese ladies do; and especially on
one occasion, when she had been invited somewhere, she begged
Lady Ippolita to plead with Lord Ermes on her behalf. Lady Ippolita
did, indeed, perform that office one day when I was with Lord
Ermes and there were only the three of us present. Lord Ermes listened to the request and answered with a smile: 'My lady, I shall not
consult Bandello, knowing him to be both your servant and my friend.
You will forgive me if I don't allow my wife to go wherever she likes or
grant her the kind of liberty that is common in Milan. I know the trot
and walk of my filly and I see no reason to take the bridle from her
neck. And I must ask you not to speak to me of this again. To this
house she can always come, day or night, as long as you're here; but
I don't want her to go visiting anywhere else.'

When he had left, Lady Ippolita and I talked at length about what
had made him speak like that, but the truth is that we could never
work it out. But now the life that the unfortunate woman lived after
the death of Lord Ermes and the way she ended up have given the lie
to all those who thought that her husband was jealous. The wise lord
knew very well what he was doing and, as he said, he knew the trot of

his palfrey. And in fact Lord Ermes was a very prudent and wise young man who governed his wife so well while he lived that she was respected as one of the most decent and proper ladies in Milan. But in one thing I think he was badly mistaken. Being, as we know, among the most prominent gentlemen of the city, noble and of great wealth, he should have married a noblewoman, high-born and reared in a noble household; instead of which he chose a woman whose blood was in no way a match for his own and whose rank depended entirely on the profits of usury. Men who want to breed a race of fine horses look for fertile mares bred from fine and noble mares. It is the same for all who love hunting, whether for birds or beasts; they look for dogs with a good pedigree and reject those who are not of good stock. And if, by any chance, their bitch gets covered by some mongrel, they drown all the puppies. What more can I say? If a man wants to buy clothes and shoes, he looks for good wool and good leather. But nowadays all that men look for in a wife is wealth—even though they should really ask who her father and mother were and think about that more than anything else. I prefer not to name one of Duke Galeazzo's most important vassals in Lombardy; he hoped to gain the duke's favour by marrying the daughter of one of his lord's captains, though she was fit for Bedlam. The result was so successful that, despite their rank and wealth, all the children he engendered with her were mad and did such completely mad things that they probably caused the ruin of the whole family.

Not long ago I heard Messer Antonio Sabino* speak on this subject. He is a cultured and experienced gentleman, an administrator for the Counts Bolognini, lords of Sant'Angelo and sons of Count Matteo Attendolo and Lady Agnese of Correggio. He had many things to say on this topic and delighted his audience by outlining all the things that one should look for most carefully in a bride, concluding that, for many good reasons, the dowry should be the last. When he turned to the particular case of Lady Bianca Maria, since she ended her days in Romagna, I begged him to satisfy my curiosity by recounting the whole story of her unhappy loves and her death; and since he is always more than ready to do whatever he can for his friends, he immediately did so. Thus, having written it down so that it can be added to my other tales and eventually read with them, I am minded to preface it with your name and offer it to you. And so, my most illustrious lady, I send it to you, humbly imploring you not to frown if I should use your worthy and illustrious name in a matter of such modest import. If you are not displeased, then our gentle Messer Mario* may one day read it to you. May Our Lord God preserve you.

The countess of Challant has the count of Masino murdered, and is herself decapitated.

My lords, you should know that the Lady Bianca Maria that we have been speaking of—I say 'lady' in respect of the rank of her two husbands—was of low birth and undistinguished ancestry, her father being Giacomo Scappardone, a plebeian* from Casal di Monferrato. This Giacomo used all the money he had for usury, lending at such exorbitant interest that, having started in the profession when he was young, he became rich enough to buy a considerable amount of property. And since he spent little, he acquired great wealth. His wife was a Greek woman who had come from Greece with the mother of Marquis Guglielmo* who was the father of the duchess of Mantua. This wife of Giacomo was a very beautiful and attractive woman, but there was a great difference in age between her and her husband, for he was already an old man while she was not more than twenty. They had only one child, a daughter who is the Bianca Maria of my story. When her father died, the little girl was brought up by her mother with a fortune in property worth more than a hundred thousand ducats. A good-looking child, as lively and graceful as any girl could be, she was about fourteen or fifteen when she became the wife of Ermes Visconti (son of that venerable patrician Battista) who led her off to Milan with all pomp and circumstance and triumphal festivities. And before she entered the city, Francesco, the elder brother of Ermes, sent her the gift of a magnificent carriage, all inlaid and decorated with gold, and covered by a pleated brocade, studded with splendid designs and embroidery. It was drawn by four coursers of great price and as white as ermine: and on this carriage Bianca Maria made her triumphal entrance into Milan where she lived with Ermes for about six years.

When Lord Ermes died, she went back to Casal di Monferrato and there, finding herself rich and free, she began to live a carefree life and indulge in all kinds of dalliance. There were many who courted her and asked her hand in marriage—the most notable of these were Lord Gismondo Gonzaga,* son of Giovanni Gonzaga, and the count of Challant,* baron of Savoy who resides in the Valley of Aosta where he possesses many castles that bring in a considerable revenue. The marchioness of Monferrato, hoping to please her son-in-law of Mantua, did everything she could to marry Bianca Maria to Gismondo, and the wedding had almost been agreed; but the count of Challant courted her so effectively and pleaded his case so well that their marriage was both celebrated and consummated in secret. The marchioness, though highly displeased and ready to play some nasty trick on Bianca Maria, still managed to hide her anger, and out of respect for the count took no further action. So the marriage was made public and the wedding took place, but with a gloomy prospect for what was to follow.

And indeed there seems to be some truth in the proverb that says 'quick to love and soon to hate', for the couple were not together long before a furious quarrel broke out between them; and whatever the cause may have been, she secretly left her husband and went to Pavia where she took over a fine comfortable house and led a very free and far from respectable life.

Now at that time Ardizzino Valperga,* count of Masino, and his brother Signor Carlo were in the Emperor's service. Happening to be in Pavia, Ardizzino caught sight of Bianca Maria, fell in love, and began serving her in everything and using every art to achieve his aim. And although he was somewhat lame in one foot, he was still a handsome and courteous young man, so that in a few days he gained possession of the lady. For more than a year he enjoyed her so fully and so openly that it was the talk not just of Pavia but of all the surrounding countryside. Then, however, she set eyes on Roberto Sanseverino,* count of Gaiazzo, a fine upstanding young man, who had just come to Pavia. She judged that he might be more vigorous and grind the corn better than her current miller with whom, perhaps, she was already sated. And so she resolved to take him as her new lover. She began to frown on Ardizzino, denying him entrance and refusing to be with him, until at last they exchanged harsh words. The young woman, bolder than she should have been and forgetting what they had done together, began to revile him, calling him a lame dog, a cripple, and many other offensive names. And Ardizzino, who was no man to bear such insults, unleashed his anger, damning her to her face as a shameless harlot, a strumpet, and a slut. And so, where there had been such great love, there was now born the most bitter hatred on both sides.

Ardizzino left Pavia and wherever he heard talk of Bianca Maria, he came out with all the insulting things that could be said of a whore in a brothel. And when she heard, as she often did, what her rejected lover was saying about her, she gave herself entirely to Count Gaiazzo, thinking that in this way she could lure him into doing whatever she wished. Thus, one day, in the midst of their amorous pleasures, when the count was obviously consumed with love for her, she begged him to do her the singular favour of killing Ardizzino who did nothing but speak ill of her. Though this proposition came as a great surprise to the count, he not only promised to do it, but vowed that he would do anything to assist her and was always ready to serve her. At the same time, however, seeing how malignant the woman was and considering that Ardizzino was a noble gentleman and his good friend, he decided to do nothing to harm him. Moreover, he reflected that Ardizzino might have some good reason to feel offended by him since, without knowing it, he had driven the count of Masino from his amorous possession of Bianca Maria. He, therefore, took his time and continued to enjoy himself with the lady.

This went on for some months until Bianca Maria saw that, though Ardizzino had been in Pavia two or three times, the count had still not attacked him or tried to have him murdered. Instead, he had greeted him as a friend and even dined in his company. And so she decided to break with the count. Whatever the reason, she now started pretending to be sick and refused to see him, finding one excuse or another. But, above all, she said that her husband Challant had sent messengers to her in view of a reconciliation and that she was eager to do whatever she could to return to him. So she begged the count of Gaiazzo to stop consorting with her, so that when her husband's emissaries came to Pavia they would give a good report of her. Whether the count believed this story or not, he certainly behaved as if he did. With no further words, he simply walked out and shook off the whole affair; and to avoid being tempted again, he left Pavia and went to Milan.

Lady Bianca Maria, seeing that he had left and remembering that she had been more free with Ardizzino who loved her so intensely, began to change her hatred for Ardizzino into love—or rather, perhaps, to change her appetite. Once she had made up her mind to go back to their old love games, she found a way of speaking to him and making her excuses, declaring that she belonged only to him and meant to remain so forever, if he agreed; and she begged him to do the same and be entirely hers as she was eternally his. This, then, was how things turned out: Ardizzino joined the dance again and resumed possession of Bianca Maria's amorous favours, remaining with her all the time, both day and night. They had been together for days on end when it suddenly struck the lady that she might have the count of Gaiazzo murdered. And if anybody had asked the reason, I rather doubt if she would have been able to find one—unless, as a witless woman who found nothing out of the way in the most wicked actions, she might have appealed to her own disordered and immoral appetites. By these, without any shadow of reason, she was not so much ruled as furiously driven—driven to the miserable end that awaited her and others, as you shall hear me tell.

With this in mind, therefore, and feeling that she could not be happy as long as the count of Gaiazzo remained alive, the only solution she could find was to persuade Ardizzino to become the assassin. One night, when she was with him in bed, in the midst of their amorous sport, she said: 'For the last few days, my lord, I've been meaning to ask you a favour, and I hope you won't deny me.' 'I'm ready to do whatever you command,' said her lover, 'however difficult it may be, as long as I have the power to see it through.' 'Tell me,' said she, 'is the count of Gaiazzo your friend?' 'Certainly,' he replied, 'I believe he is my friend, and a good one, because I love him like a brother, and I know that he loves me and would do anything to please me, as I would for him. But why do you ask?' 'I'll tell you,' she answered with half-a-dozen loving kisses, 'you are, my dearest, greatly deceived, for I'm firmly convinced that you have no greater enemy in the world. And hear how I know this, so that you don't think it's all in my imagination. Once, when he was my lover and we happened to speak of you, he swore that he would never be at ease until he'd plunged a poisoned dagger into your breast, and he hoped that before long he'd play you such a trick that you'd never eat bread again. And he went on abusing you, but would never tell me the reason, though I used all my loving charms to get it out of him. In any case, even though I was still angry with you, I kept begging him not to go through with such a thing. But he answered angrily that he was determined to do it and that I should drop the subject. So beware of him, go carefully, and watch out for yourself. But if you listened to me, I could show you how you wouldn't need to fear him and his bluster. I would act first and do to him what he wants to do to you. You're perfectly placed to deceive him, and you'll be praised and admired for it. Believe me, if you don't move first, he won't sleep, and one day, when you're not thinking of it, he'll have you murdered. Just follow my advice, have him killed as soon as you can; and you won't just be doing your duty as a knight by preserving your own dear life, but you'll also be doing me one of the greatest possible favours. If you don't want to do it for your own sake, do it for love of me, for if you gave me a whole city, it wouldn't be worth the gift of seeing that old mumbler dead. If you love me as I think you do, you'll rid the world of that puffed-up piece of pride who cares for neither God nor man.'

The woman might have persuaded Ardizzino that her story was true, had it not been for this last emotional outburst which suggested that she was moved by her special hatred for the count rather than by any love for him; and he was firmly convinced that the count had never said anything like what he had just heard. Nevertheless, he behaved as if he had taken the warning to heart, thanked her repeatedly, and promised that he would follow her wise advice. But he had no intention of doing so; instead, he meant to go to Milan and talk it over with the count, and so he did. Once in Milan, he found an occasion to speak with the count and promptly revealed everything that the woman had said to him. The count crossed himself in amazement and exclaimed: 'What a brazen whore she is! If it weren't below the honour of a gentleman to stain his hands with the blood of a woman—and especially a scandalous woman like her—I'd tear her lying tongue out of her throat. But first I'd like to hear her confess how many times she has crossed her heart and begged me to have you killed.' And so they learned from each other about the woman's vicious devices and discovered just how wicked she was—which is why, both in private and in public, they said all the ill that can be said of a guilty licentious woman, recounting her many misdeeds, and making her a common byword for vice.

When Bianca Maria heard what these gentlemen were saying about her, she pretended to take no notice; yet inwardly she was burning with anger and thinking of nothing but how she might be cruelly avenged. She then moved to Milan and stayed at the house of Lady Daria Boeta. Now in those days the Sicilian Don Pietro Cardona was also in Milan, commanding the company of Don Artale, his legitimate brother, he himself being the bastard son of the count of Collesano who died at the Battle of Bicocca.* This Don Pietro was a young man of twenty-two, well built, but with a dark complexion and a melancholy look; and seeing Maria Bianca one day, he fell passionately in love with her. Recognizing him straightaway as a prime gull who could be used to accomplish what she so longed for, she put on a smiling face and did everything in her power to dazzle him and trap him in her net. He had never loved a high-ranked lady so much, and thinking she must be among the most prominent ladies of Milan, he languished for her love. At last one night she took him to bed with her and gave him a most ardent welcome, seeming drunk with love, flattering him and mani-festing such amorous feeling in the pleasure they shared that he thought himself the happiest lover in all the world and cared for noth-ing but her. Thus he became so subject to her that soon after, having touched on certain arguments, she asked the young man if he would do her the special favour of murdering Ardizzino and the count of Gaiazzo. Don Pietro, who could not see things with any eyes but hers, made a solemn promise that he would, and wasted no time in setting about it.

Since the count of Gaiazzo was out of town, he decided to begin with Lord Ardizzino, had him followed by spies, and discovered that one night he would be dining away from home. It was winter when people dine late, so Don Pietro took twenty of his men, all armed from head to foot, and waited for Ardizzino's return. As you know, there is an arch over an alley that leads left from the Meravegli to the Corso San Giacomo. Knowing that this was where Lord Ardizzino would pass, Don Pietro and his men hid in a nearby hut and waited in ambush. And when the lookout told them that Ardizzino was coming with his brother Carlo, he stationed his men so that they closed off the alley and had the brothers surrounded. Now they began fighting hand to hand, but what could two young men and their eight or nine attendants, armed only with swords, do against so many assailants, fully armed and carrying pikes. The struggle was short; the unfortu-nate brothers were killed, as were most of their men.

That very night the duke of Bourbon,* who had escaped from France and was then representing the Emperor in Milan, managed to lay hands on Don Pietro and have him put in prison, where he soon confessed to having acted on the orders of his mistress Bianca Maria. She knew that Don Pietro had been captured and she would have had time to escape; and yet, for some reason or other, she remained in

Milan. The duke of Bourbon, having heard the confession of Don Pietro, gave orders to pick up the woman who, like a fool, took with her a strongbox containing fifteen thousand gold scudi, hoping that her cunning would get her out of prison. Don Pietro, meanwhile, had found accomplices who helped him escape from jail. But the wretched young woman, having confirmed with her own mouth the confession of her lover, was condemned to have her head cut off. When she heard the sentence she still did not know that Don Pietro had managed to break out, and she could not resign herself to death. At last she was led to the ravelin of the castle facing the square, and when she saw the block, she began to weep in despair, begging that they should let her see her Don Pietro if they wished her to die content. But she was singing to the deaf. Thus she was decapitated; and this was the end to which she was brought by her unbridled lusts. Those who desire to see her face painted from life should go to the church of Monastero Maggiore* and inside they will see her portrayed.

GIULIA OF GAZZUOLO
Novelle (Tales) 1. 8

From Bandello to the Most Illustrious and Reverend Lord, Monsignor Pirro Gonzaga, Cardinal*

IF our own days, my honoured lord, brought the same care and diligence as, for so long, the Greeks and Romans did to writing down events worthy of remembrance, I am convinced that our present age would deserve no less praise that those ancient times which writers so highly laud and celebrate. For if we talk of painting and sculpture, then our own painters and sculptors are at least equal to those vaunted names of antiquity, even if they may not be ranked above them. As for the literary works of modern times, I do not believe that they should give way before the ancient orators, poets, philosophers, and other writers, both Greek and Latin, as if they were not their peers. When were the military arts more highly valued than they are now? Think of Alexander the Great, Pyrrhus, Hannibal and Philopoemen, Quintus Fabius Maximus, those warlike Scipios, Marcellus, Pompey the Great, Caesar, and so many more famous heroes:* if they were alive today and could see our modern way of making war with sulphur and saltpetre,* they would surely take fright and yield to many of our captains, and in our simple soldiers they would see as much spirit, skill, and courage as they ever saw in their own men. But the trouble is that in these times nobody takes any pleasure in writing down what happens from day to day; and thus we lose many eloquent and shrewd observations, while a host of noble and memorable actions lie buried in dark oblivion. And yet remarkable things do happen every day, events that deserve to be enshrined for the memory of posterity. So now I shall choose one of these, something that happened a few years ago in Gazzuolo.

I had gone to pay my respects to your uncle, the noble lord Pirro Gonzaga,* and as we were talking about the various things that can happen, he asked my good friend, Messer Gian Matteo Olivo, the baritone,* to relate this little story. You were there yourself when he did so and you remarked that if this had happened in ancient times then Giulia of Gazzuolo* would be no less sung and celebrated than the famous Roman Lucrece,* were it not that she was of too lowly a birth. Now that I am assembling my tales, I want this story, which I wrote down at the time, to appear among the others armed with your noble and virtuous name so that you may know how dear you are to my memory. And how could it be otherwise since you have always loved and honoured me more than I deserve? But I could wish for some better occasion than a story to express the sincerity of my attachment to you and your illustrious family and my gratitude for the many kind attentions with which I am honoured every day. Keep well.

> *Giulia of Gazzuolo is raped, throws herself into the river Oglio, and is drowned.*

LORD PIRRO GONZAGA is marquis of Gonzaga and lord of Gazzuolo, a town that has long been owned by the Gonzaga family and that you can see from here on the banks of the Oglio facing towards the Po. It is Marquis Pirro, my gracious lord and honourable gentlemen, who has now asked me to recount the memorable death not so long ago of a certain Giulia who lived in this town. The illustrious lord could have told this tale far better himself and there are many here present who know the details as well as I do and could have told the whole story. But since he has ordered that I should be the storyteller, I am both willing and obliged to obey him. I only regret that I am not competent to praise the generous and valiant spirit of Giulia as her extraordinary deed deserves.

You should know then that while that wise and generous prince, the illustrious and most reverend Monsignor Lodovico Gonzaga,* bishop of Mantua, lived here in Gazzuolo, he kept a splendid court with many accomplished gentlemen for he well knew how to appreciate talent and spend freely. At that time there lived in Gazzuolo a young girl of seventeen called Giulia, the daughter of a very poor man of humble birth who had nothing but what his own arms could earn by toiling all day long to make a bare living for himself, his wife, and his two daughters. His wife, who was a good woman, also worked and earned something with spinning and suchlike female tasks. Now Giulia was very beautiful, having gracious manners and being altogether more lovely than was suitable for someone of her low birth. She would go out into the fields, sometimes with her mother and sometimes with the other women to dig or do whatever else was required. I remember that one day, when I was on the road to San Bartolomeo with Lady Antonia Bauzia,* mother of our illustrious lords, we met with Giulia who was coming home all alone with a basket on her head. Seeing this lovely girl, who must have been about fifteen at the time, my lady stopped the carriage to ask whose daughter she was. Giulia replied with all proper respect, giving the name of her father and answering all my lady's questions in such a fitting manner that she seemed not to have been born and brought up in a straw-roofed shack, but rather to have spent all her days being educated at court. So much so that my lady told me she wanted to take her home and bring her up with the other handmaids. Why nothing came of this I cannot say.* Coming back then to Giulia, I say that on working days she wasted no time, but was always busy whether alone or in company. On feast days, however, after dinner, as is the custom of the place, she would take some innocent pleasure and go dancing with the other girls.

Now one day, when she was about seventeen, a man from Ferrara who was a chamberlain of Monsignor the Bishop cast his hungry eyes on her as she was dancing; he thought she was the loveliest and most charming girl he had seen in a long time, and, as we have said, she seemed to have been brought up among the finest gentlefolk. He fell so madly in love with her that he could think of nothing else. When that dance, which felt very long to the chamberlain, finally came to an end, and when the musician struck up for another, he asked her to

dance with him. It was a galliard which Giulia danced particularly
well, keeping such perfect time that it was a delight to see how gracefully she moved. The chamberlain danced with her several times, and
if he had not been held back by a sense of propriety he would have
kept her for every dance, for when he was holding her hand, he
seemed to feel the greatest pleasure he had ever known. And although
she worked all day, her hand was slender, soft, and white. The wretched
lover, so suddenly inflamed, thought that by gazing on the girl's beauty
he could quench the blaze that threatened to destroy him; what he
failed to realize was that with every glance he only added kindling to
the fire. The second and third times he danced with her he started the
kind of sweet talk that young lovers try out, but she wisely replied that
he should not speak to her of love because it was not right for a poor
girl like herself to hear that kind of nonsense. And that was all the
insistent young Ferrarese could get out of her. When the dancing was
over, he followed her home so that he could find out where she lived,
and later, in Gazzuolo, he found several occasions to talk with Giulia
and express his fervent passion, making every effort to persuade her
with words that would warm the coldest heart. But nothing he said
could move her from her chaste resolve; on the contrary, she begged
him to leave her alone and stop troubling her.

The poor wretch's heart, however, was already gnawed by the pitiless cankerworm of love and the more Giulia proved hard and distant,
the more passionate he became and the more he strove to bend her to
his lust, although it was all in vain. He even got an old woman—
someone you would have taken for Saint Zita*—to talk to the girl,
and she did her office diligently enough, trying every kind of gossip
and flattery to undermine the resistance of the chaste Giulia. But the
maiden was so firm in her resolve that not a word of the bawdy old
crone could touch her heart. When the chamberlain heard this, he fell
into a deep despair, for he could not bring himself to renounce his
love for the girl; he still hoped that with entreaties, attentions, love,
and perseverance he could soften the hard heart of Giulia, convinced
that in the long run he could not fail to possess her. As the proverb
puts it, he was reckoning up the bill without the landlord.

Now when he realized that Giulia was becoming more distant every
day and that whenever she saw him she fled as if he were a basilisk,*
he decided to try whether gifts might work where his fine words and
attentions had failed, leaving force as a last resort. He went back to

talk with the wicked old woman and gave her a few rather cheap trinkets to take to Giulia for him. The old woman found Giulia alone and
turned the conversation to the Ferrarese by showing her the gifts he
had sent. But the honest girl seized all the baubles she had brought
and threw them out of the house onto the highway; and she chased
the shifty old crone back home, telling her that if ever she came back
to bother her again, she would go up to the castle and tell Lady
Antonia. The old woman picked up the things that were on the road
and went back to tell the Ferrarese that there was no way of moving
the girl and that in this case she had no idea what to do. The young
man was as upset as could be and would willingly have withdrawn
from the whole affair, but at the very idea of giving her up the poor
wretch felt as if he were about to die. At last, blinded by passion and
unable to accept that his advances were so little welcome, he resolved
that, whatever happened, if he saw the opportunity, he would take by
force what she would not give him of her own free will.

Now there was at the court a lackey of the bishop, a close friend of
the chamberlain and, if I remember well, also from Ferrara. To him
the chamberlain revealed all his fervent love and how hard he had tried
to plant a grain of pity in the maiden's breast, how she had proved
more hard and unfeeling than a rock in the ocean, and how neither
words nor gifts had ever been able to move her. 'Now,' said he, 'since
I can't live without satisfying my desires and since I know that you
love me as a friend, I'm asking you to come with me and help me to
have my way. She often goes out alone into the field, and there, where
the corn is already high, we can easily do what we mean to do.' The
lackey, without giving the matter another thought, promised that he
would always be ready to do whatever was wanted.

So the chamberlain started to spy on all Giulia's actions until one
day when she went out of Gazzuolo all alone. Immediately he called
the lackey and they went off to a field where he found the girl busy
with some task and started on his usual pleas for pity. Seeing that she
was alone, Giulia begged the young man to trouble her no longer; and,
fearing some danger, she started to go back to Gazzuolo. Determined
not to let his prey escape, the youth pretended that he and his friend
would accompany her, and on the way, with humble and loving words,
he kept begging for pity on his sufferings. The girl was in a hurry to
get back home and walked on without answering until they came to
where they had to cross a broad cornfield.

It was about noon on the day before the end of May; the sun was very hot as it usually is at that season and the field was far from any town or village. No sooner had they entered it than the young man put his arms round the girl's neck and tried to kiss her. She tried to run away and screamed for help, but the lackey caught her and threw her down on the ground where he gagged her so that she could not shout. Then the two men lifted her up and carried her some distance away from the path that crossed the field. And there, while the lackey held down her hands and she lay gagged and defenceless, the frenzied youth deflowered her. The poor girl wept bitterly, her sufferings all too clear in her sobs and groans. Despite her pleas, the cruel chamberlain mounted a second assault and took his fill of amorous pleasure. Then he removed the gag and tried to calm her with loving words, promising that he would not abandon her and that he would help her to find a husband so that she would be all right. She said nothing, asking only, with bitter tears, that they should set her free and let her go home.

Again the chamberlain tried to calm her down with sweet words and fine promises and even tried to give her money. But his words fell on deaf ears and the more he tried to console her the more she wept a flood of tears. And seeing that he still carried on talking, she said: 'Young man, you've had your way with me and satisfied your savage lust. I beg you, for mercy's sake, to set me free and let me go. Be content with what you've done, which is already far too much.' The lover, seeing that his words had no effect and fearing that her weeping might give him away, decided to let her go while he made off with his companion.

After staying a while to bewail her lost virginity, Giulia settled her poor disordered clothes, dried her eyes as best she could, and hurried back to Gazzuolo where she went straight home.

Her father and mother were away and the only person there was her sister, a girl of ten or eleven who was rather ill and could not go out. As soon as she got home, Giulia opened a coffer where she kept the few simple treasures she possessed. Stripping off all the clothes she was wearing, she took a fresh clean shift and put it on. Then she put on her starched snow-white linen gown, a collaret of white embroidered lawn, and a fine gauze apron that she usually wore only on feast days. She also put on red shoes over a pair of white silk stockings.

She arranged her headdress as carefully as she could and around her neck she fastened a necklace of yellow amber. In short, she decked herself out with all the humble finery she possessed as if she were going to show herself on the most solemn feast day in Gazzuolo.

With this done, she called her sister and gave her whatever was left of her possessions; then, taking her by the hand and closing the door, she went to the house of a neighbour, an aged woman, seriously ill and bedridden. To this good woman the tearful Giulia told the whole story of her misfortune and said: 'God forbid that I should remain alive when I have lost the honour that made life worth living. Never shall anyone point a finger at me or say to my face: "Here's the fine lass that became a whore and shamed her family; if she had any sense, she'd go and hide herself." I won't have anyone taunting my family that I gave in to the chamberlain of my own free will. My death will leave the whole world in no doubt that if my body was taken by force, my spirit remained free. I wanted to say these few words to you so that you can report everything to my poor parents and assure them that my will never yielded to the base lust of the chamberlain. May peace be with you.'

This said, she went outside and made her way towards the Oglio, followed by her little sister who was crying and had no idea what was going on. When Giulia arrived at the riverbank she threw herself head-first deep into the Oglio. Hearing the crying of her little sister and her screams that rose up to Heaven, a crowd came running, but it was too late, for Giulia had fully intended to drown herself and had let herself sink to death in that instant.

When they heard of this sad event, the lord bishop and my lady gave orders for the body to be fished out; and at this the chamberlain fled, taking the lackey with him. The body was found and when the reason why she drowned herself was revealed, the whole town was united in grief, as not only all the women but men too honoured her with abundant tears.

The illustrious and reverend bishop could not bury her in consecrated ground, but instead he had a tomb which is still there placed in the square until such time as he could erect a sepulchre of bronze upon a marble column.* That too can still be seen in the square. And truly, in my opinion, for what it is worth, our poor Giulia deserves no less praise than the Roman Lucrece; and perhaps, all things considered, she is to be preferred. One can only blame Nature for not having given such a great and valiant spirit a more noble birth. Yet that soul is to be considered noble enough who is a friend to virtue and who places honour before all things of this world.

TIMBREO AND FENICIA
Novelle (Tales) 1. 22

From Bandello to the Most Magnificent and Accomplished Lady Cecilia Gallerani,* Countess Bergamini, Greetings

LAST summer, when the extreme heat of Milan had forced you to leave Milan and take refuge with your people in your castle of San Giovanni in Croce near Cremona, I was on my way with Sir Lucio Scipione Attellano* to Gazzuolo, where we had been called by that valiant gentleman Pirro Gonzaga. Since we were passing near to your castle, we felt it would have been almost a sacrilege if we had not come to pay you our respects. I do not intend to relate how courteously you welcomed us and with what kindness you persuaded us to remain all that day and the two following days. Setting aside your precious studies of poetry in Latin and the vernacular, you spent most of the time in pleasant conversation with us.

On the second day we were joined by a number of Cremonese gentlemen who owned properties nearby and in the heat of midday we passed the time telling stories. Among these, the company particularly appreciated the tale told by our Attellano, and it was you who found the most fitting words in its praise. So it was that I decided to write it down and offer it to you as a gift; and as soon as I returned from Gazzuolo to Milan, I remembered my decision and composed this tale. And though I could not reproduce the smooth style of our fluent and eloquent Attellano, I still felt that I should not fail to send it to you. May it please you, therefore, to accept it as you habitually accept all the gifts of your friends, and to grant it the special favour of a place in your library where you keep the sweet verses and eloquent prose of so many fine scholars and where you yourself converse so highly with the Muses that you possess the first place among the learned heroines of our time. Keep well.

Scipione Attellano tells how Sir Timbreo di Cardona,* being at Messina in the service of King Peter of Aragon, fell in love with Fenicia Lionati, and the various twists of fortune that occurred before he could make her his wife.

In the year of grace 1283 the Sicilians rebelled, unwilling to bear the French yoke any longer, and in one day, at the hour of vespers, massacred all the French who were in the island with unheard-of brutality; for so it had been treacherously planned in advance throughout Sicily.

Nor was it only the French, both men and women, who were killed, but all Sicilian women who were suspected of being with child by the foreigner were slaughtered on that day; and those who were convicted later of the same fault were likewise put to death without mercy.

Thus was born that sinister term, 'the Sicilian Vespers'.* When he learned what had happened, King Peter of Aragon* moved immediately with his army and took possession of the island, having been urged to do so by Pope Nicholas III who upheld his right as the husband of Costanza, daughter of King Manfred. For many days King Peter held court in Palermo with truly royal splendour in celebration of his conquest. Then, hearing that King Charles II of Naples, son of Charles I, was approaching by sea with a great force to drive him out of Sicily, he went out to do battle with his fleet of ships and galleys. The struggle was furious and great was the slaughter, but in the end King Peter defeated King Charles and took him prisoner. And since he wanted to concentrate on the war, he moved the queen and the court to Messina as the city nearest to Italy, divided from Calabria by a narrow strait.

While he held his court there in truly regal fashion, with general rejoicing at his victory and with balls and jousting every day, it happened that one of his knights fell deeply in love. This was Timbreo di Cardona, a baron who was much esteemed and whom King Peter most particularly cherished for his personal courage and his brave conduct in the recent wars; and the young lady that he loved was Fenicia, the daughter of Messer Lionato de' Lionati, a gentleman of Messina. She was more courteous, charming, and beautiful than any other lady in the region, and little by little Timbreo fell so passionately in love with her that he could not think of living out of her sweet sight. Because he had served King Peter by land and sea ever since his childhood, Timbreo had been richly rewarded, for in addition to the many gifts already received, the king had just granted him the county of Collesano together with some other lands, so that his revenue (not counting his pension from the king) amounted to more than twelve thousand ducats.

Sir Timbreo now began to walk past the young lady's house every day, thinking himself blessed indeed when he caught sight of her. Fenicia, though still a girl, was shrewd enough to guess the reason why the knight went past so often. Sir Timbreo was universally honoured, for it was common knowledge that he was one of the king's favourites and that few at court were worthy to be compared with him; and the girl had not only heard of him, but seen him, elegantly dressed and followed by an impressive escort. He was, moreover, a truly handsome young man and showed every sign of perfect courtesy. So Fenicia, in her turn, began to observe him with pleasure and favour him with a modest bow. The knight's passion increased every day, and the more he looked on her the higher burned the flame until he felt so consumed by the fire in his heart that he vowed to possess her by whatever means he could.

But it was all in vain, for no matter how many letters and messages he sent her, she answered only that she intended to preserve her virginity inviolate for the man who would become her husband. All this left the poor lover deeply dejected, the more so because he could never persuade her to keep either his letters or his gifts. Yet still he was determined to possess her and, since she was so resolute that he could not have her without making her his wife, he considered the matter at length and finally decided to ask her father for her hand. And although he felt that he was marrying well below his rank, he knew that she was of ancient and noble blood; and such was his love for the maid that he resolved to wait no longer. Having made up his mind, he found a gentleman of Messina who was a good friend, explained his intentions, and told him what he should say to Messer Lionato. So the gentleman went off and followed his instructions to the letter. Messer Lionato heard the good news and, knowing Sir Timbreo's powerful position and worth, did not wait to consult friends or relatives before giving a gracious reply that showed how well pleased he was that the knight should condescend to such an alliance; and when he came home he informed his wife and daughter of the promise he had made to Sir Timbreo. Fenicia herself was delighted and with a devout heart she thanked God for granting such a glorious fulfilment to her chaste love; and her joy was evident in her face. But Fortune, ever hostile to human happiness, found an ingenious way of preventing the marriage that both parties so much desired. Now hear how this came about.

The news spread throughout Messina that in a few days' time Sir Timbreo Cardona was to marry Fenicia, daughter of Messer Lionato; and the news pleased the whole of Messina because Messer Lionato was much loved as a gentleman who sought to hurt nobody, but helped folk whenever he could. So almost everyone was delighted by this alliance. But there was in Messina another young knight of noble family called Sir Girondo Olerio Valenziano who had proved a valiant soldier in the recent wars and was among the most splendid and generous courtiers. When he heard the news, he was thoroughly downcast for he had just fallen in love with Fenicia's beauty and was so consumed by the flames of desire that he was sure he would die if he could not have her as his wife. He had already decided to ask her father for her hand and thought he would faint with sorrow when he heard that she had been promised to Sir Timbreo. Comfortless in his grief, he was so maddened by his passion that he lost all sense of reason and let himself be drawn into an action that would be shameful in anybody, let alone in the knight and gentleman that he was.

He had been Sir Timbreo's companion in almost every campaign and there was a brotherly friendship between them; but for some unknown reason, they had always hidden from each other their love for Fenicia. Sir Girondo now planned to sow such discord between Sir Timbreo and his beloved that the marriage would be called off; and in that case he could ask her hand with some hope of success. He lost no time in putting his mad scheme into effect, for he soon found the right man to serve his blind and reckless passion and informed him of his intentions. This fellow whom Girondo had chosen as his accomplice was a loutish young courtier who preferred evil to good. The next morning, fully instructed as to the plot he was to carry out, he went to find Timbreo who had not yet left the house, but was walking in the garden where he gave the young man a courteous welcome. After they had exchanged the usual greetings, the young man said: 'My lord, I have come to talk with you this early on a matter of the greatest importance for your honour and well-being; and since I may have to say something that offends you, I beg you to forgive me; believe me that I act with the best of intentions and let the service I render be my excuse. This I know, that if you are still the noble knight you always have been, then what I'm about to say will be of great benefit to you.

Let me come to the point: I heard yesterday that you have settled with
Messer Lionato de' Lionati to take his daughter as your wife. Beware,
my lord; think what you're doing, and have some care for your honour.
I tell you this because I have a friend who goes about two or three
times a week to lie with her and enjoy her love. Indeed, he's going
there this very evening, and I shall be going with him, as I have often
done in the past. If you can give me your word that you will do no
harm to me or my friend, I shall arrange for you to see the place and
everything else. And you ought to know that my friend has been
enjoying her like this for months. It is only my regard for you and the
many kind favours that you have done me that lead me to tell you all
this. So now you can do as you think best. For me it is enough that
I have done my duty as a man who is deeply in your debt.'

Sir Timbreo was stunned by these words. For a while he stood
silent with a thousand contrasting thoughts beating in his mind until
at last his bitter and seemingly just anger overcame the fervent and
faithful love that he bore to the fair Fenicia, and he answered with
a sigh: 'My friend, I must indeed be eternally obliged to you, since
you show such kindly concern for me and for my honour, and one day
I shall give you practical proof of my gratitude. For now I can only
give you my most heartfelt thanks. You have offered to show me what
I could never have imagined I would see, and so, by that same good
fellowship that brought you to tell me all this, I now urge you to go
freely along with your friend, and I give my word as a true knight that
I shall do no harm to either of you. Moreover, I shall keep this matter
secret so that your friend can continue to enjoy his love in peace. For
I should have been more cautious right from the start, and kept my
eyes open to look into the whole business far more carefully.' Then
the young man said: 'Tonight, my lord, at the third hour, go towards
Messer Lionato's house, hide in the ruined buildings that overlook
his garden, and keep a close watch.'

Opposite those ruins, in one wing of Messer Lionato's house, was
an ancient room where the windows were kept open day and night,
and there Fenicia would sometimes appear because it offered the best
view over the beautiful garden; but Messer Lionato and his family lived
in the other wing which was large enough to accommodate a prince's
court, let alone the household of a gentleman. The plan was now set
in motion and the young accomplice went off to see Girondo and told
him of everything that he had arranged with Sir Timbreo. Girondo

was overjoyed for it looked as if his plot were working perfectly. Then, when the time came, he took one of his servants who had already been told what to do, dressed him up as a gentleman, added a dash of perfume, and sent him to accompany the young man who had spoken with Sir Timbreo. They were closely followed by a third man with a ladder on his shoulder.

Now how could anyone give a full account of Sir Timbreo's emotions and the many conflicting thoughts that had passed through his mind during that day? For my part, I know that I would toil in vain. The credulous and unhappy knight, blinded by the veil of jealousy, ate little or nothing all day, and anyone who looked him in the face would have said he was more dead than alive. Half an hour before the appointed time he went and hid himself in the ruins where he could see anyone who passed by. He thought it hardly possible that Fenicia could have given herself to someone else, and yet he told himself that young girls are light and unstable, disdainful and avid of new things. Thus, accusing her one minute and excusing her the next, he watched and waited for the slightest movement. The night was not very dark, but very silent until at last he heard the sound of footsteps and some muffled curses. Then three men passed by and he recognized the young man who had warned him that morning, but could not identify the other two. As they went past him, he heard the one playing the perfumed lover say to the man who was carrying the ladder: 'Be sure to go quietly when you put the ladder up to the window because last time my Fenicia told me you made too much noise. So just take care and keep the noise down.' Timbreo heard these words distinctly and they were like so many sharp spears in his heart. He was alone and had only his sword, while the three men had pikes as well as swords and were heavily armed; and yet so intense was the jealousy gnawing at his heart and so fierce his burning anger that he was almost ready to spring out of his hiding place and assail them—to kill the man he thought must be Fenicia's lover or else to die and in that moment put an end to his overwhelming anguish. But then he remembered his promise and thought how base it would be to attack those to whom he had given his word. And so, bottling up his indignation, anger, and fury, he waited to see how things would end.

When the three men came under the window in the wall of Lionato's house, they set the ladder very gently against the balcony, and the supposed lover climbed up and went inside as if a mistress were awaiting him. Seeing this, and convinced that the man had gone up to lie with Fenicia, poor Timbreo was about to faint away for the sheer pain of it; but so strong was what he considered his just anger that it drove out all jealousy and not only cooled his honest and fervent love for Fenicia, but transformed it into cruel hate. Then, rather than wait for the reappearance of his rival, he left his hiding place and went back home. The young man, who had seen him leave and recognized him, guessed the state he was in, and soon signalled to the servant who had climbed up to come back down again. After which, they all went off to the house of Sir Girondo who, when they told him what had happened, was as delighted as if he were already in possession of the fair Fenicia.

Sir Timbreo, who slept very little in what remained of the night, rose early in the morning and summoned the Messinese citizen who had been his mediator when he had asked Fenicia's father for her hand in marriage. To him once again he gave his instructions, and then, fully informed as to Timbreo's attitude and intentions, that gentleman set off for Lionato's house where he found Messer Lionato walking up and down waiting for the midday meal to be served. With him was the innocent Fenicia who was embroidering silk together with her two young sisters and her mother. After Messer Lionato's courteous greeting, Timbreo's messenger said: 'Messer Lionato, I bring a message from Sir Timbreo for you and your lady and your daughter Fenicia.' 'You are most heartily welcome,' answered Lionato, 'and what is it about? Come, wife, and you Fenicia; come and hear what Sir Timbreo has to tell us.' Then the messenger spoke as follows:

'It is a common saying that the ambassador should not be punished for what he is obliged to say. I have been sent to you by someone else and I am infinitely distressed that I must bring you news that will pain you. Sir Timbreo di Cardona sends me to inform you, Messer Lionato and your lady, that you should seek another son-in law because he no longer intends to ally himself with your family. And this, not because of any fault of yours, for he firmly believes you to be loyal worthy people, but because he has seen with his own eyes something that he would never have believed of Fenicia. And for this reason he leaves you free to make other arrangements. But to you, Fenicia, he says that the love he bore you did not deserve such a reward, and that you should now look for another husband since you have already found another lover. Or rather, you should take the man to whom you gave your maidenhead. Sir Timbreo wants nothing more to do with you, since you have made him a king of cuckolds even before making him your husband.'

Fenicia stood as if struck dead by this bitter scornful message; and Lionato and his wife were in much the same condition. But then, regaining his strength and spirits, Messer Lionato answered the messenger: 'Brother, from the first moment when you spoke to me of this marriage, I feared that Sir Timbreo would not stand by his request, because I know perfectly well that I am only a poor gentleman and in no way his equal. Nevertheless, if he now regrets having asked for her hand, I think he could have simply said that he no longer wanted her. That would have been enough without slandering her as a whore. It is true that all things are possible, but I know how my daughter has been reared and I know how she behaves. One day, I trust, God, the righteous judge, will reveal the truth.'

After this reply, the citizen departed, leaving Messer Lionato convinced that Sir Timbreo had changed his mind because he considered the alliance demeaning and unworthy of his ancestry. The lineage of Messer Lionato himself was, in fact, ancient, noble, and highly respected in Messina, but his wealth was only that of a private gentleman. It was known that in bygone days his forefathers had possessed castles and held authority over many places, but the civil wars and the instability of the island had eroded their estates and those of other families like them. So now the good father, having never found his daughter less than honest and virtuous, concluded that the knight had acted out of disdain for the poverty of their present condition.

As for Fenicia, grieving and sick at heart after hearing herself so wrongly accused, she was not strong enough to withstand the shock. A delicate and tender girl, unaccustomed to the blows of hostile Fortune, she lost her self-possession and seemed more desirous of death than of life. She let herself sink under the sad burden as if she were already dead, losing her native colour and appearing more like a marble statue than a living creature. They carried her upstairs and put her to bed, where, with warm cloths and other remedies, they soon succeeded in reviving her. Doctors were called in and before long the whole of Messina knew that Fenicia, daughter of Lionato, was seriously ill and in danger of death. Many ladies who were friends and relatives came to visit her and, when they heard the cause of her sickness, vied in their attempts to console her. And, as usually happens when women get together, they had a variety of opinions about the situation; but they all agreed in laying bitter blame on Sir Timbreo. Most of them were gathered at the bedside, so that Fenicia, who had heard and understood what they were saying, showed signs of revival; and seeing that most of them were weeping, she tried to calm them, saying with a faint mournful voice:

'Dear mothers and sisters,* it is time to dry these tears since they do no good to you and only renew my suffering without improving the situation in any way. It has pleased Our Lord God that things should be as they are, and we must be patient. The suffering that I feel so acutely and that is slowly fraying the thread of my life is not because I have been repudiated, even though that is an endless pain. It is the manner of that repudiation that cuts me to the quick and has no remedy. Sir Timbreo could have simply said that I did not please him enough to be his wife, and all would have been well. But I know that the manner in which he rejects me means that the people of Messina hold me eternally guilty of a sin that not only have I never committed, but never even thought of. And yet I shall always be pointed out as a whore. I have always admitted—and still do—that my rank is not equal to that of a knight and baron like Sir Timbreo, and my family's lack of wealth prevented them from looking so high. Yet when it comes to antiquity and nobility of blood, it is common knowledge that the Lionati are among the oldest and most noble families of this island, for we are of Roman stock from before the birth of Christ Our Lord, as ancient documents attest. Now if, as I say, my lack of riches made me unworthy of such a noble husband, I can also affirm that I am most unworthily rejected in that I certainly never thought of giving to another man what the law says should be reserved for my husband. God knows that I am telling the truth: let His holy name be ever praised and revered! And who knows? Maybe this is the way His Divine Majesty has chosen to work my salvation. For perhaps, if I had made such a noble marriage, I should have become proud, scornful of others, and less aware of God's goodness towards me. Now let God do with me as He pleases and grant that this suffering may serve to save my soul. And I pray devoutly with all my heart that He may open the eyes of Sir Timbreo: not so that he may take me as his wife again— for I feel that I am slowly dying—but so that he, who cared so little for my faith, may know, along with all the world, that I never committed the folly, the shameful fault of which I am unjustly accused. Thus, even if I die in infamy, I shall be acquitted in the fullness of time. Let him enjoy whatever lady God has destined for him and long may he live with her in peace. For me, within a few hours, six feet of earth will be enough. May my father and my mother and all our friends and relatives who suffer for me have at least this small consolation: that I am completely innocent of the infamous act that is ascribed to me; and for witness of this let them take the faithful love that I give them as an obedient daughter, for there is no greater pledge or proof that I can offer at the present time. For me it is enough that I be recognized as innocent of this foul sin before Christ's just tribunal. And so to Him who gave it me I commend my soul that longs to escape this earthly prison and now sets out on its path towards Him.'

With this, so violent was the suffering that gripped her heart that, as she strove to continue, she lost the power of speech and began to babble incomprehensible words; and a cold sweat came over her, spreading through every limb until, with her hands joined in prayer, she resigned herself to death. The doctors who were still there, unable to find any relief for her grave condition, gave her up for lost and took their leave, saying that the intense sorrow had broken her heart. Shortly after, in the arms of her friends and relatives, Fenicia grew cold and her heart stopped beating, so that they all thought she must be dead. And when they called back one of the doctors, he could find no pulse and came to the same conclusion. How many then were the bitter laments, the tears, and the sighs, I leave you, tender-hearted ladies, to imagine. The poor father and the dishevelled grieving mother would have made the stones weep. And loud were the lamentations of the ladies and of all who were present.

Five or six hours had already passed and the burial was arranged for the following day. When the ladies had left, the mother, more dead than alive, remained with a relative, the wife of one of Messer Lionato's brothers; and these two, preferring to be alone, put water on the fire, shut themselves in the room, stripped Fenicia, and began to wash her body with warm water. Fenicia's vital spirits had been absent for seven hours when, as her cold limbs were being washed, they suddenly returned, and the girl began to open her eyes, giving clear signs of life. The two women were about to cry out; but, plucking up their courage, they put their hands on her heart and felt some faint pulse. This convinced them that the maiden was indeed alive; and so, with warm cloths and other methods, being careful to make no noise, they worked until at last Fenicia was almost completely herself again. She opened her eyes and sighed: 'Alas, where am I?' 'Don't you see', said her mother, 'that you're here with me and your aunt? You fell into such a deep swoon that we thought you were dead. But, praise be to God, you're still alive.' 'How much better it would be', answered Fenicia, 'if I were dead and free of all these troubles.' But her mother and her aunt protested: 'Listen, dear girl: you must live because that's God's will, and He'll put everything right.'

The mother, hiding the joy she felt, opened the door and called Messer Lionato who came immediately. One need hardly ask how overjoyed he was when he saw that his daughter was herself again; but when he had thought things over, he decided not to let anyone know what had happened. Instead, he arranged to send her out of Messina to the country villa of his brother, whose wife was with them in the room. So when he had restored the girl to her former beauty and health with delicate foods and rare wines, he sent for his brother and told him in detail exactly what he wanted. The plan worked out like this. The following night Messer Girolamo (for such was the brother's name) took Fenicia to his house where he kept her hidden for a while, with his wife for company. Then, early one morning, he sent them both out to his villa which he had already stocked with the necessary provisions. With them went one of Fenicia's sisters who was thirteen or fourteen whereas Fenicia was sixteen. This he did so that in two or three years' time Fenicia, whose looks would naturally change as she grew up, could be married off under another name.

Meanwhile, the day after Fenicia's swoon, when the news of her death had spread throughout Messina, Messer Lionato ordered a funeral worthy of her rank and had a coffin made and filled it up with something or other. This was done in the utmost secrecy, the only other person present being Fenicia's mother who certainly did not want any outside interference. Then the coffin was closed, nailed down, and sealed with pitch so that nobody would doubt that it held Fenicia's body. That evening Messer Lionato and his relatives, all clad in black, followed the coffin to the church, with both father and mother displaying as much grief as if the coffin really contained their daughter's body. Nobody remained unmoved, for the cause of death had been made known and everyone in Messina was firmly convinced that Sir Timbreo had invented the whole story of the girl's infidelity. Amid the general mourning of the whole city, a stone monument was

raised above the grave; it bore the arms of the Lionati, and the following epitaph according to the orders of Messer Lionato:

> Fenicia they gave me for a name,
> And I was promised to a cruel knight
> Who changed his mind and held his vows so light
> That he said I had sinned and was to blame.
>   An innocent virgin, wrongly put to shame,
> Doomed to be pointed out in all men's sight,
> Branded a whore: I chose to die outright
> Rather than bear this stain to my fair fame.
>   No sword was needed when I came to die,
> For suffering did all a sword could do
> When I heard those foul falsehoods heaped on me.
>   But yet I prayed that when the time was due
> God would reveal the calumny, since he
> Who broke his pledge cared not that I was true.

After the funeral rites, people everywhere continued to talk about the
cause of Fenicia's death, discussing it at length and expressing their
compassion since they regarded the accusation against her as completely unfounded. And Sir Timbreo himself began to feel great sorrow
and a strange tremor in his heart that he would not have thought possible. Yet still he thought that he was not to blame, for he had certainly
seen a man climbing up a ladder and entering the house. But by now
his anger had cooled and, as he gave more reasonable consideration to
what he had witnessed, he reflected that the man who entered the house
might have done so for some other woman or could have been a thief.
Then he remembered that Lionato's house was very large and that
nobody actually lived in that part of it. Fenicia, in any case, slept with
her sisters in a room adjacent to that of her parents and would have
found it impossible to reach the other wing without passing through
her father's bedroom. And these thoughts gave him no rest.

Sir Girondo was in a similar state. When he heard how Fenicia had
died, he recognized that he was her assassin, partly through his mad
passion for her, but above all, as the instigator of the injury she had
suffered. His heart was breaking with sorrow and his despair was such
that more than once he came close to plunging a dagger into his
breast. Unable to eat or sleep, he was like a man possessed or one who
had lost his wits, and as he grew ever more frantic, he could find no
peace. At last, on the seventh day after Fenicia's funeral, he felt that

he could no longer go on living unless he went to Sir Timbreo and confessed the evil that he had done. Hence, at the hour when most people go home to dine, he went towards the royal palace and met Timbreo returning from the court. 'Sir Timbreo,' he said, 'if it is no trouble, would you grant me the favour of your company?'

Timbreo, who enjoyed the company of Girondo, walked along with him for a while, talking of this and that, until they reached the church that held Fenicia's tomb, where Girondo told his servants to wait outside and asked Timbreo to do the same. Timbreo agreed, and the two of them went into the church alone and found it empty. Girondo led Timbreo to the chapel that held the supposed tomb of Fenicia and, kneeling down, unsheathed his dagger and put it, with naked blade, into the hand of his friend who was astonished and stood wondering what all this was about, for he had still not realized whose tomb it was. Then Girondo, his voice broken with sobs and tears, began to speak:

'I have done you an infinite injury by the advice I gave, and I have not come here to beg forgiveness, for my fault is too great to forgive. But if ever you hope to do something worthy of your valour as a noble knight, if ever you look to do something acceptable to God and pleasing to the world, then take this dagger and plunge it into my criminal breast, and with my vicious and abominable blood offer a fitting sacrifice to the sanctified bones of the innocent, ill-fated Fenicia. For it is Fenicia who was buried in this tomb a short while ago, and it is I alone who am the cause of her undeserved and untimely death. And if, with more pity for me than I have for myself, you refuse, then with my own hands I shall exact the last vengeance for my crime. But if you are still the true knight that you always have been, impatient of the slightest stain upon your honour, then you will avenge with one blow both Fenicia and yourself.'

Realizing that this was indeed where the fair Fenicia's body had been buried, Sir Timbreo was stunned by Girondo's words and could not imagine what they might mean. Yet moved by some strange impulse, he began to weep bitterly; and throwing the dagger aside, he begged Girondo to rise and tell his story more clearly. At last Girondo gave way, stood up, and spoke:

'You must know, my lord, that I was so passionately in love with Fenicia that even if I were to live for a hundred years, I could find no comfort, since this very love caused the cruel death of that unfortunate maiden. First I saw that she could never give me a kind glance or the slightest sign of encouragement; then, when I heard that she was promised to you, blinded by my unbridled desire, I thought that if I could find a way of preventing that marriage, it would be easy to ask her father for her hand and get her for myself. Unable to imagine any other satisfaction for my burning love and careless of what might follow, I devised a vile plot and tricked you into seeing a man going into her house at night. That man was, in fact, one of my servants. And as for the fellow who came to tell you that Fenicia had given her love to someone else, he was suborned by me to take that message. And so it was that the following day you repudiated Fenicia; and as a result she died and was buried here. That is why, as the butcher and executioner who has done such harm to you and to her, I beg you yet again with outstretched arms'—and here he knelt again—'to take fitting vengeance on my wickedness, for when I think of the evil I have caused, I scorn to live any longer.'

When he heard this, Sir Timbreo wept bitterly. But knowing that the fault was irreparable and that Fenicia, once dead, could not return to life, he felt there would be no point in taking vengeance on Girondo, whereas by pardoning him he could restore Fenicia's good name and give her back the honour that had been so brutally taken away. He urged Girondo to stand up and, after many sighs and tears, he spoke as follows:

'How much better it would have been for me, dear brother, if I had never been born. Or if born, then born deaf so that I could never hear such a heavy and hateful thing. Now I can never find happiness in life, knowing that by my credulity I have caused the death of one whose love and Heaven-born gifts and virtues deserved a better reward than foul infamy and untimely death. But God, against whose will not a leaf falls from a tree, has allowed this to happen, and since things past are sooner blamed than mended, I do not mean to take revenge on you. To lose one friend and then to lose another would be adding grief to grief and would still not bring the blessed soul of Fenicia back to the chaste body that has ended its earthly race. But for one thing I must blame you so that you never make the same mistake again: you should have told me that you loved Fenicia since you knew that I was in love with her myself and completely unaware of your intentions. For then, instead of asking her father for her hand, I would have abandoned my amorous enterprise and given way to you. Conquering myself, as noble and generous minds do, I would have placed our friendship before my own desire. Or perhaps, after hearing me out, you would have been the one to give way and this tragedy would have been averted. Now what is done is done and cannot be undone. Only in one matter I ask you to gratify me by doing as I say.'

'Command me, my lord,' said Girondo, 'I shall do everything you say, without reserve.'

Timbreo continued: 'Since it is our fault that Fenicia has been falsely accused of being a harlot, I want the two of us to do everything we can to restore her good name and render her the honour she deserves—first before her grieving relatives and then before the people of Messina, for the fact is that what I said about her has been repeated here and there, so it may well be that the whole city believes she was a whore. If we fail in this, her angry ghost will always be before my eyes, crying to God for vengeance.'

Girondo answered: 'It is for you to command, my lord, and for me to obey. I was first bound to you by friendship; and now am made your eternal slave by the injury I have done you and by the pardon that you, as a virtuous loyal knight, have offered to me, a faithless villain.' After this, still weeping bitterly, both men knelt before the tomb with out-stretched arms, imploring forgiveness from Fenicia and from God, the one for the evil he had done and the other for his credulity. Then, when they had dried their eyes, Sir Timbreo asked Girondo to go with him to the house of Messer Lionato.

So they went off together and found Messer Lionato who was just leaving the table after dining with some relatives. He was surprised when he heard that the two knights wished to speak with him, but nonetheless he went to meet them and bade them welcome. And when they saw Messer Lionato and his wife clad in black, they were moved yet again by the cruel memory of Fenicia's death and could hardly speak for weeping. Chairs were brought and when everyone was seated, Sir Timbreo, his speech broken by sighs and sobs, told all those present the sad story of the events that had caused the untimely death (or so he thought) of Fenicia; and he and Girondo threw themselves pros-trate on the ground and begged the father and mother to forgive them. With tears of tenderness and joy Messer Lionato embraced them both, forgave the injuries they had done him, and thanked God that his daughter's innocence had been recognized.

After further exchanges Timbreo turned to Messer Lionato and said: 'Father, since hostile fate has prevented me from being your son-in-law, as I heartily desired, I beg you—and, indeed, oblige you, insofar as I can—to make use of me and of all that is mine just as if that alliance had indeed gone ahead, for I shall always show you the respect and reverence that a loving obedient son owes to his father. And if you deign to command me, you will find that I shall suit the deed to the word, for truly I know of nothing in the world, however difficult, that I would not do for you.' The good old man thanked Timbreo with loving words, and then said: 'These are courteous and generous offers, and since adverse Fortune has barred me from an alliance by marriage, I make bold to ask of you something that you will find easy to grant. Which is this: I pray you, by the loyalty that governs all you do and by the love you bore to my Fenicia, that when you decide to choose a wife, you will be so kind as to let me know; and if I can propose a woman who pleases you, you will take her.' Assuming that the grieving old man was seeking some small reparation for the great loss he had suffered, Sir Timbreo took him by the hand, kissed him on the mouth, and answered: 'Dear Father, you ask me a very easy thing, considering my far greater obligations towards you: and to show you how eager I am to please you, not only will I never take a wife without informing you, but I shall marry only the lady that you advise me to take. And this I swear before all these gentlemen.' With similar fair words Girondo also promised that he would always be ready to do whatever might please Lionato. Then the two knights went off to dine, and the news soon spread throughout Messina that Fenicia had been falsely accused. That same day Lionato sent a special messenger to tell his daughter what had happened. She was overjoyed to hear it and devoutly thanked God that her honour had been restored.

A year passed and Fenicia remained in the country where things were so well managed that nobody knew she was still alive. Meanwhile Sir Timbreo remained in close contact with Lionato who kept Fenicia informed of what he was getting ready to do. During this time Fenicia had grown beautiful beyond belief; she was now seventeen and had developed in such a way that nobody would have taken her for the Fenicia they once knew, especially since they believed that Fenicia to be dead. Her sister was with her, a maid of about fifteen, aptly named Belfiore, for she seemed indeed a flower of a girl and hardly less beautiful than her elder sister.

Messer Lionato, who often went out to visit them, decided that he had waited long enough. So one day, when he was with the two knights, he said to Timbreo with a smile: 'The time has come, my lord, when I can release you from the kind obligation towards me that you once undertook. I think I have found you a well-born and beautiful young bride and I believe that once you have seen her, you will be perfectly satisfied. And even if, perhaps, you cannot take her with as much love as when you sought the hand of Fenicia, I can assure you of this much: you will not find in her any less beauty, any less nobility, or any less kindness. With all other womanly qualities and refined ways she is, thank God, abundantly adorned. You shall see her and then be free to do whatever you feel is to your best advantage. On Sunday morning I shall come to your lodgings with a group of chosen relatives and friends, and you and Sir Girondo should be ready to go with us about three miles outside Messina to a villa where we shall hear Mass. There you will see the young woman we have been speaking about, and afterwards we shall dine together.'

Sir Timbreo accepted the invitation and the instructions and when Sunday came he and Sir Girondo rose early and made ready to ride off. Then Messer Lionato arrived with a group of gentlemen, having already set up everything needed for a proper reception at the villa. As soon as Timbreo was told of Lionato's arrival, he and Girondo and their attendants mounted their horses; and after the usual exchange of greetings, the whole party rode out of Messina. Talking of this and that on the way, as people usually do on such outings, they arrived at the villa before they knew it and were given a courteous welcome. After hearing Mass in a church near the house, they all returned to the main hall which was splendidly furnished with Alexandrian tapestries and carpets. When they were all assembled, several ladies joined them from an inner room, among them Fenicia and Belfiore; and Fenicia seemed indeed like the moon in a clear sky, outshining the stars. The two knights and the other gentlemen greeted them with all due respect, as gentlemen should always greet ladies. Then Messer Lionato took Timbreo by the hand and led him to Fenicia, who had been called Lucilla ever since she had been smuggled out into the country. 'Sir knight,' said he, 'here is the lady Lucilla whom I have chosen to be your wife, if she pleases you. And if you follow my advice, you will marry her. Nevertheless, you remain free to take her or leave her.'

Timbreo was wonderfully taken with her, for one glance was enough to show him that she was truly beautiful; and since he had already decided to satisfy Messer Lionato, after a brief pause for thought, he answered: 'Father, not only shall I accept the young lady you present to me, who seems to be a princess, but I would have accepted any other lady you might have offered me. And to show how much I wish to satisfy you and to prove that my promise was not made in vain, I shall take this lady and none other as my lawful wife, provided that her wishes agree with mine.' To these words the young lady herself replied: 'Sir knight, I stand ready to do whatever Messer Lionato tells me.' 'And for my part, fair maid,' added Lionato, 'I urge you to take Sir Timbreo as your husband.' Then, with no further delay, they called on a learned priest who was present to pronounce the customary words according to the rites of Holy Church. The priest performed his office with proper gravity, and with those words Sir Timbreo married his Fenicia, thinking her to be Lucilla. Yet when Timbreo first saw the young lady emerging from the inner room, his heart had trembled with a strange ineffable emotion, for there was something in her features that recalled his Fenicia. He gazed on her as if his eyes could never have enough, and he felt that all his love for Fenicia was being transferred to this new young maiden.

After the nuptials, water was brought for them to wash their hands. The bride was placed at the head of the table and on her right was seated Sir Timbreo; opposite him was Belfiore and beside her was Sir Girondo. And so the whole seating was arranged with men and women side by side. The food was highly refined and carefully prepared and the whole banquet was calm, sumptuous, and elegantly served. There was no lack of pleasant conversation, witty banter, and good-humoured amusement until at last, when the seasonal fruits had been served, Fenicia's aunt, who had been with her in the villa for most of the year and was sitting next to Timbreo, seeing that the meal was coming to an end, turned to him as if she had heard nothing about his past and said gaily: 'Sir bridegroom, have you never had a wife before?' At the matron's question Timbreo's eyes filled with tears which began to fall before he could answer; but overcoming the tenderness of his nature, he gave this answer: 'My lady aunt, your kind question brings to mind something that is always in my heart and will soon, I think, end my days. For although I am very happy with Lucilla, there is, nonetheless, another lady whom I once loved and who, now that she is dead, I love more than myself. And what constantly torments me and slowly gnaws at my heart like a grievous worm is the fact that I alone was the cause of her unjust death.'

At this Girondo attempted to intervene, but was hindered by repeated sighs and tears until at last he managed these halting words: 'No, sir, I was to blame. I, with my treachery, was the instigator and assassin; I caused the death of this ill-fated maid whose rare gifts made her worthy of a far longer life. You were in no way to blame, for all the fault was mine.' This exchange brought tears into the eyes of Timbreo's bride as she remembered all the bitter pains she had suffered. Meanwhile her aunt persisted and asked her new nephew: 'Now, sir knight, since we have nothing else to talk about, would you kindly tell me the story of how these things happened that have you and the other gentlemen still weeping so tenderly?' 'Alas, lady aunt,' said Timbreo, 'you ask me to renew the greatest distress that I have ever suffered and the very thought of it is enough to unman and unmake me. It is a tale of my own credulity that adds nothing to my honour and everything to my eternal woe. But for your satisfaction I shall tell you everything that happened.' And so, to the astonishment and compassion of his hearers and not without burning tears, he told the whole sad story from beginning to end. The matron commented: 'This is a strange and tragic story, sir knight, and perhaps nothing like it has ever happened in the world before. But tell me this with God's help: suppose that before you were given the wife you now have, you had been able to resurrect this lady that you loved, what would you have done to have her alive again?' Timbreo answered: 'I swear to God, my lady, that I am very happy with my wife and hope to be more so every day. Yet had it been possible, I would have given half my lifetime and all its wealth to bring back that maiden from the dead, for truly I loved her as much as any man alive could love a woman. And were I to live for a thousand years, I would still love her, dead as she is, and for her sake I shall always revere her family and kin.'

At these words, the father of Fenicia was so relieved that he could no longer hide his joy; and weeping for the overwhelming emotion, he turned to his son-in-law and said:

'Dear son-in-law—for so I must now call you—your deeds fall somewhat short of your words, for you have actually married this Fenicia you love so much and you have been sitting next to her all morning; and yet you still do not know her. Where has all your ardent love gone? Has she changed shape? Are her looks so altered that you no longer recognize her?'

With these words the eyes of the loving knight were opened at last and, throwing his arms around her neck, overcome with infinite joy, he gave his Fenicia a thousand kisses and gazed at her as if he could never have enough. Yet at the same time he wept gently, unable to speak but reproaching himself for having been so blind. Then, to their great surprise and delight, Messer Lionato told the whole company how this had come about. Sir Girondo then rose from the table and threw himself at Fenicia's feet, begging forgiveness with all humility. She greeted him kindly and without hesitation, repaying with friendly words the injuries he had done her. After which, turning to her husband who was still blaming himself, she begged him in the sweetest way never to speak like that again, since he had not sinned and had no need of pardon. And there in an excess of happiness they remained, kissing each other and drinking warm tears.

Now while everyone was enjoying the occasion and preparing to celebrate with song and dance, Sir Girondo went up to Lionato, who looked as happy as if he could touch the heavens with his fingers, and asked him whether he could do him a great favour, a favour that would bring him a wonderful happiness. Messer Lionato replied by asking him to name it, for if it were in his power, he would do it willingly and with pleasure. 'Then,' said Girondo, 'I ask to have you, Messer Lionato, as my father-in-law and kinsman, along with the lady Fenicia and Sir Timbreo as my sister-in-law and brother-in-law, and the lady Belfiore as my lawful loving wife.' The good father, almost beside himself with the addition of such new and unhoped-for joy, hardly knew whether he was dreaming or whether what he heard and saw was sober truth. But since he knew that he was not sleeping, he thanked God with all his heart for this great and undeserved reward and replied that whatever pleased Girondo would please him also. With no more ado, he called Belfiore: 'You see how things are, my daughter: this knight wants you as his wife; if you want him as a husband, I shall be most happy and you shall have your wish; so tell me freely how you feel.' The lovely girl trembled as she answered in a low modest voice that she was ready to do whatever he wished. Girondo waited no longer, and with the consent of all her relatives and with the proper matrimonial rites and vows, he gave the fair Belfiore his ring. The joy of Lionato and his kinsfolk knew no bounds; and because Timbreo had married his dear Fenicia under the name of Lucilla, he solemnly wedded her again as Fenicia. And so the whole day was spent in dancing and other pleasures.

The fair and gentle Fenicia* wore a snow-white gown of finest damask and a headdress that was a wonder to see. She was suitably tall for her age and well formed, though young enough to be still growing. Beneath a delicate veil of finest silk her breasts could just be seen, perfect in their separation, urging forward and upward like two round apples. To see the lovely colour of her face was to behold a pleasing and pure whiteness tinged with a comely virginal blush—those crimson touches painted not by art but by the masterly hand of Nature, now more and now less according to her changing motions and emotions. The swelling breast seemed a living expanse of pure white marble and the rounded throat was like snow. But he who saw her gentle mouth opening and closing as it formed her sweet words could surely say that he had seen a priceless treasure-house girt with the finest rubies and filled with the richest and loveliest orient pearls that were ever sent to us by the fragrant East. But then if you saw those two shining eyes, or rather two bright stars, or rather two dazzling suns, as her glance went here and there, then surely you could swear that within those serene lights dwelt Love, sharpening his arrows in that luminous splendour. And how splendid was that crown of blond curls that played above her broad high forehead like threads of fine gold, wantonly waving at the slightest breath of wind! Her arms were fairly shaped, with two elegant hands so well proportioned that envy itself could not have found anything to improve. To sum up, her figure was lovely and slim, and so sweetly formed by Nature as to lack nothing. And then the motions of her limbs or of her whole body were so rhythmical and so smooth that every step, every gesture, every nod or beck was of an infinite grace and seemed to steal the hearts of all who gazed on her. She was rightly called Fenicia in that she was indeed a phoenix whose beauty surpassed that of all other women. Nor, however, was the presence of her sister Belfiore any less admirable, except insofar as she was still too young to have a bearing of the same majesty and grace.

So the whole day was spent in revelry and joy and the two bridegrooms could never have enough of gazing on their brides and conversing with them. But it was Sir Timbreo whose happiness seemed beyond all measure for he could hardly believe that he was truly there where he was and wondered whether it might not be a dream or the result of some magic spell.

When that day was over and the morrow came, they got ready to return to Messina where the marriages could be celebrated with the solemnity appropriate for two gentlemen of their rank. They had a friend who was particularly close to the king, and to him they forwarded messages post-haste, explaining these events and giving him instructions as to what he should do. So that very same day he went to pay homage to King Peter on behalf of the two knights and told him the whole story of their loves from beginning to end. The king was more than a little pleased and had the tale repeated all over again before the queen who heard it with great wonder and satisfaction; and when it came to the sufferings of Fenicia, she could not refrain from tears.

Now in those days King Peter embodied courtly generosity more than any other prince, and he best knew how to reward those who deserved it; and since the queen was no less courteous and kind, he opened his mind to her and told her what he meant to do. And when she heard how splendid his intentions were, she was full of praise for her lord and husband. And so, having carefully prepared the whole court and invited all the gentlemen and ladies of Messina, the king commanded that his eldest son, Don Giacomo Dongiavo, should lead a great company of noble barons, knights, and gentlemen out of Messina to meet the two bridal sisters. So they rode out of the city in fine orderly fashion and had not gone a mile before they met with the two brides and their husbands and many other folk who were coming gaily towards Messina. When they came near, the two knights dismounted to pay their respects to Don Giacomo, but he told them to remount and, in the name of his father, courteously congratulated the two fair sisters. He was greeted with all due respect; and no less courteously given than received was the welcome that the courtiers and company from Messina extended to the brides and their husbands. The two knights and their wives expressed proper gratitude to everyone, but reserved the greatest possible thanks for Don Giacomo. Then they all set off together towards the city, chatting and joking as people do on such happy occasions. Don Giacomo himself spent much of his time entertaining Lady Fenicia or Lady Belfiore with pleasant witty conversation.

The king had been kept informed and when he thought the time was ripe, he mounted his horse and, with the queen and an honourable retinue of gentlemen and ladies, rode out to meet the other goodly company at the entrance to the city. And when they had dismounted and made obeisance to the king and queen, they were all graciously received. The king then made them remount and took his place between Messer Lionato and Sir Timbreo; the queen rode between the fair Fenicia on her right and Belfiore on her left, while Don Giacomo was beside Sir Girondo. All the other gentlemen and ladies followed in good order, and, as the king wished, the whole troupe proceeded to the royal palace. There, after a sumptuous banquet, Sir Timbreo, at the king's command, told the whole story of his love before the assembled guests. Then came the dancing, and for a week the king held open court, insisting that throughout that time everyone should eat at the palace.

When at last the festivities were over, he called Messer Lionato and asked what dowries he had promised for his daughters and how he meant to bestow them. Messer Lionato answered that there had never been any discussion of dowries and that he would give them as fair a settlement as he could afford. Then the king said: 'We wish to give your daughters the dowries that are worthy of them and of my knights, without any further expense on your part.' So the generous king summoned the two bridegrooms and their brides and made them formally renounce any claim they might have on the estate of Sir Lionato. This he then confirmed by royal decree, and his decision was warmly commended not only by the Sicilians but by all those who heard of it. Immediately afterwards he gave substantial dowries to the brides as if they were his own daughters rather than the children of a subject; and he increased the allowance that the two husbands already received from him. No less liberal and munificent than the king, the queen made the two brides ladies of her court and from her own revenue accorded them a generous annual allowance. She continued to cherish them; and they, being naturally noble, behaved in a way that soon won the approval of the whole court.

As for Messer Lionato, the king gave him a most honourable public office in Messina, from which he derived no small profit; and since he was already old, he arranged with the king for one of his sons to have the reversion.

This then is what happened to Sir Timbreo as the result of his faithful love; and the evil that Sir Girondo sought to do was converted into good; and both of them enjoyed their ladies in perfect peace for many long years, often recalling with pleasure the misadventures of the fair Fenicia.

This Sir Timbreo was the founding father of the noble house of the lords of Cardona that in Sicily and in the kingdom of Naples still boasts men of no little fame. In Spain also the noble blood of the Cardona continues to flourish, breeding soldiers and counsellors who are in no way unworthy of their ancestors. But what shall I say of the two noble brothers, Don Pietro and Don Giovanni di Cardona, both truly valorous and excellent lords and warriors? Among those present here I see some who knew Don Pietro, count of Collesano and grand constable and admiral of Sicily, whom the incomparable Lord Prospero Colonna* honoured and admired for his wise counsel. And certainly the count of Collesano was a remarkable man. He died at the Battle of Bicocca, to the general sorrow of all Lombardy. And his brother Don Giovanni, marquis of the Palude, was slain before the walls of Ravenna,* fighting bravely in the battle between French and Spaniards. But now, without noticing it, I have passed from telling stories to composing panegyrics.

THE DUCHESS OF AMALFI
Novelle (*Tales*) 1. 26

Bandello to the Most Courteous and Magnificent Lord, Count Bartolomeo Ferraro, Greetings

How good it would be if here in our regions we could adopt certain customs of those new worlds which, they say, the Spanish and Portuguese are discovering, though it was the Italians who opened the way.* Then all the evil that we do would cease and we would not keep hearing: here's a man who murdered his wife because he suspected she was making him a prince of Hornland;* and there's one who smothered his daughter for getting married in secret; and there's yet another who had his sister killed because she didn't make the marriage he wanted. It is surely very cruel that we men want to do whatever comes into our head, and that we do not let poor women get their way in anything. And if they do anything that we don't like, then immediately out we come with chains, sword, and poison. How much good it would do us if a turn of the wheel gave them such power over men! Think of the revenge for the abuse and injuries inflicted upon them by cruel men. And yet we could at least count on some relief in that women are naturally soft-hearted and merciful and would soon relent and become receptive to our prayers, for their tender nature has little love for blood and poison, death and tears. Truly I think men very foolish to think that their honour and the honour of all their family depends upon the lust of a woman. If a man makes a mistake, however grave, his kin do not lose their nobility on this account. If a son strays from the path of virtue traced by his forefathers, those worthy men do not lose their dignity. But we make the laws, we interpret them, we gloss them, and we promulgate them as we please. Now there's a count—I won't say his name—who takes the daughter of a baker for his wife, and why? Because she has bags of money. And yet nobody says a word against him. Then there's this other count, noble and rich, who marries the daughter of a muleteer without any dowry whatsoever, simply because he feels like it. And now she has the rank and status of a countess, and he is still the count he was before.

Quite recently there was the case of the Duchess of Amalfi.* She was the daughter of Enrico of Aragon and sister of the Cardinal of Aragon,* and the Duke of Amalfi was her first husband. When he died, she married Antonio Bologna,* a noble, virtuous, and wealthy gentleman who had been steward to King Frederick of Aragon. And because they considered that she had married beneath herself, the brothers launched a crusade against her and did not stop until they had savagely murdered her, along with her husband and some of her children—truly a most pitiable event. It is still less than a year since Antonio was wretchedly murdered here in Milan, and not so long ago Lord Girolamo Visconti told the story of that marriage and that death to many guests assembled in his magnificent palace, the Casa Bianca, just outside the city. So I, who had already heard it all recounted in detail by the worthy lord Cesare Fieramosca,* wrote the tale that now I give you. Your leisure, I know, is filled with worthy activities, yet still I hope that when sometimes you withdraw from your public duties you may read and keep it for my sake, whose debt to you is so much greater than this tale can repay.

And I recommend myself to you. Keep well.

Antonio Bologna marries the Duchess of Amalfi and both of them are murdered.

Antonio Bologna, a Neapolitan, as many of you may know, was in the service of Lord Silvio Savelli* during his residence in Milan. Then, when Lord Silvio departed, he took up with Francesco Acquaviva, the marquis of Bitonto who had been captured at the Battle of Ravenna and kept prisoner by the French in the castle of Milan. But when the marquis had given reliable guarantees he was released and lived in the city for a considerable time. Finally, after paying a large ransom, he returned to the kingdom of Naples. Bologna, therefore, entered the household of Alfonso Visconti along with three servants and could often be seen in elegant attire, riding through the streets of Milan. He was a courteous and cultured gentleman, handsome, brave, and an excellent horseman. He was also well versed in literature and could sing sweetly to his own lute. I know that there are some here who heard him sing, or rather lament his state, one day when he played and sang at the urging of Lady Ippolita Sforza.*

Now Frederick of Aragon,* after being driven out of Naples, had taken refuge with King Louis XII and received a generous welcome. Bologna, having served as King Frederick's faithful steward in France for many years, at last returned to reside in his native Naples and in his own home. But it was not long before the Duchess of Amalfi, daughter of Enrico of Aragon and sister to the Cardinal of Aragon, asked him to become her steward; and because he was accustomed to life at court and had always supported the Aragonese faction, he accepted. The duchess had become a widow very young and was now charged with governing the duchy of Amalfi and bringing up the son she had borne to her husband. Still young, high-spirited, beautiful, and living a comfortable life, she was reluctant to get married and confide her son to the rule of someone else; and so she thought of finding, if she could, a worthy lover with whom to enjoy her youth. Among her subjects and in other company she saw many men who seemed courteous and noble, but on close consideration of their bearing and behaviour, she could find no one who could compare with her steward, for he was indeed a handsome man, tall and well built, with refined elegant manners and endowed with many good qualities. Thus she fell in love with him and as, day by day, she observed and admired his courteous ways, she burned with such a passion that she felt she could not live without seeing him by her side. Bologna was indeed neither stupid nor sluggish and, though conscious that he was not her equal in rank, perceived the love she bore him and so cherished her in the secret of his heart that he thought of nothing else. In this way, they loved each other until the duchess was struck by a new idea. Wishing to offend God as little as possible and anxious to avoid the blame she might incur, she resolved that, without telling anyone of her passion, she would become not the lover of Bologna, but his wife. Thus they could enjoy their love in secret until such time as she felt obliged to publish the marriage. Having made this decision, she called Bologna into her room one day and, seated with him by the window, as was her custom when she needed to discuss household affairs, she began:

'If I were speaking to anyone but you, Antonio, I would think a lot before saying what I have decided to tell you. But I know that you are a discreet gentleman, naturally endowed with a strong intellect, educated and trained in the royal courts of my relatives, Alfonso II, Ferdinand, and Frederick.* And therefore, I am convinced (and the thought pleases me) that when you have heard my honest reasons, you will share my opinion. For were this not so, I would be forced to believe that you do not possess the acute insight that everyone sees in you. As you know, I became a widow very young on the death of my husband, the late duke, of happy memory; and since then I have lived in such a way that nobody—not even the sharpest and most austere of critics—could accuse me of straying a hair's breadth from the path of virtue. At the same time I have governed the duchy so well that when my son is old enough to rule he will find it in a better state than when the duke left it. Moreover, when I had paid off fifteen thousand ducats of debt incurred by that good soul during the recent wars, I bought a profitable barony in Calabria so that now I don't owe a penny and the needs of the household are amply provided for. I used to think that I would continue to live as a widow, governing the duchy and dividing my time between town and castle and Naples; but now I'm inclined to change and lead a different kind of life. For truly I think it much better to take a husband than to act like some other women who offend God and incur public shame by giving themselves up to lovers. I know very well what they say about a certain duchess of this kingdom, though her lover is one of the greatest barons in the land; and I know you understand me. Now, coming back to my own case, you see that I am still young, not cross-eyed nor crippled, nor as ugly as the Baronci* so I need not fear comparison with others. And since I live in the comfort that you see every day, I cannot avoid thinking of love, even against my will. I can hardly find a man of the same rank as my first husband, unless I take some callow youth who would chase me from his bed as soon as he got tired of me and put whores there instead. And right now there is no baron of a suitable age who is in need of a wife. That is why, after much careful thought, it struck me that I might choose a well-qualified gentleman and take him as my husband. But there would be a risk of scandalous gossip and of being put to shame by my relatives, especially my brother the cardinal, and to avoid this I would like to keep the marriage secret until such time as it can be revealed with less danger. The man I wish to marry has an income of about a thousand ducats, and I have my dowry which, added to what the duke left me, makes over two thousand, plus the furnishings of the house which belong to me. And if I cannot keep up my rank as duchess, I will be happy to live as a gentlewoman. Now I would like to hear what you advise.'

After this long speech from the duchess, Antonio hardly knew what to say. He was sure that she loved him, and he loved her with a real passion; but now he feared that she was contemplating marriage as a way of putting an end to this love. So he remained speechless, with a changed countenance, simply sighing instead of giving a firm answer. The duchess, who guessed the thoughts of her lover and was not unhappy to see these signs of his ardour, decided to put him out of his agony, and rather than leaving him in suspense, she said: 'Antonio, be of good heart and have no fear, for if you consent I have decided that you shall be my husband, come what may.' At these words, her lover returned from death to life and, having approved her intention with all appropriate terms, he offered himself not as a husband but as her most faithful and humble servant. Then, assured of their mutual affection, they discussed the situation at length and finally fixed on a plan to live together in the best possible and most secret way.

The duchess had confided her feelings to a young girl who was in her service and who happened to be a daughter of the nurse who had cared for her from the very cradle. She now called this girl to be a witness* as, with nobody but the three of them present, she was wedded to Bologna. The marriage remained secret for many years, during which time they slept together almost every night; and since they continued to share this pleasurable practice, the duchess became pregnant and gave birth to a son, managing the matter so well that nobody at court knew anything about it. Bologna had the child properly nursed and gave him the baptismal name of Federico. After this, as they continued in their loving intercourse, the duchess conceived a second time and gave birth to a lovely daughter.

But with this second birth they could not hide things so success-fully, and many people were aware that the duchess had been preg-nant and borne a child; and as the various rumours spread, so at last the affair reached the ears of her two brothers, the Cardinal of Aragon and his younger brother Carlo. Hearing that their sister had given birth to a child and not knowing who the father was, they decided that they could not abide the shame of it and set about using all possible means to spy on the duchess's every move. Since the court was now buzzing with gossip and swarming with people sent by the two broth-ers for no other purpose than to find out about the affair, Bologna began to fear that the handmaid might reveal the way things really stood, and so one day he said to the duchess: 'You know, my lady, that this second birth has aroused your brothers' suspicions and how per-sistently they attempt to discover the whole truth. I fear they already have some proof that I am involved and one day they will have me killed. You know their character better than I do and how heavy-handed one of them can be. I don't think they will ever be so cruel with you and I'm convinced that once they have murdered me, they will go no further. That is why I've decided to go first to Naples and, when I have settled my affairs there, to take refuge in Ancona where my revenues can be sent. I shall stay there until it becomes clear that your brothers no longer have this business on their minds. After which, time will be our best counsellor.'

They talked the matter over for a long time, and then, to the great distress of his wife, Bologna departed. As he had planned, he put his affairs in order, confided them to the care of a cousin, and took refuge in Ancona where he rented a suitable house and lived a respectable family life with the son and daughter he had taken with him and whom he looked after with the greatest care.

The duchess meanwhile, who was with child for the third time and could not bear to live without her dear husband, was so distressed as to be on the verge of madness. Brooding constantly on her wretched state and fearing that the brothers would play her some nasty trick if they heard of this third birth, she decided to go and join her husband and live as a private gentlewoman rather than remain a duchess with-out him. And after that, there are still those who say that love is not all-powerful! But who can deny that the force of love is immense? In fact, its power is greater than anything we can imagine. Don't we see every day that love produces the most strange and astonishing effects and that it overcomes all obstacles? That is why men say that there is no such thing as love in moderation. For when love so wishes, it can make kings, princes, and noblemen subject to the most depraved women—not as lovers, but as slaves. But let us drop this topic and return to our story.

The duchess had secretly informed her husband that she intended to join him and now she arranged to send ahead to Ancona as much money and as many belongings as she could. She then announced that she had made a vow to visit the shrine of Loreto.* With all these measures taken, and making sure to leave in good hands the education of her son who was to inherit the duchy, she set out with a numerous and honourable retinue and a large mule train. At Loreto, she ordered a solemn High Mass to be sung and made many rich gifts to that venerable and revered sanctuary. Then, when they all assumed that they would be returning to the kingdom of Naples, she said to them: 'We are only fifteen miles from Ancona and I have heard that it is a fine ancient city. It would be good to spend a day there.' Everyone agreed with the duchess, and so the mule train was sent on ahead and the whole party took the road to Ancona. Bologna had been informed of everything in advance and had refurbished the house in a fitting manner and prepared a suitably abundant reception for them all. His mansion gave onto the main street so that they were obliged to pass by his door. The butler, who had come early in the morning to organize the meal, was led inside by Bologna and told that lodgings had been prepared for his lady the duchess. This was enough for the butler, for although Bologna had left the court, nobody knew exactly why and he was very well liked. When the time seemed right, Bologna mounted his horse and, with a goodly company of gentlemen from Ancona, rode almost three miles out of the city to meet the duchess. When the duchess's people saw him they began to shout with joy: 'Look, lady! Look, duchess, it's our Antonio Bologna'—and they all rejoiced to greet him. He dismounted, kissed the hands of his wife, and invited her back to his house with all her company. She accepted and he led her to his home—not as his wife but as the lady he served. There, when they had all dined, the duchess, knowing that it must eventually come to this, decided to drop the pretence and called all her people into the hall where she addressed them as follows:

'My gentlemen and all who serve me, the time has come when I must reveal to the world something that I once did in the sight of

God. Being a widow, I wished to remarry and to take as a husband the man my own judgement had chosen. That is why I tell you that some years ago, in the presence of my handmaid who is here now, I married Signor Antonio Bologna whom you see. He is my legitimate husband, and because I am his wife I intend to stay with him. Until now I have been a duchess and your lady, and you have been my faithful vassals and servants. In the future take good care of the duke my son and be faithful and loyal to him as you should. You will accompany these maids of mine to Amalfi; before I left the kingdom I deposited their dowries with the bank of Paolo Tolosa and the documents are all in the monastery of San Sebastiano with the abbess and the nuns. For the time being I want no woman with me except this handmaid. Lady Beatrice, who has been my maid of honour so far, has been given full satisfaction, as she well knows. All the same, in the documents I just mentioned, she will find enough to make a dowry for one of the daughters she has at home. If there is among you anyone who wishes to stay and serve me, he will be well treated. Any other business will be settled in the usual way by the steward when you get to Amalfi. To conclude, I prefer to live privately with my husband Signor Antonio rather than to remain a duchess.'

On hearing this announcement, the whole company was stunned, speechless, and almost senseless. But when they saw that it was really happening, that Bologna had brought in his son and daughter by the duchess and that she kissed and embraced them as their joint off-spring, then they all decided to return to Amalfi, except for the maid of honour and two grooms who remained with their mistress. After much discussion, with everyone having his say, all the others left the house of Bologna and went to stay at the inn, because once they had heard how matters stood, nobody dared stay with the duchess for fear of the cardinal and his brother. Indeed, they agreed that the next morning one of the gentlemen should go to Rome and inform the cardinal who was there with his brother. And this was done. The rest of them made their way back to the kingdom of Naples.

The duchess remained with her husband, sharing a life of perfect happiness and a few months later gave birth to another son who was given the name Alonso. But while the couple lived in Ancona, more in love every day, the Cardinal of Aragon and his brother, who could not bear the thought that their sister had married in this way, used their influence with the cardinal of Mantua, Gismondo Gonzaga,* who was Pope Julius II's legate in Ancona. This succeeded so well that Bologna and his wife were banished from the city. They had been in Ancona about six or seven months and although the legate did everything he could to have them expelled, such were the devices of Bologna that the affair dragged on for some time. But knowing that in the long run he would be expelled and not wanting to be taken by surprise, he sought the help of a friend in Siena and obtained a safe conduct from the government of that city and permission to reside there with all his family. In the meantime he sent his children on ahead and settled his own affairs so that when the Anconitans ordered him to leave within a fortnight, he and his wife and their followers were able to ride off to Siena that very day. Hearing of this, the Aragon brothers, who had hoped to ambush them on the way, understood that they had been duped. So they turned for help to Alfonso Petrucci,* cardinal of Siena, whose brother was head of the Sienese government; and once again Bologna was expelled. After much thought about where he might find refuge, he decided to take the whole family to Venice.

So they set out, passing through Florentine territory on their way towards Romagna where they hoped to take ship to Venice. They had already reached the outskirts of Forlì when they realized that they were being followed by a large body of horsemen—something they had already been given reason to suspect. At first they were overcome by fear, more dead than alive, hardly knowing what to do, seeing no way to escape death. Yet the same fear urged them on and they made what haste they could towards a small farm not far off in the hope of finding safety inside. Bologna was mounted on a fine Barbary horse, as swift as the wind, and he had put his elder son on another excellent Barb.* His second son and his daughter were in a litter and his wife was riding a good palfrey. He and his son could easily have escaped, but the love that he bore his wife held him back. But she, firmly convinced that their pursuers threatened no one except her husband, urged him with tears to escape, saying: 'My lord, save yourself, for my brothers will do no harm to me or to our children; but if they catch you, they will put you to a cruel death.' And pressing on him a large purse full of ducats, she kept begging him to flee in the hope that with time, God willing, her brothers might be pacified. Her poor husband saw that their pursuers were drawing so near that there was no way his wife could escape. In great distress and bathed in tears, he took a sad leave of her and telling his men to save themselves, gave spur to his

Barbary horse. His son, seeing his father flee, boldly followed him with free rein, so that finally Bologna, his son, and four of his mounted escort managed to escape and, instead of going to Venice, made their way to Milan.

The band who had come to murder Bologna, captured the woman, her little son, her daughter, and all the rest of the group. Now whether he was carrying out the orders of her brothers, or whether he was acting on his own initiative to calm things down and make the lady come quietly, the chief of the pursuers said to the duchess: 'My lady, your brothers have sent me to bring you back to the kingdom and to take you home so that you can care for your son the duke instead of wandering here and there. For that Antonio Bologna was the kind of man who would have cleared off and left you destitute as soon as he got tired of you. Take heart and have no fear.' The lady seemed greatly relieved by these words for she thought they confirmed what she had said before, that her brothers would not torment herself and her children. In this belief, she travelled on for a few days until they came to a castle belonging to her son, the duke. Once there, she, her little children, and the maid of honour were all made prisoner and held in the keep of the fortress. What happened to the four of them was not known for some time. All the others were set free, but, as became clear later on, the duchess and the maid and the children were all wretchedly put to death in that keep.

The duchess's unfortunate lover and husband, with his son and their followers, came to Milan where they remained several days under the protection of Signor Silvio Savelli at the time when he was besieging the castle of Milan in the name of Massimiliano Sforza;* and indeed the castle did surrender a little later. Savelli then went to set up camp before Crema where he stayed for a few days. Bologna meanwhile took refuge with the marquis of Bitonto and, when the marquis left, with Signor Visconti. The Aragon brothers had used their influence in Naples to have all his goods confiscated. Bologna, for his part, sought only to appease the brothers, being absolutely unwilling to believe that his wife and children had been killed. There were some gentlemen who warned him more than once to be on his guard since he was not safe in Milan. But he listened to nobody, and some evidence that I obtained at the time leads me to think that he was persuaded to stay on by some secret assurances that he would see his wife again. Buoyed up by this vain hope and feeding on it from one day to the next, he remained in Milan for more than a year. At this same time a gentleman from the kingdom of Naples, who commanded some men-at-arms in the duchy of Milan, told the whole story to our Delio,* affirming that he had been commissioned to have Bologna assassinated, but that he had no wish to serve others as a butcher. He therefore managed to warn Bologna to stay out of his way, and also confirmed that the duchess and her children and the maid of honour had all been strangled.

But one day when Delio was with Lady Ippolita Bentivoglia, Bologna played the lute and sang a piteous complaint that he himself had composed and set to music. When Delio, who had never met Bologna before, learned that he was the husband of the Duchess of Amalfi, he was moved to compassion and took him aside to tell him that his wife was dead, adding that he knew for certain that there were men in Milan who had come to murder him. Bologna thanked Delio and told him: 'Delio, you are wrong about this, because letters from my people in Naples tell me that the authorities will soon restore what they confiscated, and from Rome too comes good hope that my most reverend and illustrious lord the cardinal is no longer so angry with me—and his brother even less; and I shall surely be reunited with my lady wife.' Delio, knowing how he was being deceived, said what he thought was fitting and left him.

Now those who sought to murder Bologna saw that nothing was being done and that the Neapolitan with the men-at-arms seemed lukewarm about the project. So they hired a Lombard gentleman, urging him to do everything possible to carry out the assassination. Delio had already told Signor Lucio Scipione Attellano the whole story up to this point, saying that he intended to use it in one of his tales, for he was sure that poor Bologna would be murdered.

Lucio Scipione Attellano and Delio were in Milan one day, standing where they faced the Monastero Maggiore, when who should come by but Bologna, riding a fine jennet,* on his way to hear Mass at the church of San Francesco. He had two attendants, one carrying a pike and the other a book of hours of Our Lady. 'Here comes Bologna,' said Delio to Attellano. Attellano thought he saw fear in Bologna's face and exclaimed: 'By God, he should have that attendant carry another pike instead of that prayer book, in danger as he is.' Attellano and Delio had not reached San Giacomo before they heard a great noise: it came from where Bologna, even before arriving at the church,

had been attacked by Captain Daniele de Bozola* and three of his
armed men; he was pierced through and through, and brutally murdered before anyone could come to his aid. And the men who had
killed him departed undisturbed and went their various ways as they
pleased, for there was nobody who could be bothered to take legal
action against them.

NICCOLÒ D'ESTE
Novelle (Tales) 1. 44

Bandello to the Most Magnanimous and Virtuous
Signor Count Baldassare Castiglione*

NOT so long ago that noble lady Bianca d'Este,* widow of Signor
Amerigo Sanseverino, came to Milan and remained there for several
days in order to settle certain legal disputes. She was very honourably
received and welcomed by many Milanese gentlemen with sumptuous
banquets, music, and other fitting entertainments. And among those
who honoured her so splendidly there was Benedetto Tonso, an amiable lawyer who was pleading her cause. There was also Signor Lucio
Scipione Attellano, a courteous and virtuous person, as you know,
who generously held a Lucullian dinner and supper in her honour
and invited a number of noble ladies and honourable gentlemen. It
was the month of July when the dog days are often unpleasantly hot.
A farce was performed—not very long, but thoroughly delightful—
which kept the joyous company highly amused for some time. Then
came dancing and many pleasant games, but since it was about midday the air was excessively hot. They were in a room on the ground
floor where the windows faced east and offered some coolness, but even
so the happy group gave up dancing and began to discuss various topics.

Signora Camilla Scarampa,* who can truly be called a Sappho of
our times, suggested that it might not be unfitting to spend such a hot
and tiresome hour in pleasurable storytelling.

Everybody was delighted with the idea, and Signora Camilla herself began with a very entertaining story, after which other ladies and
gentlemen followed suit. Finally Lady Bianca recounted a tale about
events that I thought particularly remarkable. And that is why, being
present on that occasion, I noted it down and transcribed it for

inclusion among my other stories. Now, since I think the subject matter makes it worthy to end up in your hands, I send it to you as a proof of my love and reverence for you, for I know of no other way to show you my devotion and bear witness of it to the world. I also feel that since you sent me your lovely elegy, I should send you some little thing of my own—not as an exchange, for my gossip cannot be compared to your learned muses, but so that everybody should know that you are and always will be in my thoughts. Keep well.

Marquis Niccolò III d'Este* catches his son committing adultery with his stepmother and has both of them decapitated on the same day in Ferrara.

As the whole of Europe knows, my paternal grandfather, Marquis Niccolò III d'Este, was an exceptional and most generous lord who often acted as an arbitrator whenever there was a dispute or a war between the princes of Italy. And because he was not legitimate, he was fiercely opposed by his first cousin Azzo IV d'Este. But with Fortune's favour and the help of the Venetians, Florentines, and Bolognese, he succeeded in packing Azzo off to Crete (which is now called Candy) and establishing a long and peaceful rule in Ferrara. He then married Gigliola, daughter of Francesco the Younger of Carrara who ruled Padua at that time. By her he had one child, a fine son, who was given the name Ugo, count of Rovigo.* But the mother did not long survive his birth; struck down by a grave sickness, she passed into the next life, to the great distress of the marquis who had loved her alone. Count Ugo was educated as befits the son of such a prince and excelled for his age in everything he did.

The marquis now took many lovers and, being young and secure in his power, thought of nothing but having a good time. So much so that he produced enough bastards to make an army—which is why in Ferrara they still say: 'Three hundred bastards of Marquis Niccolò have hauled the ships along the River Po.' The first of these bastards was Lionello,* who was born of a lovely girl called Stella and who later succeeded his father as ruler in the city of Ferrara. The second was the famous Borso,* born of a Sienese gentlewoman of the ancient and noble family of the Tolomei: Pope Paul II raised him from the rank of marquis to that of duke of Ferrara and the Emperor Frederick of Austria made him duke of Modena and Reggio.

But why should I list one by one the sons that Marquis Niccolò had by his various lovers? It would take me far too long. And I am not speaking of all the sons because we simply do not know how many there were, but only of those who were recognized as his. I myself saw about ten of them when I was a young girl in Ferrara.

But enough of the sons. Let me tell you that Marquis Niccolò decided to marry for a second time and, having considered many matches in Italy and abroad, he chose a daughter of Carlo Malatesta,* then the powerful lord of many cities in the Marches and Romagna, and considered in Italy as a great master of the art of war. The bride was still a young girl, not yet fifteen, very beautiful and charming. She arrived in Ferrara with an honourable escort from the Marches and from Romagna and was received by the marquis with great splendour. But she had not been long with him before she realized that he was still the cock of Ferrara and that she was losing his attention, for he was indeed the greatest womanizer of the age and could not look at a woman without wanting to have her. It was never said, however, that he possessed any of them by violence. Now when his wife the marchioness saw what he was like and that, by neglecting her, he was saving what he would spend elsewhere, she decided not to waste her youth by standing still with her arms folded. Having observed the manners and customs of the courtiers, she had the misfortune to set eyes on her stepson, Count Ugo, who was indeed very handsome and gracious in every way. He pleased her so much that she fell madly in love, finding neither happiness nor rest except in his company and conversation. The young count, who could not think of any such villainy, treated his stepmother with the same respect and deference that any good obedient son would show to his real mother. But she was looking for something more than deference and in her infatuation multiplied the signs and gestures that would make him understand the amorous fire that consumed her. Yet still Count Ugo, a youth of sixteen or seventeen years of age, paid no attention to her lascivious motions for he was far from imagining anything of the kind. And seeing this, she became deeply depressed and dared not tell him of her immoral and criminal appetites; and even though sometimes she tried to force herself to speak, she was tongue-tied with shame and could not utter a word. So she went on, in this most unhappy state, not knowing what to do and finding no relief from her cruel torments which grew greater from hour to hour. After several days of this torture, she saw clearly that only shame prevented her from speaking out and revealing her love to Count Ugo. Since she had already opened her breast to such immoral passions, she resolved also to open her mouth and, banishing all shame, to find a remedy for her ills, confiding in nobody, but going in person to reveal everything to Count Ugo.

When she had taken this decision, it happened that Marquis Niccolò was called by Duke Filippo Visconti* to Milan where he would have to stay several days. On one of these days the marchioness was in her room, brooding over her fierce desires. At last, unable to restrain herself and finding the moment ripe for her purpose, she sent for Count Ugo as if she had matters of some importance to discuss. With thoughts very different from those of his stepmother, he hastened into her presence, greeted her with proper respect and, at her invitation, sat down beside her, waiting for what she had to say. She hesitated for a while, torn between love and shame. Finally, spurred on by love which had now driven out all shame and reserve, with flushed cheeks and frequent sighs, with trembling voice and broken words, impeded by tears and sighs, she began to speak as best she could:

'I don't know, sweet lord, if you have ever thought of the unpraise-worthy life led by Marquis Niccolò, your father, and of his behaviour which causes me such constant unhappiness. When he was left a wid-ower by the death of your lady mother of happy memory, he began chasing women so regularly that in Ferrara and throughout its terri-tory there is hardly a district where he hasn't left a bastard son. Everyone thought that marrying me would change his behaviour, but it has done nothing to temper his evil habits. Just as before, he cannot see a woman without wanting to possess her. I really think he would prefer to die rather than give up the pleasure he takes with these women as long as he can find them. And since he's the lord, who is going to deny him? But what feels worse for me is that he has more care for these whores and coarse women and for the children he gives them than for me, or indeed for you, the child of such a virtuous and noble lady. If you have ever thought about it, you must have realized this. When I was still at home with my father I heard a counsellor who loved to read old chronicles say that among our forefathers there was a certain Fresco who became enraged against his father Azzo II and killed him because he had brought a stepmother into the house—and this even though she was the daughter of Charles II, king of Naples. I am not suggesting that you should stain your hands with the blood of your own father by becoming his murderer, but I'm warning you to keep your eyes open and watch out that you don't end up fooled and defrauded with a reed in your hand instead of a sceptre. Haven't you heard how your father obtained the marquisate of Ferrara, although he was illegitimate and it belonged by right to Azzo IV? He gathered his friends together and, with the help of the Venetians, drove Azzo out of the land and into exile on the island of Candy where that unfortunate lord died a wretched death. Beware lest you share the same kind of fate and that one out of that crowd of bastards doesn't leave you, as the saying goes, out in the cold like a scarecrow. As for me, if anything should happen to your father, I would risk all my worldly wealth and life itself to ensure that the power remains, as it should, in your hands. And although people often say that stepmothers don't love their stepsons, you can be sure that I love you more than myself. If only Heaven had granted me the destiny that was already my hope! For when my lord father spoke of a Ferrara marriage, it was of you he spoke and not of your father. I don't know why that plan was changed. May God forgive whoever made that bargain! You and I, my lord, are of the right age to be united in marriage; and we would have made a far better couple than I make with the marquis. My life would have been happier with you as my lord and husband—all the more so because I loved you long before the marquis, since I was given hope that I would be yours and you mine. And to tell you the truth, I have always loved you deeply and I still love you more than my own soul; nor could I ever turn my thoughts towards anyone else, so firmly rooted are you in my heart. Therefore, my sweet lord and light of my eyes...' With these words, since they were alone in the room, she threw her arms around his neck and kissed him passionately on the mouth two or three times: 'Have pity on me and on yourself. Ah, my lord, behold my grief and be mine as I am eternally yours. Thus, without doubt, you will become the lord of this land and transform the dejected wretch that I am into the happiest woman in the world.'

Count Ugo, who was waiting to see what she was leading up to with her speeches, was so stunned by these last words and by her sweet and passionate kisses that he could neither answer her nor go away; instead, he remained there, unmoving, more like a marble statue than a living man. Her beauty was enchanting, daring, and sensual, enhanced by the ardour of two captivating eyes. Indeed, I firmly believe that if Phaedra had been so lovely and charming, she would surely have won

over her beloved Hippolytus.* Now when the marchioness saw that
Count Ugo was not offended and that he did not get up, but rather
stayed there immobile and said nothing, she decided to strike while
the iron was hot without leaving him time to summon up courage to
reply or to consider the villainy that was being suggested, the shame
and ignominy of the offence to his father, and the danger to himself.
Since the opportunity offered, she once again wrapped her arms round
his neck and showered him with lascivious kisses and a thousand other
indecent touches and caresses, together with sweet murmured words.
Dazzled and entrapped, the unfortunate youth felt a certain swelling
down below, and, as the reins of reason gave way to his lustful appetite,
he began to return her lascivious kisses and bites, putting his hands
into her snow-white bosom, and fondling her lovely firm round
breasts. But why should I go into detail? They would willingly have
satisfied their desires there and then, but that the place seemed too risky
and at last they settled on somewhere more suited to their mutual
pleasures. They also decided that unless she confided in one of her
women, it would be impossible to enjoy each other without grave
danger. With this in mind, the marchioness considered all her maids
and, having assessed their various qualities, chose the one who seemed
to be most suitable. So, one day, she found the right moment to reveal
her intentions, and argued so persuasively that the woman promised
to carry out all her orders.

Ugo, meanwhile, having left the room, remained so drunk with
ardent love for his stepmother that he could think of nothing but her
beauty. And if she longed to be with him again, his own craving was
no less. Shortly after, with the help of the faithful chambermaid, they
were able to come together and enjoy the ultimate delights of love, to
the infinite pleasure of them both. And although the courtiers noted
some familiarity between them, nobody thought there was anything
wrong in that. So this amorous intercourse went on for more than two
years without arousing any suspicion until, at last, the chambermaid
fell ill, took to her bed, and died. The lovers, however, carried on with
less discretion before so that finally a manservant of Count Ugo
became aware of it, though I do not know how. And to be quite sure,
he began to observe everything his master did and somehow managed
to climb up above the room where the lovers took their pleasure. At
a time when he could not be heard, he made a little hole in the ceiling
through which once or twice he watched the unfortunate couple

making love. Then, having witnessed that abominable crime, he took the first opportunity to show everything to Marquis Niccolò through that same hole. The marquis was distressed beyond all measure by such a grievous offence, and his love for his wife and his son was replaced by a violent hatred as he resolved to take cruel revenge upon them both.

It was the month of May, in the early afternoon, when the marquis saw the lovers at their sport; and so, at about four o'clock, while the unfortunate Count Ugo was playing ball in the square, he called up the captain of the guard with his men and gave orders that they should be armed. Many of the first gentlemen in Ferrara were in the palace at the time and, when the captain arrived, they were amazed to hear the marquis command that they should go straightaway to seize Count Ugo and chain him up in the tower that gives on to the Porta del Leone—the same tower where the duke's brothers, Don Ferrando and Don Giulio,* are imprisoned today. Then he ordered the warden of the castle to arrest the marchioness and to put her in the other tower. After which he explained to all those present the reasons that had led him to take these measures.

As I have said, the unfortunate Count Ugo was playing ball, and since it was a holiday when the common people do not work, all Ferrara was there to see him play. The captain arrived in the square with his sergeants and, right in front of the clock, laid rude hands on Count Ugo to the general sorrow of all those who witnessed the cruel spectacle; then he was bound and led away to prison. Likewise the marchioness was imprisoned by the warden of the castle.

That same evening the cruel father sent two friars from the convent of Santa Maria degli Angeli to tell Count Ugo that he should prepare for death. When he heard the reason for this unexpected news and for his tragic fate, he wept over his sin and with great contrition made himself ready for the death he had deserved, spending the whole night in pious conversation and detestation of his offence. He even sent to his father to ask forgiveness for the injury he had done him. The marchioness, when she found herself in prison and learned that Count Ugo was also held captive, begged to speak to her husband, but without success. She then sent another message to say that she alone was guilty, she alone had led Count Ugo astray, and she alone should be punished for the crime they had committed. But when she heard that they were both to have their heads cut off, she was seized by an unbridled fury which clearly showed that she could not bear to think of the death of Count Ugo, though she cared little or nothing for her own. Day and night she did nothing but call her lord Ugo, not ceasing to invoke his name throughout the three days that she remained in prison. To her also the marquis sent two friars to give her comfort and to prepare her to suffer with patience the pain of death, but their efforts were all in vain.

The young man, for his part, persevered in his repentance for three days, attended by the two friars, conversing of holy things and ever more fully making ready for his approaching death. After the third day, early in the morning, one of the friars said Mass for his intention, and he received the most sanctified body of Our Saviour, shedding copious tears and asking God and the world to pardon his sins. That evening, as dusk was falling, in the same tower, on his father's orders, his head was severed by the executioner. At that very hour, in the other tower, the woman's head was cut off. But she showed absolutely no repentance for the crime she had committed and steadfastly refused the sacrament of confession. On the contrary, she kept on begging them to let her see her lord Ugo for one last time. And so, with the cherished and beloved name of Ugo on her lips, the wretched and unfortunate lady was decapitated. The next day the marquis had both bodies, carefully washed and nobly dressed, placed in the middle of the palace courtyard where anyone who wished could see them. Then, when evening came, he gave them a solemn funeral and had them laid together in a single tomb in the church of San Francesco.

The marquis, finding himself without a wife and without legitimate children, married for a third time and took for his wife Riccarda, daughter of the marquis of Saluzzo, who gave birth to Duke Ercole, father of Duke Afonso and of Lord Sigismondo my father. I know that some think the unfortunate Count Ugo was not the son of Marquis Niccolò's first wife, but the firstborn of his bastards. But they are quite wrong about this, for Ugo was indeed legitimate and was count of Rovigo, as I heard my late father say many times.

ANTON FRANCESCO GRAZZINI (IL LASCA)

INTRODUCTION
Le cene (The Suppers)

IT was more than fifteen hundred years since the fruitful incarnation
of the Blessed Son of the Virgin Mary, the fortieth year of the century
being passed and the fiftieth not yet reached—in the time, that is,
when, as vicar of Christ and successor of Peter, Paul III governed the
Holy Mother Church, when Charles V with eternal glory loosened or
tightened the bridle of the ancient empire of the warlike sons of
Mars,* and when the Gauls were guided and ruled by Francis I, most
serene king of France. In that year,* then, in the fine and flourishing
city of Florence, on the last day of January, on a feast day, after dinner,
four of the city's most prominent and high-born young men were
gathered in the house of a widow who was worthy and noble, rich and
beautiful. They had come to pass the time and relax in the company
of her brother, who had few rivals for culture and courtesy, not only
in Florence but in all Tuscany. Over and above his other gifts, he was
a perfect musician and had a music room full of songbooks and excellent instruments of all kinds; for all those young men, to a greater or
lesser extent, knew how to play something or sing.

Now as they were preparing to enjoy themselves with music, the
weather grew worse and it began to snow so heavily that in a few
hours it was six inches high. Seeing this, the young men left the room
where they were singing and playing, went out into a spacious courtyard, and started throwing snowballs. When the spirited and charming lady of the house heard this, it struck her that she might mount
a pleasant assault against her brother and the other young men; and
without delay she called up four young ladies who for various reasons
were in the house with her at the time. These were her two stepdaughters, her niece, and a neighbour—all four married and all noble
and beautiful, blithe and graceful. Their husbands were absent, those
of the two stepdaughters on commercial affairs in Rome and Venice,

that of the niece on official business, and that of the neighbour out in the country. Then the lady of the house said: 'My dear girls, I think we should go straight up onto the roof and, together with all the maids, make a big pile of snowballs. Then we can go down to the windows that overlook the courtyard, and while the young men are fighting with each other, we shall bombard them most terribly. They'll try to turn and reply, but since they are down below, they'll be hit so often that for once they will end up as losers.'

Her words pleased them all, so they promptly made themselves ready and went up first to the terrace and then to the roof, where in time they filled three trays and two baskets with well-made solid snowballs. Then quietly they came down to the windows that gave onto the courtyard where the disorderly young men were still fighting with each other; and putting down their trays or baskets on the floor, they came forward, bare-necked and bare-armed, and began to pelt the young men, who found this all the more remarkable and astounding because it was so unexpected.

In the first moment, taken by surprise and not knowing what to do, they just stood still and looked up, so that the well-aimed snowballs hit them on the forehead or in the face or on the chest or anywhere on the body. Then, understanding that the ladies were in earnest, they turned round, shouting and laughing, and began the most hilarious skirmish ever seen. But they soon got the worst of it, for as they bent down they got badly hit and in trying to avoid one snowball they would get struck by another; and often they slipped and fell so that eight or ten balls would get them at the same time—all this to the great delight of the ladies who, with enough snowballs for about twenty minutes, had the time of their lives. At last, when their stock ran out, they closed the windows and hurried off to change and warm themselves, leaving the young men sodden and bedraggled in the courtyard.

Seeing that the ladies had vanished and that the windows were closed, the young men gave up their game and went inside where they found that a good fire had been lit. Some went to dry themselves, some took off their stockings; others went to bed, and there were even those who had to change their shirts. But when they were all dry and warm, they could not accept the fact that they had been so thoroughly trounced by the women and began to think about revenge. So with one accord they all stole back into the courtyard and gathered armfuls of snowballs; then, believing they would catch the women unprepared by the fire, advanced on tiptoe to get their revenge. But they could not climb the staircase so stealthily as not to be heard and seen by the ladies who immediately ran to lock the door, so that the young men, baffled yet again, went back to their room. And since it had stopped snowing, they started to discuss where they could go to amuse themselves. But while they were making up their minds, as so often happens, the snow turned into rain and there was such a downpour that they decided to stay where they were for the rest of the evening. Lights were brought in because it was already growing dark; the fire was rekindled, and they began to sing madrigals for five voices by Verdelot and Arcadelt.*

The ladies, having warded off disaster, were warming themselves by the fire and laughing at the foe; and as they were chatting about cheerful and pleasant matters, they happened to hear the men singing, but could only make out the tune when they would have liked to hear the words as well. And since there were those among them who loved and understood such music, they decided unanimously to call the young men who were all relatives or neighbours or friends, and therefore used to being in their company. The lady of the house was chosen as their messenger. The young men were more than happy to accept the invitation and accompanied her to the room where the other ladies gave them a most honourable, cheerful, and fitting reception. And when they had sung six or seven madrigals to the great satisfaction and pleasure of the whole party, they went to sit around the fire. Now one of the men had brought into the room a copy of the *Decameron* which he held under his arm so that a lady asked him what book it was. To which he replied that it was the most beautiful and useful book ever written: 'These', he said, 'are the tales of Messer Giovanni Boccaccio, or rather Saint Giovanni Boccadoro.'* 'Fine,' giggled another lady, 'I like that *saint*.'

Since the young man had a good voice and a pleasant way of reading, they asked him to choose some stories to read aloud; but he kept refusing until one of the ladies intervened to say that they should select a day, then each of them might read one story and, since they were a party of ten, everyone would have a turn.

The proposal met with general approval and they started to argue about which day to choose: some wanted the fifth day, some the third, some the sixth, some the seventh. At last it struck the lady of the house that she might try out an idea that had just come into her mind; and without saying anything, she got up from the fire and went into the next room where she summoned an attendant and a servant and gave them precise orders as to what she wanted them to do. Then she returned to where the company were still debating which day to choose and spoke as follows in her bright festive manner: 'Fine young men and fair young ladies, since necessity, rather than your wisdom or my foresight, has brought us together so unexpectedly to talk before the fire this evening, I'm obliged to ask you a favour. It's the men I am asking, because I have complete faith in the courtesy of my ladies to do whatever I wish.'

When the young men swore that they would do everything they could to suit her, she continued: 'You can hear how it's not simply raining, but absolutely flooding down, so the favour I ask is that you shouldn't think of leaving, but agree to stay for an informal supper with me and with your great friend, my brother. In the meantime the rain will have stopped; and even if it continues, there are so many rooms ready on the ground floor that we could easily put up a much bigger party than you are. But while we are waiting for supper, I have an idea, if you agree, about how we can spend the time most pleasantly: and this will not be by reading the tales written by Boccaccio, even though there are no others quite so splendid, so lively, and so instructive. Instead, each in his turn, we should find and tell our own stories, which, if not as good as those of Boccaccio, won't have been so often read and heard. And since we have among us people who are clever, subtle, imaginative, and original, they should offer us, for once, some real utility with no little pleasure and happiness. As for you, young men, you've all had a good literary education and are familiar with the poets, not just Latin and Tuscan, but Greek as well, so you shouldn't be lacking in manner or matter, and my ladies too will strive to do themselves honour. What's more, it will soon be the Carnival season when even the monks are allowed to have fun, and the friars play football, act comedies, and dress up as women to play and dance and sing. And the nuns too, in the shows they put on when they celebrate these feast days, feel free to dress as men, with velvet caps, tight stockings, and sword on thigh. Why then should it be considered unfitting or improper for us to take pleasure in telling stories? Who can honestly blame us? Who can reasonably condemn us? Today is Thursday and, as you know, not next Thursday, but the Thursday after that will be Fat Thursday;* and so on these two coming Thursdays I am asking you to do me the favour of dining with my brother and me, just as you are doing this evening. Tonight, since we've had little time to think, our tales will be short, but on the two other evenings we shall have had a week to prepare, so for the first one I think we should have tales of medium length and for the second, which will be Fat Thursday, we shall have the long ones. In this way, each of us will show his or her skill in three different kinds of tale: the short, the middle-sized, and the long. Moreover, the number three is the most perfect of all, since it contains within itself beginning, middle, and end.'

FAZIO THE GOLDSMITH
Le cene (*The Suppers*) 1. 5

Guglielmo Grimaldi is wounded at night, runs to the house of Fazio the goldsmith, and dies there. Fazio wickedly robs him of a large sum of ducats and buries him in secret. Being an alchemist, he pre-tends to have made silver and goes with the money to France. Then, feigning to have sold the silver, he returns to Pisa a rich man. Accused by his jealous wife, he is put to death; after which she kills her children and herself.

GALATEA'S brief tale pleased everyone and was much praised. No sooner had she finished than Leander* began to look affectionately around the merry band: 'Gentle ladies,' he said, 'and you, amorous youths, I think that Heaven must have chosen me to tell this kind of story because of my pseudonym, since the man who truly bore that name ended up badly and drowned while swimming across to his lover's house. And so I reluctantly agree to tell of unfortunate and unhappy events, a sad and piteous case that is truly worth your tears, and perhaps as grim and fearful a story as ever occurred. And although it did not happen in Greece or Rome, nor to persons of noble ancestry or royal blood, still it came about exactly as I shall tell you. You will see that tragic passion may be found in low and humble dwellings no less than in proud palaces and under golden roofs. And you will learn how a woman who was neither an empress nor a queen nor a princess caused the desperate and bloody death of her husband, her children, and herself. Listen, therefore.' And he began:

We read in the old Pisan chronicles* how there once came to live in Pisa a certain Guglielmo Grimaldi, exiled from Genoa because of the factional strife in that city. A young man of twenty-two, without much money, he rented a modest house, lived very soberly, and began to lend money at interest. In this usurious profession, he did rather well; and since he spent little, he soon became quite rich. And as time went on and he continued in the same business, he became very rich indeed, for the more money he made the more he wanted to make. So it was that he became an old man worth several thousand florins who had never moved house and avoided expense by living completely alone, trusting his savings to nobody, and keeping all his florins carefully locked up at home. He loved money so much that he would not have spent a scudo to save a man's life, and this made him despised and hated in all Pisa.

Now Guglielmo was still leading this kind of life when one evening he went out to dine with some friends. It was already late as he made his way home and in the pitch-black night he was suddenly assaulted and received a stab-wound above his left nipple. The attack may have come from a personal enemy or he may have been mistaken for someone else; but the poor man ran away, knowing only that he had been badly wounded. In that precise moment a thunderstorm broke out and it began to rain so heavily that he had run little more than a bowshot before he was already soaked through; it was then that he saw a house with an open door and a roaring fire and made his way inside. In that house lived Fazio, a goldsmith who had recently turned to alchemy and spent much of his fortune trying to turn lead and pewter into fine silver. That evening he had kindled a huge fire and was about to start refining the metals; and because it was summer and the room was hot he had left the door open. So when he heard footsteps he turned and recognized the intruder: 'Guglielmo,' he exclaimed, 'what are you doing at this time of night and in such terrible weather?' 'Alas,' answered Guglielmo, 'I've been attacked and wounded, and I don't know who did it or why'—and with these words he collapsed and passed from this life to the next.

Fazio was astounded and scared out of his wits. At first, thinking that Guglielmo must have fainted, he undid his jerkin to give him some air, tried to raise him up, and called him by name. But there was no motion and no heartbeat. Then he discovered the wound in his breast, so mortal that there was no longer any flow of blood, and at last he felt certain that Guglielmo was dead, as was indeed the case. As chance would have it, Fazio was all alone, for his wife, with their twin sons who were about five years old, had gone to look after her father who was on his deathbed. And so he rushed to the door in a panic and began to call the neighbours. But there was not a living soul to be seen on the road, and what with the noise of the pouring rain and the thunder, he soon realized that no one could hear him and gave up. Quick to change his mind, he locked the door and went back inside where the first thing he did was to open the dead man's purse to see if there was any money. He found four lire in small change, and, amid a lot of worthless rubbish, a bunch of keys. These, he guessed, must serve to open the street door of Guglielmo's house and then of all the rooms, coffers, and strongboxes, for the old man was widely thought to be extremely rich, especially in hard cash which he kept locked up at home. As he thought this over, astute and intelligent as he was, he suddenly realized that he might pull off something so brilliant that it would change his life for good and all:

'Now why shouldn't I take these keys and go over to his house straightaway, since I'm sure that there's absolutely no one there? Who is there to stop me taking all his money and bringing it quietly back here? Luckily for me, it's raining, bucketing down, and what's more it's past midnight, so there's nobody out and about. They're all locked up, safe and sound, sleeping in the quiet of their homes. I'm alone in this house, and as for the man who stabbed Guglielmo, once he'd done the job, he must have run away to hide somewhere, and he won't have seen Guglielmo coming in here. And if I hold my tongue and don't speak of it to a living soul, who can ever think that Guglielmo Grimaldi came here wounded and died like this? The Lord God sent him here for my benefit. And then who knows, if I told the true story of this business, would I be believed? Maybe they'd think I killed him because I meant to rob him, and then got cold feet. Who can say that I wouldn't be arrested and sentenced to death? And how would I defend myself? Those interrogators aren't known for being tender, and I could be given a taste of the strappado* if not worse. So what can I do? All told, the best thing is to try my luck, since they say that Fortune favours the bold. We'll see if I can get myself out of trouble for once.'

That was it. With a good felt cloak on his back and a wide-brimmed hat on his head, with the keys close to his chest and a lantern in his hand, he set off amid the rain, thunder, and lightning, and in less than an hour he reached Guglielmo's house which was not all that far off.

With the two largest keys he opened the door and entered a room where he went straight to a huge coffer. After trying many keys, he finally found the right one and inside he saw two strongboxes which he just about managed to prise open. One of them was full of gold objects such as rings, chains, and bracelets and also precious jewels and pearls; in the other there were four bags brimful of the finest gold ducats and stitched on each bag there was a label saying 'Three thousand scudi in cash'. Fazio was perfectly happy to take only that strongbox and to leave the gold objects and the jewels for fear that one day they might be recognized. Then, leaving everything else in its proper place, and making sure that the whole room was exactly as he had found it, he locked up and went out with the keys at his belt and carrying the strongbox on his head. He came home without being seen by anyone, thanks to the weather which had never been worse than that year, for the heavens held nothing back and the rain kept pouring down amid thunder and lightning.

The first thing Fazio did when he arrived safely home was to put the strongbox into his room and to get changed. And since he was strong and vigorous he lifted up the corpse and carried it into the cellar. Taking the right tools for the job, he dug a ditch, eight foot deep, six foot long, and four foot wide, and in it he placed Guglielmo fully dressed, together with the keys. He then filled the ditch with earth which he levelled, pressed down, and covered with some rubble that he found in a corner, so that the place looked as if it had never been touched.

Back in his room, Fazio opened the strongbox and emptied one of the bags onto a table. He was almost dazzled by the sight which confirmed that all the coins were gold florins. It was the same when he examined and weighed the other bags; just as the label said, each bag was worth three thousand scudi. With joy in his heart, he carefully sealed the bags again and locked them in a cupboard in his study, and the strongbox he put in the fire and waited until it had been reduced to ashes. Then, leaving the furnaces and the lead and the alembics in disorder, he went to bed, for morning was breaking and the rain had stopped. Tired out by his hectic night, he slept until evening.

When he awoke, he went to the main square and the trading quarter to hear whether anyone was talking about Guglielmo, but there was nothing said that day or the next. On the third day, however, when Guglielmo had still not appeared in the places where he usually did business, people started to ask questions; and especially when they saw that the doors and windows of his house were barred they suspected that something serious must have happened to him. The friends who had dined with him gave a full account of that evening up to the time when he left them—after which, nobody knew what he had done or where he had gone. Faced by this prolonged absence, the judicial authorities reckoned that he might be dead and sent their officers round to his house where they forced open the door and went in. They found everything in perfect order, but there was no sign of Guglielmo. This set them wondering, and since they had found no keys, they sent for locksmiths who, in the presence of witnesses, opened all the doors, coffers, and strongboxes. The gold objects, the inventories, and the account books were all taken away by the authorities and deposited in a safe place; and the house was left as it was.

Notices were circulated immediately, threatening severe punishments for those who withheld information and promising rich rewards to anyone who might find Guglielmo dead or alive. But it was all in vain and three months passed without any news. Guglielmo had no heirs in Pisa and the war that had broken out between Genoa and Pisa meant that none of his relatives could turn up to lay a claim. So the authorities confiscated all his property, wondering only why they had found no money. Some people thought that he had taken it with him to God, others that he had buried it somewhere out of the way, and many more reckoned that the authorities had, in fact, taken it but did not want to say so.

Fazio, in the meantime, had kept his head down, delighted to see that things were going from good to better. His family were now back home with him, but he had told his wife absolutely nothing and was determined not to do so. He would have done well to stick to his decision, for doing the opposite turned out to be the ruin of himself, his wife, and his children.

Now the Guglielmo affair had died down and people had stopped discussing it, so Fazio let it be known that he had succeeded in making several ingots of silver and intended to sell them in France. Most people laughed at this since he had already tried twice and wasted his efforts, time, and money when the metal failed the test of the hammer.* Above all, his relatives and friends tried to persuade him, arguing that he should test the metal in Pisa. If it passed the test, he could sell the silver in Pisa just as well as in Paris; and if it failed, as they thought it would, he would have saved himself the trouble and expense of a journey. But nothing had any effect, for Fazio was determined to go; and if he did not want the metal to be tested in Pisa, it was because he knew that this time it was perfectly genuine silver. Pretending that he lacked money for the journey, he mortgaged a small farm for the sum of one hundred florins—fifty to cover his expenses and fifty for his wife to live on until his return. People could say what they liked, but he had already made arrangements with a Ragusan ship* bound for Marseilles. When his wife heard this, she began to weep and scream:

'So that's it, husband. So you're going to leave me alone with two children, just like that? And you'll go off to waste what little we've got left so that your wife and children can die of hunger! Damn your bloody alchemy and whoever put it into your head! How much better off we were when you stuck to your trade as a goldsmith and did some real work!'

Fazio tried to comfort her and calm her down, promising her all kinds of marvellous things when he returned; but she carried on: 'If this silver is so fine and good, it will be just as fine and good here as in France and you can sell it in the same way. But you're clearing off and you don't mean to come back. That's just my luck! And when I've spent the fifty ducats you're leaving me, I'll have to take the children and go begging.' And so she went on, crying and complaining day and night.

Now Fazio loved and cherished her like the apple of his eye and more than his own life, and in the end he felt so desperately sorry for her that he decided he would cheer her up by telling her the truth. So one day, after they had eaten together, he called her into his room and recounted the whole story of what had happened to Guglielmo, beginning at the beginning and neglecting no detail; then he took her by the hand and led her to his study and showed her the bags full of gold ducats.

The wonder and joy of Fazio's wife as she kept kissing and hugging her beloved husband can hardly be imagined, let alone expressed in words. He spoke to her at some length, insisting that, above all, she should keep silent, telling her what he intended to do, and describing the comfortable life he planned for them after his return. His wife was delighted and happily gave him permission to leave, only adding that he should try to get back as soon as possible.

Having settled things with his Pippa, Fazio set out the following morning. He had ordered a new strong coffer with a double lock and in the bottom of it he put three of the money bags, leaving the fourth with his wife in case some emergency should arise. On top of the bags he placed a dozen or more ingots of lead, pewter, mercury, and various alloys. He then had the coffer taken to the ship, while his father-in-law, relatives, and friends expressed their disapproval. Even his wife joined in, though her tears were feigned. All Pisa was there to mock and laugh at him; and some people who in the past had known him as shrewd and intelligent now thought that he had been driven mad, as men often are, by that curse of alchemy. The ship put to sea and set out on its voyage with a prosperous wind. Pippa, still feigning distress, remained behind to watch over the house and take care of the children.

In due time, the ship arrived at Marseilles, and there, at night, Fazio threw all the alchemical ingots into the sea. Leaving the ship and taking his coffer with him, he went with the traders' wagons to Lyons* where, after a stay of several days, he took his money bags to be counted by the first bank that would accept them and then had two letters of credit made out for banks in Pisa—the Lanfranchi and the Gualandi.* After this, he wrote to his wife to tell her how he had fared, informing her that he had sold his silver and would soon be returning to Pisa as a rich man. Pippa showed the letter first to her father and then to the other relatives and friends of Fazio, who were all amazed. And many simply refused to believe his success because they had expected the opposite. Not long after, Fazio left Lyons with his letters of credit and went to Marseilles where he embarked on a ship carrying grain that took him first to Livorno and then on to Pisa. The first thing he did on his arrival was to go and find his wife and children, and in an ecstasy of joy he hugged and kissed everyone who met him on the way, telling them that with God's help he had come home a rich man because his silver had been proved perfectly genuine by any standard. He took his letters of credit to the Lanfranchi and Gualandi banks and they counted out and paid him nine thousand gold ducats which he then had carried to his house amid the wonder and joy of his relatives and friends, who simply could not stop celebrating and complimenting him on his enterprising spirit.

Fazio found himself very rich for a man of his class and, seeing that by now everyone in Pisa believed his wealth had come from alchemy, he thought it was time to put it to use and start spending. First, he paid off the mortgage on his farm and bought a fine house that stood opposite his old one, and four of the best plots in the region of Pisa. He also bought some official positions in Rome* for two thousand scudi, and invested another thousand in a textile business at ten per cent. All told, he was living like a prince, and to go with his new house he took on two manservants and two maids and kept two horses, one for himself and one for his wife. The children were dressed as befitted their new station, and Fazio and his Pippa lived a calm, relaxed, and happy life.

Pippa, who was not used to such wealth and luxury, began to get above herself and decided to take in an old woman she knew, together with her wonderfully lovely daughter of about sixteen or seventeen; and she managed to persuade Fazio by telling him that the girl was just what she needed in the house to cut, sew, and mend shirts, shifts, and bonnets. And so, happy with her husband and her children, she passed her time in peace and quietness.

But envious Fortune, ever the enemy of those who are happy and of all worldly pleasures, saw to it that their joy would soon be turned to sorrow, their sweetness into a bitter taste, and their laughter into tears. For Fazio fell ardently in love with Maddalena (for such was the name of the old woman's daughter) and sought every opportunity to fulfil his desire until at last, by supporting his pleas with money, he corrupted the old woman, who was very poor, and had carnal knowledge of her daughter.

As the affair went on, without his wife knowing anything about it, Fazio became more infatuated with the girl every day. He had promised her mother and the girl herself that he would soon find her a husband and provide her with a good dowry; in the meantime he intended to take his pleasure and have a good time. And so he secretly enjoyed his Maddalena, even if it meant spending a few florins now and then. But they could not manage things so carefully as to prevent Pippa from finding out. First came harsh words and violent quarrels with her husband; and then, more seriously, she set about Maddalena and the old woman. One day, when Fazio was out, she sent them both packing with bag and baggage and a flood of insults only fit for dogs. Fazio made a furious scene when he heard of it, and as his disordered lust increased, he began to provide for the two women in their own home. Life with his wife was now nothing but quarrels and conflict.

He no longer troubled her at night because he had already shot his bolt with Maddalena during the day; and this drove Pippa so wild with rage and jealousy that her screams and complaints made the house unliveable. Fazio tried scolding her, coaxing her, threatening her, but nothing worked until at last he gave free rein to her fury and his own burning love by going off to his house in the country and calling Maddalena and her mother to join him. There he could happily concentrate on satisfying his desires, without being driven crazy by his nagging wife.

Pippa was left so miserable and distressed that she did nothing but weep and sob day and night, complaining bitterly about her unfaithful husband, the immoral old woman, and that hateful girl. A month had already passed and Fazio had still not come back home and showed no sign of doing so, as he passed the time frolicking with his sweetheart, overwhelmed with incomparable joy and delight. Pippa knew all this and burned with such an excess of fury and anger against her husband and the two women that she made a fateful decision. Without measuring the harm it might do, she resolved to accuse her husband of having made his money not from his alchemy but by robbing Guglielmo Grimaldi; this was where the money came from and not from the silver that he pretended to have sold in France. 'And in this way,' she said to herself, 'I shall punish my ungrateful husband and those two nasty women.'

Without further reflection, she spruced herself up, and set off immediately, urged on by her anger and alone without a single servant for company. It was almost evening when she came into the office of the magistrates charged with administering justice, like the Eight Judges* here in Florence. There she recounted the whole story of her husband's doings exactly as he had told it to her, saying they should go and see where Guglielmo had been buried in the cellar of the old house. And she directed them to the precise spot. Their first reaction was to have the woman detained, since they could not be certain whether her story was true or false; and then, promptly and discreetly, they sent out a team who discovered the body of Guglielmo exactly where Pippa had said they would. That very night the Bargello's men* seized a surprised and unsuspecting Fazio whom they found in bed with his lover. Before dawn he was led to the prison, and there he remained in great distress until day came and he was taken to be questioned. He refused to confess to anything, but they confronted him with his wife, and when he saw her he shouted out: 'Serves me right!', and then, turning to her, 'Too much love for you, that's what brought me here.' After which, addressing the magistrate, he told the whole story exactly as it had happened.

But they kept frightening and threatening him, saying they were convinced that he was the one who had deliberately stabbed and killed Guglielmo in order to steal his money and enjoy it himself, as in fact he had done. Then, with cruel insistence, they put him to the torture, inflicting such dreadful and unrelenting sufferings that before they left they had made him confess whatever they wanted. So the magistrates condemned him to be dragged round the main streets of Pisa, have his flesh torn with pincers, and then to be quartered while still alive—the sentence to be carried out the following morning. And all Fazio's goods were confiscated immediately. Guglielmo's body was exhumed from the cellar and buried in consecrated ground, to the wonder and astonishment of all who saw it. Officers were despatched without delay into the countryside where they took possession of all Fazio's estates and drove everyone out. Maddalena and her mother returned as wretched as ever to their poor house in Pisa.

Pippa, when she had been dismissed, made her way back home, thinking that she was still the great lady of the house; but she could not have been more wrong, for she found that the maids and the menservants and the children too had been driven out by the bailiffs. Half dead with grief, she gathered them to her and entered the empty house with tears and lamentations, understanding too late the mistake that she had made.

In the meantime the news had spread throughout Pisa, leaving everyone shocked and bewildered as they blamed the cunning villainy of the alchemist no less than the wicked ingratitude of his faithless wife. And when her father and some other relatives went to visit her, they also put the blame on her and reproached her bitterly, saying that she and her children would die of hunger because of her cruel and inhuman betrayal of her poor husband. Then they left her in an agony of weeping.

The next morning came and at the appointed hour, the wretched Fazio was drawn on a cart round the main streets of Pisa until they came to the square where he was placed on a specially erected scaffold. There, cursing himself and his wicked wife, he was quartered by the executioner in the presence of a great crowd. Then the severed limbs were put back in place to form a body which lay exposed there for the rest of the day as a warning to cruel and evil men.

When Pippa heard the terrible news, she was plunged into the depths of anguish; and realizing that it was through her own anger and jealousy that she had lost both her husband and her entire fortune, she decided to show due penitence for her sin in her own way. Blinded by anger and knowing what she meant to do, she waited until most of the crowd had gone to dine and then, taking her two children by the hand, made her way to the square. There were not many people about, and those who recognized her shouted a couple of insults and rebukes, but let her pass by. And so she came to the foot of the scaffold where there were hardly any people left; and the few who knew her had no idea what she intended to do and made way for her. Still weeping, she climbed the cruel ladder with her children as if she meant to embrace and mourn her dead husband, provoking a storm of execration: 'Evil woman! She got what she wanted, she arranged the whole thing, and now she's crying her eyes out!'

Pippa scratched her face with her fingernails and tore her hair, weeping all the time and kissing the face of her dead husband. She made her tender young children bend down, saying: 'Embrace and kiss your unfortunate father'; and the tears of the children made all the onlookers weep in their turn.

But in that moment the cruel mother drew a sharp pointed knife from her breast and suddenly stabbed one of her children in the throat, killing him on the spot. Then, more vicious than a trodden viper, she whipped round to the other child and did the same so quickly that people hardly realized what was going on. And finally, in her fury, she turned against herself and plunged the bloodstained knife into her own throat and fell dying upon the bodies of her children and her dead husband.

Seeing this, all the bystanders cried out and rushed to the scaffold in time for the last convulsions of the desperate mother and the two ill-fated little brothers, lying there with their throats cut like innocent lambs. There was an uproar of screaming and shouting and the horrible news soon spread throughout Pisa. People came running, with tears in their eyes, to see the fearful ghastly spectacle where father and mother with two such lovely blond sons lay savagely stabbed and wallowing in their blood, one dead body stretched out over another.

Let Thebes and Syracuse, Argo, Mycenae and Athens with all their horrors, let Troy and Rome fade before unhappy, ill-fated Pisa,* fountain and vessel, mother and dwelling-place of cruelty. The city wept and cried out and lamented as if it were the end of the world.

Above all, people mourned the death of the two innocent little brothers who, for no fault or sin of their own, lay unnaturally stained with the blood of their father and steeped in that of their wicked mother. They were stretched out as if they were sleeping, their tender throats gaping wide with the wound and dripping warm red blood, so that all the onlookers were moved to sorrow and compassion; for truly it must be said that the man who could withhold his tears would be made of stone or iron rather than human flesh. Indeed, the brutal wicked spectacle would have aroused the spirit of pity in the breast of cruelty personified. At last, with permission from the authorities, some friends and relatives of Fazio and Pippa came and put the bodies of husband and wife into a coffin. They could not be buried in sanctified ground because they had died without the sacraments, so they were interred by the city wall. But the two little brothers, amid the infinite sorrow of all the Pisans, were buried in the church of Santa Caterina.

LAZZERO AND GABRIELLO
Le Cene (*The Suppers*) 2. 1

Lazzero, son of Master Basilio of Milan, goes to see Gabriello fishing and is drowned. Because there is such a resemblance between them, Gabriello assumes Lazzero's identity and tells those who come running that Gabriello has been drowned. Then, as if he were truly the owner, he takes over Lazzero's property. Pretending to do so out of compassion, he marries his wife for a second time and with her and the children lives a long life, happy and respected.

IN days gone by, as you may have read and heard a thousand times, Pisa was one of the most populous and prosperous cities not only in Tuscany, but in all Italy; and many of its citizens were noble, worthy, and rich. Now long before the city fell under the domination of Florence,* a Milanese doctor came there from Paris where he had studied and learned the art of medicine; and, as Fortune would have it, he remained a while and began to treat some gentlemen whose lost health he rapidly restored as it pleased God. Thus, seeing the gradual improvement in his credit, reputation, and earnings, and finding that he liked the city and the customs and habits of its citizens, he decided not to return to Milan, but to remain in Pisa. A few days before his arrival, he had learned of the death of his aged mother, the only relative he had left in Milan; and so, having no prospects there, he placed his hopes in Pisa where he chose to reside and practise medicine. In a short time he proved so useful that he became wealthy; and he called himself Master Basilio of Milan.

So it was that many Pisans sought to give him a wife, and many candidates were offered to him before he was satisfied. In the end the woman that pleased him had neither father nor mother; she was of noble blood, but poor; and all that she could bring as a dowry was a house—into which the doctor was delighted to move once he had celebrated and consummated the marriage; and there, steadily increasing in property and progeny, they lived happily for many years. They had three sons and one daughter who was honourably married in Pisa when she came of age. A wife was found for the eldest son and the youngest received a literary education; but the second son, whose name was Lazzero,* had struggled with his studies and found no pleasure in them since he was, in any case, lazy and slow-witted. He was melancholy by nature, dreamy, solitary, taciturn, and so stubborn that once he had said no, the whole world could not make him change his mind. So his father, knowing him to be awkward, boorish, and obstinate, arranged to get him out of the way by packing him off to the country, not far from town, where he had bought four good farms. There Lazzero lived happily, preferring peasant ways to those of the city.

Ten years after Master Basilio had sent Lazzero to the country, Pisa was invaded by a strange and dangerous sickness which wasted people with a burning fever and then plunged them into a deep sleep from which, being unable to awake, they eventually died. Moreover it was contagious like the plague. Master Basilio, eager to make money, as were other doctors, was among the first to start treating the disease, with the result that after a few cases he caught the vicious poisonous sickness himself. Syrups and medicines were of no avail, and in a matter of days, it killed him. And so cruel and contagious was the disease that it infected all the other members of his household until, to cut a long story short, it sent them all underground, one after the other, until only an old serving-woman remained alive. Its ravages were enormous throughout Pisa, and would have been even worse had not many people left the city. At last spring came and with it the end of the evil influence of that deadly disease which in those days was called the worm-sickness. Feeling safe again, people returned to the city to resume their old activities and go about their usual business.

Lazzero was called back to Pisa and to a great and rich inheritance which he took over with only one extra assistant, plus the old serving-woman. His steward was confirmed in the management of the farms and the crops. In the meantime the whole city wanted to find him a wife, not considering his stubborn character and boorish ways; but when he replied firmly that he meant to stay a bachelor for four years and that only then would he think of marriage, they realized what kind of man he was and dropped the subject. Lazzero, in the meantime, seeking only a quiet life, avoided familiar contact with all mortal men the way devils avoid the cross.

It chanced that opposite Lazzero's house there lived a poor man called Gabriello, with his wife Santa and two children, a boy of five and a girl of three years old. Their only possession was a little shack, but Gabriello was an excellent fisherman and bird-catcher and a perfect master in the art of making nets and traps; and so, by sweating away at fishing and bird-catching he managed to provide for his family as best he could—with the help, however, of his wife who wove linen cloth. Now Gabriello, as God willed, looked so much like Lazzero that it was a wonder to see. They were both red-haired and their beards were of the same length, cut, and colour, so that they seemed like twins; and not only did they have the same figure and stature, but they were of the same age and, as I have said, so alike that if they had dressed in the same way it would have been difficult to tell them apart; and even Gabriello's wife would have been deceived, for truly it was only the clothes that made the difference, since one of them wore rough cloth and the other only the finest material.

Lazzero, then, seeing this strong resemblance, thought that it must have some great cause and could not be mere chance; and so he became more sociable and often sent over food and drink to Gabriello and his wife; and frequently he invited his neighbour to dinner where the two of them talked about a thousand things. Gabriello would tell Lazzero the most wonderful stories in the world, for although he was poor and of humble birth, he was nonetheless wise and astute, and well knew how to flatter and entertain his host until Lazzero could hardly live without him.

On one of these occasions, when they were dining together and the main course had already been served, the conversation turned to fishing and Gabriello instructed Lazzero in all the different ways of catching fish until at last he came to the technique of fishing with square nets* hung around the neck. This, he said, was the most effective and pleasant way of fishing and he praised it so highly that Lazzero begged him to show how it was done, since he longed to see how one could fish by diving underwater, catching big fish not only with hand and net, but even with the mouth. Gabriello answered that he was ready to satisfy him at any time, even right now, for it was the height of summer and he could easily arrange things. So they agreed to go immediately, left the table, and went out; and Gabriello took the square nets and went with Lazzero through the west gate towards the Arno and along a boardwalk supported by piles where rows of high-branching poplars and alders offered a sweet refreshing shade. Once there, Gabriello told Lazzero to sit in that cool shade and watch him at work. And stripping naked, he fixed the nets around his arms while Lazzero sat on the bank and waited to see what he would do. Gabriello, who really was a master of the art, had no sooner entered the river and dived underwater than he re-emerged with eight or ten good-sized fishes in his nets. When Lazzero saw how well one could fish underwater, he found it almost miraculous, and he was immediately seized by a violent urge to look at closer quarters; moreover, since the burning sun was now high in the sky, wounding the earth with its fiery rays, he thought that he might cool himself in the river. So Gabriello helped him to strip off and led him to where the water reached up to the knees, flowing pleasantly just before the place where he would be out of his depth. Then he showed him the pile that was furthest out and told him not to go beyond that point; after which, he carried on with his fishing. Lazzero, splashing about, felt wonderfully relaxed and completely refreshed as he watched Gabriello who kept coming up to the surface with his nets and hands full of fish, sometimes jokingly putting one in his mouth so that Lazzero, who had never dived in his life, was astounded and thought that there must certainly be some light under the water, since it would be impossible to catch so many fishes in the dark. And he was so eager to find out how it was done that when Gabriello dived again he also bowed his head and, without thinking, let himself go under and came near to the furthest pile so that he could be sure where exactly he was. He sank down to the bottom like lead and since he did not know how to hold his breath and could not swim, he panicked and struggled violently to rise up to the surface. But the water came in not only through his mouth but through his nose and ears; and though he fought with flailing arms, it was all in vain, for the more he thrashed about, the more the current bore him out of his depth so that he soon lost consciousness.

Gabriello had let himself down into a great hole amid the piles where the water came up to his navel, and since he felt that there might be many fishes there to fill his nets, he was in no hurry to come out. Poor Lazzero meanwhile rose to the surface half dead two or three times; the fourth time he did not rise again and so, drowning wretchedly, ended his life.

At last Gabriello, judging that his catch was large enough, came out of the water with a full net and looked cheerfully around for Lazzero; but as he looked here and there and could not see him anywhere, he became perplexed and frightened. And as he stood there in a daze he saw Lazzero's clothes on the green riverbank. Frantic with worry and even more distressed than before, he began to look into the water and there at last he saw the body washed up on the shore by the current. Anguished and trembling, he rushed to the place and, finding Lazzero drowned, was so overcome with grief and fear that he almost lost his senses and stood there immobile like a stone. Thus he remained for some time, thinking things over and uncertain what to do. He was afraid that if he told the truth, people would say that he himself had drowned Lazzero in order to rob him. Finally, making a virtue of necessity and rendered bold by despair, he resolved to carry out a plan that had only occurred to him in that very moment.

There were no witnesses since almost everybody had gone indoors to seek the cool shade or to sleep, so the first thing he did was to put his nets and the fishes into a box made for that purpose; after which, he hoisted the dead body of Lazzero onto his shoulders and, although it was heavy, carried it to the wet riverbank and laid it there on the green and flourishing grass. He removed the drawers that Lazzero had been wearing and put them on himself and then, slipping off his own square nets, he bound them tightly to the arms of the drowned Lazzero; and picking the body up again, he dived with it into the water and took it to the bottom where he tied it to the pile, entangling it round with the nets in such a coil that it could hardly work loose. That done, he climbed back up the bank and put on the shirt left by Lazzero and then all his other clothes right down to the shoes. He sat down having decided to try and test his luck, first in order to save his skin, and then to see whether, after all, he might not escape poverty and make his likeness to Lazzero serve as the source of great happiness and lasting prosperity. And since he was wily and bold, judging that it was the right moment to begin his daring and dangerous enterprise, he began to shout as if he were Lazzero: 'Help, help, good people! Hurry to help a poor drowning fisherman!' He shouted so loudly that at last the local miller and a group of peasants came running at the noise; and Gabriello, feigning Lazzero's rustic accent and almost weeping, explained how the fisherman had dived again and again and caught plenty of fish; but that the last time he had been underwater for almost an hour, so now he was very much afraid that he had drowned. And when they asked him where exactly he had dived, he pointed out the pile where he had entangled Lazzero in the way you know.

The miller, who was a good friend of Gabriello, stripped off immediately and, being a good swimmer, dived to the base of the pile where he quickly found the dead man, entangled and bound to the pile. At first he tried to pull him up, but then, unable to get him loose, he went back up and cried out in anguish: 'The poor devil's at the base of this pile, entangled in his nets—dead drowned, that's for sure!'

The great grief of his companions was clear from their words and gestures. Two of them stripped and with the miller's help managed to fish out the body and bring it up from the water and onto the riverbank. Their arms were strained and almost broken by the square nets which they blamed for causing that terrible death by entangling the victim. And so, as the news spread, a priest came, and at last the corpse was carried in a coffin to a little church nearby and placed in the middle of the aisle so that everybody could see it and bless it, thinking that it was Gabriello.

The sad news had already reached Pisa and come to the ears of Gabriello's unfortunate wife who set off with her two children and some of her closest relatives and neighbours. Seeing the man who was lying dead in the little church, she really believed it was her husband and threw herself on the body, weeping and wailing. As if she could never have enough of kissing his face and embracing him, she lay outstretched upon him, loudly lamenting, with disordered dress and dishevelled hair, grieving together with her little children who wept so tenderly that all those who stood by were moved to compassion. At this, Gabriello, who dearly loved his wife and children, was so overcome by pity that he could not hold back his tears. Pulling Lazzero's hat down over his eyes and covering his face with a handkerchief to dry his tears so that everyone would think he was indeed Lazzero, he spoke to comfort his sad afflicted wife, affecting a rustic accent and saying so that all could hear: 'O lady, don't despair, don't weep, for I'm not going to abandon you; it was out of love for me and to give me pleasure that your husband came fishing with me against his will, and so I think that I'm partly to blame for his death and your harm. That's why I shall always be there to help you and provide for you and your children: so now weep no more and go home in peace and quiet, for you shall want for nothing as long as I live; and if I die, I'll leave you enough to be well-off by the standards of your class'; and these last words he said weeping and sobbing as though he were overcome by grief for the death of Gabriello and by the harm done to her. And so, as if he were Lazzero, praised and commended by all, he went his way.

When the time came for the body to be buried, Santa, having tired her eyes with weeping and her voice with mourning, returned home to Pisa with her relatives, somewhat comforted by what she had heard from the man whom she firmly believed to be Lazzero. Gabriello, who resembled Lazzero and had taken his identity, entered Lazzero's house as Lazzero, for he was perfectly familiar with the place and knew all its master's habits. Greeting nobody, he went straight to a luxurious room which overlooked a lovely garden; there, taking the keys from the leather pouch of the dead master, he began to open all the coffers and chests which contained smaller keys for safes, strong-boxes, caskets, and drawers. In these, not counting the tapestries, he found clothes of wool, linen, and velvet and other rich garments that had belonged to the brothers of the drowned Lazzero and to his father, the doctor. But what pleased him most, apart from the golden objects and jewels, was a sum of about two thousand gold florins and four hundred* in small change. He could hardly contain himself for joy and could think of nothing but how he might hide his real identity from the household and pass himself off as Lazzero. Since he knew Lazzero's temperament so well, he left his room at supper time almost in tears. The butler and the servant who had heard of Santa's tragedy and how Lazzero was largely to blame, assumed that he was weeping for Gabriello; but he called the butler and had him take six loaves of bread and fill two flasks of wine; and with these and half the supper, he was sent off to Santa. Yet they gave little cheer to the poor woman who did nothing but weep. On his return, the butler gave orders for supper to be served, and Gabriello, having eaten little in order to resemble Lazzero, left the table without saying a word, locked himself in his room (this also being Lazzero's custom) and did not come out until nine the following morning. To the serving-man and the maid it seemed that his speech and complexion were somewhat changed, but this they put down to his grief at the tragic fate of the poor fisherman, and after dining as usual, they went to bed when it suited them.

Poor Santa meanwhile managed to eat something with her children, comforted by some relatives or other who saw good reason to hope in the victuals she had just been sent. Then she went to bed, and her relatives took their leave.

That night Gabriello hardly slept a wink for the ideas that came crowding into his mind, and in the morning he arose happily at Lazzero's usual time, and, well knowing his habits, went on imitating him as best he could, always taking care that his Santa lacked for nothing. But when his servant told him that she continued to weep and to mourn her husband as one who had loved her as dearly as any husband ever loved a wife, Gabriello grieved for her grief, and thought how he might comfort her. And having decided what to do, one day after dinner, he went over to her house where, since it was so soon after the tragedy, he found her in the company of her cousin. When Gabriello made it known that he had come to speak with her on a matter of some importance, the cousin, who knew of his charitable actions and did not want to disturb him, took his leave with the advice that she should listen to her compassionate neighbour.

As soon as the cousin had left, Gabriello locked the door, went through into a little chamber on the ground floor, and beckoned to Santa to follow him. But she, concerned for her honour should she remain alone with him like that, was uncertain whether to join him or to stay where she was. At last, thinking of all the practical benefits that she had already received and hoped to receive in the future, she took her eldest son by the hand and went through into the chamber. There she found Gabriello lying on the couch where her husband always used to lie when he was tired. She stood stock still with amazement. Seeing that she had brought her little son with her, Gabriello smiled with joy at this proof of his wife's purity, and addressed her with a special term that he very often used with her. More astounded than ever, Santa was all on tenterhooks. Then Gabriello, taking up the child and kissing him, said: 'Your mother doesn't understand and that's why she weeps for your good fortune and the happy lot of herself and her husband.' Yet not trusting such a young child, he carried him into the larger room, put him down just inside, and gave him some coins to play with. Then, returning to his wife, who had almost recognized him by his words, he bolted the door of the chamber and told her who he was and everything he had done, all in the proper order; and the woman was overcome by surpassing joy as the story was confirmed by many intimate things that were known to them alone. Nor, in her bliss, could she have enough of clasping and embracing him, with as many kisses for the happiness of finding him alive as she had given the corpse for sorrow when she believed him dead. And weeping together tenderly for the overwhelming joy, each drank the tears of the other—until Santa, to be all the more certain and to make up for past sufferings, burned to taste the ultimate sweetness with her dear husband. He, in his turn, was nothing loath, having perhaps an even greater desire for her. And so by this, more than by anything else, she knew him as Gabriello the fisherman, her legitimate husband. But when they had taken their pleasure and talked at length, Gabriello warned her that she should dissimulate and say nothing. He showed her how happy their life could be and, to her great satisfaction, told her once again of the riches he had found and of all he intended to do. And when they had left the room and Gabriello was already out in the street, Santa pretended to weep and called after him so that the neighbours could hear: 'For pity's sake, take care of these poor children.' He told her to have no fear and returned home, thinking how best he could carry out his plans and achieve his aims.

Evening came and, just as before, once he had dined he went straight to his room without saying a word and lay down to sleep. But he could hardly close his eyes all night with thinking about what he meant to do; and no sooner had dawn appeared in the east than he got up and went to the church of Santa Caterina where he asked to see a venerable friar called Angelico, a kind and devout man whom all the Pisans looked upon as a saint. Gabriello said that he badly needed to talk and receive good counsel on an important and unusual event in his life. The good father, though he did not know him, led him into his room; and there, announcing himself as Lazzero, son of Master Basilio of Milan, the visitor, who knew it all so well, recounted his whole ancestry and how the deadly plague had left him without relatives, and many other things until gradually he came round to Gabriello. He went over everything that had happened: how he had persuaded Gabriello to go fishing against his will because he wanted to see how it was done; and how, in fishing to give him pleasure, the man had drowned. He spoke of the sad consequences for the wife and children who, having neither goods nor property, had lived entirely on what their father earned. And, since he felt that he was largely to blame for their troubles and their father's death, his heart was heavy and his conscience heavy-burdened. Therefore, as inspired by God, he intended, despite her poverty and low birth, and provided that she and her relatives consented, to take Santa as his wife and to adopt the children of the dead fisherman as if they were his own issue, to bring them up and care for them and to make them his heirs no less than any other children that might be born to him. In this way he thought that he might the more easily obtain pardon from God and praise from men.

To the spiritual father this seemed a most pious work, and he exhorted him to carry out that holy intention as soon as possible, saying that if he did this, he could be quite certain of God's mercy. Gabriello, in order to obtain the friar's help more readily and quickly, opened his purse and laid out thirty silver pounds, saying that he wanted the Mass of Saint Gregory* to be sung on three successive Mondays for the soul of the dead fisherman. At this sweet spectacle, the venerable friar, for all his holiness, was overjoyed, and taking the money, he said: 'My son, the Masses will begin next Monday: all that's left is the marriage, and for that I shall help as best I can; and don't worry about wealth or nobility, for you need have no care for such things. Rich you are already, by the grace of God; and as for nobility, you should give it no thought, since we're all born in the same way of a father and a mother and the only true nobility lies in virtue and the fear of the Lord. I know the young woman and she is not without these virtues; and the same goes for most of her family.'

'I came here for no other purpose,' replied Gabriello, 'so please show me how I should go about it.' 'When do you want to give her the ring?' asked the friar. 'This very day, if she agrees.' 'Then in God's name,' replied the friar, 'leave it to me: go home and stay there, for before dinner-time I hope we shall have this blessed wedding.' 'Indeed, it's all I ask of you,' said Gabriello, 'and I count on you.' Then, having received a blessing, he left the friar's room and returned home where he waited confidently for things to turn out as happily as he had planned.

Having put away the thirty pounds, the reverend father went with one of his brethren to see Santa's uncle, who was a cobbler and her cousin, a barber; and when he had told them the whole story, they all went off together to Santa's house. They explained everything to her and she feigned some reluctance; however, they implored her so strongly and produced so many reasons why it would be a happy outcome for her and her children that finally she agreed to the marriage, almost weeping and vowing that she did so only for the good of her children and also, perhaps, because Lazzero was so like her Gabriello. Shall I tell you briefly what happened next? The same morning, thanks to the good work of the friar, in the presence of several witnesses and of the notary, all gathered in the house of Lazzero, Gabriello, under the guise of Lazzero, gave his ring to Santa for the second time. And Santa, no longer wearing widow's weeds, was resplendent in a lovely rich robe which had belonged to the wife of drowned Lazzero's brother and was chosen among many others because it fitted her so perfectly. And so that morning they enjoyed a fine meal and in the evening a splendid supper. Then, when it was over and the guests had taken their leave, the bride and groom went off to bed where they talked things over happily, laughing heartily at the simplicity of the friar and the credulity of relatives, neighbours, and everyone else before spending the joyful night in mutual pleasure and play. The maidservant and the butler were amazed to see such great expense, blamed it on the wedding, and were less than happy with this union.

The bride and groom arose late next morning and, when they had drunk raw eggs,* received visits from Santa's relatives and made a sumptuous meal. Gabriello had provided clothes for the children that suited their new honourable condition, and thus the festivities continued for four days. Santa, who found herself ascended from earth to Heaven and from Hell to Paradise, decided, on her husband's advice and to his great satisfaction, to engage more servants; and, to be on the safe side, they arranged to dismiss those they already had. So one morning Gabriello called them all together and gave them the news: to the old serving-woman who had been in the house for many years, in addition to what she was owed, he gave three hundred pounds as a dowry for her niece; and to the steward, who had not been there for long, he gave a good bonus on top of his wages and packed him off in peace, so that both of them went on their way happy and contented. And when the house was well provided with new maids and servants, he lived there peacefully with his twice-wedded wife in calm and quiet. They had two more sons to whom he gave the new family name of De Fortunati;* and from their seed were born many men renowned for their prowess in arms and letters.

PIETRO FORTINI

ANTONIO ANGELINI
Le giornate delle novelle de' novizi
(Tales for Beginners) 2

Antonio Angelini falls in love with a Flemish woman and, as he enjoys her for a considerable time, learns something of her language. Once back home, he jokingly uses some Flemish words when he is with his wife. One day, seeing a pilgrim pass by, she remembers one of these phrases without knowing what it means, and thus invites the young man to mount an assault; only her screams prevent her from being defeated and disgraced at the first onset.

NOT long ago there lived in Siena a young artisan called Antonio Angelini who made his living by selling drugs and medicines and with this he managed very well. He was a handsome, well-built, and well-dressed young man, and having adopted this profession he gave it his full attention. Now it happened that another artisan who had a number of daughters to marry off thought that this might be the man he was looking for. He was impressed by the fine clothes of Antonio who always wore a satin jerkin, embroidered taffeta-lined stockings, and other fripperies, as young men of his kind usually do; all this expense and elegance led him to think that the young man was much richer than in fact he was, and so he made up his mind to give Antonio one of his daughters as a wife. A friend served as a go-between to make the offer, and Antonio was no less willing to take her than the father was to give her away. He had, in fact, seen the girl several times and found her very attractive for she was indeed a beautiful creature. In short, he began to think far more about the girl than about the shop, and indeed his breast was so inflamed with love that he gave no thought to anything else. Urged on by the father of the fair and tender maid, the go-between kept pleading for this alliance, and since the young man was already even keener on it than the father, the deal was soon made. Both parties were happy with it, and everything was set up for the wedding.

It need hardly be said that, for his part, the delighted and dashing bridegroom made sure he was splendidly turned out—rather more so than befitted his social status. Thus, with all the rites completed, the bride dressed and the nuptial Mass said, he led his wife to her new home, as the custom is. And for many, many days he hardly thought about the shop or anything else. But after a few weeks, as husbands usually do, he began to think about the dowry and raised the question with his in-laws. His father-in-law, who knew it was due, had the whole sum ready and paid it to him according to the contract.

Once he had the money, the young apothecary thought it was time to refurbish his shop and put things in order; so a few months later he decided to travel to Venice to buy drugs, as is the habit of apothecaries if they have enough to spend. After a long conversation with his wife, he set out and, by way of Florence, Bologna, Ferrara, and Padua, finally arrived in that great and famous city. As a foreigner who had never been in Venice before, he did not know where he could find good lodgings, and, as he asked around, he told people where he came from. So it was that, as he was still searching, he came across one of our fellow countrymen who lived in Venice and whose name was Giovanni Manetti. Antonio told him why he had come to Venice and asked if he could direct him to some place where he could find good food and decent lodgings. Now Manetti, who was always very ready to help his fellow Sienese and, indeed, all kinds of foreigners (we Sienese are like that, more helpful to foreigners than to each other), sent him to a house kept by a Slav friend* who offered lodgings to any respectable visitor who came his way—this being, so I have heard, the custom in Venice where both the gentlemen and the common people take in lodgers. Recommended as a personal friend of Manetti and with a servant to show him the way, Antonio found the house of the Slav and took up lodgings.

When he had been in Venice for five days, Antonio was at table one Sunday morning with the Slav after breakfast; and as they were talking of this and that, he said: 'You know, Messer Zanobi'—for that was the Slav's name—'I must ask you to do me a favour today.' The Slav, who was a pleasant and obliging man, answered: 'What is it? You only have to ask.' Then Antonio: 'If it's not too much trouble, since today's a holiday, I'd like us to go for a walk in Venice and spend the whole day sightseeing. You show me what there is to see, because I don't know the city and I can't find my way through all these small streets and

canals.' The Slav, as I have said, was a very obliging fellow, and after
more talk, the two of them went out together and, leaving the Slav's
house which was near the church of the Madonna della Fava,* took
a long roundabout walk through Venice. Then they gave threepence
to a gondolier to take them for a trip in and out of the canals as they
pleased. But when they had been in the gondola for some time,
Antonio said to the Slav: 'Messer Zanobi, why don't we go to one of
those houses where there are girls who offer pleasure for payment;
you know, the kind they call "courtesans" in Rome?' 'Let's do that,'
said the Slav, 'but now it's too late because they'll all be in church*
for the benediction; when that's over we'll find plenty of girls, and
good-lookers too. In the meantime we can have a quick trip down the
Grand Canal and turn round at the Rialto until we're nearer the right
time.'

While they going down the canal the Slav suddenly remembered
a certain Flemish girl and said: 'Messer, how about going as far as
Calaballotte* to see if we can find Giachena Fleming? I promise you
she's one of the loveliest creatures I've seen in a long time and I'm
sure you'll like her; and then when we've seen her, we can go wherever
you want.' With this, they made their way towards Calaballotte and
when they reached the Fleming's house, the Slav knocked on the
door. When she heard the knocking, Giachena came to the window
and when she saw the Slav, who was an old friend, she opened the
door by pulling on a rope. The Slav, who knew this routine, dismissed
the gondola and entered the house, taking Antonio with him.

They climbed the stairs and came to a tapestried room where the
Fleming came forward and gave them a cheerful welcome. She was
indeed a lovely creature, the fairest in all Venice: besides her tall elegant figure, she had fine features and her skin was as white as snow,
with a delicate tinge of red, like a blend of milk and blood; her flesh
looked like nothing so much as orient pearls, or rather, a bunch of
roses and violets born in the shade and plucked at daybreak. As I have
said, she gave them a sweet-voiced welcome and seated them on
chairs of gold and green velvet—obviously meant for gentlefolk; and
she sat in the middle as they chatted about this and that; and although
the lady was Flemish, she spoke Italian very well.

Her beauty went hand in hand with the brilliance of her mind
which was great and noble. And when they had talked for some time,
she turned to her maid, who was Flemish like herself and spoke to her

in their own language, and in no time at all the girl set out a little table with everything for a genteel refreshment, with many different dishes and rare wines. And so, as they carried on the conversation, they ate very well and had a very pleasant meal.

When they had finished drinking, the Slav decided to leave the field free for his young friend and said: 'Would you believe it? When we went out, there was something I completely forgot, something I have to see about in Chioggia.* Messer Antonio, wait for me here at least an hour, if it isn't too much trouble. You stay here and enjoy a chat with Madonna Giachena. I won't waste any more time.' And he added: 'Look, Messer Antonio, you'd better wait until I get back because you'll never find your way home by yourself.' With this, he left Antonio alone with Madonna Giachena. The young man who desired nothing else and felt as if he were sitting next to a queen, began to whisper a thousand sweet nothings and took her by the hand. And when he had used up his armoury of blandishments, Antonio ventured to put his hands on those firm white breasts, kissing her on the mouth and sweetly toying with her. The gallant woman was nothing loath to give as good as she got with amorous kisses. And after much wanton playing, both roused to a peak of lust, they embraced and went into a luxuriously furnished chamber. There they threw themselves on a rich bed and before long their embraces had touched the height of pleasure no less than four times. After which they returned to the room they had left where they joked together and enjoyed a very intimate conversation. Aroused as they were, they agreed to pass the night together, and for this time Antonio, not wishing to appear a scoundrel, paid for the pleasure he had received from such a fair lady by giving her a gold scudo (which was much appreciated).

Now when the two had been together for some considerable time, the Slav thought he had been away long enough and went back to the house of the Fleming where he asked Antonio if he wanted to go back home with him. Antonio, given the pleasure he had tasted, had forgotten the Slav, the schools, his business, his homeland, and his wife, and in that moment he hardly knew what to say, but the Fleming understood the situation and said: 'Messer Zanobi, this evening I want Messer Antonio to stay and have supper with me.' The Slav, acting in the young man's interest, answered: 'Madonna, you should know that this evening we have to go to Mellone on this young man's business, it's an affair of valuable goods; but as soon as we've settled

it, I'll bring him back to you.' The Fleming believed the Slav was
telling the truth and turned to Antonio: 'Well then, Messer Antonio,'
she said, 'I shall expect you for supper.' Antonio had no idea what the
Slav was on about, but he took leave of the Fleming with a firm promise
to come back soon. The two men then went off, leaving the Fleming
delighted with herself, convinced that she had acquired the custom of
some rich noble and eagerly awaiting his return.

Antonio was already outside with the Slav, and as they talked their
way up the Caraballotte, Messer Zanobi said: 'You know, my friend,
that I dragged you out of that house for your own good, because the
Fleming takes you for some rich Venetian gentleman, and that's why
I reckon you shouldn't go to supper or spend the night there if you
haven't first left any money you're carrying in a safe place. Because if
you're unlucky enough to meet a real gentleman in that house and
he realizes that you're just a tradesman, then she'll leave you without
a penny in your purse. And if you still want to go there, first leave your
money with Manetti or somewhere else where it will be safe. Only
then can you go there with nothing to worry about. Because if they
should take your money or do anything like that, you'd stand no
chance against them in a law court.' Although Antonio had fallen in
love with the Fleming, he appreciated these wise words, thanked the
Slav for the good advice and immediately followed it; and since he
thought Zanobi was a trustworthy fellow, he left all his valuables in
a sturdy chest in the room where he lodged. Then, without spending
much longer with Zanobi, he turned round and had himself taken
back to the house of his beloved Giachena where he stayed for supper,
as the Venetians say on such occasions. And as he made love with her,
she pleased him more than ever, and he pleased her no less. In short,
as Fortune would have it, they were so overwhelmed with love for each
other that they could hardly spend an hour apart. Thus entangled,
Antonio gave himself up to love and to amorous encounters where for
many days he enjoyed the sweet fruits of his desire.

Poor simple-minded Antonio was captivated by the beauty of the
Fleming and also by her extraordinary elegance (not a quality one
usually associates with the Flemish); and then there was the pleasant
and cheerful welcome she always gave him, and he was indeed so
caught up that he forgot all about Siena and his wife and thought of
nothing but his dear Fleming. So he went on, a blind and foolish
lover, entangled in that net and hardly leaving Giachena's side. This

crazy love affair had already lasted for two full months, with Antonio wasting all his time with the Fleming; and because she was a lively and witty woman, she often tried to teach him a few words in her own language. And among the many phrases she taught him is how a man asks a woman to do you-know-what, and how she answers if she agrees. So every time they wanted to give each other a good time, she would say *Ansi visminer?* and Antonio, who had learned his lesson very well, would answer *Io*. And when he did not feel like it, either because he was tired or for some other reason, he would say *Nitti sminere*. So whenever he went to the Fleming's house, he would greet her with *Ansi visminere?*,* chuck her under the chin and kiss her mouth; and since she was eager to please him, she always answered *Io*. So much so that the poor youth was almost fainting from overwork and could hardly stand up; and if it had not been for the good hearty meals that she kept making for him, he would surely have collapsed from excess of love. The poor fellow seemed not to know who he was and, as I have said, had forgotten his homeland and his wife; it never struck him that his home was elsewhere, for he felt as if he had been born in Venice and that all he valued could only be there.

While he was delaying his return to Siena far longer than was normal, he began to receive letter after letter from his wife, from his brothers and friends, and from many other people moved to write to him out of compassion for the lovely young woman he had abandoned. Antonio, who could not take his mind off Giachena, replied to none of them; but still, when he heard anyone speak of Siena, the poor devil was racked with doubt. At last, one day, convinced by the repeated urging of so many letters and messages, he understood the wrong he had done and made arrangements to return to the homeland he had forgotten; and in a few days, with the little money that was left to him, he bought what drugs he could and, together with several boxes of glass bottles, packed them up and shipped them off to Pesaro. He settled everything with the Fleming, and took his leave, excusing himself with good sound arguments. There were tears on both sides and close embraces, and then, with many vows and promises to return, he went his way. The separation was distressing for both of them, but somewhat less so for him, since he was, after all, determined to leave. So he entered the waiting gondola and set off for his old homeland.

He soon arrived home and was greeted with rejoicing and celebration by his wife who was delighted to see him back after she had been without him for so long. He sold his goods without wasting time and made a fine exhibition of his new glass bottles, drugs, and a few medicines before getting back to work in his shop.

But even when he had been home in Siena for some time, he still could not forget his beloved Giachena; and even though he had a wife of rare beauty, the poor fool still could not get the Fleming's embraces out of his mind and he would try to enjoy his wife in the same way, seeking to drive out one nail with another. Toying with his wife so that he could imagine himself with his lover, he would take her in his arms, chuck her under the chin and say *Ansi visminere*, and then, kissing her mouth and caressing her firm alabaster breasts, he would take his fill of pleasure. Not knowing what the words meant, but hearing them so often, the girl sweetly asked: 'What does *sminere* mean?' Her husband, caught unprepared and with a sudden tug at his heartstrings, heaved a great sigh as he remembered his Giachena and replied: 'It means, would you like something to eat?' The simple woman laughed and said: 'Oh, I thought it meant something naughty, even though I've heard it so often.' These words encouraged Antonio to let her take the Fleming's place in his quest for pleasure, since in those moments he could almost believe that they were one and the same; and so, sporting together, they enjoyed the greatest mutual satisfaction.

The wife believed what her husband had said and since she heard him say it so often when they were dining, at supper, or in bed, she took to using the phrase herself, and sometimes she would come out with *Ansi visminere?* and Antonio, who remembered the answer all too well, would reply *Io* and give her mouth a sweet juicy kiss. She liked this game so much that soon not a day went by without her renewing his old wounds, unaware of her mistake.

Things between them went on like this for some time, until one day in high summer when the fair wife of the foolish apothecary was sitting and sewing outside the house in a sheltered area. Now, as everyone knows, in that season there are many travellers on the road because the days are longer; and in this case there was the Holy Jubilee Year as well. The lovely girl was sitting there doing her domestic duty while trying to escape the unpleasant heat of the day. She was wearing a sleeveless white smock which made her look like a heaven-born angel, and stockings of white silk needlework which her husband had brought her from Venice and which, drawn tight, did not quite cover her legs, but revealed the loveliest and daintiest feet that ever a woman had, fitting snugly into a pair of black embroidered velvet shoes. On her head she wore a shawl of gold and silk and round her neck a slender collar of the finest embroidered silk. Just so this angel sat sewing on a low chair next to the door of the house; and as she leaned forward and bowed her head she showed the loveliest pair of breasts that were ever seen on any woman at that time—not very large, but as white as pure fresh snow and firm as marble, seeming truly to be made of pearls and rubies.*

Now it happened that while the lovely girl was sitting there like that, some Flemish travellers passed by on their way to Rome to obtain an indulgence in the Jubilee Year,* and among these pilgrims was a young gentleman who was making this journey in fulfilment of a vow. He was in his prime of youth, being not yet twenty-five and appearing even younger than he was. He was spending his own money on that journey and was able to live within his means. As he passed by with the others, his glance fell on the fair and delicate girl who, as I have said, was sitting by the door and sewing. When the young pilgrim saw this lovely creature, he thought she must have come down from Paradise, for such beauty surely seemed more than human. And to contemplate her more closely, he stopped and, in a youthful impulse, asked her something that he had asked of no one else on that journey, begging alms of her in the name of God, as he stood entranced before her. When the young woman saw this Flemish pilgrim begging for alms, she judged him to be a well-born person, as indeed he was; and, remembering her husband's phrase, she said *Ansi visminere?* The pilgrim was amazed to hear these words, for the invitation did not seem one that could come from a respectable woman. He hardly knew what to do and simply stood there stunned and astonished, thinking that only by some miracle could she have made him such an offer; and since he spoke no word of our language, all he could do was gaze at her with shining eyes as if she were more divine than human, as he stood there silent, struck dumb by her beauty.

Faced by this silence, the woman repeated her invitation with the same phrase; and at this second offer the young man felt sure that this was some kind of joke and that she was having him on. But this was not enough to quench the raging fire in his youthful breast. Already tormented by love, he began to let his imagination wander, boldly going so far as to think that she must be a whore—which was what her invitation and her seductive dress suggested. This did not stop him

gazing at her with imploring eyes which soon moved the woman to
charity so that she invited him for the third time. The young pilgrim,
having by now lost all piety and fear of the Lord, had forgotten all
about Saint Peter and Saint Paul and concentrated all his energy on
the young woman, for after looking at her for so long he was already
feeling a distinct resurrection of the flesh. He said nothing, but simply dropped his hand to his hose, untied them, lowered them, and
rushed over to the doorway to take the girl in his arms. Nearby was
a chest full of bottles which her husband often placed there so as not
to overcrowd his shop which was opposite the house. And there, with
passionate luscious kisses, the pilgrim tried to force the woman to
pleasure him while with one hand he did the best he could to insert
his sturdy staff. This situation was completely new to the girl who
had never been found doing such a thing in such a place; so at first
she hardly knew what to do, but soon she decided to scream, raising
her voice and shouting: 'Help! Help! Antonio! Antonio!' The poor
pilgrim had already stripped down enough to get on with the job
and was on the point of putting in his massive staff when the girl,
stupid as she was, started screaming; and though he did not understand the language, he understood the fear and saw that her actions
belied her invitation. And since, as a foreigner, he was afraid of getting
into serious trouble, he ran away like some fleeting ghost, unhappy but
unhindered.

Antonio, whose shop faced the house, heard the screams and knowing it was his wife, came running and thinking that, as often happens,
it must involve some kind of low prank, he rushed through the door
in a furious rage. He was not quick enough to see the pilgrim who had
already escaped, but what he did see was his wife sprawled across the
chest exactly as the Fleming had left her, with her skirts pushed up
over her waist, unable to speak, and half fainting with fear—or rather,
we should say, with anger. Her husband, seeing her in that state, went
as pale as death, assuming that his honour was gone for good, and
asked her what had happened. His wife, all worked up by something
that was no longer fear, said: 'May God above blast you for what it
was!' Not knowing what she meant, Antonio asked her again, and this
time she answered: 'A plague on you! I can hardly breathe for the
scare I've had.' Her husband insisted: 'Just say it, say what happened
and stop messing about.' Settling her shawl and smoothing down her
skirts, she replied: 'In all my life, I've never known anything worse,

but by God's cross, it would have served you right if he'd done what you've been asking for.'

Her husband was desperate for an answer: 'Why can't you say just what happened?'; and then she burst out: 'What did you teach me? Why don't you say it? You taught me a heap of filthy things and told me they were good, and then I'm not supposed to scream!' Antonio still had no idea what she was on about and asked her yet again: 'Come on, say it, don't keep me in suspense.' Then, at last, she told him all about the pilgrim, and when he heard it, Antonio changed his tack as he realized that he alone had caused the whole scandal. 'Listen, never say those words ever again to anyone but me, because what they mean is: how would you like to come and do it with me?'

She turned on him with an angry look: 'And I tell you that's a fine sense of decency you've got—teaching me all those filthy things!', and she followed up with a virulent barrage of the worst insults that ever a wife inflicted on her husband. Knowing that he was in the wrong, he answered nothing until at last, when the tirade had gone on and on, he said: 'Well, be wiser next time, and thank God that this time it ended all right.' After which, he returned to his shop and as he turned his back on her, she said: 'You're the one who should thank Him, and you'll never hear me saying those words or any other unless first I know exactly what they mean; and no foreign words either. So when you want to ask me you-know-what, you'd better speak the way we do round here.' And Antonio went off with a tetchy: 'Do that, and you'll be all right,' leaving his wife in a foul mood for the rest of the day. She no longer wanted to stay sewing at the door, and took her anger back into the house. So it was that at one and the same time three people were left offended, worked up, and burning with rage.

CRISTOFORO ARMENO

THE METAMORPHOSES OF AN EMPEROR
Il peregrinaggio di tre figliuoli del re di Serendippo (*The Travels of the Three Sons of the Emperor of Serendip*)*

THERE was once in the land of Becher* a wise and prudent Muslim Emperor who had four wives, one being the daughter of his uncle and the other three daughters of great princes. Now because he was a man of much learning, he made it a habit to show great courtesy and signs of affection to worthy men, and whenever he heard that they were visiting his country he honoured them with rich and magnificent gifts. So it was that he was always surrounded by a great number of such men and whenever he could spare time from his public duties, he spent it discussing various and virtuous topics with them. One day, as he was discussing the fair and wondrous works of nature with a philosopher who was famous for his infinite knowledge, the Emperor asked to be told of some especially remarkable example, being convinced by the man's advanced age and considerable learning that he would come up with something quite exceptional.

And he was not disappointed, for the philosopher was keen to please him: 'My lord,' he said, 'since I see that you are so eager to hear some admirable secret of nature, I shall tell you of one more extraordinary than anything else I ever saw or heard of in all my life. A few years ago, I happened to be in western parts where I had gone in the hope of learning something, since I had heard that in those lands there are many men of high and noble intellect. I was accompanied by a wise and knowledgeable young man who went with me from town to town. On the way we used to talk of the various wonders of nature, and one day he declared that he knew of one such marvel that was greater than all the others. And it was this: that whenever he pleased, he could kill an animal of any species whatsoever, and afterwards, with a few words pronounced over the dead body, pass into the animal,

giving it life with his own vital spirits while his human body was left
for dead. Then, when he had inhabited the animal's body for as long
as he pleased, he needed only to say the same words over his own dead
body and immediately his vital spirits would return to it. The senseless beast would fall down dead and he himself return to his original
state and be just as he was before. I thought the thing quite impossible,
but when he saw that it was so hard to convince me, he gave me proof
by performing the deed in my presence. Since I had never seen
anything more marvellous, I was soon burning with curiosity to learn
how it was done; and finally, after long incessant entreaties, I got him
to teach me what I wanted.'

'That sounds quite impossible,' said the Emperor when the philosopher had finished his tale, 'how can I believe it without proof?'
'Well, let's try it out,' replied the philosopher, 'and in this way you'll
find it quite easy to believe. Bring me some animal and I shall show
you everything.' The Emperor hurried to have a sparrow sent in and
gave it to the philosopher who drowned it and threw it on the ground;
after which he whispered a few words over the corpse. Immediately
the philosopher fell down dead and the sparrow, restored to life,
began to fly around the room. After this had gone on for some time, it
perched on the dead body of the philosopher and chirped for a while,
thus bringing the philosopher back to life while the bird itself fell
dead as before.

The Emperor was full of wonder and, like the philosopher before
him, burned with desire to learn the secret words; and the philosopher,
who could hardly deny so great a prince, revealed everything to him.
From then on, now that he possessed the secret, the Emperor had
a bird brought to him almost every day. Then he would kill it, enter it
with his own vital spirits, leave his own body for dead, and enjoy himself until such time as he chose to re-enter and revive his own body
and leave the bird a corpse. With this device he was able to learn the
intentions of many of his vassals so that he could punish the wicked,
generously reward the good, and maintain the empire in perfect peace.

Now the Emperor's chief counsellor became aware of this practice,
and knowing how highly the prince valued him, he revealed the fact
one day as they were talking together. Since he already knew so many
of his lord's secrets, thanks to the Emperor's confidence in him, he
now begged to be given this secret as well, so the Emperor, because
he loved him dearly, taught him the secret formula. The counsellor

tried it out immediately, and it was clear that he had learned his lesson very well.

Now one day, when they were out hunting together and had became separated from their companions, the Emperor and his counsellor met with two deer and killed them. The counsellor saw in this a good opportunity to carry out a wicked plan that had been in his mind for some time. 'My lord,' he said, 'since we're so far from our companions, why don't we enter into these two deer with our vital spirits and enjoy ourselves roaming over these green hills?' 'Certainly,' said the Emperor, 'that's a very good idea and there's no doubt that we shall have a lot of fun with this kind of game.' And with these words, he dismounted, tethered his horse to a tree, and went straight to stand over the dead deer where he said the secret words and entered into the animal, leaving his own dead body behind. As soon as the counsellor saw this, he also dismounted and without stopping to tether the horse, hurried to the dead body of the Emperor and said the secret words. Immediately he entered into the Emperor's corpse and, leaving his own body for dead on the ground, mounted his master's horse and rode off to join the rest of the company; and as he drew near to the city, since he bore the form and aspect of his master, he was greeted by everybody as if he were indeed the Emperor. Once at the royal palace, he asked among his barons if there was any news of his counsellor and when he heard that nobody had seen him, he put on a show of great grief, pretending to believe that the man had been devoured by wild beasts after getting separated from the rest of the group.

Now that he ruled over the empire, he began to assume all the functions of the true Emperor. But since God above will not allow any fraud to remain hidden for long, it so happened that when he had lain with three of the imperial wives, he turned on the fourth night after his return from the hunt to the one who was the daughter of the Emperor's uncle, and she noticed that the way he made love to her was different from that of the Emperor. She also knew that her lord possessed the secret of how to pass into any kind of animal with his vital spirits; and, being a highly intelligent woman, when she recalled that the counsellor had never returned from the hunt, she understood the whole deception and the misfortune that had befallen the Emperor. Thus, although the counsellor had the body of the Emperor, she immediately got out of bed and, without letting on that she had discovered the fraud, said: 'My lord, just before you lay with me I had a horrible monstrous vision which I am forbidden to describe to you in this moment. But the result is that I have decided to live in chastity from now on and so I beg you not to lie with me in future; and if you choose to deny this request, then I would rather kill myself than consent to pleasure you.' These words greatly upset the false Emperor, but nonetheless, because he loved her ardently and feared that she would take her own life, from then on he abstained from sleeping with her; and, since only that was forbidden, he was content with looking at her and talking with her. But everything else in the empire he continued to order as if he were the true and just Emperor.

The true Emperor, transformed into a deer, was subjected to every kind of misadventure, pursued by the male deer and often savagely beaten by other brute beasts, until at last, hoping to escape from such misery and return to his own body, he decided to steer clear of the other animals and walk by himself. So it was that in the fields one day he found a parrot who had died a few days before; and thinking that he might have a less troublesome life if he entered that corpse with his vital spirits, he said the magic words. Immediately, leaving the deer dead on the ground, he became a parrot, and in that form, together with many other parrots, he met with a bird-catcher from the capital who happened to be spreading his nets. He reckoned that if he let himself be caught, it might help him back to his original human condition, and so he settled in a place where the net would cover him, and in this way managed to get himself captured by the bird-catcher, together with many other birds and parrots.

Now he was in a large cage with the other birds; but since he was endowed with reason and understanding, as soon as the bird-catcher went off to see to his nets, he used his beak to lift a little latch and open the door of the cage. All the other birds flew off and he alone remained inside. He did not have to wait long before the return of the bird-catcher who, seeing the cage empty and the birds all flown, began to complain bitterly that all his work that day had been wasted. But when he came up to close the little door of the cage and prevent the one remaining parrot from escaping, the bird began to comfort him with wise and prudent advice. At first the bird-catcher was astonished because he thought it almost impossible that a parrot he had only just caught should be able to talk so wisely; but then he cheered up as he considered how much money he could earn with a bird like that. So he continued the conversation, and when he heard the bird's acute replies, he stored away his nets and set off with the parrot towards the city, reflecting as he went that he would surely acquire great riches with an animal who could speak with such wisdom and intelligence.

Now he was already in the city and had stopped to talk with some friends in the main square when suddenly a big row broke out not very far away. The parrot asked his master what the noise was all about, and his master, who knew the whole story, explained that there was a famous and very beautiful whore who dreamed that she had slept the night before with a gentleman of that city; and meeting him in the square she laid hold of his cloak and demanded a hundred scudi, swearing that she had never slept with a man for anything less. And because the gentleman refused, she was now kicking up such a fuss. When the parrot heard this, he said: 'It's truly regrettable, master, that they should quarrel so violently when all you need to do is to bring them here before me, for I could certainly make peace between them.' So the bird-catcher, knowing how wise the parrot was, left his friends to look after the cage and went straight across to where the row had broken out between the whore and the gentleman. There, with a few words, he managed to calm them down a little, and taking them by the hand he led them to the parrot and said: 'If you agree to submit your quarrel to the arbitration of this animal, I can promise that he'll judge fairly between you.' All the bystanders scoffed at this because it seemed impossible that an animal without reason could do what the bird-catcher had said. But the gentleman declared himself eager to see such a miracle and turned to the whore: 'If you agree,' he said, 'I'm ready to put my faith in the parrot's judgement to solve our problem.' The whore also accepted the proposal and so the parrot questioned them about their dispute, listened to everything they had to say and heard that they were ready to accept his judgement. Then he had them approach the cage and gave orders that a large mirror should be placed in front of it. When this was done, with the mirror brought to him and placed on a table, he asked his master to hold it absolutely vertical; then, turning to the gentleman, he ordered him to lay out on the table the hundred scudi that the whore had demanded. The whore was overjoyed at the idea that she could fill her purse with them, and the gentleman unwillingly doled out the money in front of the mirror. 'And now, my lady,' said the parrot, 'don't touch the scudi counted out on the table, but take the hundred that you see in the mirror: because since you were with this gentleman in a dream, so it's only fair that the payment you demand should also be dreamlike.'

All the bystanders were astonished and found it hard to believe that an animal without reason could pronounce such a wise judgement. The parrot's fame soon spread throughout the city until at last it reached the ears of the Empress. Convinced that an animal endowed with such wisdom and prudence must contain the spirit of her husband the Emperor, she immediately gave orders that the bird-catcher and his parrot should be brought before her. The order was swiftly carried out, and when the bird-catcher arrived at the royal palace he was taken straight before the Empress. After questioning him at length about the powers of the bird and how it had been captured, she offered to buy the bird, saying that, if he agreed to sell, she would make him so rich that he would never need to go bird-catching again. 'My lady,' he answered, 'both the bird and I are in your power, and the greatest favour I can ask is that you should accept the bird as my gift, because I value your grace more highly than any great riches it might bring me.' The Empress was greatly impressed by these words and could hardly believe that the bird-catcher had such a noble soul. She accepted the parrot and promptly granted the bird-catcher an annual revenue of five hundred scudi as a reward for his generous spirit. For the bird she made a rich and comfortable cage which she had placed in her room, and there she now spent most of the day, discussing various topics with her parrot.

Now the bird had been with the Empress day and night for two months and in all that time had never seen the false Emperor come to lie with her, a fact which delighted him, even in his wretched imprisoned state. One morning, when the Empress was alone with him in her room, she said: 'The truth, you wise and prudent animal, is that you talk to me all day in such an intelligent and perceptive way that I simply can't believe that you lack the power of reason: indeed, I'm convinced that you are the spirit of some noble person who has been transformed into a parrot by black magic. Tell me, I beg you, if I am right in thinking so.'

When the Empress had finished speaking, the parrot, for the love he bore her, could no longer hide his true identity and told her the whole story from the beginning and how it was the faithless and disloyal counsellor who had reduced him to this wretched state. In reply, the Empress told him how she had been made suspicious by the new way the false Emperor tried to make love to her and how she had then threatened to kill herself rather than lie with him. 'If such is your wish,' said the parrot, 'you can solve the whole problem very quickly, restore me to my original state, and take revenge on the wicked and perfidious counsellor.' The Empress could wish for nothing better and begged him to show her how it could be done. 'In future,' said the animal, 'when the false Emperor cosies up to you with my body, put on a cheerful smiling face; and as you start to caress him, say: "I must be the most unhappy woman in the world because, loving you as I do, I still find myself unable to enjoy you as I used to. All this because I was struck with a strange suspicion about your identity when I saw that you no longer amuse yourself as you once did by passing with your vital spirits into the dead body of an animal. And that's why I'm almost dying with grief." Now more than anything else he wants to lie with you, and so you can count on it that he will try to satisfy you and prove that he is the real Emperor by passing into some dead animal; and that will give us an opportunity to take a merciless revenge for his perfidy. Because when he does this, you will open the cage and I will fly over my own dead body, re-enter it with my vital spirits, and recover the form I had before. And from then on we shall live a calm and happy life.'

He had hardly finished speaking before the Empress hastened to carry out his instructions. That very evening the false Emperor came to her room, and as they talked of this and that as they usually did, she managed to repeat the speech that the parrot had taught her. And because he desired nothing so much as her love and favour, he protested: 'For far too long, my lady, you have done great wrong both to me and to yourself. Since that was the reason why you doubted my identity, you should have told me of it well before now and I would have removed all your suspicions. But bring me a hen and I'll soon show you how wrong you were.' The order was given immediately and a live hen was brought into the room; after which, all the servants were dismissed and the couple remained alone with the parrot. The false Emperor stifled the hen with his own hands, said the magic words over the dead body and passed into it, leaving his own body for dead upon the ground. When she saw this, the Empress hurried to open the cage and released the parrot, who flew out, hovered over the dead body and, through the power of the magic words, entered into it, leaving the parrot dead. The Empress was overjoyed and wept for happiness, clinging to her husband, the Emperor. Then she seized the hen who was beginning to realize its predicament, cut off its head, and threw it into the fire that was burning in the room. Nobody at the court was aware of what had happened, for the Emperor and the Empress gave out that the parrot had died; and when they came out of the room, they ordered great festivities with the ladies and their knights for the following day. And when the feast was over, the Emperor dismissed three of his wives and kept only the daughter of his uncle; and having recovered his imperial authority, he lived with her in perfect peace and happiness for many long years.

GIOVAMBATTISTA GIRALDI CINZIO

THE MOORISH CAPTAIN
Hecatommithi 3. 7

A Moorish captain takes a Venetian citizen as his wife. His ensign accuses her of adultery and the Moor tries to arrange for the ensign to kill the man he takes for her adulterous lover. He himself kills his wife and is then accused of the crime by the ensign. The Moor does not confess, but, given the clear proofs against him, is banished. The ensign, seeking to harm others, brings about his own wretched death.

THERE was once in Venice a very valiant Moor* who combined personal bravery with such proofs of prudence and skill in warfare that he was held in great esteem by the authorities of that city who exceed the rulers of all past republics in rewarding noble actions. It so happened that a virtuous and wonderfully beautiful lady called Disdemona fell in love with this Moor, moved not by female sensuality but by his worthy character; and the Moor, conquered by the beauty and virtuous mind of the lady, fell likewise in love with her. And although the lady's relatives did whatever they could to make her take a different husband, Love proved so favourable to the couple that they were joined in matrimony; and for as long as they remained in Venice they lived in such calm and concord that no deed or word that was less than loving ever passed between them.

Now the Signoria of Venice were about to rotate the troops that were garrisoned in Cyprus* and chose the Moor as commander of the new contingent. He was pleased with this promotion for such a high-ranking position was only given to men who were noble, strong, and loyal and had given proof of their worth. His satisfaction faded, however, when he thought of the distance and dangers of the voyage and how it might harm Disdemona. But the lady, who cared only for the Moor, was delighted that her husband's worth had been recognized by such a noble and powerful republic and could hardly wait to see him set off with his men and take up such an honourable post. She fully intended to go with him and was distressed to find that the Moor seemed rather troubled. Not knowing the reason, one day, as they were dining, she said: 'Why is it, my Moor, that just when the Signoria has raised you to such an honourable rank, you become so melancholy?' The Moor answered: 'What disturbs my pleasure in this honour is the love I bear you; because I see that the result must be one of two things: either I take you with me to risk all the perils of the sea, or, to spare you such danger, I leave you here in Venice. The former would surely weigh heavily upon me, for I would be worried out of my mind by whatever troubled or threatened you; and as for the latter, leaving you behind would be a torment to me because it would mean parting from my very self.'

When Disdemona heard this, she exclaimed: 'Listen, husband: however did such ideas get into your head? Why should such a thing disturb you? I mean to come with you wherever you go, even if I have to go through fire in my shift. Instead of which I shall be sailing with you across the sea in a safe and comfortable ship. And even if we really meet with toils and trouble, I still want to share them. And I would think that you loved me less if you left me in Venice to avoid the bother of having me with you at sea or if you convinced yourself that I'd rather stay safely here in Venice than share the danger with you. So get yourself ready for the voyage, and do it cheerfully because that's what your high rank deserves.' Then the Moor threw his arms round his wife's neck and kissed her, saying: 'May God keep us long in this love, dear wife.' Shortly after, having donned his armour and made everything ready for the journey, he embarked in his galley together with his wife. They cast off, set sail, and after a perfectly calm voyage arrived in Cyprus.

In the Moor's company there was an ensign of very handsome bearing, but with the most villainous nature in the world. The Moor thought very highly of him and had no idea of his wickedness, for although the man had a base mind, he knew how to hide the vileness of his heart with his impressive presence and proud high-sounding words, as if he were, indeed, another Hector or Achilles. Like the Moor, this evil man had come to Cyprus with his wife, a good-looking and honest young woman who spent much of the day with the Moor's wife who loved her dearly because she was an Italian. Also in the company was a lieutenant who was very dear to the Moor. He often went to dine with the Moor and his wife at their home, and the lady, who knew how well her husband liked him, was especially kind towards him. This the Moor saw and appreciated.

The wicked ensign, setting aside the vows he had made to his wife, heedless of friendship, faith, and his obligations to the Moor, fell ardently in love with Disdemona and began to think of nothing but how he might enjoy her; but he dared not show his passion for fear that if the Moor came to know of it he would kill him on the spot. And so, as discreetly as he could, he sought ways of letting the lady know that he desired her, but all her thoughts were with the Moor and not with the ensign or anyone else. Nothing he did to attract her had the slightest effect and he might just as well have saved himself the trouble. It then struck him that the cause of this must be that she was already enamoured of the lieutenant, and he began to think of how he might remove that attraction from her sight. That was not all, for the love he had once felt for the lady now changed into the most bitter hate, and he concentrated his mind on a plan which would involve not just killing the lieutenant, but making sure that if he himself could not enjoy the lady, then neither should the Moor. He considered various courses of action, all equally vile and vicious, and at last hit on the idea of accusing the lady of adultery and convincing the husband that her lover was the lieutenant. He recognized, however, that the Moor's love for his wife and his friendship with the lieutenant would always prevent him from believing such accusations unless he could be deceived by some cunning stratagem. With this in mind, the ensign was prepared to wait until time and place offered an opening for his evil enterprise.

Not long after this the Moor demoted the lieutenant from his rank for having drawn his sword and wounded a soldier while on guard-duty. Disdemona was upset by the affair and kept trying to persuade her husband to a reconciliation. And thus it was that the Moor confided to the wicked ensign that his wife was giving him so much trouble over the lieutenant that he feared he would eventually be forced to reinstate him. The wicked ensign seized on this as a chance to carry out his cunning plans, and said: 'Maybe Disdemona has a good reason for wanting to see him.' 'How so?' said the Moor. 'I wouldn't want to come between husband and wife,' replied the ensign, 'but if you keep your eyes open, you'll see for yourself.' And although the Moor persisted in questioning him, the ensign would say no more. Those words, however, left such a sharp thorn in the Moor's mind that he kept going over them and wondering what they meant until he fell into a deep melancholy.

One day his wife was trying yet again to calm his anger towards the lieutenant, begging him not to let one small fault cancel out so many years of service and friendship, especially since the wounded soldier and the lieutenant had now made peace. Suddenly the Moor burst into a fit of anger: 'There must be some great reason, Disdemona, why you take such trouble over this man; he's not your brother or your kinsman, so why should he matter to you so much?' The lady's answer was courteous and humble: 'I don't want you to be angry with me; I have no other motive but sorrow at seeing you lose such a good friend as you know the lieutenant has always been. Surely his offence is not so great as to deserve such hate. But you Moors are so hot-blooded that any little thing moves you to anger and revenge.' At these words the Moor grew even more angry: 'Those who don't believe it will soon see the proof. I shall revenge the wrongs done to me with a vengeance that sates my thirst.' The lady was dismayed by these words and seeing that her husband, unlike his usual self, was so incensed against her, she humbly replied: 'I spoke with the best of intentions, but rather than make you angry with me, I shall never say another word about it.'

The Moor, however, seeing that his wife had intervened yet again in favour of the man he had dismissed, concluded that what the ensign had said must imply that Disdemona was in love with the lieutenant. In a dark mood, he went off to that villain and tried to persuade him to speak more openly. The ensign, intent on injuring the unfortunate lady, began by feigning reluctance to say anything that might displease his commander; but in the end, as if overcome by the Moor's pleading, he said: 'I must confess that it pains me, pains me incredibly, to have to tell you something that will hurt you more than anything else. But you have asked me to speak and I am spurred on by the regard I have for your honour as my commander. I shall not fail to do my duty in answering your request. You should know, therefore, that if your lady is so upset to see the lieutenant in disgrace, it is simply because she takes her pleasure with him every time he comes to your house. And she has had enough of your blackness.'*

These words pierced the Moor's heart to the very core. But he still wanted to learn more, although his rooted suspicions had already convinced him that what the ensign said must be true. With a fierce look, he exclaimed: 'I don't know what keeps me from cutting out the insolent tongue that dares to speak such infamy of my lady.' And the ensign: 'I expected no other reward for my loving service; but since my duty and my concern for your honour have taken me so far, I shall tell you that things are exactly as you have just heard. If the woman's pretence of love has dimmed your eyes so much that you can no longer see what you should, that doesn't mean that I am not telling the truth. Because, in fact, the lieutenant himself told me, the way men do who can't believe their happiness complete unless they tell someone else about it.' And he added: 'When he told me that, I would have killed him as he deserved, if I hadn't been afraid of your anger. But since I get such a reward for telling you what concerns you more than anyone else, I shall say nothing from now on. If I'd been silent from the start I wouldn't be in your bad books now.' The Moor could not contain his anguish: 'Unless you let me see with my own eyes what you've just told me, I'll teach you that you'd have been better off born dumb.' 'That would have been easy when he used to come to your house', said the scoundrel, 'but now that you've driven him out—not for the right reason, but for something so trivial—it can only be rather difficult. I'm still sure that he enjoys Disdemona whenever you give him the chance, but he does it much more discreetly than before, now that he knows how you've come to hate him. And yet I haven't lost hope of showing you what you would rather not believe.' And with these words they parted.

As if pierced by the sharpest of arrows, the wretched Moor went home to wait for the day when the ensign would show him a sight that would make him miserable forever. But the cursed ensign was no less troubled because he had observed the lady's chastity and doubted that he would ever find a way of getting the Moor to believe his lies. At last, after racking his brain, the scoundrel came up with a new cunning ruse.

The Moor's wife, as I have said, often spent the best part of the day in the house of the ensign's wife; and he noticed that she sometimes took with her a handkerchief, finely embroidered in the Moorish fashion. It had, in fact, been given to her by the Moor and both of them treasured it. This handkerchief the ensign planned to steal so that he could use it to compass her downfall. He happened to have a three-year-old daughter who was much loved by Disdemona. One day he took the little girl in his arms and held her out to that unfortunate lady who happened to be in the house at the time. Disdemona took her and pressed her to her breast, and in that moment the trickster slipped the handkerchief from her girdle with such perfect sleight of hand that she felt nothing. Then he took his leave exulting.

Disdemona went back home, unaware of what had happened, and soon had so many things to think about that she did not realize the handkerchief was missing. But a few days later, she looked for it, and when she failed to find it she grew frightened that the Moor would ask after it, as he often did. Meanwhile, the wicked ensign, seizing the right moment, had gone to the lieutenant's room and, with cunning malice, dropped the handkerchief at his bedhead. The lieutenant did not notice it until the following morning when, as he got out of bed, he trod on the handkerchief which had fallen on the floor. He had no idea how it had come into his house, but he knew it belonged to Disdemona and decided to take it to her. So he waited until the Moor was out of the house, went to the back door, and knocked.

Fortune seemed to have conspired with the ensign to cause the poor woman's death, for in that very moment the Moor came home, heard the knocking at the door and went to the window where he asked angrily: 'Who's that knocking?' The lieutenant, hearing the voice and fearing that the Moor might come down to assault him, took to his heels without answering. The Moor ran down the stairs, opened the door, and went out into the street, but when he could see nobody, he went back inside in a foul mood and asked his wife who had been knocking down below. She answered truthfully that she did not know, but the Moor said: 'It looked to me like the lieutenant.' 'I really don't know', said she, 'whether it was him or someone else.' The Moor kept himself in check, though he was burning with rage, and decided to do nothing until he had spoken with the ensign, which he did without delay. He told the ensign everything that had happened and asked him to find out whatever he could from the lieutenant himself. And the ensign, delighted at how things were turning out, promised to do so. He chose to speak to the lieutenant on a day when the Moor was standing where he could see them talking together and, as he chattered about things that had nothing to do with the lady, he laughed heartily and made gestures of surprise with his head and his hands as if he were hearing something quite extraordinary. As soon as the Moor saw them separate, he went to the ensign to learn what the lieutenant had told him; and the ensign, after much persuasion, finally said: 'He hid nothing from me, and he told me he's been enjoying your wife every time you give him a chance by being out of the house; and the last time he was with her she gave him the handkerchief which was your wedding gift.' The Moor thanked him and concluded that if he found his lady no longer had the handkerchief, then it would be clear that everything was as the ensign had said.

One day, therefore, when they had dined and he was talking of this and that with his wife, the Moor asked her for the handkerchief. This was what the unhappy woman had been so afraid of; she grew red in the face and tried unsuccessfully to hide her blushes from him by running to a chest and pretending to look for it. And after much rummaging around, she said: 'I don't know why I can't find it; have you taken it by any chance?' 'If I'd taken it,' said he, 'why would I be asking you for it? But you can look for it better some other time.'

As he left her, the Moor began to think how he might kill his wife, and the lieutenant too, in a way that would leave him clear of any blame. This thought obsessed him day and night and inevitably his wife became aware that his attitude towards her was not what it used to be.

'What's wrong with you?' she often asked, 'what's troubling you like this? You used to be the most cheerful fellow on earth and now you're the gloomiest man alive.' The Moor answered with various excuses, but the lady was far from satisfied. And although she knew that she had done nothing wrong that could have troubled the Moor, yet still she feared that after a surfeit of lovemaking he was growing tired of her. Sometimes she said to the ensign's wife: 'I don't know what to think of the Moor; he used to be all love, but in the last few days he's become a different man. I really am afraid that I shall serve as a warning to young girls not to marry against their parents' wishes; and that Italian women will learn from me not to join themselves to men who are divided from us by Nature, Heaven, and custom. But since I know that he's a good friend of your husband and confides in him, I beg you to let me know if he tells you anything: I count on your help.' And she wept bitterly as she spoke.

The ensign's wife knew everything already, for her husband had wanted to make her an accomplice in the death of the lady, though she would never agree. But she was so afraid of him that she dared not say anything except: 'Take care not to give your husband any grounds for suspicion, and do your best to show how loving and faithful you are.' 'That's just what I am doing,' said Disdemona, 'but it gets me nowhere.'

The Moor, in the meantime, was looking for further confirmation of what he would rather not have known, and he asked the ensign to arrange for him to see the handkerchief in the lieutenant's possession; and although this was difficult, the villain still promised to do what he could to provide him with that proof.

Now the lieutenant had a woman at home who excelled in embroidering on lawn. When she saw the handkerchief and heard that it belonged to the Moor's wife and would soon be returned to her, she set about making a copy. While she was working, the ensign noticed that she was sitting at a window where she could be seen by every passer-by. So he showed her to the Moor who, convinced that his virtuous lady was indeed an adulteress, arranged with him to kill both his wife and the lieutenant. As they discussed how this might be done, the Moor begged the ensign to earn his undying gratitude by murdering the lieutenant, but the ensign at first refused, thinking that the lieutenant's skill and courage would make the task difficult and dangerous. Finally, the Moor's entreaties and a large sum of money persuaded him to say he would take the risk.

Not long after this decision, the lieutenant was attacked as he came out of the house of a courtesan where he often went to have a good time. It was a dark night and the ensign assaulted him, sword in hand, slashing at his legs to make him fall. A cut through the right thigh brought the victim down, and the ensign pounced to finish him off. But the lieutenant was a brave man and accustomed to blood and death: wounded as he was, he drew his sword and defended himself, shouting: 'Murder! I'm being murdered!' When the ensign heard people come running, and among them some soldiers who were quartered nearby, he began to run away so as not to be caught there. Then, turning back, he acted as if he had just run there himself on hearing the noise. Mingling with the crowd, he saw that the lieutenant's leg had been severed and judged that he would soon die of the wound, even though he was not dead yet. And though inwardly he rejoiced, outwardly he grieved for the lieutenant as if he were his brother.

In the morning the news spread throughout the city and when it came to the ears of Disdemona, she showed openly how deeply grieved she was by what had happened, for her tender heart had no idea that this display of emotion could cause her any harm. The Moor interpreted this in the worst possible way and went off to see the ensign: 'You know,' he said, 'that idiot of my wife is so upset by what has happened to the lieutenant that I think she'll go mad.' 'What else could you expect,' said the ensign, 'since he's her very heart and soul?' 'Her soul, eh?' said the Moor, 'I'll tear her soul out of her body. I wouldn't think of myself as a man if I didn't rid the world of that evil woman.'

They had started to discuss how to kill Disdemona, unable to make up their minds between poison and the knife, when the ensign said: 'I've just thought of a way that will satisfy you and arouse no suspicion. This is it: the house you live in is very old and the ceiling of your bedroom is full of cracks; I suggest that we fill a stocking with sand and use it to beat Disdemona to death. That won't leave any traces on her body. Then, when she's dead, we'll bring down part of the ceiling and break the lady's head so that it will seem that she has been killed by a falling rafter. That way nobody will have the slightest suspicion about you, and everyone will think her death an accident.'

This cruel plan pleased the Moor, and they waited for a suitable occasion. One night he was with her in bed and had hidden the ensign in a closet which opened off from the bedroom. As they had planned, the ensign made some kind of noise, and when the Moor heard it, he said to his wife: 'Did you hear that noise?' 'Yes, I heard it.' 'Get up, then, and go and see what it is.' The unhappy Disdemona got up and as soon as she came near the closet, the ensign sprang out and, being strong and muscular, gave her a terrible blow in the small of her back with the sand-filled stocking. The lady fell down on the spot, almost unable to breathe; but with what little breath she had, she called on the Moor to help her. He jumped out of bed and exclaimed: 'You wicked woman, here's your reward for being unfaithful: this is how to deal with women who pretend to love their husbands and then put horns on their heads.'

The ensign had already given the wretched lady another blow, and when she heard these words, knowing that her end was near, she called on Divine Justice to bear witness to her fidelity since earthly justice had failed her. As she called on God for help, the third blow fell and there she lay, slain by the wicked ensign. They then put her on the bed and smashed in her head; after which, as they had planned, they brought the ceiling down on her, and the Moor began to call for help, shouting that the house was collapsing. The neighbours came running and found the lady dead under the fallen rafters. Everyone was grieved by her death as they remembered what a good life she had led.

The next day Disdemona was buried amid the general sorrow of those people. But God, who in His justice knows all hearts, would not let such a great crime pass without condign punishment. So it was that the Moor, who had loved the lady more than his own life, now that she was taken from him, began to long for her so intensely that he wandered around the house, looking for her like a man who had lost his wits. Realizing that it was the ensign who had caused him to lose his lady and with her all the joy of life and his own real self as well, he came to hate the villain so much that he could not stand the sight of him. And if he had not feared the implacable justice of the Venetian lords, he would have killed him openly. But since he could not do this safely, he demoted him and would not accept him in the company. The upshot was a bitter enmity between them, so great and deadly as to be unimaginable.

The ensign, that worst of scoundrels, now thought of nothing but how he might harm the Moor and went to find the lieutenant who had recovered and went around with a wooden stump to replace the leg that had been cut off. 'Now's the time', he said, 'for you to take revenge for the leg you lost; and if you come with me to Venice, I'll tell you who's to blame. There are many reasons why I wouldn't dare to say it here; but in Venice I shall bear witness for you in court.' The lieutenant, who felt deeply wronged but did not know the facts of the case, thanked the ensign and went with him to Venice. Once there, the ensign told him that it was the Moor who had cut off his leg because he had somehow got it into his head that the lieutenant was sleeping with Disdemona; and that for the same reason he had murdered his wife and then told everyone that she had been killed by the collapse of the ceiling. When he heard this, the lieutenant went before the Signoria and accused the Moor both of cutting off his leg and of murdering the lady. As a witness he called the ensign who said that both accusations were true because the Moor had told him all his plans and tried to persuade him to commit both crimes. He went on to say that, after killing his wife in a fit of bestial jealousy, the Moor had told him exactly how he carried out the murder.

The Venetian lords, when they heard of the cruelty inflicted by the barbarian on one of their citizens, had the Moor arrested in Cyprus and brought to Venice where they tortured him to find out the truth. He bravely resisted every kind of torment and denied all the accusations so steadfastly that they could get nothing out of him. But although he escaped the death sentence by his stubborn courage, he spent many days in prison and was eventually condemned to perpetual exile. In exile, finally, he received his just deserts and was killed by the lady's relatives.

The ensign went back to his own country where, true to his habit, he accused a companion of having tried to persuade him to murder one of his enemies who was a nobleman. The man he accused was arrested and put to the torture, and when he denied everything, the ensign also was tortured so that their two stories could be compared. After being stretched by the rope so violently that his intestines were ruptured, he was released from prison and taken home where he died a miserable death. Thus God avenged the innocence of Disdemona. All these events were recounted, after the ensign's death, by his wife who knew the facts as I have told them to you.

NIGELLA AND THE DOCTOR
Hecatommithi 3. 9

> *A doctor is in love with his servant Nigella, but she will have none of him and complains to his wife. When the wife does not believe her, the girl finds a way to show him up and put him to shame.*

FERRARA,* as they used to say, is very much a newcomer among Italian cities, but this does not make it any the less admirable. Leaving aside the great spiritual knowledge and wisdom with which its private citizens govern their lives, I believe the character of Ferrara derives from its rulers who do everything they can to make their people not only happy but endowed with all those virtues that give nobility to free men. And this they do by encouraging serious literary studies, which is why there have always been so many citizens who are learned in every branch of knowledge. Nor do these illustrious lords only make use of the excellent home-grown talents, though there are plenty of them; they also pay high salaries to bring in highly reputed foreigners so that the souls of our youth will be more inflamed with virtue.

Now a foreign doctor of high reputation in his profession, being appointed to this kind of public office, brought with him his wife and his whole household which included a pretty maidservant, sweet-faced and slender, spirited, fresh, and fifteen years of age. The doctor, though he had a beautiful young wife and was already old and grey himself, fell madly in love with this maidservant and waylaid her whenever he had a chance—sometimes with jokes and chat and sometimes letting his hands do the talking, but always one way or another urging her to be kind and give herself to him. Nigella (named like that because she was rather on the dark side) kept brushing him off, saying: 'Sir, I'm not ready to give myself to any man who isn't my husband, however rich and powerful he may be; so please stop trying me out because I'm not for you and you're not for me; and you'd do well to be satisfied with your wife who's done nothing to deserve being scorned by you and harmed by me.'

But these words did not stop the doctor from pestering her and growing so bold that one day, when he found her in a nice quiet corner, he put his hand on her breast, snatched a kiss, and said: 'Listen, honeymouth, if you let me have my way, I'll give you a dowry of a hundred lire.' Nigella answered: 'You can give your hundred lire to someone else, and I'll keep my honour for myself.' And then, all upset, she left him and went straight to tell her mistress what the doctor had said and done and how she could hardly take a step without finding him in her way to pester her. And finally, she asked the lady to do something to rid her of this nuisance. The lady knew that her husband could be rather playful, perhaps more than was fitting for a man of his age, and so she said: 'Nigella, you're a fool: you know my husband's a very playful type, and if he sometimes tries it on with you, it's all a joke; he does it for fun, and not because he's trying to get you to do something immoral. He's not such a proud cock that he suddenly needs two hens: he's got more than he can handle with me.' 'You're wrong about that,' answered the maid, 'because if I agreed to what he keeps asking, he'd already despise me and I would have done you harm at his request. For it's not just that my honour is precious to me, but that I couldn't bear to give you cause for complaint by such behaviour. And I can tell you right now that if he carries on like this and you do nothing about it, then I shall have to find another mistress, because this sort of trouble can be very bad for a girl of my age, and I won't put up with it.'

But the lady had so much confidence in her husband that, despite what the maid had said about his behaviour, she still thought it more likely that he was joking than that he was acting out of some lustful desire. 'Nigella,' she said, 'believe me, my husband's only making fun of you; and even if he were looking for something else, let me tell you that men are men and women are women; and men don't get from women anything that women don't want to give; and a woman's just as able to defend herself from a man as he is ready to assault her. It's easier to kill a woman than to rape her when she really doesn't want it. And so, my girl, however often my husband comes round to pester you, he'll never get what you don't want to give him. And let me tell you that if you leave me, as you say you might, you could easily be running into the trap you're trying to escape. So simply wait and keep your wits about you, and you'll have nothing to fear.'

Nigella thought it very strange that the lady's faith in the doctor was so strong that whereas other women are often fiercely jealous even when their husbands give them no cause, she chose to believe nothing when she had heard things that should have been a source of infinite suspicion. And since she did not want the lady to think that she had been talking nonsense, she decided to wait for an opportunity to show her mistress that the truth was nothing less than what she had said. With this in mind, she was more patient in putting up with the doctor's harassment which was growing worse every day. As for the doctor, he thought that Nigella's new-found patience gave him some hope of satisfying his desire and he waited for Fortune to offer him a suitable time and place. The opportunity came when Nigella went up to the storeroom to sift the flour needed for making bread on the following day. Taking the sieve, she set about separating the bran from the flour with great thumping shakes. Now the doctor had put on his scarlet gown and hood and was ready to go out to the college when he heard Nigella sifting the flower in the room above. A sly sidelong glance into his wife's room showed that she was completely absorbed in her woman's work, and it struck him that this might be the right time and place for him to enjoy Nigella without being caught. Instead of going downstairs and off to college, he went into the room where Nigella was sifting the flour, put his arm round her neck and kissed her, saying: 'Dear heart, it's time you stopped tormenting me. Who should have the flower of your virginity if you don't give it to me—me who loves you and wants to do you so much good? Anyway, you'll be deflowered by some poor devil of a husband who'll care more about the hundred-lire dowry I give you than all the virginity you could bring. And what's more, whenever you want to get married, I'll arrange for you to be so dressed up that you'll look as much a virgin as if you'd just come out of your mother's womb.'

Reckoning that now was the time when she could undeceive her mistress, Nigella answered: 'You make me so many promises, sir, and use so many strong arguments that this time I can't say no, and I'm ready to do as you please; but I wouldn't want to risk having my mistress come in here. I left her idling in her room, and you know how the slightest noise can be heard down there; so if she doesn't hear me shaking the sieve, she could come up here and find me with you. And what a scandal that would mean for both of us! So please take the sieve and keep shaking it while I go down; and if I find her so busy that I've got nothing to fear, then I'll come straight back to you and give you your fill of pleasure.'

The doctor was pleased with these last words, and since he knew that his wife had been quite busy when he left her, he was happy to let the maid go off and make sure, thinking that afterwards he would be able to enjoy her at his leisure. So he said: 'Go then, and come back quickly so that I have time to go to the students who are waiting for my lecture; and bring a brush with you so that people won't see all the flour on my gown that comes from shaking the sieve. 'I'll do that, sir,' said the clever little minx, and with a hop, skip, and jump she was down the stairs to see her mistress, who was puzzled to see her all white with flour while she could still hear the noise of the sieve.

'What's going on, Nigella?' she said, 'you're down here with me and I can still hear the sieve upstairs.'

'Please, my lady, would you mind coming upstairs because I want to show you a new sifter who shakes the sieve and separates the bran so well that you'll be as amazed as I was?'

'What kind of wonder is this?'

'I just want you to see it for yourself.'

'Go on, then, and I'll follow you because this is a miracle I really must see.'

While the two women were talking, the doctor was giving the sieve a good shake, wallowing in the thought that he had brought the maid round to satisfying him at last; and at every little sound, he thought it must be her coming back. And overjoyed to recognize Nigella coughing and spitting as the two women climbed the stairs, he exclaimed: 'Here she comes!' But Nigella had remained a little behind while her mistress had already reached the top step, and the doctor, thinking it must be Nigella, said: 'You come in God's good time; I'm already covered in flour and it will be your job to clean me up, believe you me.' Then, turning round, he saw his wife instead of Nigella; and as he saw that she had caught him out, he almost collapsed with embarrassment. But the lady, who could have imagined anything but finding her husband in that situation, was enraged and said: 'Well, husband, it serves you right. From being a doctor you've made yourself into a sifter and from being master of the house you've become the skivvy of your maid. What on earth were you thinking of?' The doctor blushed more scarlet than the gown he was wearing, and although he was very eloquent when he lectured, he now seemed struck dumb while his wife showered him with bitter reproaches.

But then, plucking up his courage, he tried to calm her down with soft talk, begging her to forgive what was, after all, a very human weakness, because there's not much a man can do to resist when an enemy as fierce as Love mounts an all-out attack.

'If that's the way it is,' said the lady, 'what about me, a member of the weaker sex and more liable to fall than you are? I'm still a young woman, so what if I did with some young spark what a greybeard like you wanted to do with Nigella? Shouldn't you forgive me?'

'I could never think that of you, dear wife, because I know that you're armed against any such assaults by the shield of your honour, which I'm sure is dearer to you than life itself.

'But if—which God forbid!—if that should happen, yes, I would forgive you then just as I ask you to forgive me now.'

'That's very gracious and very kind of you; but you don't need my forgiveness because you've harmed yourself, not me. If you hadn't made such a fool of yourself, I wouldn't say another word about it on my own account. But you're a man who knows so much and teaches others how to live a decent and reasonable life, and it pains me to see how, at an age when you should know better, you've let yourself be so blinded by lust that you've become the laughing stock of a servant-girl as if you were some wretched skivvy. What a wretch you are!

'How do you think anyone will come to you for legal advice when they see that you've given up law for sifting flour. If this gets out, you'll have all the children mocking you, and you won't be able to walk down the street without people shouting insults behind your back.'

The doctor saw that what his wife said was all too true and behaved so humbly that she began to feel more sorry for him than angry.

Together they went down to their own room where she cleaned him up and brushed off all the flour, for he was as white as if he had been caught in a snowstorm. That done, he sent a message to his students saying that unforeseen circumstances prevented him from giving his lecture that day. As for his wife, although she praised Nigella's virtuous conduct, she preferred not to keep seeing the girl who had made such a fool of her husband. So she arranged for her to have a dowry and married her off to a blacksmith who took her away to his home in Mantua. And there, forgetting the whole episode, she lived quietly with her husband.

IURISTE AND EPITIA
Hecatommithi 8. 5

Emperor Maximilian sends Iuriste to Innsbruck where he arrests and condemns to death a young man who has violated a virgin. The young man's sister tries to obtain his liberty and Iuriste gives her hope that he will marry her and give her back her brother. She lies with him and that very night Iuriste has the young man's head cut off and sent to his sister. She complains to the Emperor who commands that Iuriste should first marry her and then be put to death. But the lady procures his freedom and lives with him most lovingly.

THOSE to whom God has given the government of the world should punish ingratitude, whenever it comes to their knowledge, no less than they punish murder, adultery, and robbery—crimes which, though serious, deserve perhaps a lesser punishment. It was in this spirit that Maximilian,* the great and worthy Emperor, chose to punish at one stroke both the ingratitude and the unjust conduct of one of his ministers. And his decision would have been carried out if the lady who suffered the injustice of the ungrateful minister had not, in her eminent courtesy, freed him from the sentence, as I shall now tell you.

While this great lord, who was a rare example of courtesy, magnanimity, and outstanding justice, happily reigned over the Roman Empire, he sent out his ministers to govern the states that flourished under his rule. And among other appointments, he sent to Innsbruck a man called Iuriste* who was especially dear to him. And as Iuriste was about to leave, the Emperor told him: 'Iuriste, the good opinion that I have formed of you while you have been in my service leads me to send you as governor to the noble city of Innsbruck. There are many instructions I could give you, but I will condense them all into one, which is that you should have a strict regard for justice, even if it means passing judgement against me who am your lord. I could forgive any other faults that you might commit out of ignorance or negligence (though you should do everything to avoid them); but I will never forgive any action that goes against justice. No man can be good for everything, and if perhaps you feel that you cannot be the kind of governor I want, then renounce this position of authority and remain here at court as my dear friend in your usual functions; for if, in your government of the city, you ever failed to serve justice, it would be my painful duty to punish you as justice demands.' And with that, he fell silent.

Iuriste's happiness at being called to this position was greater than his self-knowledge. He thanked his lord for the kind advice and said that though he was already intent on maintaining justice, yet the Emperor's words had kindled an even greater eagerness to do so, making him determined to govern so well that His Majesty would find no occasion for anything but praise. The Emperor was pleased with Iuriste's words and said: 'Truly, there will be no cause for anything but praise, if your actions are as good as your words.' And giving him the letters patent that were lying ready, he sent him off to Innsbruck.

Iuriste began his rule of the city with great wisdom and diligence, taking especial care to keep the scales of justice evenly balanced, not only in passing judgement, but also in official appointments and in rewarding virtue and punishing vice. As time went by, his moderation earned him ever-greater favour from his lord and the affection of the whole city. And he would have been considered the happiest of men if he had continued to govern in this way.

It happened that a young man of that country called Vieo raped a girl who was herself a citizen of Innsbruck. An accusation was lodged with the governor who immediately had the man arrested; and when he confessed that he had indeed violated a virgin, Iuriste sentenced him in accordance with the law of the city which stipulated that such a criminal should be beheaded even if he were prepared to marry the victim.

Now the young man had a sister, a virgin no more than eighteen years of age, who was not only extremely beautiful, but also had a very sweet way of speaking and a most charming presence imbued with female chastity. When this virgin, who was called Epitia, heard that her brother had been condemned to death, she was overcome with distress and decided to try whether she could, if not set her brother free, at least soften the sentence. Together with her brother (who had made no good use of the teaching), she had studied philosophy under the direction of an old man whom her father kept in the household for that purpose. With this preparation, she now went to Iuriste and begged him to have pity on her brother. She argued that he was no more than sixteen years of age and that his youth should be considered as some excuse; and then she pointed out that he had little experience of life and was moved by the sharp spur of love. The wisest men were of the opinion that an adultery provoked by the force of love and not intended to injure the lady's husband deserved a lesser punishment than one designed to cause harm. So surely the same argument should apply in the case of her brother who had not meant to cause any harm, but had been urged on by an ardent love to do that deed for which he was now condemned, and for which he was ready to make amends by taking the girl for his wife. And even though the law might say that this argument cannot apply to those who violate virgins, yet Iuriste, wise as he was, could still soften the severity of the sentence, which indeed was more like cruelty than justice. For in that city, by the authority given to him by the Emperor, he was himself the living law; and she trusted that His Majesty had given him this authority to be used fairly and tending more to clemency than to harshness. And if ever moderation was called for, it was surely in affairs of love, and especially when the honour of the victim could be preserved, as in the case of her brother who was perfectly ready to make the girl his wife. She believed that this law had been created as a fearful deterrent rather than as a sentence to be actually carried out, for she thought it a cruel thing to punish with death a sin that could be honourably and religiously amended to the full satisfaction of the injured party. And with these and other arguments* she tried to persuade Iuriste to pardon her wretched brother.

Epitia's sweet speech had charmed Iuriste's ears no less than her beauty delighted his eyes, and, eager to see and hear more of her, he asked her to repeat what she had said. Taking this as a good omen, the lady went over the same arguments, but this time to much greater effect. Overcome by Epitia's eloquent discourse and rare beauty and stirred by a lustful appetite, he began to think of how he might commit the same sin for which he had condemned Vieo to death, and said: 'Epitia, your arguments have served your brother so well that whereas he was due to lose his head tomorrow, I shall postpone the execution until I have had time to consider all the points you have raised; and if I find that they justify setting your brother free, then my happiness in doing so will be as great as my sorrow would have been to see him led to death by the letter of a harsh law.'

Epitia took good hope from these words, thanked him warmly for being so courteous with her, and said she would be eternally grateful to him, assuming that since he had been so kind as to prolong her brother's life, he would also be ready to set him free. She added that she firmly hoped that what she had said would convince him to do so and thus make her perfectly happy. And he replied that he would think it over and, if it could be done without breaking the law, he would do as she wished.

Full of hope, Epitia left and went straight to her brother and told him everything about her meeting with Iuriste and how heartened she was after this first discussion. This news was very welcome to Vieo in his desperate circumstances. He begged his sister not to cease her efforts to set him free and she promised to do everything she could.

Iuriste meanwhile had the lady's beauty deeply imprinted in his mind and, lecherous as he was, he thought of nothing but how he could enjoy Epitia; and so he waited eagerly for her to come back and speak with him. After three days she came back and with all due courtesy asked him what he had decided. Iuriste caught fire as soon as he saw her and said: 'You are welcome, fair maiden. I have thought hard to see how far your arguments could help your brother, and I have sought a few new ones as well in the hope of giving you satisfaction. But I find that everything points to his death, for there is a universal law that when a man sins, not simply out of ignorance, but from culpable ignorance,* there can be no excuse for his sin, because he ought to know what all men universally should know about how to lead a good life. And a man who sins through this kind of ignorance deserves neither excuse nor compassion. Your brother should have known very well that the law prescribes death for the rape of a virgin, and this being the case he must die, and I have no justification for showing him mercy. Nevertheless, the fact is that I would like to make you happy, and since you love your brother so much, if you let me enjoy you, I am ready to spare his life and commute his death sentence into something less severe.'

Epitia blushed fiery red at these words and answered: 'The life of my brother is very precious to me, but even more precious is my honour, and I would rather save him by losing my life than by losing that honour. Give up this immoral proposal. But if I can save my brother in any other way, then I will be most happy to do so.'

'There is no other way and you need not be so reluctant because once we have been together you may well become my wife.'

'I refuse to put my honour in danger.'

'Why in danger? Do you think that what I say could never happen? Think it over and I shall be waiting for your answer tomorrow.'

'I can give you your answer right now. Even if you make my brother's freedom depend on it, you are wasting your words if you think you can have me without making me your wife.'

Iuriste repeated that she should think it over and then bring him the answer; she should consider carefully who he was and all he could do and how useful it might prove to be his friend—not just for her but for anyone else, given the authority and power vested in him.

Epitia left in a state of great agitation, went to her brother, and told him what had happened between her and Iuriste, concluding that she was not ready to lose her honour in order to save his life. In tears she begged him to patiently endure the lot that fixed fate or ill fortune had reserved for him. But Vieo began to weep, begging his sister not to consent to his death, since she could free him in the way proposed by Iuriste. 'Epitia,' he said, 'would you see me with the blade at my neck, see them cut off a head that came from the same womb as yourself, engendered by the same father? The head of one who grew up with you, who studied with you—would you see it cast on the ground by the executioner? Ah, sister, surely the promptings of nature, of blood, of the abiding love between us will bring you to deliver me from this wretched ignominious end, since it is in your power to do so. I have sinned, I confess it. You have the power to atone for that sin, dear sister; do not withdraw your helping hand. Iuriste said he might take you for his wife: why should you assume that this cannot happen? You are very beautiful and endowed with all the graces that Nature can give to a noble lady, you are charming and attractive, you have a wonderful power of speech. Any one of these gifts—let alone the combination of them all—would make you precious not just to Iuriste but to the Emperor of the world. You have no call to doubt that Iuriste is about to make you his wife, and so you will save both your own honour and the life of your brother.'

Vieo wept as he said these words and Epitia wept with him, clinging to his neck. And before she left, overcome by her brother's tears, she had promised to give herself to Iuriste as he suggested, provided he spared her brother's life and confirmed his intention of making her his wife.

With this agreed between them, the following day the maiden went to Iuriste and told him that two things had convinced her to put herself entirely in his power and give herself to him: first, the hope that, once they had been together, he would take her as his wife; and second, her desire to free her brother not only from the death sentence but from any other punishment that his crime might deserve. Above all, it was the safety and release of her brother that she wanted Iuriste to promise.

Iuriste thought himself the happiest man in the world since he was about to enjoy such a charming and lovely girl and so he repeated the promise he had made her and said that she would have her brother back and freed from prison the morning after he had slept with her.

So, after dining together, Iuriste and Epitia went to bed and the villain took his fill of pleasure with the lady; but before he went to lie with the virgin, instead of releasing Vieo, he gave orders that he should be beheaded without delay.

In her eagerness to see her brother freed, the lady could hardly wait for daybreak, and never, it seemed, had the sun been so slow to bring the dawn as it was that night. When morning finally came, Epitia slipped out of Iuriste's arms and urged him in the sweetest way to make her his wife in fulfilment of the hope he had given her. And in the meantime he should release her brother and send him back to her. He answered that he had thoroughly enjoyed being with her and was glad that she had derived such hope from his words; and moreover, he would soon send her brother back home. And with this, he summoned the jailer and said: 'Go to the prison and bring out the brother of this lady and take him back home.' Epitia was overjoyed to hear this and went home to wait for her brother's release. The jailer placed the body of Vieo on a bier, put the head at his feet, covered it with a black cloth, and walked ahead as he had it carried to Epitia. And when he entered the house, he called the maiden: 'This is your brother,' he said, 'who has been released from prison and sent to you by the lord governor.' And with these words he uncovered the bier and presented Epitia with her brother in the state I have described.

I do not think that speech can say or the human mind comprehend the depth of her distress or the intensity of her grief when she was offered the corpse of her brother—her brother whom so joyfully she had expected to see released from prison and free from any further punishment. But, ladies, I have no doubt you can imagine that the wretched woman's suffering exceeded every other kind of anguish. But she hid the pain deep in her heart for philosophy had taught her how the human spirit should react to the vicissitudes of Fortune; and where any other woman would have wept and cried, she seemed unmoved and said to the jailer: 'You may tell your lord and mine that as he has been pleased to send my brother to me, so I receive him. And since he has chosen to follow his own inclinations and not to do as I wished, I am content to conform my will to his and to think that what he has done was justly done. So commend me to him as being always most ready to please him.'

The jailer told Iuriste what Epitia had said, and added that she had shown no sign of distress before such a horrible spectacle. Iuriste was inwardly happy to hear this and it struck him that he might possess the young woman as he pleased just as well as if she were his wife and he had restored Vieo to her alive.

Epitia meanwhile, as soon as the jailer had left, threw herself on the body of her dead brother with a flood of tears, protesting long and bitterly, cursing the cruelty of Iuriste and her own simplicity in giving herself to him before seeing her brother released. And after much weeping, she buried the corpse and withdrew to her room where alone, moved by righteous anger, she said to herself: 'So then, will you, Epitia, suffer this? First this villain robs you of your honour in exchange for a promise to restore your brother alive and free, and then he sends you back that brother as a miserable corpse. Will you allow him to boast of how cunningly he took double advantage of your simplicity and not inflict on him the punishment he deserves?'

With such words she kindled the fire of her revenge, saying: 'My simplicity made it easy for this scoundrel to satisfy his filthy lust. Now I shall make his lechery serve my revenge, and even if revenge will not bring my brother back to life, it will at least help me to overcome my grief.' Agitated and obsessed with this idea, she waited for Iuriste to send for her so that he could lie with her again. She had decided that she would hide a knife, which she would keep with her, waking or sleeping, until she found the right moment to bleed him and, if possible, cut off his head and take it as an offering to her brother's tomb. But on second thoughts, she saw that though she might succeed in killing the deceiver, people might conclude that she was an evil-minded harlot who had acted out of rage and anger rather than because he had betrayed her faith. And so, knowing the Emperor's regard for justice, she decided to go to Villach where His Majesty then was and denounce the ingratitude and injustice of Iuriste, being confident that the excellent monarch would inflict a fitting punishment on that villain for his crimes. Dressed in mourning clothes, she set out secretly and alone. And when she had requested and obtained an audience with Maximilian, she threw herself at his feet and, with a voice as sad as her dress, addressed him as follows:

'Most sacred Emperor, I am driven to come before Your Majesty by the savage ingratitude and incredible injustice inflicted on me by Iuriste, Your Imperial Majesty's governor in Innsbruck. I speak in the hope that your justice, which has never failed the poor and weak, will be such as to punish Iuriste. I have suffered endlessly for the unheard-of wrong he has done me; let your justice prevent him from taking pride in having so foully murdered me. Allow me to use that word before Your Majesty for, however harsh it seems, it still falls short of the cruel and unprecedented shame brought on me by this evil man, who has treated me both ungratefully and most unjustly.'

After which, with sighs and tears, she told His Majesty how Iuriste, by suggesting he would marry her and promising to release her brother, had taken her virginity and then sent her the dead body of her brother on a bier, with the severed head at his feet; and here her eyes filled with tears and she gave out such a cry that the Emperor and all the lords who were with him were shaken by the pity of it.

But though Maximilian had great compassion for Epitia and raised her up when she had finished speaking, nonetheless, after listening to her, he wanted to hear the governor's version; and so, after telling her to rest, he summoned Iuriste, with strict instructions to the messenger that, as they valued his favour, neither he nor any of the others who were there should say a word about the matter to Iuriste.

Iuriste, who could have imagined anything but that Epitia had gone to the Emperor, arrived in a high good humour and when he came into His Majesty's presence, he bowed low and asked why he had been sent for.

'You will know soon enough,' said Maximilian, and immediately sent for Epitia.

When he saw the woman whom he knew he had wronged so gravely, Iuriste had such a sharp pang of conscience that he began to tremble and almost lost his senses. When Maximilian saw this he knew for certain that Epitia had told him nothing less than the truth, and turning to Iuriste with the severe aspect that befitted such a heinous crime, he said: 'Hear this young woman's complaint against you,' and asked Epitia to repeat her accusation. This she did, telling the whole story as it had happened from beginning to end and concluding, as before, by a tearful appeal to the Emperor for justice.

When he had heard the accusation, Iuriste tried to cajole the lady and exclaimed: 'I never thought that you, whom I love so much, would come and accuse me before His Majesty like this.' But Maximilian would permit no such blandishments and said: 'This is no time to play the lover. Just answer the accusation she had made against you.' Iuriste now dropped the counter-productive jovial manner: 'It is true', he said, 'that I had her brother beheaded because he had kidnapped and raped a virgin, and this I did because I would not violate the sanctity of law and because I wished to serve the justice that Your Majesty had recommended to me—a justice that would not have been observed if he had remained alive.'

'And if you thought that was what justice required,' said Epitia, 'why did you promise to deliver my brother alive, and then use this promise and the prospect of marriage to take my virginity? If my brother, for one sole sin, deserved to feel the severity of the law, you deserve it far more for your double crime.'

Iuriste was like a man struck dumb. 'Do you think', said the Emperor, 'that in this you have preserved justice? Or have you not rather wounded and almost murdered justice by your unheard-of, wicked, and ungrateful treatment of this noble lady? But you will not get off lightly, believe me!'

Then Iuriste began to beg for mercy and Epitia, on the contrary, to demand justice.

Now that Maximilian understood the innocence of Epitia and the wickedness of Iuriste, he immediately began to think how he could serve justice and, at the same time, preserve the honour of the lady. And when he had made up his mind, he announced that Iuriste should marry Epitia. The lady objected that she could expect nothing from Iuriste but evil deeds and betrayal, but Maximilian insisted that she should accept his decision.

Having married the lady, Iuriste believed that his troubles were over, but this was not how things turned out, for no sooner had the Emperor given Epitia permission to return to her lodgings than he turned to Iuriste who remained behind and said: 'You committed two crimes, both very serious. First you put this young lady to shame in such a deceitful way that one must say it amounted to rape: second, you broke your word and killed her brother. And even though he deserved to die, yet still, since you were ready to break the law, surely it would have been better to keep the promise you had made to his sister in your dissolute lust. Indeed, this would have been better than dishonouring her and sending her brother back to her as a corpse. I have seen to it that you atone for the first crime by making you marry the lady you violated. As for the second, just as you had her brother's head cut off, so your own will be forfeit.'

How wretched Iuriste felt when he heard the Emperor's sentence is easier to imagine than to describe. He was handed over to the sergeants to be executed the following morning in accordance with the sentence and was now fully prepared for death, with nothing to expect except that the executioner should come and put an end to him.

Epitia, meanwhile, who had been so fierce against him, was moved by her natural kindness when she heard the sentence. She reflected that the Emperor had given her Iuriste as a husband and that she had accepted him as such; to now consent that he should die on her account would be unworthy of her and might well seem the result of a cruel thirst for vengeance rather than any desire for justice. Intent, therefore, on saving the villain's life, she went straight to the Emperor, was granted audience, and spoke as follows:

'Most sacred Emperor, the injustice and ingratitude of Iuriste prompted me to beg for Your Majesty's justice upon him; and you, as is just, have pronounced fitting judgements on the two crimes he committed: for stealing my virginity he has had to take me as his wife; and for putting my brother to death, despite his promise, he is condemned to death himself. Before I was his wife, I desired that death sentence which you have so justly pronounced; but now, since it has pleased you to bind me to Iuriste by the holy bonds of matrimony, if I were to consent to his death, I would deserve to be held in eternal infamy as a cruel and pitiless woman. And this surely goes against

Your Majesty's intention which was to preserve both justice and my honour. Therefore, most sacred Emperor, to fulfil your good intention and to preserve my honour without stain, I humbly and reverently implore you: withdraw the sentence and let not the sword of justice so cruelly sever the knot by which you have tied me to Iuriste. And whereas Your Majesty's sentence, by condemning him to death, has clearly demonstrated your justice, so now, I beg you to show your mercy by restoring him to me alive. For one who holds the reins of power, as Your Majesty so worthily does, the exercise of mercy is no less praiseworthy than that of justice; for while the latter shows that he hates and therefore punishes all vices, the former makes him similar to the immortal gods. If your kindness grants this special grace to me, your humble servant, I shall offer ceaseless prayers to God that He grant Your Majesty many long and happy years in the exercise of justice and mercy to the benefit of mortals and to your own immortal glory and honour.' And here Epitia ended her plea.

Maximilian was amazed that she should set aside the great injury she had suffered from Iuriste and pray for him so warmly. And he thought that he should reward such great goodness as he saw in this woman by restoring to her alive, in the name of mercy, the man he had condemned to death in the name of justice. So, having summoned Iuriste in the very hour when he expected to be led to death, he said: 'You evil man, the goodness of Epitia has worked on me so powerfully that whereas your wickedness deserved not one but a double death, she has persuaded me to grant you your life. You must know that you owe that life to her and since she agrees to live with you, I also consent that you should live with her in that union which I ordained. And if ever I hear that you have treated her as anything less than a most kind and loving wife, then I shall make you feel the weight of my displeasure.' And with these words, he took Epitia by the hand and gave her to Iuriste.

Then Epitia and Iuriste together gave thanks to the Emperor for the grace and the favour he granted them, and Iuriste, recognizing how great was Epitia's generosity towards him, held her dear ever after, so that she lived with him happily for the rest of her days.

GIAMBATTISTA BASILE

CINDERELLA
Il cunto de li cunti (The Tale of Tales) i. 6

Zezolla is persuaded by her teacher to murder her stepmother and thinks that she will be cherished for helping that teacher to marry her father; but she is put to work in the kitchen until, thanks to the fairies and after many adventures, she wins the hand of a king.

YOU should know, then, that once upon a time there was a prince who had been left a widower with an only daughter whom he loved so much that he had no eyes for anyone else. He found her a first-class teacher who taught her chain-stitch and hem-stitch, back-stitch and front-stitch, and cherished her more than words can say. But the father had just remarried and taken for his wife a fiery wicked devilish creature, a cursed woman, who soon began to feel sick in her stomach at the sight of her stepdaughter. Then came sour looks, ugly grimaces, and glowering frowns so fearsome that the poor little lamb went crying to her teacher about how badly she was being treated, saying: 'You're the one who gives me all the hugs and cuddles; why couldn't you be my mummy?'

And she kept singing the same old song until at last, blinded by some evil spirit, the teacher too got that bee in her bonnet and said: 'Look, if you do what my crazy mind is thinking, I'll be your mother and you'll be like the apple of my eye.' She would have said more, but Zezolla (for that was the girl's name) said: 'Forgive me if I cut you off. I know you love me, so it's lips sealed and *sufficit*:* teach me how to go about it, because I'm just a simple country lass; you write and I'll sign.' 'Right then,' answered the teacher, 'now listen carefully; prick up your ears and your bread will come out white as flowers. As soon as your father goes out, tell your stepmother that you want one of those old dresses that are in the big chest in the storeroom so that you can spare the one you're wearing. She loves to see you in rags and left-offs, so she'll open the chest and tell you: "Hold the lid up." You'll hold it, and while she's rummaging inside you'll suddenly let it fall and break her neck. Once that's done, you know that your father would forge florins to make you happy, so when he's hugging you, you beg him to take me for his wife, and, lucky you, you'll have my service for life.'

Zezolla could hardly wait; every moment seemed an eternity until she had followed the teacher's instructions in every jot and tittle. Then, after proper mourning for her stepmother's accidental death, she began to play on her father, touching all the right keys to make him marry the teacher. At first the prince thought it must be a joke, but his daughter kept knocking until the door gave way. Zezolla's words had done their job, and, with great celebrations, he married Carmosina the teacher.

Now one day, while the newly-weds were having a quiet romp, Zezolla went out onto a balcony of the house, and a little dove flew down, perched on the wall, and said: 'Whenever there's something you want, send a message to the fairies' dove on the island of Sardinia, and you'll get it straightaway.'

For five or six days the new stepmother practically smothered Zezolla with attention, seating her in the best place at table, giving her the best titbits, and dressing her in the finest clothes. But that short time was hardly over before all the favours she had received were set aside and forgotten (it's a sad soul that dwells in a wicked mistress!), and she began to push forward her six daughters that she had kept secret until then. And she was so successful in getting round her husband that he opened his heart to those stepdaughters and closed it to his own child, so that from one day to the next Zezolla was demoted from the chamber to the kitchen, from the canopied bed to the humble hearth, from gold and silks to wretched rags, from the sceptre to the spit; and not only her status but even her name was changed—from Zezolla to Cinderella, the Cinder-Cat.

It happened that the prince had to go to Sardinia on official state business and so, one by one, he asked his six stepdaughters, Imperia, Calamita, Fiorella, Diamante, Colombina, and Pasquarella, what they would like him to bring them on his return. One asked for showy dresses, one for ornaments to deck her head, one for rouge for her cheeks, one for toys to pass the time away, one for one thing and one for another, until at last, almost in mockery, the prince asked his own daughter: 'And what would you like?' She replied: 'Only this, give my regards to the fairies' dove and ask her to send me something; and if you forget, may you be unable to go forward or backward. Remember what I say: cross your heart and hope to die.'

The prince departed, settled his business in Sardinia, bought everything his stepdaughters had asked for, and forgot all about Zezolla. But when he had embarked and was about to set sail, the ship proved unable to leave port, just as if it had been blocked by a lamprey. The captain of the ship, who was almost in despair, was so tired out that he fell asleep, and in a dream he saw a fairy who said to him: 'Do you know why you can't leave port? It's because the prince that you have on board hasn't kept the promise he made to his daughter and has remembered everyone except his own flesh and blood.' The captain woke up and told his dream to the prince, who was highly embarrassed and went straight to the grotto of the fairies where he passed on his daughter's regards and asked them to send her something.

And lo and behold, a young woman, bonny and bright as a banner, came out of the cave and told him to thank his daughter for her kind regards and that Zezolla should be happy for love of the fairy. So saying, she gave him a date tree, a hoe, a golden pail, and a silk cloth, and told him that the tree was for planting and all the other things were to help it grow. The prince, amazed at these gifts, took leave of the fairy and went back to his homeland; there he first gave his step-daughters everything they had asked for and then at last presented his daughter with the fairy's gift.

So delighted that she could hardly stay in her skin, Zezolla planted the date tree in a fine big pot and hoed it, watered it, and dried it every morning and evening with the silk cloth until, after four days, it had become as tall as a grown woman. Then a fairy came out of it and said: 'What is your wish?' Zezolla answered that sometimes she would like to go out of the house, but without the six sisters knowing it. The fairy answered: 'Whenever you feel like it, just go to the pot and say:

> *O my lovely golden date-tree,*
> *I've weeded you with a hoe of gold*
> *I've watered you from a pail of gold,*
> *I've dried you with this silk I hold,*
> *Now strip yourself and then dress me.*

And when you want to undress, change the last verse and say:

> *Now strip me and dress yourself.*'

Now a feast day came round and the teacher's daughters went out, all dolled-up, all perfumed, powdered and painted, all buttons and bows, baubles and bells, all roses and posies. Zezolla immediately ran to the pot, and no sooner had she said the words that the fairy taught her than there she was, got up like a queen and mounted on a fine steed, accompanied by twelve trim slim pages. Then she went off to the same place as her sisters who foamed at the mouth with envy when they saw the beauty of this shining dove.

But, as chance would have it, the king turned up in that very place and when he saw the extraordinary beauty of Zezolla, he was immediately enchanted and asked his most trusty servant to see how he could find out more about this lovely creature, who she was and where she lived.

The servant went after her right away, but she had spotted the ambush and threw down a handful of gold coins that she had procured from the date tree for that purpose; and when he set eyes on the shining money, the servant forgot about following the horse and preferred to stuff his pockets with fistfuls of small change. Zezolla rushed off home and undressed in the way the fairy had taught her—just before the ugly sisters arrived, intent on making her miserable by telling of all the splendid things they had seen.

The servant, meanwhile, reported back to the king who, when he heard about the coins, flew into a frightful rage saying that for four shitty little coppers he had sold off his master's royal pleasure and that, when the next feast day came round, whatever the cost, he had better find out who the lovely girl was and where the pretty bird had its nest.

The next feast day arrived and the six sisters went out all dressed up to the nines, leaving poor despised Zezolla at the hearth. She immediately ran to the date tree and repeated the formula, and lo and behold, out came a whole band of damsels—one with a mirror, one with a flask of squash water, one with a curling iron, one with a rouge cloth, one with combs, one with pins, one with clothes, and one with a diadem and pendants. Then, when they had made her as splendid as the sun, they put her in a coach drawn by six horses, accompanied by footmen and pages in livery; and off they went to the same place where the other feast had been held and where once again she struck astonishment into the hearts of the sisters and fire into the breast of the king.

But when she left and the servant began to follow her, she threw out a handful of pearls and jewels to prevent him catching up with her; and while that fine fellow stopped to snap them up (for it wasn't stuff you'd want to lose), she had time to drag herself home and get undressed in the usual way. With a hang-dog look, the servant returned to the king, who said: 'I swear by the souls of my ancestors that if you don't find her, I'll give you a good thrashing and a kick in the arse for every hair in your beard.'

Yet another feast day arrived, and when the sisters had gone out, Zezolla returned to the date tree, repeated the magic formula, and was immediately dressed in splendid clothes and placed in a golden coach, attended by so many servants that she seemed like a whore caught parading down the street and surrounded by policemen.* So she went off to the feast, made the sisters green with envy, and then left, with the king's servant practically stitched onto the back of the coach. Seeing that he was still at her heels, Zezolla said: 'The whip, coachman, the whip!' And the coach surged forward at such a furious speed that she lost one of her high cork shoes, one of the prettiest things you ever saw. The servant couldn't keep up with the flying coach, but he picked up the shoe, took it to the king, and told him what had happened.

Taking the shoe in his hand,* the king exclaimed: 'If the foundation is so lovely, what must the house be like? O sweet candlestick where once the candle burned that now consumes me! O fair tripod of the cauldron where my life is boiling! O precious cork on the line that the fisherman Love has cast to snare my soul! See, I embrace you, I hold you close; and if I cannot reach the plant, I will adore the roots, and if I cannot have the capitals, at least I will kiss the plinth. Once you supported a white foot and now you wound a black heart. Thanks to you, the tyrant who rules my life became ten inches taller, and thanks to you my life also grows in sweetness as I behold and possess you.'

And with this he called his scribe and summoned his trumpeter and *tantara, tantara*, he issued a proclamation that all the women in the land were invited to the great public feast and banquet that he suddenly felt like providing. And when the day came, O lord alive, what a blowout! what a beanfeast! Where did they come from, all those pastries and pasties? all those stews and meatballs? all those macaroni and ravioli? There was enough to feed a whole army.

All the women came flocking in, nobles and commoners, rich and poor, old and young, beautiful and ugly; and when they had stuffed themselves, the king gave a toast and then set about trying the shoe on all the guests, one by one, to see if he could find a foot where it would prove a perfect skintight fit. In this way he thought he could use the form of the shoe to find the woman he was seeking; but there was no foot that matched the shoe, and he was beginning to despair.

Nonetheless, silencing them all, he said: 'Come back tomorrow and do penance with me again; but if you love me, don't leave any woman at home, whoever she may be.' Then the prince said: 'I have a daughter, but she stays at home to look after the hearth; she's a miserable little thing and not fit to sit at the table where you eat.' The king answered: 'Put her first on the list, for such is my will.' So they all took their leave and came back the following day; and along with the daughters of Carmosina came Zezolla. As soon as he saw her, the king had the impression that she was the one he was looking for, though he gave no sign of it.

But when everybody had finished nattering, it was time to try on the shoe; and it had hardly been brought near to Zezolla before it leaped of its own accord onto the foot of that egg painted by Love himself, like iron attracted by a magnet. When the king saw this, he ran to clasp her in his arms, made her sit under the royal canopy, and put a crown on her head, commanding everyone to bow and curtsey before her as their queen. The sight made the stepsisters livid with anger and so heartsick that they slunk away to their mother's house, admitting, in spite of themselves, that *only a madman fights the stars*.

SUN, MOON, AND TALIA
Il cunto de li cunti (The Tale of Tales) 5. 5

Talia is killed by a scrap of flax and left in a palace where a passing king has two children by her. His jealous wife gets hold of them and gives orders that they should be cooked and served up to the king while Talia is burned. But the cook saves the children and Talia is set free by the king who throws his wife into the fire that she had prepared for Talia.

ONCE upon a time there was a great lord who had a daughter called Talia. When she was born he summoned all the wise men and soothsayers of his kingdom to foretell her future; and after much confabulation they concluded that she would run into grave peril because of a scrap of flax. So to ward off this dangerous encounter he commanded that no flax or hemp or anything of the kind should ever enter his house.

But one day, when Talia was already almost grown up and was standing at the window, she saw an old woman who was spinning as she passed by. And since she had never seen a distaff or spindle, she was fascinated by all that winding and made the woman come up. She herself took the distaff in hand and was beginning to draw the thread when by some accident a scrap of flax got lodged under her fingernail and she fell down dead.

The old woman saw what had happened and scurried back down the stairs. And when the wretched father heard of the terrible accident and had paid for that bucket of bitter wine with a barrel of tears, he left his daughter in that country mansion, seated on a velvet chair under a canopy of brocade. Then he closed the doors and abandoned forever the place that had given him so much pain, hoping to cancel from his mind every trace of this tragedy.

But some time after this a falcon escaped from a king who was out hunting and flew straight through the open window of that palace. And since the bird did not return when called, the king had his men knock at the door, for he thought that someone must be living there. But when he had been knocking for a long time, he decided to see for himself what was inside the house. He got hold of a harvester's ladder, climbed up, went in, and looked all around without finding a living soul. For a while he stood stock still like a mummy, but at last he came to the room where Talia sat enchanted, and at first sight, thinking she must be asleep, he called to her. But since she did not awake however much he shouted and shook her, he picked her up and carried her to a bed where, inflamed by her beauty, he plucked the fine fruits of love. Then he left her lying there and went back to his own kingdom where, for a long time, he forgot everything that had happened.

After nine months Talia pushed out two babies, one a boy and the other a girl, who seemed like precious jewels. They were looked after by two fairies who had appeared in the palace and who put them at their mother's breasts, and one day, when they wanted to suck and could not find the nipple, they grasped her finger and sucked so hard that the flax came out from under the fingernail. Then Talia felt as if she were waking from a long sleep and, seeing those two jewels next to her, she suckled them and held them as dear as life itself.

She still did not know what had happened to her or how she found herself alone in that palace with two babies by her side and folk she could not see who brought her things to eat. But meanwhile the king had remembered Talia and seized on another hunting-trip as an opportunity to go and look for her. And when he found her awake, with those two gorgeous painted dolls, he was mad with joy and told Talia who he was and what had happened. And so they struck up a friendship and formed a close bond. He stayed with her for a few days and then, promising to return and take her with him, he went back to his kingdom. Once there, he never missed a chance to talk of Talia and the children; even when he was eating it was as if he had Talia in his mouth, and the Sun and the Moon as well, for these were the names he had given the twins and he called on them both when he lay down to sleep.

Now the king's wife had already become a bit suspicious when it took her husband so long to return from his hunting-trip, and when she heard him going on about Talia, the Sun, and the Moon, she burned with a fever that was not caused by sunstroke. So she called her secretary and said: 'Listen up, son: you're between Scylla and Charybdis,* the jamb and the door, a rock and a hard place. You tell me who my husband's in love with and I'll make you rich; hide it from me and by the time I've finished you won't know whether you're dead or alive.'

The compliant servant was torn between two emotions—sick to death with fear and at the same time itching with sheer self-interest which is a blindfold on the eyes of honour, a veil on the face of justice, and a jemmy that breaks the lock of the given word. So he answered her with bread for bread and wine for wine; and the queen sent the secretary off to tell Talia, in the name of the king, that His Majesty wanted to see his children. Talia was delighted to send them; and then that heart of Medea* ordered the cook to cut their throats, make them into all kinds of snacks and appetizers, and serve them up to her wretched husband. But the cook was a bit of a softie and when he saw those two golden apples, he felt sorry for them and gave them to his wife to hide while he prepared two young goats in a hundred different sauces.

When the king came home, the queen had the food served in a high good humour; and the king ate it with great gusto saying: 'By jingo,

this is good stuff! Oh, and this is tasty, by my granddad's soul!' And
all the time his wife kept egging him on with: 'Eat up, eat up; after all,
what you're eating is yours.' When the king had heard this refrain two
or three times and she kept on repeating the same old tune, he finally
snapped: 'Yes, I know that I'm eating what's mine, because you certainly didn't bring anything into this house!' Then he got up in a rage
and stormed off into the countryside to vent his anger.

The queen meanwhile was still not satisfied with what she had done
and called her secretary again, telling him to summon Talia with the
excuse that the king was waiting for her. She came straightaway, eager
to find the light of her life and unaware that what awaited her was the
fire. But when she came before the queen, she was greeted by a face as
furious as that of Nero and a voice that said: 'You're very welcome,
Lady Slut! So you're the fine dolled-up piece of trash, the stinking
weed that my husband enjoys so much! You're the bitch who's been
giving me all these splitting headaches! Well, make yourself at home,
because this is Purgatory where I'll make you pay for the harm you've
done me.'

When Talia heard this, she began to apologize because, after all,
it wasn't her fault and the king had invaded her little country nook
when she was spellbound and asleep. But the queen would hear no
excuses, and there in the courtyard of the palace she had a great fire
kindled and ordered them to throw Talia into the flames. Seeing that
things had taken a turn for the worse, Talia knelt down and begged the
queen to give her at least enough time to take off the clothes she was
wearing. 'Strip off then, that's all right with me,' said the queen—not
because she had the slightest pity for the poor girl, but because she
wanted to get her hands on those gowns embroidered with gold and
pearls. So Talia began to get undressed, and with every garment she
took off, she let out a scream. Off went her gown, her skirt, and her
jacket, and when she came to her petticoat she gave one last shriek as
they dragged her off to become ashes for the laundry where they wash
Charon's breeches.*

But in that very moment the king came back, and when he saw what
was going on, he insisted on knowing the whole story. And when he
asked about his children, she began to blame him for his infidelity,
and at last he heard from her own mouth how she had arranged for
him to gobble them up. At this news, the hapless king was overwhelmed by despair: 'So I was the wolf man for my own little sheep!

Ah, why didn't my veins recognize the springs of my own blood? O you renegade Turk, what bestial ways are these? But just you wait. You'll soon be compost for cabbages, and I won't be sending that bossy face of yours to do penance in the Colosseum.'*

And with that he commanded that she should be thrown into the same fire that had been kindled for Talia, and along with her went the secretary who had given her a hand in the cruel game and had helped to weave that wicked web. He was just about to do the same with the cook who had, he thought, made mincemeat of his children, but the man threw himself at the king's feet and said: 'To be quite frank, my lord, the service I've done you would deserve some better pension than a fiery furnace and a support more solid than a pole up my arse. I can think of a jollier entertainment than burning and shrivelling in that fire, and I don't see much profit in mixing the ashes of a cook with those of a queen! This isn't exactly the great thanks I expected for saving your children from that heap of dogspew who wanted to kill them and send them back into the body they came from.'

When the king heard all this, he was struck almost senseless; he thought he must be dreaming and could hardly believe his own ears. But at last he turned to the cook and said: 'If it's true that you've saved my children, you can be quite sure that I'll free you from turning the spit; instead, I'll put you into the kitchen of my heart and there you'll turn my desires the way you please and give yourself a prize that will make you feel like the happiest man in the world.'

While the king was speaking, the cook's wife, having seen how things were going with her husband, brought the Moon and the Sun before their father, who started playing the game of three with his wife and children, doing the round of kisses from one to the other. And when he had given the cook a large reward and made him a gentleman-in-waiting, he took Talia as his wife. She lived a long and happy life with her husband and the children and recognized that, despite all the trials she had endured, she was one of those lucky people on whom *the good rains down even when they are sleeping*.

FRANCESCO PONA

ARMILLA
La lucerna (The Lamp),* First Evening

Eureta: Now when you came out of Argenis whom did you possess?

Lantern: In Udine, a city no less warlike than splendid, there once
lived a knight of noble blood who possessed many castles and was rich
in all the delights that Fortune could grant a man who ranked only
a little lower than a prince. He left one son, his only heir, a more
handsome youth than could be found in any other city of the region,
endowed with such a fine and noble intellect that it exceeded even the
dignity inherent in his high birth. In the knightly exercises that he
practised he surpassed all the other youths of his age and attracted the
eyes of women no less than the applause of men.

Among all the girls of Udine, Love made me the most charming
and attractive in the eyes of Tebaldo (for that was the name of the
noble youth) and although I was far inferior to him by birth, he began
to court me openly, but in such a pure and honourable way that everyone thought he meant to marry me, given that there was no paternal
authority to hinder him. But he had other things in mind. One
evening, accompanied by four strong well-armed young men to make
doubly sure, he seized me as I was walking by his castle with my
mother. And leaving my mother sick with anxiety, he took me off to
his chambers. And since he was so powerful, my mother, who was
a poor widow, could only put up with the situation—but with such
a devouring sorrow that she soon closed her eyes in the sleep of death.

The citizens of Udine were amazed to think that this outrage had
been committed by Tebaldo who was otherwise so mild and virtuous,
and he was often reproached for it by those who knew him best. But
he insisted that all the blame belonged to Cupid's bow; it was true that
he had surrendered to the violence of love's arrow and the flames of
passion which had finally forced him to ravish me; but this was only

after he had already tried flattery, entreaties, and gifts without success; and moreover, in all other matters he had remained as virtuous as before.

I had now left off my virginal bashfulness and was utterly captivated by the sweet embraces of my fine lusty lover. Forgetful of my mother, who had died with the death of my honour, I lived a joyous life, flattered and served like a queen. And already the love that reigned peacefully in the mind of Tebaldo began to govern like a tyrant in mine, filling me with jealousy whenever he went into town on business or for amusement. Already I feared the rivalry of every other woman, however withered or ugly. And I felt that the handsome man who had become the idol of my heart must be equally adored by other hearts. The more tender Tebaldo seemed in his kisses and lovemaking, the more I suspected that he was putting on an act to hide his interest in some other woman. This suspicion roused an unbearable tumult in my breast until, with a storm of tears, needing to give some vent to my passion, I chose to reveal at least a part of my suffering to an old Greek woman who was closer to me than any of the other servants. Having spent her whole youth in love affairs, she expressed her sympathy; and to gain my favour she not only wept with me but also offered her help. And she explained at great length how safe, useful, and easy it would be to make use of the magic arts (in which she happened to be an expert) to bind Tebaldo firmly in the chains of my love.

Tebaldo, meanwhile, had been away from me in the city for three whole days, so that I was almost consumed with anxiety, as if I foresaw the evil that was being prepared for me. For, in fact, under the pressure of his closest relatives, Tebaldo in those days had begun to arrange his marriage to a neighbouring baroness, a maiden of sixteen and said to be the most beautiful girl in that part of the country. The negotiations had gone ahead so smoothly that both parties were ready to agree on every detail, the respective relatives had given their consent, and on the third day the matter was concluded.

It was the fourth year after Tebaldo had ravished me, and how passionately I loved him you can judge from what I have already said. When he returned to the castle, I saw that his manner had changed in that instead of rushing to embrace me, he simply gave me a polite greeting and announced that he would sleep that night in the same room as his friend—a cousin of his new wife, as I found out later. It was enough to make me mad, desperate, suicidal; the ravings of a maniac could not compare with mine that night. The spectres I saw were not only weird and outlandish, but also creatures unknown to nature and stranger than the metamorphoses of Proteus. I awoke with the sun, or rather before sunrise, but not earlier than Tebaldo who, with a friendly greeting, told me to get dressed because he wanted us to go out to one of his estates. I sprang to do his bidding, decking my tormented and fading beauty with all those ornaments that might, I thought, hide something of my suffering. So we rode away, together with three soldiers, the Greek servant, and the friend who had deprived me of rest the night before. As we went on for about thirty miles, Tebaldo told me all about his forthcoming marriage which was to take place in a few hours' time; and then, giving me five hundred gold scudi together with the clothes and ornaments that I had taken with me, he left me, desperately unhappy to lose him, with the old Greek woman in another castle.

There would be no point, Eureta, in me trying to describe the thousandth part of the pains I endured; only the direct experience of love shows it to those in despair. I was so afflicted that if I remained alive, it was only because grief does not kill. Tears were my drink and bathed the little food that I ate. I shall not say that they accompanied my sleep, because for nights on end my eyes remained as open to tears as my jaws were open to howling and my heart to the wounds of jealousy and woe.

I was reduced to such a state that anyone seeing me would have thought that in the same moment he beheld Echo changed into a mere voice and Egeria* transformed into a fountain. Far from lessening my pain as she intended, the words and tears of the Greek woman only increased my suffering until at last, having run out of soothing arguments, she dried my eyes and said:

'Armilla'—for that was my name—'by the limits imposed on us by Nature, or rather by the tyrannical education inflicted by our fathers, we are denied the use of arms and the shedding of blood to avenge our wrongs. But that does not mean that we are left without another safer and more wonderful way of overcoming our weakness; and if the powers of Heaven are not moved by our wrongs and our prayers, we can still move the powers of Hell.

'Remember our magic arts. Be bold. Have a manly heart, take my advice, and let's kill your rival so that you alone will have your

Tebaldo. Loosened from her arms, he'll remember the old sweet pleasures and run back to yours.'

These words she spoke in such a frank and fervent manner that my spirit was roused from cowardice to courage as I listened to her; and, determined as I was to remove my rival from my sight, I breathed anew and began to plot with Gebra (for so the Greek woman was called) how to take the life of Tebaldo's bride, Clerinda. We decided that once we had sold the most cumbersome furniture we should go back to live in the village surrounding Tebaldo's castle where he was obliged to pass by fairly often. There, inventing some reason why we had returned from the place where he left us, we would wait to see him and be seen.

Everything went as we had planned. Tebaldo came through a couple of times and, since I seemed so cheerful, asked to speak with me and expressed his satisfaction with the decisions I had taken, frankly offering to protect and support me whatever might happen. And because I let slip not a word or a hint about our love affair, almost as if I were another woman, he began to frequent my house quite regularly and stay to talk with me. He seemed to enjoy this transformation of love into kindness and was happy that, without betraying his wife, he could have the company of the woman he had once loved to excess.

The relationship went on like this, truly prudent and chaste, until at last I found an opportunity to carry out our plan. I brought the conversation round to his wife and asked about her beauty, and when he replied that she was indeed very beautiful and so sweetly mannered that it would be impossible to find her peer, I begged him to let me see her, for so far he had never let her put a foot outside the castle. He refused, saying that he had good reasons for doing so, for his wife unfortunately knew about his past love affairs and he did not want to give her any cause for jealousy. But I insisted and asked about Clerinda's beauty in some detail: how were her eyes, her cheeks, her hair? Finally, I begged him to let me have at least a lock of her hair so that I could see whether it was more or less lovely than my own golden tresses. He promised he would do so, and left.

Meanwhile the Greek woman, rejoicing with me that everything had gone so easily, busied herself preparing magic plants, strange stones and roots, unburied bones and deadly spells, so that we could use them on that lock of hair to work the death of the innocent Clerinda. But when he returned to the castle, Tebaldo, like the cautious man he was, started to wonder why I had been so interested in his wife's hair. He distrusted Gebra whose magic spells were already the subject of vague rumours and he began to suspect that in asking for the lock of hair I might have some evil end in mind. Then he remembered that he had a good thick lock of my own hair that he had cut off when we were playing around at the beginning of our love affair, and it struck him that, whatever might come of it, he could take it to me. And this he did, with the result that you shall hear.

On his return, therefore, he enriched my hand with the fine threads of gold, and I was happier to have that ringlet than Nisus' daughter was to have the curl cut from her father's head or Delilah* the locks of her simple-minded lover. As if all I wanted was to compare Clerinda's hair with mine, I kept some of it and gave the rest back to him, saying that it was indeed beautiful and that he had done very well to love a woman who bore a mine of such fine and noble gold upon her head. Then, with no further words, impatient to carry out my wicked intentions, I let Tebaldo take a hurried leave.

Already the night that precedes the day of Venus, the night that favours whispered magic spells, was spreading its dark veil and its broad skirts of shade above the earth, when Gebra and I, naked and dishevelled, went up to a high loggia. There, in the open air, carrying blackened candles of pure wax, we entered a large circle inscribed around and within with various names and signs and began to call forth silent Hecate and the other terrible gods from the soundless shades and the furthest recesses of Stygian night.

At the sound of our horrid spells and frightful blasphemies we saw the stars lose their radiance, threatening to fall with wrack and ruin, flashing here and there, and streaking down the sky. At one moment the moon would hide from us behind a livid sable cloud; and at another, with face blood-red from anger or flaming with dark fire, rain down sparks and piercing rays rather than kind refreshing dew. The heavenly blue was changed into a murky green that threatened lightning and storm so that fear began to take hold of me. Then Gebra, with three waves of her potent wand and uttering the great name feared and revered in Styx, with terrible wild gestures cast the lock of hair into the deadly fire, swearing and adjuring that the lady who produced that hair should shrivel and burn just like the hair itself.

And see, Eureta, no sooner does that fair lock of hair begin to catch fire than I feel my heart burning with a sudden heat, my blood drying up, my flesh shrivelling, and my limbs failing; as Gebra stands by transfixed with fury and astonishment, I fall to the ground, writhing in agony, until at last, with shuddering and groans, I set free from skin and bone a soul that has been cheated of its vengeance.

Eureta: A well-deserved punishment for a criminal intention. But when you had come out of the jealous girl, where did you go next?

LINDORI
From *Ormondo*

MY native land was Crete* and my parents were notables of that famous island. My education was the best that country could offer to a well-born youth. Atropos* robbed me of my father when I was hardly twelve years of age, and my loving mother, who had no other child to share her tenderness, took over the duties of her late husband and saw to the sound management of the family's wealth, which was not small. For my part, I studied hard to follow those paths that lead to solid happiness.

Now as Love would have it, my attention was directed to a noble young lady whose house was next to mine; and she was attracted by my looks and perhaps no less by my conduct and manners, such as they were—and this at the very same time as I enthroned her in my heart as the idol of all my desires and with reciprocal affection made myself subject to her beck and call. The warmth of her passion was incomparable and she expressed it in ways that were more than great. But the more her ardour increased, the more I felt my own flame burn lower as if my sentiments were rendered weak by the growing strength of hers. Or it may be that surrender gives rise to contempt and that finding her an easy prey diminished the attraction that is born from what is forbidden. Our love, in any case, reached the point where, when we found a way of being alone together, she placed her trust in my discretion and allowed me to steal the flower of her virginity—but not before I had promised Lindori (for that was her name) that we would be united by the bonds of marriage. As we came together more often, so my passion and my pleasure decreased; but with Lindori it was quite the contrary, perhaps because when a maid gives herself to a man she acquires something of his superior masculine vigour, and that is why a woman seldom falls out of love with her first lover. But by now we had aroused the suspicions of her mother who, somewhat late in the day, began to keep a close watch over her. She spied on us to find the secrets of our love, and since she believed that everything was still at the level of intentions, she made it very difficult for us to meet and we were forced to rely on letters or even gestures to convey our shared emotions.

Now while my passion for Lindori was cooling, it happened that a senator who governed the island in the name of the Queen of Republics was kind enough to appreciate the qualities that I possessed and asked whether I would be ready to go to the city of Venice and wed a young lady of singular beauty and considerable wealth, for such was the niece whose marriage it was his task to arrange. Offered such a profitable and desirable settlement, I gave my full agreement, dismissing Lindori from my mind and setting aside the faith I had pledged—crimes typical of changeable young lovers, though after so many years they still bring a blush to my cheeks. And so, having fixed everything with the uncle of my future bride and received letters confirming the conditions, I decided to embark for Venice and take happy possession of the lovely, noble, and rich young lady.

My plans, however, could not be entirely hidden from a valet in my service who soon got wind of them. Whether he had been bought by Lindori or whether he felt sorry for her I do not know, but the fact is that he went and told her what was going on. I would have thought it far too cruel simply to clear off without taking leave of her; and so, as soon as I found an opportunity to speak to her, I explained as best I could that I had to go to Venice on very serious legal business, but that I would marry her on my return. She had such strength of character and such skill in dissimulation that she seemed to be completely convinced and gave no sign that her affections were in any way altered. On the contrary, she announced that for as long as I was away, she would shut herself up in a convent to await my return; and I myself saw her taken there under the protection of an aunt.

It was already the day when I was due to embark and Lindori, kept fully informed by the valet, benefited from the total complicity of her shrewd loving aunt who instructed her to do what I shall now recount to Your Highnesses.*

I embarked, then, on a ship that, with a fair wind, soon reached our first port of call on the island of Zakynthos* where we stopped over to refresh ourselves. We had gone out to take the air and were walking happily along the beach when my eye suddenly fell on a fisherwoman who, with a soul-ravishing voice, was singing a sweet and joyfully rhythmic tune. And as I turned to look, I discovered the most marvellous beauty glistening through the purity of a white smock. I drew near, and I saw the face of the Lindori I had abandoned. She looked at me as if she had never seen me before and went on towards the sea with her fishing gear, leaving me confused and floundering like someone in a dream. I followed her and she turned round; I greeted her, and with a charming but bashful modesty, she rewarded my greeting with a timid acknowledgement. I was certain that she could not be Lindori whom I had left shut up in a convent and in no condition to go fishing.

After seeing to some necessary provisions and trading some merchandise, in a ship heavy with new passengers, we set sail with a fair wind for Corfu. There we stayed for three days while the ship was cleaned up and more of our cargo exchanged. As I strolled around the city, at the coolest time of the day, I saw many coaches and in one of them there was a beautiful woman so like Lindori that Lindori was not more like to herself. I gazed at her and the longer I looked the more I discerned the features that I knew so well, so that I no longer trusted myself to judge whether it was Lindori or not. I approached her, I stared at her, I bowed to her and observed how she reacted to my respectful greeting. With an unsmiling air, as if she were acknowledging a mere commoner, and with no more than a fleeting glance, she gave a slight nod and turned away. I lay in wait for her in several other places, and as I looked at her more closely, I found that she had a somewhat darker complexion or a slightly fuller figure or a more melancholy regard; and at last, for all these quibbles, I saw nothing in her but Lindori, though I firmly believed that she was not Lindori. And so, more dazed than ever, I wondered how two different women could look so alike. I would have liked to make further enquiries, but being a foreigner made me cautious and the coach vanished round a corner in the street making it impossible for me to ask anything without being indiscreet.

These two visions, whether waking dreams or phantasms of a sound mind, had created a great turmoil in my heart, stirred as I was by a sweetly painful inner commotion. The voyage had already made me pensive and taciturn, and the kind of wit that salts everyday talk struck me as insipid, so that I could neither respond to others nor take the initiative myself. Before the eyes of my soul stood Lindori, the fisher-woman, and the lady of Corfu—three women with one face, a wonder of fearful aspect.

After a swift voyage of some six hundred miles, driven by the sirocco, we reached Rovigno,* a port where large vessels occasionally dock for repairs. Passengers decide for themselves whether they want to rest on board the ship or go ashore to a small tavern. I was already feeling sick from the voyage, but even more sick in my mind; and so to find some relief from my melancholy thoughts, I went ashore along with two of the wealthier passengers and made my way to the inn. And there I was assailed by new wonders—or rather, new horrors! For there, emerging to greet her guests and invite us in to dinner with a charming Cretan accent, came the hostess, a young woman of exceptional beauty, wearing the most fanciful headdress and the strangest-looking gown that artless seduction could devise. Yet in her face there was Lindori; and though the voice struck me as rather dif-ferent, yet the likeness was such that I could hardly persuade myself that this was not Lindori. But the place, the profession, and the free-dom of manner strongly suggested otherwise. I drew near to engage her in conversation and was assaulted by flashing and over-familiar glances while, with skilled deception, she wove me such a splendidly credible web of lies about who she was that I was forced to think that she simply could not be Lindori. At the same time I was left so stunned by the exact resemblance that I swore to myself that nowhere else in the world could be found two faces so alike.

I began to fear that perhaps some vindictive god was intent on pun-ishing my perfidy by sending this succession of ghosts to reproach my breach of faith. Running through my mind was the suspicion that some dark sorcery was behind the appearance of the identical faces, exploiting those illusions to damage and disturb my normal visual faculty. My journey was like that of fame, which grows in strength the further in travels. The nearer I drew to Venice and to a profitable settlement that would better my situation, the more perplexed I became. Thus it was that shortly before we docked, I saw a tartane* approach-ing with a group of young people; and fishing with them was a girl so similar to Lindori that no Apelles or Zeuxis* could copy her features in such a lifelike way. They sailed skilfully around our ship, coming as near as they could without risking an accident; and as I observed more closely her glance, her smile, the swell of her breast, her swift gestures, her features, I felt obliged to think that this was surely Lindori. My wonder grew to a point where I was not so much bewildered as completely stunned. There were fishes swimming around the boat and sometimes showing their heads above water, and I began to fear that even among that silent shoal I would be shown the face of Lindori. I no longer dared to look the other travellers in the face for fear that at any moment they might be transformed into the accusing vision that tormented me.

At last, after three days, wafted by a fair wind, we reached the famous city where, amid the vast host of beauties, I hoped to find some relief from my anxieties, as at every window and in every street I beheld faces worthy of Venus herself. But that hope was soon dashed. Three days earlier I had given a servant some letters and sent him on ahead with letters to arrange lodgings for me with one of my kinsmen; and no sooner had I found the house and knocked on the door than a well-dressed young man came out to meet me and ask what I wanted. He had a gallant bearing and his face was as beautiful as could be; his eyes were unbelievably bright and loving; with his sword at his side and a splendid plume on his hat, he exhaled an air of grace and ardour. Only the voice seemed unfitted for that blend of qualities, for it was soft and struck one precisely with that soothing harmony that proceeds from the throat of a virgin with all her charms. Indeed, it was a voice that breathed out all the sweetness and graces that belonged to the speech of poor betrayed Lindori, just as the youth's features were the same as those that pleased me when first I fell in love. It froze my heart's blood. Confused as I was, and taking a her for a him, I started up a conversation, but there was no way I could get the youth to let fall any clue that would confirm the evidence of my eyes and ears. Instead he apologized for the absence of my uncle, the master of the house and, once my luggage had been taken to my room, invited me to join him in a walk round Venice and enjoy looking at so many things that were new to me. He led me from one street to another; we visited the major churches, and when we had seen some of the most notable things in Venice, he put me in a little boat and whispered something I could not catch in the boatman's ear. I did, however, understand that I was to be taken to the waterside entrance of his house where he would soon join me with his uncle. I was taken round the salt waters for a whole hour and had time to enjoy the many magnificent sights—not, however, without wondering why the canal way to my lodgings was taking so long. But, as I was to learn later, the delay was not without a hidden purpose.

The boat left me at my lodgings and there to meet me, excusing the absence of her husband the senator who was busy, came a young matron, dressed in a fashion that encourages thoughts of love; and in her features too I saw Lindori, save that she had a fuller figure, seemed slower and more affected in her speech, and was less forthright in her greeting.

But quite apart from these differences, any doubt as to her identity was largely dispelled when I recalled that Lindori was a young woman living in seclusion, who had never left her native land and was now safe in a cloister, unaware (as I believed) of my plans to get married despite the faith I had pledged to her. I believe, noble princes, that I would lose your esteem if I could not plead as an excuse my repentance and amendment of life, and even more my tender age and inexperience, in addition to the assaults of those who urged me on. The fair young lady directed me to my room; and in the meantime, though I had no suspicion of an understanding between them, my valet was using one pretext after another to go to her chambers and give her a full account of all my most secret concerns.

I stayed there for another two days before moving to the house of my promised bride where I received a lavish reception from the senator who had charged the governor of Crete to find a husband for his daughter. When the time came, I was married to the maiden and the sight of her in the torchlight filled me with such astonishment and confusion that I thought I was going mad; for even in those splendid festive trappings, I perceived the natural likeness of my ever-present Lindori. At this, overcome by pangs of conscience, I broke out into tears of repentance and emotion; and with a loving address to the woman whom I still believed to be far away, I confessed my fault and told the bystanders the whole story without the shadow of untruth. Then the young woman, giving way to tenderness and accompanying my tears with a warm flood of her own, revealed the sequence of events—how, when she heard about the marriage I was planning at the expense of her honour and her love, she had consulted her aunt, and how, the day after my departure, with letters from that same aunt, she had embarked in a frigate with four other ladies and sailed to Zakynthos, where she had time to prepare her performance as a fisherwoman. Then she had gone on to Corfu as the noble lady who appeared to me in the coach; and from there to Rovigno where she had persuaded the landlady to let her take over for the day. And finally she had come to the kind-hearted senator who, when he heard about the wrong I had done her, willingly renounced the idea of giving me his daughter and, with admirable deceptions, set about ensuring that Lindori retained possession of the man she loved. Then, with renewed tenderness and love, after solemnly celebrating the marriage that had already taken place in secret, I soon returned to my native land with Lindori. There, not long after, Atropos stole her from me and I made a vow to remain forever a widower. I became a courtier, reserving for you, my noble princes, whatever may serve to demonstrate my most devoted service.

EXPLANATORY NOTES

3 *Prince Galahalt*: see Introduction, pp. xv–xvi.

noble love: the youthful passion of Boccaccio's Neapolitan years, reflected in his creation of the fictional character Fiammetta.

5 *fables or parables or histories*: see Introduction, pp. xi–xii.

deadly plague: the plague struck Florence in 1348 and is thought to have killed about half the urban population.

Panfilo's story: the tale of Cepparello, a mendacious scoundrel who becomes revered as a saint after making a false deathbed confession.

the queen: Pampinea, chosen as queen for Day One of the *Decameron*.

7 *better teachers*: unlike Rome, medieval Paris was renowned for theological studies.

9 *Capsa*: Gafsa in Tunisia.

Theban deserts: in the third century Christian hermits sought the solitude of the desert around the ancient Egyptian city of Thebes.

13 *Tancredi, prince of Salerno*: though the name was popular among the Norman rulers of southern Italy, there is no record of any Tancredi, prince of Salerno.

20 *soul...cherished*: medieval medical theory situated the soul in the blood and therefore in the heart.

21 *Gerbino*: princely protagonist of Elissa's tale.

San Gimignano: small town in Tuscany, still famous for its towers.

24 *Baronci family*: old Florentine family noted for their ugliness.

25 *Pugliesi... Guazzaliotri*: prominent families in Prato.

27 *final prayer*: the previous tale ends with a comic prayer addressed to a ghost.

Avorio district: Boccaccio knew Naples well, having lived and worked there for over a decade (*c.*1328–40). The Scrignario family lived near the Avorio district and are mentioned in a document of 1324. It is typical of Boccaccio to add verisimilitude to his fictions by using the names of prominent families.

29 *Saint Galeone*: in the Avorio district there was a chapel dedicated to Saint Eucalion (San Galeone in Neapolitan).

30 *Parthia*: Rome waged many wars against the Parthians whose military strength was often associated with the vigour of their horses and the skill of their cavalry (See Ovid, *Fasti* 5. 580–94).

31 *'The good man... Torello'*: the good man is a character in an earlier tale (*Decameron* 7. 1) whose wife succeeds in convincing him that her lover is a ghost by performing an exorcism; Torello, the protagonist of the preceding tale (*Decameron* 10. 9) is reunited with his wife just as, believing him to be dead, she is about to remarry.

31 *Saluzzo*: Piedmontese town south of Turin.

36 *Panago*: modern Panico, near Bologna.

39 *jiggle her muff*: this jarring obscenity ends the tale on a deliberately ambiguous note. See Introduction, p. xvii.

40 *Scali*: Florentine banking family who specialized in public finance.

  Tanais: Greek city at the mouth of the River Don, site of the modern Azov.

43 *third hour of the day*: counted from daybreak.

47 *a Jew at Mestre*: Mestre is the urban extension of Venice on the mainland. Jews were present on Venetian territory from the tenth century, but were not allowed to reside in the city until 1366.

55 *Pistoia*: Tuscan town, 25 miles north-east of Florence.

  Magistrate's Court: Palazzo del Podestà (It.), the *podestà* being the chief magistrate of the city; today the building houses the Bargello National Museum.

  Abbey Church: Badia Fiorentina (It.), founded in 978, one of the oldest churches in Florence, facing the entrance to the Bargello.

  Prato: Tuscan town about 12 miles north of Florence.

  Agliana bridge: in the province of Pistoia, about 7 miles from Florence.

58 *ambassadors of Casentino*: comic rustic notables in another of Sacchetti's tales (*Trecentonovelle* 31).

  moneylending . . . damnation: though moneylending flourished in Florence, usury (the taking of interest) was officially condemned by the Catholic Church. Dante places usurers in the seventh circle of Hell. The friar manages both to fulfil his promise and to uphold traditional doctrine by distinguishing between the act of lending money and the taking of interest.

60 *qui in coelis est*: (Lat.) who is in Heaven.

61 *not in the name*: the tale concludes with an exuberant list of euphemisms for usury.

63 *Pozzuoli*: town west of Naples, famous for its *solfatara*, a shallow volcanic crater.

66 *Charles the Lame*: Charles II, king of Naples (r. 1285–1309).

68 *Salimbeni . . . Montanini*: prominent Sienese families.

70 *purse never opened before*: metaphoric assertion of Angelica's virginity.

74 *Tomaso Pecori*: the Pecori family played a prominent role in Florentine politics, many of them serving as priors in the government of the city.

  Manetto: Manetto Ammannatini (1381–1450), woodworker and inlayer.

  Piazza di San Giovanni: square in the historic centre of Florence, site of the famous Baptistery.

75 *Filippo di Ser Brunellesco*: Filippo Brunelleschi (1377–1446), architect; celebrated for his construction of the dome of Santa Maria del Fiore.

  believe that he is someone else: some scholars affirm that this prank really took place, but perhaps the real *beffa* lies in the very existence of the tale, in the fact that Manetto was the sort of man of whom such a story could be believed.

76 *Santa Maria del Fiore*: the cathedral of Florence.

Polverosa: village near Florence.

77 *Donatello*: Donato di Betto Bardi (1386–1466), major sculptor of the period; his provocatively erotic David can be seen in the Bargello Museum.

Calandrino: a gullible simpleton who appears in four tales of the *Decameron*.

Merchants' Court: Tribunale della Mercatanzia (It.), a court dealing with trade disputes, fraudulent commercial practice, and unpaid debts.

79 *Rucellai*: prominent political and banking family: the Palazzo Rucellai in Via della Vigna Nuova is one of the most notable buildings in Florence.

80 *a judge*: possibly Giovanni Gherardi da Prato, presumed author of *The Paradise of the Alberti*, who was known to be heavily in debt at the time.

81 *Apuleius*: Latin novelist (*c.* AD 124–70), author of *The Golden Ass* in which Lucius (not Apuleius himself) is magically transformed into an ass.

Actaeon: the huntsman who saw Diana bathing naked and was transformed into a stag to be devoured by his own hounds (Ovid, *Metamorphoses* 3. 165–252).

Circe: the sorceress whose magic potion transforms the crew of Odysseus (Ulysses) into swine (Homer, *Odyssey* 10).

83 *Angelus*: prayer commemorating the Annunciation (Luke 2: 26–38), recited three times a day at fixed hours in the morning, at midday, and in the evening.

84 *Santa Felicità*: church on the south bank of the Arno, near the road still known as the Costa San Giorgio.

89 *Mercato Nuovo*: the New Market, near Via Porta Rossa.

94 *Empoli*: Tuscan town 20 miles west of Florence.

Charterhouse: Carthusian monastery of Galluzzo, 4 miles south of Florence.

96 *apse*: the architectural details remind us that Brunelleschi's prank reaches its triumphant conclusion in the very church that he will later transform by his famous dome.

97 *Counsellors*: members of a consultative body offering regular advice to the nine priors who made up the Signoria (see note to p. 130).

99 *Hungary*: Manetto Ammannatini worked in Hungary from 1410 (the year after the prank) until his death in 1450.

Pippo Spano: Filippo Scolari (1369–1426), mercenary soldier, general in the service of King Sigismund and also patron of the arts. His portrait by Andrea del Castagno can be seen in the church of Sant'Apollonia in Florence.

Sigismund: Sigismund of Luxembourg (1368–1437), son of Emperor Charles IV, became king of Hungary in 1387 and was elected Holy Roman Emperor in 1433; he encouraged the diffusion of humanist ideas by promoting cultural and commercial links between Florence and Hungary.

102 *Antonio ... many others*: the list of those involved in the transmission of the
     story indicates how deeply it became embedded in the collective memory
     of Florence's artistic community. They are, in the given order: Antonio
     Gamberelli, sculptor (1427–79), also known as Rossellino; Michelozzo
     (1396–1472), sculptor and architect; Andrea Cavalcanti da Buggiano
     (1412–62), sculptor and architect, adopted son of Brunelleschi; Giovanni
     Guidi (1407–80), also called Scheggia, painter, brother of Masaccio; Feo
     Belcari (1410–84), poet and author of sacred drama; Luca della Robbia
     (1400–81), sculptor, famous for his glazed statuary; Antonio Guidotti
     (*fl.* 1450s), architect; Domenico di Michelino (1417–91), painter, pupil
     of Fra Angelico.

103 *Giovanni Pontano*: (1429–1503), prominent humanist scholar and neo-Latin
     poet.

104 *Friars Minor*: religious order founded by Saint Francis in 1209. The fail-
     ure of the Franciscans to live up to the ideals of their founder provided
     abundant matter for satire in the fourteenth and fifteenth centuries.

     Saint Bernardino: Saint Bernardino of Siena (1380–1444), fanatical Franciscan
     preacher, inveighed against frivolity, usury, witchcraft, and sodomy; can-
     onized 1450.

106 *Saint Griffin*: an invention of Masuccio. In an early draft of the story the
     saint was Bernardino. The griffin is a fabulous animal with the head and
     wings of an eagle and the body of a lion. The final procession bearing the
     drawers of Saint Griffin may have a parodic relation to a passage in Dante's
     Purgatorio (canto 29) where a griffin, presumably symbolizing the two
     natures of Christ, appears in a procession which the poet witnesses in the
     Earthly Paradise.

108 *good hound*: the phrase sets off a somewhat ponderous sequence of sexual
     metaphors.

109 *in promptu*: (Lat.) immediately.

111 *Veni Creator Spiritus*: Gregorian Latin hymn, 'Come, Creator Spirit'.

     Avicenna: Ibn Sina, famous Persian philosopher and physician (*c.*980–1037).

112 *Enrico of Aragon*: (*c.*1451–78), marquis of Gerace, illegitimate son of King
     Ferrante of Naples. He died after a meal of poisonous mushrooms; his son
     Luigi was the cardinal who ordered the murder of the Duchess of Amalfi
     and her husband Antonio Bologna (see pp. 207-18).

113 *Bologna*: great medieval university, founded in the late eleventh century, as
     famous for its studies in law as Paris was for theology or Padua for medicine.

115 *Trayques*: possibly the Piedmontese town of Entracque near Cuneo.

118 *virtuous deeds*: the subsequent story is one of high-minded courtesy: the
     king of Portugal grants an unconditional release to a captured Arab gen-
     eral whose wife has come to plead for him; the general then vows to serve
     the king.

119 *Monte San Savino*: small town in the Tuscan province of Arezzo.

120 *Samson…David…Solomon the Wise*: Old Testament figures: Samson revealed the secret of his strength to Delilah; David sinned with Bathsheba, wife of Uriah; Solomon's wives turned his heart towards strange gods.

120 *following letter*: parodic example of Petrarchan rhetoric.

124 *Sodom and Gomorrah*: cities of the plain destroyed by God as punishment for homosexual practices (Gen. 19: 1–29).

125 *Minos and Rhadamanthus*: two of the three sons of Zeus (the other is Aeacus) who are demigods and judges in the Underworld. Early Christianity recast the pagan gods as devils.

Pluto: king of the Underworld.

126 *Belphagor*: name derived from Baal, god of the Moabites and Midianites.

Ognissanti: western district of Florence around the church of Ognissanti (All Saints).

Aleppo: great Syrian trading city, a magnet for Florentine merchants.

127 *John the Baptist*: patron saint of Florence; his feast day is on 24 June.

128 *Peretola*: village 4 miles north-west of Florence.

129 *Zenobius…Gualberto*: Saint Zenobius was a fifth-century bishop of Florence; Saint John Gualberto (d. 1073) was the founder of a Benedictine congregation known as the Vallumbrosians. A manuscript in the Laurentian Library of Florence recounts how in 1466 the head of Saint John Gualberto was used to exorcize a girl possessed by an evil spirit. The head then profited from the occasion to reveal the sins of local monks.

130 *Charles of Naples*: Charles d'Anjou (1226–85).

Louis VII: anachronism; the only King Louis contemporary with Charles d'Anjou would be Louis IX (1214–70).

Signoria: governing body of Florence (also in Venice).

135 *city of Poland*: here a remote fantasy land of chivalry and magic.

141 *Spolatina*: given the Dalmatian setting of the story, this should probably be Spalatina, from Spalato, the Italian name for the Croatian port of Split.

Ragusa: Italian name for modern Dubrovnik.

Middle Island: Lopud, about 3 miles north-west of Dubrovnik.

146 *Bartolomeo della Scala*: the Della Scala family ruled Verona (birthplace of Da Porto) from 1277 to 1381. Bartolomeo I (r. 1301–4) gave shelter to the exiled Dante who rewarded him with a place in his *Paradiso* (17. 71–3).

Azzo d'Este: Azzo VI, ruled Verona from 1207 to his death in 1212.

150 *pleasures of life*: the implication is that Fra Lorenzo relies on the support of young nobles like Romeo to protect him from the consequences of some sexual indiscretion.

152 *Lodrone*: town in the province of Trentino.

154 *Our Saviour's body*: the medieval laity did not receive Holy Communion as frequently as modern Catholics; hence the need for an exceptional spiritual preparation, including confession.

158 *Conventual... Observants*: after the death of Saint Francis in 1226 the order that he had founded split into two major currents: the Observants sought to follow the original strict rule; the Conventuals, as the name suggests, modified the rule to allow for the foundation of large religious houses. The two factions finally separated in 1517.

160 *Pygmalion*: legendary sculptor who fell in love with his statue and persuaded Venus to transform it into a living woman (see Ovid, *Metamorphoses* 10. 243–97).

165 *our city*: Venice.

167 *Corfu*: Venetian possession from 1401 to 1797.

169 *Isabella d'Este, Marchioness of Mantua*: (1474–1539), daughter of Ercole I of Ferrara and wife of Francesco II Gonzaga, marquis of Mantua. Bandello was attached to the Gonzaga family who gave him refuge for seven years (1515–22) after the French capture of Milan.

countess of Challant: Bianca Maria Scappardone (1501–26), wife of Ermes Visconti and then of René de Challant. Decapitated 20 October 1526.

Ermes Visconti: first husband of Bianca Maria, executed in Milan for plotting against the French (1519).

Sforza Bentivoglio: Ippolita Sforza (1481–1520), wife of Alessandro Bentivoglio, lord of Bologna. After the Bentivoglio family were expelled from Bologna by Pope Julius II, they took refuge in Milan which is where Bandello first met Ippolita. He considered her as one of the most learned women of her time and credited her with having inspired him to write the *Novelle*.

170 *Antonio Sabino*: literary friend of Bandello.

171 *Messer Mario*: Mario Equicola (1460–1525), Italian humanist and neo-Latin author, friend of Bandello, secretary and Latin tutor of Isabella d'Este. Having died the year before the execution of Bianca Maria, he could hardly have read the story, as Bandello suggests.

plebeian: Bandello alters the facts to support his theory of inherited moral qualities; Giacomo Scappardone was not a plebeian, but a member of the minor nobility: his wife was Italian, not Greek.

Marquis Guglielmo: marquis of Monferrat. The connection between Monferrat and the Gonzaga rulers of Mantua is evident later in the story where the marchioness of Monferrat seeks to ensure the hand of Bianca Maria for Sigismondo Gonzaga.

Gismondo Gonzaga: Sigismondo Gonzaga (1499–1530), mercenary captain (*condottiero*) who served Emperor Charles V in his Italian wars against the French.

172 *count of Challant*: René de Challant (1502–65), second husband of Bianca Maria; later became a distinguished soldier and diplomat, faithful to the interests of the dukes of Savoy.

Ardizzino Valperga: count of Masino in Piedmont, lover of Bianca Maria, murdered 1526.

Roberto Sanseverino: count of Gaiazzo, scion of a Neapolitan military family. Bandello dedicates a story to him (*Novelle* 3. 33).

176 *Bicocca*: battle near Milan (1522) where the French were defeated by the troops of Emperor Charles V. An ancestor of the Sicilian Cardona family is the protagonist of Bandello's tale of Timbreo and Fenicia (p. 184).

duke of Bourbon: Charles III, duke of Bourbon and Auvergne (1490–1527); in the Italian Wars he changed sides and abandoned the French in order to serve with the imperial forces of Charles V. He was killed during the Sack of Rome (1527). The sculptor and goldsmith Benvenuto Cellini claimed to have been among those involved in the fatal episode (*My Life*, 1. 34).

177 *Monastero Maggiore*: the frescoes by Bernardino Luini (*c.*1480–1532) can still be seen in the monastery church of San Maurizio in Milan. It was once thought that Bianca Maria was the model for Saint Catherine in a decapitation scene, but modern researchers have suggested that we should look for her in the image of Saint Lucy.

Pirro Gonzaga, Cardinal: nephew of Pirro Gonzaga, marquis of Gazzuolo.

famous heroes: among the less familiar figures in this list are the Roman general Marcellus (268–208 BC), who captured the Sicilian city of Syracuse during the Second Punic War, and the Greek Philopoemen (253–183 BC), successful commander of the Achaean League in the war against Sparta.

saltpetre: the use of gunpowder had transformed warfare in Italy during Bandello's lifetime.

178 *Pirro Gonzaga*: marquis of Gazzuolo and soldier in the service of France. Bandello helped to arrange his marriage to Camilla Bentivoglio and acted as tutor to his two daughters Lucrezia and Isabella.

baritone; nothing is known of Gian Matteo Olivo.

Giulia of Gazzuolo: almost certainly a true story; Bandello would have heard it spoken of in the Gonzaga circle at Gazzuolo. An earlier and shorter version of it is to be found in Castiglione's *The Courtier*, bk III, where Giulia is given the more plebeian name of Maddalena Biga.

Lucrece: chaste Roman matron who killed herself after being raped by Sextus Tarquinius; her death provoked the expulsion of the Tarquin dynasty and the birth of the Roman Republic (Livy 1. 57–9).

179 *Lodovico Gonzaga*: noted for organizing performances of classical drama at Gazzuolo.

Antonia Bauzia: mother of Camilla Bentivoglio and mother-in-law of Marquis Pirro.

179 *I cannot say*: the remark adds an extra touch of pathos to the story by reminding us of how Giulia's beauty so nearly became her fortune rather than her downfall.

180 *Saint Zita*: pious domestic servant whose body was preserved in the cathedral of Lucca. The old woman in Bandello's tale resembles her in decayed appearance, but not in morality.

basilisk: legendary reptile whose glance was thought to kill.

183 *marble column*: as a suicide, Giulia cannot be buried in consecrated ground; her tomb resembles a pagan monument.

184 *Cecilia Gallerani*: (1473–1536), poet and friend of Bandello, mistress of Lodovico Sforza, duke of Milan; model for Da Vinci's celebrated portrait, *Lady with an Ermine*.

Lucio Scipione Attellano: Milanese patrician, supporter of the Sforza faction; close friend of Bandello, frequently mentioned in the *Novelle*.

Sir Timbreo di Cardona: ancestor of the Sicilian Cardona family, counts of Collesano.

185 *Sicilian Vespers*: a particularly bloody popular revolt that chased the Angevin rulers from the island in 1282.

King Peter of Aragon: Peter inherited the throne of Sicily through his marriage to Constance, daughter of Manfred, son of the Holy Roman Emperor Frederick II Hohenstaufen (1194–1250) who was also king of Sicily. He renounced the throne on his deathbed in 1285. The story starts as he celebrates a naval victory over Charles of Anjou in 1284.

192 *Dear mothers and sisters*: an elaborate exercise in the Female Complaint, a fashionable and tearful Renaissance genre inherited from Ovid's *Heroides*.

204 *The fair and gentle Fenicia*: a literary set piece, following the criteria for ideal feminine beauty derived from the Petrarchan tradition and codified by Agnolo Firenzuola in his dialogue on the beauties of women (*Dialogo delle bellezze delle donne*, 1548).

207 *Prospero Colonna*: military leader much admired by Bandello; captain-general of the Milanese forces of Massimiliano Sforza and later commander in chief of Emperor Charles V's armies in Italy.

Ravenna: Battle of Ravenna (1512), French victory over Spanish and Italian forces.

Italians who opened the way: Columbus and Vespucci.

prince of Hornland: a cuckold; in the original *vicario di Corneto*, a play on the word *corno* (horn).

208 *Duchess of Amalfi*: Giovanna of Aragon (1478–1510), married to the duke of Amalfi, regent of the duchy after the duke's death in 1498; secretly married to her second husband, the household steward Antonio Bologna.

Cardinal of Aragon: Cardinal Luigi of Aragon (1474–1518), trusted adviser of Pope Julius II, noted for his patronage of writers and the opulence of his feasts.

Antonio Bologna: 1475–1513, second husband of Giovanna of Aragon, duchess of Amalfi, grandson of noted humanist Antonio Beccadelli (the Panormite). Bandello portrays him as a model of probity, culture, and courtesy.

Fieramosca: lieutenant under Prospero Colonna; it is unusual for Bandello to introduce a second source for his story.

Silvio Savelli: active in the Italian wars; after serving with Florentine forces, he became commander of the Milanese infantry.

209 *Ippolita Sforza*: see note to p. 169.

Frederick of Aragon: king of Naples, driven from his kingdom (1501) by an alliance between his cousin, King Ferdinand of Aragon, and Louis XII of France.

210 *Alfonso II, Ferdinand, and Frederick*: three kings of Naples who reigned in rapid succession between 1494 and 1501.

Baronci: see note to p. 24.

211 *witness*: the Catholic Church regarded a marriage of this kind as illegal but not invalid; the presence of a priest became obligatory only after the Council of Trent.

213 *Loreto*: small town south of the port of Ancona, famous for the shrine containing the Holy House of the Virgin Mary, miraculously transported by angels from Nazareth to Loreto in order to save it from profanation by the Muslim conquerors of Palestine.

214 *Gismondo Gonzaga*: cardinal in 1505, bishop of Mantua in 1511, later papal legate in Bologna and Ancona. Not to be confused with mercenary soldier of the same name.

215 *Petrucci*: Cardinal Alfonso Petrucci (1491–1527), member of the powerful Petrucci clan of Siena, imprisoned and probably murdered for his opposition to Pope Leo X's control of the city.

Barb: short for 'Barbary horse'.

216 *Massimiliano Sforza*: ruled Milan 1512–15; his success in driving the French out of the castle of Milan was short-lived. After the decisive victory of Franco-Venetian forces at Marignano (1515) he ceded all his rights in the city to the French king Francis I in exchange for a generous pension.

217 *our Delio*: pseudonym for Bandello himself.

jennet: small Spanish horse.

218 *Daniele de Bozola*: the Bosola of Webster's *Duchess of Malfi*.

Castiglione: Baldassare (or Baldesar) Castiglione (1478–1529), author of *Il libro del cortegiano* (*The Book of the Courtier*, 1528; English translation by Sir Thomas Hoby, 1561), a crucial Renaissance text set in the court of Urbino and presenting, through a series of discussions and debates, an ideal of courtesy and courtly behaviour. Bandello would have met him at the court of Mantua between 1518 and 1520. The influence of Castiglione's idealized picture of the Urbino court is felt in the relaxed and cultured audience enjoyed by Bandello's narrators.

218 *Bianca d'Este*: narrator of the tale and granddaughter of its protagonist, Niccolò III, marquis of Ferrara.

Camilla Scarampa: minor poet, prominent in Milanese aristocratic circles, much admired by Bandello who sees her and Cecilia Gallerani as 'two lights of the Italian language in our time'.

219 *Marquis Niccolò III d'Este*: (1393–1441), illegitimate son of Alberto whom he succceeded as lord of Ferrara; fought off a challenge by his cousin Azzo who was captured and exiled to Crete.

Ugo, count of Rovigo: not, as Bianca claims, the legitimate heir, being, in fact, like his brothers Lionello and Borso, an illegitimate son of Niccolò by Stella Tolomei; executed at the age of 20 in 1425.

Lionello: Lionello d'Este (1407–50), succeeded his father as lord of Ferrara in 1441.

Borso: Borso d'Este (1413–71); succeeded his brother Lionello in 1450 and was named duke of Ferrara and Modena by Emperor Frederick III in 1452. A great patron of the arts, he ordered the allegorical frescoes by Cosimo Tura that adorn the Palazzo Schifanoia in Ferrara.

220 *Carlo Malatesta*: Bandello is mistaken. This should be the *condottiero* Andrea Malatesta (1373–1416); his daughter, whom Bandello does not name, was Parisina who became the second wife of Niccolò III at the age of 14. It said that she found no less than eight of her husband's illegitimate sons in her new household.

221 *Duke Filippo Visconti*: Filippo Maria Visconti (1392–1447), duke of Milan, sought the help of Niccolò in his struggle against Venice. Niccolò was looking for confirmation of his own possession of Reggio.

223 *Phaedra... Hippolytus*: in the Greek myth, dramatized by Euripedes and Racine, Phaedra, wife of Theseus, falls in love with her stepson Hippolytus. Unlike Ugo, Hippolytus remains unmoved and is destroyed by the angry goddess Aphrodite.

224 *Don Ferrando and Don Giulio*: sons of Duke Ercole I, imprisoned by Duke Alfonso I for conspiring against their brother Ippolito (1506).

226 *ancient empire... Mars*: the Holy Roman Empire.

that year: the elaborate opening is imitated from the *Decameron*; the references to Pope Paul III, Emperor Charles V, and King Francis I give us a date between 1540 and 1547.

228 *Verdelot and Arcadelt*: Philippe Verdelot and Jacques Arcadelt, madrigalists, both active in Florence in the 1530s.

Boccadoro: golden mouth, a translation of the Greek *chrysostom* as applied to the Church Father Saint John Chrysostom (*c.*349–407). No wonder a lady giggles at this association between the author of bawdy tales and a revered Church Father.

229 *Fat Thursday*: last Thursday before Lent.

230 *Leander*: the narrator's pseudonym. In the Greek myth Leander is drowned in the Hellespont as he swims over to his lover Hero (Ovid, *Heroides* 17–18).

old Pisan chronicles: the story is set sometime in the second half of the thirteenth century, but the details of Fazio's financial dealings reflect the situation of a later date.

232 *strappado*: a form of torture where the victim's hands are tied behind his back and he is then suspended by a rope attached to his wrists.

234 *test of the hammer*: the alloys produced by the alchemists were notoriously brittle and would reveal their origin when struck by a hammer.

235 *Ragusan ship*: the Dalmatian republic of Ragusa (now Dubrovnik), maintained a sizeable merchant fleet.

236 *Lyons*: as an important financial centre, sixteenth-century Lyons had strong connections with Italian banks.

Lanfranchi... Gualandi: Pisan bankers (see Dante, *Inferno* 33. 32).

237 *positions in Rome*: in Grazzini's time Vatican finances were kept afloat by the sale of largely fictive positions, offering a fixed revenue and sometimes an honorific title. Fazio would have seen it as an expensive but profitable long-term investment.

238 *Eight Judges*: Florentine tribunal for civil and criminal cases.

Bargello's men: guards in the service of the Bargello, a functionary roughly equivalent to a modern chief of police.

240 *Thebes... Pisa*: see Dante's denunciation of Pisa (*Inferno* 33. 79–90).

241 *domination of Florence*: Florence annexed Pisa for the first time after a siege in 1406 and definitively in 1509.

242 *Lazzero*: Lazarus, appropriate name in that he will, in a certain sense, rise from the dead when Gabriello assumes his identity.

243 *square nets*: this kind of fishing is attested by Boccaccio, *Decameron* 10. 6.

247 *two thousand... four hundred*: the estate of a wealthy Florentine merchant in Grazzini's time.

250 *Saint Gregory*: (*c.*540–604), reputed to have had 30 Masses said to free from Purgatory the soul of a monk who had broken his vow of poverty by possessing three gold pieces.

251 *raw eggs*: old Italian custom, presumably to help the newly married couple recover from their nocturnal exertions.

De Fortunati: not uncommon Italian family name, obviously fitting in the case of Gabriello.

253 *Slav friend*: by trading down the Dalmatian coast, Venice developed close links with the Slav world. A major waterfront is still called Riva degli Schiavoni.

254 *Madonna della Fava*: church in the Castello district of Venice. A literal translation might be 'Our Lady of the Bean', but Fava was probably the name of the family who financed its construction.

in church: ironic reference to the legendary piety of prostitutes.

Calaballotte: in the port area of Venice.

255 *Chioggia*: small town at the entry to the lagoon, about 16 miles from Venice.

257 *Ansi visminere?*: Fortini's distorted version of a Flemish phrase; we are left in no doubt as to its meaning.

259 *pearls and rubies*: the description offers a pleasant contrast between the tempting provincial freshness of Antonio's wife and the more opulent attractions of Giachena.

indulgence in the Jubilee Year: the Church rewarded acts of piety, such as a pilgrimage to Rome, with a cancellation of the temporal punishment due to sin in Purgatory. The abuse of this system led to Luther's rebellion against papal authority. The Jubilee Year is probably that of 1525 proclaimed by Pope Clement VII.

262 *Serendip*: Ceylon, modern Sri Lanka.

Becher: possibly Bechar in Algeria.

270 *valiant Moor*: Cinzio does not name the Moor, the ensign, or the lieutenant (Shakespeare's Othello, Iago, and Cassio respectively).

Cyprus: Venetian possession from 1489 until 1571 when it was captured by the Turks.

273 *blackness*: unlike Shakespeare's Iago, Cinzio's ensign does not draw much attention to the Moor's blackness, but this one occasion when he does so is particularly vicious in its implication that Disdemona's attraction to him was no more than a passing sexual caprice.

280 *Ferrara*: Cinzio's birthplace, a significant centre of humanist culture under the rule of the Este family in the fifteenth and sixteenth centuries. Its fortunes declined after its absorption into the Papal States in 1598.

285 *Maximilian*: Maximilian I Habsburg (1459–1519), Holy Roman Emperor from 1493.

Iuriste: the name identifies him as a representative of the law. Iuriste, Epitia, and Vieo are the Angelo, Isabella, and Claudio of Shakespeare's *Measure for Measure*.

287 *these and other arguments*: Epitia puts her education to good use; her speech is less an emotional plea for mercy than a brilliant piece of legal argument involving some of the basic principles on which justice should be based.

288 *culpable ignorance*: the Italian text makes a distinction between sinning out of ignorance (*per ignoranza*) and sinning ignorantly (*ignorantemente*). Vieo cannot plead ignorance of the law as an extenuating circumstance because he has sinned against the basic moral laws that all men should know.

296 *sufficit*: (Lat.) it is enough.

300 *surrounded by policemen*: Neapolitan courtesans were often arrested for parading in carriages along the Posillipo beach which was the daily promenade of the nobility.

Taking the shoe in his hand: the king's apostrophe to Zezolla's shoe is a parody of the metaphorical excesses of mannerist love poetry.

303 *Scylla and Charybdis*: two sea monsters situated on either side of the Strait of Messina separating Sicily from the mainland (see Homer, *Odyssey* 12), generally accepted as personifications of a dangerous reef and a whirlpool.

Medea: princess of Colchis who helped Jason to obtain the Golden Fleece and became his wife; when he abandoned her, she killed their children.

304 *Charon's breeches*: Charon ferries the souls of the dead across the River Styx to Hades.

305 *Colosseum*: great Roman amphitheatre, considered as a site of atrocious cruelty.

306 *The Lamp*: the student Eureta possesses a lamp which contains an evil spirit whose migrations from one tortured character to another provide the frame for the collection. Here the evil spirit passes from Argenis to Armilla.

308 *Echo...Egeria*: the nymph Echo pined away for love of Narcissus until she was reduced to a mere voice; Egeria wept for her husband Numa Pompilius, legendary second king of Rome, until at last she was transformed into a fountain (see Ovid, *Metamorphoses* 3. 357–401 and 15. 479–551).

310 *Nisus' daughter...Delilah*: Scylla, daughter of King Nisus, cut off the golden lock that gave him life and power and gave it to his enemy Minos (Ovid, *Metamorphoses* 8. 11–151). Delilah cut off Samson's hair which held the secret of his strength (Judges 16: 4–20).

311 *Crete*: under Venetian rule from 1204 to 1669.

Atropos: in Greek mythology one of the three Fates (*Moirai*); she cuts the thread of life that has been spun by Clotho and measured by Lachesis.

312 *Your Highnesses*: one of five insert-stories in Pona's romance *Ormondo*, the tale is recounted by a courtly gentleman to a group of high-born passengers on board a ship.

313 *Zakynthos*: small Greek island in the Ionian Sea.

314 *Rovigno*: port in Istria, now Rovinj (Croatia).

tartane: small one-masted Mediterranean vessel.

Apelles or Zeuxis: famous painters of ancient Greece, approx. fourth and fifth centuries BC; nothing of their work survives.

The Oxford World's Classics Website

www.worldsclassics.co.uk

- Browse the full range of Oxford World's Classics online

- Sign up for our monthly e-alert to receive information on new titles

- Read extracts from the Introductions

- Listen to our editors and translators talk about the world's greatest literature with our Oxford World's Classics audio guides

- Join the conversation, follow us on Twitter at OWC_Oxford

- Teachers and lecturers can order inspection copies quickly and simply via our website

www.worldsclassics.co.uk